Linux—Unleashing the Workstation in Your PC

3rd edition

Springer

New York
Berlin
Heidelberg
Barcelona
Budapest
Hong Kong
London
Milan
Paris
Santa Clara
Singapore
Tokyo

Stefan Strobel & Volker Elling

LINUX

Unleashing the Workstation
in Your PC

3rd edition, revised and enhanced

Foreword by Jürgen Gulbins
Translation by Robert Bach & Aileen Derieg

 Springer

Stefan Strobel
Schlegelstraße 19
D-74074 Heilbronn
Germany

Volker Elling
Dr.-Maria-Moormann-Str. 12
48231 Warendorf
Germany

The authors can be reached at the following e-mail address:

linux@hn-net.de

Library of Congress Cataloging-in-Publication Data
Strobel, Stefan, 1970–
    [Linux—vom PC zur Workstation. English]
    Linux, unleashing the workstation in your PC / Stefan Strobel &
    Volker Elling ; foreword by Jürgen Gulbins ; translation by Robert
    Bach & Aileen Darling. — 3rd ed., revised and enhanced.
        p. cm.
    Includes bibliographical references and index.
    ISBN 0-387-94880-5 (alk. paper)
    1. Linux.   2. Microcomputer workstations.   I. Elling, Volker.
    II. Title.
    QA76.5.S78513   1997   97-10096
    005.4'469—dc21

Printed on acid-free paper.

Production managed by Bill Imbornoni; manufacturing supervised by Rhea Talbert.
Typeset in TEX from the authors' files.
Printed and bound by Hamilton Printing Company, Rensselaer, NY.
Printed in the United States of America.

9 8 7 6 5 4 3 2 1

ISBN 0-387-94880-5 Springer-Verlag New York Berlin Heidelberg   SPIN 10552782

Foreword

U NIX achieved its widespread propagation, its penetration of the university domain, and its reach into research and industry due to its early dissemination by AT&T to all interested parties at almost no cost and as source code. UNIX's present functionality emanated not just from AT&T developers but also from many external developers who used the product and contributed their own further developments, which they then put at AT&T's disposal. (Consider the contributions of the University of California at Berkeley, for example.) With the rising commercialization of UNIX by AT&T (and the current owner, Novell) since 1983, and with the philosophical wars between the large UNIX vendors such as Sun, HP, Digital, IBM, SCO, and the UNIX laboratory, as well the more rhetorical than factual discussions between OSF and UNIX International, such creative and cooperative continuing development became increasingly restricted, and UNIX source code today has become unaffordably expensive and de facto inaccessible.

Linux has changed the situation. Linux provides interested computer scientists and users with a system that revives the old UNIX tradition: Linux is available for free, and everyone is heartily invited (but not obliged) to contribute to its continuing development. When I wrote the foreword to the first edition of this book in 1994, Linux, because it ran on PC systems, had begun to penetrate the workrooms of many computer science students and computer freaks. This triumphal advance is nearly complete, and Linux is beginning to play a more serious role in commercial environments.

The functionality, completeness, and compatibility to commercial UNIX products that Linux has meanwhile achieved is truly impressive. The rate of development is so rapid that it proves difficult to remain up to date. Today Linux can hold its own against proprietary UNIX. In fact, in certain respects, such as support of PC expansion boards and peripherals, Linux has outstripped its proprietary competitors. What is of utmost importance to systems programmers and in stark contrast to commercial UNIX systems, Linux source code is freely available.

This book can contribute to making this rich source of software more readily accessible for users and programmers and to help readers obtain an overview. This is the task of this book, which seeks to complement the readily available Linux Manual Pages by means of an overview and numerous notes and additions. This will permit the Linux novice a more rapid initiation, better utilization of the system, and a look at areas that were unfamiliar or could not be found. Especially the instructions for installation and administration— which unfortunately vary greatly from one UNIX system to the next—will prove helpful to most Linux users.

Linux overview

As a sort of UNIX veteran, I am pleasantly surprised that Linux, far beyond the initial euphoria, has managed to rekindle the pioneering spirit of the early UNIX years and, for the benefit of the commercial UNIX peddlers with their often ridiculous, unresolved, and truly proprietary discussions, really shows what is possible and useful. May this book contribute to this effort.

pioneering spirit

J. Gulbins

Note from the authors

This book evolved from the experience that we gathered through various courses that we taught and from the questions that we repeatedly encounter on the subject of Linux. We have seen that novice users, in order to facilitate their getting started, frequently need a broad overview of the Linux system and its many tools rather than large amounts of precise knowledge of technical details. As such, instead of serving primarily as a reference, this book strives to impart to the reader the necessary basic knowledge that makes it possible to tap additional sources independently.

Acknowledgments

We wish to expressly convey our gratitude to the following persons, who actively contributed to the production of this book: Christian Lotz and Henner Zeller, without whose help we could never have found the time to complete the second edition and Stefan Middendorf, who contributed CD-ROMs and valuable advice for the third one. Dirk Höfle, Sascha Runge, Rainer Maurer, Maren Mecking and Roland Uhl contributed criticism and corrections. We owe special thanks to the director of the computing center at Heilbronn College, Dr. G. Peter, and his staff. We are obliged to J. Gulbins for contributing the foreword.

We also thank our translators, Bob Bach and Aileen Derieg, for the synergy and the brutal night shifts that they shared with us in the final stages of preparing the manuscript for production.

Contents

## Chapter 1

Introduction

For some time 32-bit machines have been a hot topic in the world of PCs. It seems that more powerful operating systems will soon be displacing DOS. Meanwhile, at least in the professional literature, lively discussion has been raging about what the future standard will be. Two alternatives seem to be emerging for the domain of server operating systems: Windows NT, and UNIX variants such as Solaris 2, UnixWare, and NextStep 486. In this context OS/2 plays no significant role since it is seen more as a competitor to Windows.

UNIX vs. Windows NT

We cannot yet predict which system will finally predominate. However, the significant rise in the power of hardware in recent years has unleashed the demand for a modern operating system that makes use of these developments. Under a modern server operating system, the borderline between classical UNIX workstations and high-end PCs will tend to become more fluid.

workstations

1.1   Historical perspectives on Linux

An extremely powerful alternative to the above proprietary systems has evolved far from all the big debates on strategy. The system is Linux, a UNIX system for Intel processors that is available for free.

Linux was developed by a young Finnish student named Linus Torvalds. His initial goal was not to develop a full-scale operating system, however. At first he only wanted to acquaint himself with and understand the special task-switching commands of the 80386 processor. To compile his test program, he used MINIX, a pedagogical operating system by Andrew Tannenbaum for teaching and learning operating systems.

386 processor

1

Yet, due to its didactic orientation, MINIX had some shortcomings. The ambitious student soon exhausted the possibilities of the UNIX-like system. From his test program, he began step by step

kernel to develop a small operating system (kernel) that ran in the protected mode of the 80386 and thus optimally exploited the processor.

After the task switcher, Torvalds wrote a simple keyboard driver to allow him to work interactively with the system. At this point Linux still relied on parts of the MINIX system, but that was soon to change.

To avoid having to develop a new file system as well, Torvalds

MINIX file system decided to adopt the MINIX file system. This not only saved him a great deal of work, but also provided from the start a stable system for managing the hard disk. After a few months the developer considered the system to be mature enough to present it to the general public.

In August 1991 the complete source code of Linux appeared

FTP server for the first time on Finland's largest FTP server (Internet address nic.funet.fi). It was announced as a "freely distributable MINIX clone" and caught the attention of only a few interested parties on the network. Only two months later, Torvalds published the next version (0.02), which contained some rudimentary UNIX commands. The accompanying GNU compiler (gcc) permitted the compilation of small C programs and thus enabled the porting of a UNIX shell (bash).

POSIX The early decision to adhere to POSIX, a family of standards of the Institute of Electrical and Electronics Engineers (IEEE), played a deciding role in ensuring the portability of standard UNIX software to today's Linux. However, it took until the end of the year before Linux received more widespread notice. The breakthrough came on January 5, 1992, with version 0.12. Linux had attained sufficient power to interest a larger community of developers. The system

swapping had meanwhile acquired a swapping mechanism that gave it an unequivocal edge over MINIX.

interested developers Over time an ever-increasing number of interested developers were sending corrections and suggestions for improvements to Finland and thus participating in the improvement of the Linux system. Early developments contributed in this way include the

POSIX Job Control in version 0.12 and the switchable virtual consoles.

The Internet proved to be an important tool for the rapid development of Linux. The Internet is a wide-area network (WAN), an information highway connecting more than six million computers and allowing the fast exchange of all kinds of information. The Internet permits Linux developers to exchange comments, improvements, and programs.

Early on, Torvalds was bombarded with over 60 e-mail messages per day, which he could hardly read and answer. Only after several discussion groups for Linux were set up did the flood of mail subside. Today there are several newsgroups concerned with Linux. The most important is `comp.os.linux.announce` (c.o.l.a.), where new developments and program versions are announced. Mailing lists were set up for Linux developers to permit a similar kind of information exchange.

In addition to letters and information, files can be exchanged via the Internet, which makes it possible to organize the distributed development of larger software systems, as Linux so impressively demonstrates.

The rapid flow of information proves to be a tangible advantage not only for developers but also for users of Linux. If the user encounters any problems during installation or detects errors during operation, then with a little luck and the Internet, an adequate solution is only a couple of hours away. Even commercial service contracts seldom provide such extensive support.

Naturally, not every Linux user has access to the Internet, but even then the user is not deserted. Many mailbox networks have set up Linux discussion groups, so that a modem suffices for keeping on top of things.

An interesting aspect of Linux history is that there was never a strict hierarchy or authority that managed the development in any way. Rather, the project has been fueled by the enthusiasm of many individual Internetters who continue to contribute new improvements and suggestions. These are often professional developers or employees of large institutions who contribute their free time.

Internet

discussion groups

mailing lists

support

mailboxes

participatory
development

3

Although Linus Torvalds continues to handle the concrete further development of the kernel, quite a few competent allies have taken over other areas of the system. Such areas include the porting and maintenance of the GNU C compiler and the C libraries for Linux, the maintenance and adaptation of the X Window System, and networking. Other Linux devotees are working on user and system documentation, or assembling an installable system on diskettes or CD-ROM.

GNU C

X Window System

Free source code is available not only for the kernel but also for most application programs. They come primarily from the huge UNIX freeware archives on the Internet. Periodically via the Internet a software catalog (Linux Software Map) is distributed; it currently contains some 1300 software packages. There is scarcely a domain for which some suitable software cannot be found.

source code

software catalog

Since much development at American universities is carried out with UNIX, and such developments become public domain, many implementations in the area of research are available for Linux. One example is compilers for both well-known and more obscure programming languages. Also, the database systems Ingres and Postgres from the University of California at Berkeley have been ported to Linux.

public domain

Although the emphasis remains on freeware, commercial applications are also available, such as a Modula-2 compiler, a Smalltalk development system, an interface builder, CAD software, several database systems, and the OSF/Motif graphical user interface that has become a standard in the UNIX world.

OSF/Motif

1.2   Versions

The further development of Linux is currently experiencing big leaps similar to the first implementation of the kernel. Version 1.0 was scheduled for December 1992 but was delayed—not because of a lack of stability, but because the functionality had not yet matched that of proprietary UNIX systems.

Version 1.0

Thus the release of Version 1.0 was repeatedly delayed. In retrospect, Torvalds says that he should have declared the first stable and usable version 0.12 as version 1.0, for the zero in the version number apparently scared off many potentially interested parties from delving deeper into the system.

The final version 1.0 was released in March 1994, and developments continued with the version numbers 1.1x. This system of numbering led to a great deal of confusion among users and interested parties. Various CD producers have also contributed to the confusion by selling several Linux distributions with their own version numbers. Linux itself, however, is only a small component that easily fits on a disk several times when compiled. Asking about the Linux version on a CD is thus misleading. Instead, you should ask about the version of the kernel, the C library, the compiler, or X11.

distributions

Another popular misconception is that the higher the version number, the better or more stable the software. This is not the case, however. For a long time, the Kernel 1.0 Patchlevel 9 (or 1.0.9 for short) was the only stable kernel; the kernels with 1.1.x numbers still contained many new and not yet completely polished functions. They were intended for developers and often changed several times in a single week.

Linux 1.2 provides a new island of stability. For a long time, Linux 1.2.13 was the kernel of choice for systems that had to work reliably. In parallel thereto, the "hacker" line 1.3.* integrated new features into the kernel. At the end of 1995 the 1.3 kernel was frozen: no new code was integrated; only bugs in existing code were fixed. In June 1996 the kernel had attained sufficient stability: Linus Torvalds released Linux 2.0 (see 3.7). Since then Linux development has progressed in the 2.1 line; from time to time Linux 2.0 is extended with drivers that are considered to be reliable.

The situation is similar with the versions of the GNU C compiler: version 2.5.8 was by far more stable than version 2.6.0. So it is not possible to determine the quality of a Linux distribution solely by the numerical value of the version number. We recommend the Slackware or the Linux Universe distributions.

GNU C

The current version of Linux has all the important features of its commercial competitors, and due to its efficient design, it extracts much higher performance from a given hardware configuration. This applies to the graphical user interface as well as to the kernel.

maturity

1.3   Features

An option that may prove particularly interesting for use in commercial areas is the possibility of running programs for other

COFF, ELF   PC-based UNIX variations in COFF or ELF format under Linux. The Linux user has access to a practically unlimited supply

iBCS2   of professional applications with the iBCS2 emulator that was specifically developed for this purpose. DOS programs also run with

DOS   a DOS emulator. Likewise there is an emulator called Wine for MS-Windows programs; this emulator runs a number of Windows applications.

Contrary to many other UNIX systems, Linux already employs

X Window System   the newest version of the X Window System, X11R6. Additional Linux features that proprietary UNIX systems seldom provide include the support of INMOS transputer boards and the option to run TCP/IP via the serial or parallel port. Direct kernel support for ISDN boards for fast network connections over long distances makes Linux interesting for communication tasks. However, since there is no road map for the further development of Linux, the system will surely provide some surprises along the way.

pronunciation   Even insiders often mispronounce the word "Linux." Many users consider it an American term and pronounce it with an English long i and short u. The Finnish pronunciation is the correct one, amounting to "lee-nooks" for an English speaker.

1.4   UNIX development and standards

Ritchie & Thompson   The history of UNIX dates back well into the 1970s. In 1971 Dennis Ritchie and Ken Thompson at AT&T's Bell Laboratories developed the first version. With the availability in 1973 of the compiler

C   language C, which had evolved from BCPL and B, most of the UNIX system was rewritten, which later proved to be a great advantage for porting the system to other processors.

AT&T   Due to an agreement with the U.S. government, AT&T could not market its quite successful system. Therefore, AT&T gave UNIX as source code, although without support, to universities, where its popularity grew. With Version 7 in 1979, AT&T announced a change in its licensing policy: UNIX source code would only be provided for a fee. This prompted the University of California at Berkeley to develop its own variant, BSD (Berkeley Software Distribution) UNIX. In 1983 AT&T announced the marketing of its enhanced System V. The System V Interface Definition specified the programming interface to this system.

BSD UNIX

System V

Companies like Sun Microsystems, Microsoft, and DEC developed their own versions of UNIX (SunOS, Xenix, ULTRIX), which in time unnecessarily encumbered the porting of software between these systems. In order to merge the two main branches of UNIX (BSD and System V), in 1990 AT&T propagated its Release 4 of System V as a new standard that encompasses all previous variants of UNIX.

System V Release 4

Other institutions also have recognized the need for a standardization of UNIX. The Institute of Electrical and Electronic Engineers (IEEE) developed the POSIX standard for UNIX-related operating systems. This standard is divided into several parts. POSIX 1003.1 describes only the lowest-level system interface; 1003.2 will define a standard for shells and commands; 1003.7 covers the possibilities of system administration. Although POSIX is actually based on the UNIX system interface, this standard will also be supported by other operating systems (e.g., Windows NT).

standardization

POSIX

A body consisting primarily of UNIX manufacturers has released another standard. Although the X/Open Portability Guide is based on POSIX 1003.1, it provides extensions in certain points. Within the realm of the COSE Initiative (Common Open Software Environment), the importance of the X/Open Consortium rose significantly. Meanwhile we also have the standardized user interfaces and programming interfaces CDE (Common Desktop Environment) for important UNIX platforms (HP-UX, AIX, UnixWare, Solaris 2). Linux adheres to the POSIX standard.

X/Open

1.5   The Free Software Foundation

In addition to its orientation to the POSIX standard, Linux is also largely subject to the General Public License (GPL) of the Free Software Foundation (FSF). FSF was founded about a decade ago

General Public License

7

Richard Stallman

free software

by Richard Stallman, the developer of the legendary GNU Emacs editor. The organization "aims to make high-quality free software available to everyone." Note that *free* in the title of the organization refers to "freedom," not "zero dollars."

This kind of freedom means that copying and distributing software, including the source codes, is not to be restricted. This makes free software fundamentally different from public domain software or shareware. It is protected by copyright, and the license requirements are regulated by the GPL.

commercial distribution

Software that is subject to the GPL may also be commercially distributed, but it must be possible for anyone to copy it and pass it on. The source code must be included. If developers use free software as the basis for their own developments, then this development must also be made available under the GPL. This does not apply to software that was compiled with the GNU C compiler or edited with the GNU Emacs editor, but rather to programs using a source code that is subject to the GPL.

quality

Objective-C

A frequent result of this practice is an increase in the quality of software, from which everyone benefits. For instance, the Next Company used the GNU C compiler as the basis of its Objective-C compiler. So what was available to them was a relatively mature and freely accessible compiler. Under the GPL, the new additions were made available to the general public, so now the GNU C compiler works not only with ANSI C and C++, but also with Objective C.

GNU

The GNU project represents FSF's attempt to develop a complete operating system that can be freely copied and is largely compatible with UNIX. GNU, by the way, stands for "Gnu's not UNIX." In addition to the GNU C compiler and the Emacs editor, numerous UNIX-compatible commands and tools were developed in the course of this project that are currently used in almost all Linux distributions. What the FSF and GNU project have been lacking is an operating systems core. Although the GNU kernel (Hurd) was already in the works before Linux emerged, it cannot be employed yet by users. Hurd is based on the Mach-3 microkernel, and someday it may well be technologically superior to Linux.

Hurd

Since quite a few UNIX commands and utilities originated in the GNU project or are at least subject to the GPL, Linux has profited

from the project. At the same time, Linux fulfills the aim of the GNU
project, as the Linux kernel, together with the FSF tools and other   Linux & FSF
freely accessible utilities, represents a complete UNIX system that
is free of charge.

Currently, the further development of such essential elements   further developments
as the C compiler and the C library is done in collaboration and
is coordinated by GNU and Linux developers. Popular FTP servers   FTP server
now offer the interested programmer an overwhelming multitude
of software that is subject to the GPL. In addition to programming
languages such as C, C++, Smalltalk, Lisp, and Fortran, there are also
various editors, debuggers (gdb), and even a PostScript interpreter
(Ghostscript).

1.6   An overview of Linux features

To give the reader a better orientation, we offer the following
summary of Linux's most important features:

- **A full-fledged, 32-bit multi-user/multitasking UNIX system**.   multi-user
  Linux permits multiple users to execute (different) programs   multitasking
  simultaneously and thereby fully exploits the capacity of the Intel
  80386 processor and its successors. The resulting performance is   performance
  definitely comparable to a classical RISC workstation.
- **Orientation to common UNIX standards** (POSIX). This
  provides an ideal environment for developing portable software.
  Available software that adheres to existing UNIX standards usually
  can be ported to Linux without problems.
- **Network support** (TCP/IP and others). A Linux machine can   network
  easily be integrated into a TCP/IP network, LanManager, Windows
  for Workgroups or Novell network. Linux supports common
  Ethernet adapterss and TCP/IP connection via modem (SLIP/PPP).
- **Graphical user interface** (X11 Window System). The Linux   X11R6
  system includes the current version (Release 6) of the X Window
  System. OSF/Motif, the standard user interface for proprietary   OSF/Motif
  UNIX systems, can be purchased as an add-on product.

9

GNU

- **GNU utilities and programs**.   Many of Linux's commands and utilities emanate from the GNU project and contribute much functional enhancement.

compatibility

- **Complete UNIX development environment**.   Linux permits the development of programs that run problem-free on other UNIX systems. In addition to the GNU C/C++/ Objective C compiler, numerous editors, and several version control systems, there are many other software development tools.

Basics

I n order to understand the following chapters, the reader will need some knowledge of computer science in general and UNIX in particular. To ease the transition into this material for readers who are newcomers to UNIX, we present some of the most important concepts and terms in this chapter.

2.1   Multi-user operation

In classical data processing, a central mainframe handles all required DP tasks. Serial connections link terminals (simple text-oriented consoles with keyboards) to this mainframe. Many users sharing a single mainframe necessitates a system of access control and user management to achieve fair distribution of the shared resources. UNIX is such a *multi-user system*.   mainframe
terminals

Unambiguous user names, also called *login names*, form the basis of this system. Each user is assigned a login name, which can be an abbreviation of the user's natural name, e.g., bsheehan for Betty Sheehan. In order to start a new session, the user must enter this login name and the associated password; we call this logging in. Each login name carries with it certain permissions for file access and other privileges.   login names

Actually, a user is identified by a number, the *user ID (UID)*. The kernel (operating system kernel, see Section 2.4) itself recognizes only UIDs, and even the file owners in the file systems are stored as UIDs. Only the outer layers offer mechanisms to translate login names to UIDs and vice versa. This is the purpose of the file /etc/passwd, which saves a record for each user with the login name, UID, password, and other information. Most UNIX commands   user ID and programs that at some point require identifying the user do accept the login name (or both the login name and the UID). A user can work problem-free without ever knowing the UID.

All multi-user systems have one privileged user who administrates the system. This user is called the *system administrator* or superuser. Under UNIX this privileged user has the name root and the numerical ID 0. This user's permissions are unlimited. The administrator can create new users and assign permissions. Chapter 7 explains the tasks of the system administrator in more detail.

Users are assigned to various *groups*. Typical groups include users (all normal users), root (users with root permissions, which is usually the user root alone), and ftpadm (users maintaining the FTP server).

If a file server is used by the staff of various projects and departments, then it makes sense to create a group for each project and department. A user can belong to multiple groups. The *primary group* is specified in the file /etc/passwd; in addition, the user can be assigned to other groups in the file /etc/group.

In addition to an *owner*, each file also has a user group that can be granted additional permissions beyond normal users. Thus we could assign all users that maintain the WWW server to the group webmaster; this group would have write permissions in the directories where Web pages reside. All files created by the staff of a certain project could be assigned to this project group and might not even be readable for other users. In addition to a name (such as users), groups have an identifying number, the *group ID* (or *GID*). Translating the GID to a group name occurs via the /etc/group file.

In recent years hardware prices have fallen while performance has risen. The possibilities afforded by decentralized systems with their graphical user interfaces led to a decline in the acceptance of mainframes. Instead of a central mainframe with many terminals and numerous users, today's trends reveal an increasing number of workplaces where each user has sole use of one or more computers. These computers are connected via a network to each other and to other computers and servers to permit the easy exchange of data.

superuser
root

groups

/etc/group

owner

group ID

from central
mainframe to network
multiple terminals

A similar development has occurred in the area of UNIX: the purely text-oriented UNIX system has evolved into a graphical desktop UNIX workstation. The trend that a single user might use multiple computers at the same time in order to simultaneously access various programs and data is also reflected in *virtual terminals*. This feature allows a user to log in to the same computer repeatedly, even though the user physically has only one monitor; a special key combination makes it possible to switch between various virtual terminals.

UNIX workstation

virtual terminals

2.2 Multitasking

Newer multi-user systems are usually multitasking systems as well. They are capable of processing many tasks quasi-simultaneously, which simple multi-user systems cannot necessarily do.

The smallest unit that can be handled in parallel in such a system is called a *process* or *task*. In UNIX, which is both a multi-user and a multitasking system, we generally speak of processes. Processes that execute in parallel on a UNIX system could be programs from different users or programs that always run in the background (so-called *daemons*).

process

daemons

A significant characteristic of modern multitasking systems is the availability of *interprocess communication* (*IPC*). This encompasses functions for synchronization and data exchange between processes.

interprocess
communication

On conventional computers with only one processor, the CPU must be allocated alternately among the individual processes in order to give the user the impression of simultaneous execution. This task is managed by the *scheduler*, a special process that maintains a list of the normal processes and sees to it that the processor handles the next process at certain time intervals.

scheduler

There are various strategies that a scheduler can use to determine which process to handle next. One very simple strategy (*round robin*) selects the next respective process in the list at regular intervals (e.g., 50 ms) and puts it at the end of the list after the allocated time if the process is not yet finished. Another strategy assigns each process a

scheduling strategies
round robin

13

priority, whereby processes with higher priority are allocated more CPU time.

nice levels

UNIX employs *nice levels*, which allow the user to influence the internal priorities of processes. This allows the user to reduce significantly the encumbering of the system by programs running in the background. Likewise, the system administrator can also raise the priority of important processes to ensure faster execution.

2.3 Memory management

Memory management in today's UNIX systems differs substantially from that of a simpler operating system. For instance, a UNIX operating system may pretend to provide more main memory to the programs than is actually available.

The method used to implement virtual memory management in Linux is called *paging*. With the help of tables, the operating

logical address space
physical address space

system maps a large *logical address space* onto a smaller *physical address space*. When processes demand more main memory than is physically present, individual segments of logical memory that have not been referenced recently are relocated onto the hard disk

swapping

(*swapping*).

When a program accesses a logical address that is currently located on the hard disk, the respective memory segment (called a *page*) is loaded into main memory, while another memory segment must be written to the hard disk to compensate. Due to the significantly higher access time of a hard disk compared to main memory, there is naturally a price to be paid in terms of execution

speed

speed.

swap files

In order to be able to use the hard disk for virtual memory management and the logical main memory, *swap files* or *swap partitions* must be created on the hard disk. Without such partitions or files, main memory is limited to its actually available physical size.

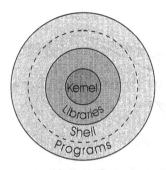

Figure 2.1. Schematic structure of a UNIX system.

2.4   Shell model

The structure of a UNIX system is often depicted as a *shell model* (Figure 2.1). The *kernel* of a UNIX system contains components like the scheduler and the *device drivers*. These routines permit access to the interface hardware and external devices. The memory management also resides in the kernel.

    The processes in the kernel are different from the processes running in the shell around the kernel. User processes can be interrupted at any time; they are subject to the control of the scheduler; and a certain region of memory is allocated to each of them. If a user process attempts to access a region of memory outside its own, the process is aborted with the error message `segmentation fault`. The contents of the current memory for the process may then be written into a file called `core` (a *core dump*). This file can be useful for the developer looking for errors.

    By contrast, *kernel processes* have unrestricted access to all resources of the computer. Hence we speak of two different modes in which processes can run: the *user mode* and the *kernel mode*. The outer shell of a UNIX system consists of programs that directly make contact with the user. This outer shell includes the *command shell*, which executes operating system commands, as well as application programs such as word processing and databases.

    Between the outer shell and the kernel are the various *libraries* that provide access to their library functions (usually written in C) and

shell model
kernel
device drivers
hardware

user processes

segmentation fault
core
core dump
kernel processes

command shell

libraries

15

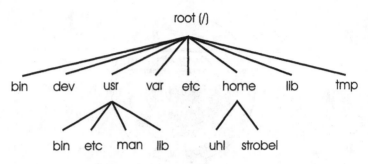

Figure 2.2. Excerpt from a UNIX file tree.

linking   to kernel routines. These libraries are normally linked to a program after its compilation, thus adding the library routines to those of the program itself.

statically linked   Since these *statically linked* programs demand a large amount

shared libraries   of memory, modern programmers usually employ *shared libraries*, which consist of two parts. A small part containing only references to the library is linked to the program. The library itself is actually loaded only when the program is executed. This allows multiple programs to use the routines in shared libraries simultaneously, which also saves memory. You can find additional information on the shared libraries, in general and under Linux, in Section 7.10.

Another advantage is the possibility to exchange a shared library

version upgrade   for a newer version without having to relink the programs relying on it. However, this assumes that the routines in the new library are invocation-compatible with those of the old version.

2.5   File systems

hard disk   A file system manages data stored on a hard disk. Although every computer system has such mechanisms, they can differ substantially. Modern file systems have a hierarchical structure (Figure 2.2). The user can distribute files in various directories, making it easier to

path   maintain an overview. The user accesses the files via the *path*. Contrary to DOS, UNIX uses the slash (/) as the delimiter with a path.

Under UNIX, paths can be specified as absolutely (with a / at the beginning) or relatively to the current directory. A user's *home directory* is particularly important here. Personal data are stored in this directory, and this is where the user lands after logging in.

home directory

DOS addresses disk drives and the partitions of a hard disk with a drive letter. UNIX merges all of these to a single file system and does not assign them separate designations. This means that the user can no longer distinguish the individual drives and partitions. Only one large drive with a single file system appears to exist. Problems arise in the management of diskettes and other removable storage media since these are not permanently in the drive. Before access to a removable storage medium is possible, it must be linked to the system using the `mount` command, which normally only the system administrator can do.

no drive letters

diskettes

The management of files and free blocks differs considerably under DOS and UNIX. DOS creates a File Allocation Table (FAT) on each drive to record the free and allocated sectors. Another sector contains the *root directory*. Besides the names of the contained files, a DOS directory also contains their attributes, such as size and date.

FAT

By contrast, UNIX allocates an *i-node* for each file, in which the most important attributes are stored, such as name, permissions, and start block. Directories thus contain only references to the respective i-nodes. Because it is both more economical in terms of storage space and more efficient regarding access, such a structure proves better suited to the management of larger file systems than a FAT system.

i-node

Permissions

When a file is created under UNIX, the operating system stores not only the file name and the date of creation but also the user ID of its creator (or owner) as well as the group that owns the file. To be able to protect the files of a file system against undesired access, the permissions for each file are stored separately. Thus access to a file can be limited to its owner or to a certain user group. It is also possible to define general permissions. We further distinguish among read, write, and execute permissions, which are reflected in the output of the `ls` (list) command by the letters r, w, and x. The position of the letters in the output indicates whether the permissions apply to

owner

file access

read, write, and execute

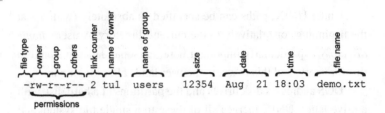

Figure 2.3. Displaying permissions using the command ls.

the owner of the file, the group owners of the file, or everyone else (Figure 2.3).

directories Subdirectories are an exception. Read permission suffices only to read their contents. In order to change to a subdirectory, however, a user must possess both read and execute permissions for that subdirectory.

Links

Another feature of the UNIX file systems is the possibility to create *links*. If access to a file is to take place from various points in the file systems, this file could simply be copied. Naturally this approach would mean a waste of storage. In such cases under UNIX, the creation of a link proves a more practical alternative.

hard links UNIX links to a file can be either *hard links* or *symbolic links*. A hard link is an additional reference from a directory to a file or its

link counter i-node. The *link counter* tabulates the number of such references. If a file to which several links refer is to be deleted, then the link counter is decremented by one. Only after the link counter reaches the value one can the file be deleted physically.

Since the numbers of i-nodes are unambiguous only within a file system, hard links cannot be created for files intended for use outside a given file system. By contrast, symbolic links can reference any directory entries (subdirectories or files). Whether the referenced file actually exists plays no role in the creation of the symbolic link. The output of the ls command indicates the difference between these two kinds of links:

```
linux1:/etc> ls -l hosts passwd
lrwxrwxrwx 1 tul   users   10 Aug 21 18:05 hosts -> /etc/hosts
-rw-r--r-- 2 root root    863 Aug  9 15:00 passwd
```

Symbolic links are represented with an l (el for link) in the column for the file type and a visible reference to the original file. Hard links can only be recognized by the increased link counter in the second column (after the permissions).

file types

Virtual file system

In order to support the development of different file systems, Linux provides an additional layer, the *virtual file system*, between the kernel and the actual routines of a file system, as in proprietary UNIX systems. The virtual file system defines a number of routines that must be available in every file system, for opening, reading, writing, and closing files. This unambiguous interface enables the problem-free coexistence of different file systems.

file system
virtual file system
routines

2.6   Devices

UNIX maps hard disks as well as terminals and other devices onto special files in the directory /dev of the file systems. Thus the programmer can access such devices in the same way as normal files.

/dev

This file-like view of devices also has advantages for the user. If the user wants to output a file to the printer instead of to the console, then it suffices to redirect standard output to the respective device (/dev/lp1).

advantages

```
linux2:/home> cat output.txt >/dev/lp1
```

Likewise the floppy disk drive (/dev/fd0), the mouse (/dev/ mouse), and the hard disk are addressed via an entry in the /dev directory (see Figure 2.4).

mouse
device drivers

Files in directory dev and the respective devices are associated via two numbers, the *major device number* and the *minor device number*. These also form the interface to the kernel. In addition,

major and minor
device numbers

19

device file	description
/dev/console	system console
/dev/mouse	serial mouse
/dev/hda	first AT-bus hard disk
/dev/hda1	first partition of first AT-bus hard disk
/dev/hda2	second partition of first AT-bus hard disk
/dev/hdb	second AT-bus hard disk
/dev/hdb1	first partition of second AT-bus hard disk
/dev/sda	first SCSI hard disk
/dev/sdb	second SCSI hard disk
/dev/lp0	first printer port (LPT1)
/dev/null	null device (all output is suppressed)
/dev/ttyN	virtual console
/dev/ptyN	pseudoterminal for login from network
/dev/ttySN	serial port

Figure 2.4. List of the most important devices

character and
block devices

there are two kinds of devices, *character devices* and *block devices*. The former are character-oriented and are used primarily for devices like terminals and serial ports. The latter are used for transferring large data blocks for hard disks and other data storage devices. For block devices, the access position can be changed (seek). The major and minor device numbers are evident in an **ls -l** output.

```
linux1:/dev> ls -l
...
brw-r-----  1 root    root    3,  0 Aug 29  1992 hda
brw-r-----  1 root    root    3,  1 Aug 29  1992 hda1
brw-r-----  1 root    root    3,  2 Aug 29  1992 hda2
...
crw-rw-rw-  1 root    root    4,  0 Aug 16 12:26 tty0
crw--w--w-  1 tul     users   4,  1 Aug 21 15:15 tty1
...
linux1:/dev>
```

device driver

The major device number (fifth column in the above listing) specifies the type of the device. Normally each major device number has a corresponding *device driver* in the kernel. When multiple devices of the same type are connected, they are distinguished by their minor device number (sixth column in the above listing) and served by the same driver.

2.7 Shells

The *shell* provides the interactive interface between the operating system and the user. Even in this era of graphical user interfaces, many UNIX users still prefer to enter commands this way.

We can compare the tasks of the shell with those of command.com under DOS, although a UNIX shell affords significantly more features than the DOS command interpreter.

command.com

Standard shells

Most proprietary UNIX systems include three kinds of shells: a Bourne shell (sh), a Korn shell (ksh), and a C shell (csh). The Bourne shell was the first UNIX shell; thus it affords little in the way of comfort. The Korn shell is an extension of the Bourne shell and appears relatively often with proprietary UNIX systems.

sh, ksh, csh

Like BSD UNIX, the C shell was born at the University of California at Berkeley. In contrast to the Bourne and Korn shells, the C shell offers a simple *history function*, allowing the UNIX user to return to commands that have already been entered on the command line. *Alias substitution* makes it possible to automatically replace certain commands that were entered in an initialization file or interactively. Due to its C-like syntax, this shell variant has been a particular favorite among programmers.

history function

Alias substitution

When it is started as login shell, the C shell executes the commands of the .login, which must be located in the home directory for this purpose. Since a user normally possesses only one active login shell, the contained commands are executed only once at login. On the other hand, a shell script that is executed at the start of each new C shell is the file .cshrc, which likewise must be located in the home directory.

.login

.cshrc

Interactive use

UNIX commands such as ls, cd, and man, which are entered in the normal command line, are not executed by the UNIX operating system itself; instead, they are programs that are usually located in the directories /bin and /usr/bin. A user entering such commands is not in direct contact with the UNIX operating system, but only with its outermost shell, a program named shell.

After logging in, UNIX system users normally find themselves in an interactive shell. The shell only recognizes a few commands

standard input

and spends most of the time reading user input from the standard input device, i.e., the keyboard, and starting the respective program. With the input of **ls -l**, for example, the shell invokes the program /bin/ls with the option -l, and the contents of the current directory are displayed on the console:

```
zeus:/home/uhl> ls
Disktools        Help       News          demo.txt
Documents        Motif      UsrAdmin      demo.tex
zeus:/home/uhl>
```

options

Most commands also allow parameter transfer. Thus data and options can be transferred to a program that can evaluate them.

```
zeus:/home/uhl> ls -l
total 1516
drwxr-xr-x      3 uhl      users        1024 May 14  1994 Disktools
drwxr-xr-x      2 uhl      users        1024 May  1  1994 Documents
drwxr-xr-x      2 uhl      users        1024 Aug  8 12:28 Help
drwxr-xr-x      2 uhl      users        1024 Dec 24 17:27 Motif
drwxr-xr-x      2 uhl      users        1024 Jul 31 12:56 News
drwxr-xr-x      3 uhl      users        1024 Mar 27  1994 UsrAdmin
-rw-r--r--      1 uhl      users     1474560 Dec 29 21:10 demo.tex
-rw-r--r--      1 uhl      users     1474560 Dec 29 21:10 demo.txt
zeus:/home/uhl>
```

With the ls command, the parameter -l leads to a more comprehensive version of the table of contents.

Enhanced shells

As a rule Linux does not employ any of the above shells. Instead,

more comfortable

Linux uses enhanced variants of these shells. These more comfortable shell variants, which are available for free for almost all UNIX systems, render the original shells obsolete. The Bourne Again shell

bash and tcsh

(bash) has displaced the Bourne shell sh, and the tcsh shell has supplanted the C shell. System administrators usually use a Bourne shell because most administration scripts require it. The following explanations thus refer primarily to this shell variant.

bash The bash (Bourne Again shell) evolved, like many other programs, from the GNU project of the Free Software Foundation. It can be considered an extension of the Korn shell, which shares many of the features of the tcsh (see the next section). Furthermore, the scroll keys allow activation of practical special functions like automatic name and path extension and history scrolling. The following example explains this feature in more detail.

GNU

tcsh

To change from the directory /home/stefan to the directory usr/src/linux, the command **cd /usr/src/linux** could naturally be entered manually, letter by letter. With automatic path recognition in bash it suffices to specify directories only enough to assure that they are unambiguous. Entering (Tab) then automatically extends the path.

automatic path recognition

```
/home/stefan> cd /usr/s
```

After entry of (Tab) the above line becomes:

```
/home/stefan> cd /usr/src/
```

Then an **1** (el) is entered:

```
/home/stefan> cd /usr/src/l
```

After entry of (Tab) the above line becomes:

```
/home/stefan> cd /usr/src/linux/
```

In order to edit the makefile of the Linux kernel in this directory, it suffices to enter only a few characters:

```
/usr/src/linux> emacs M
```

After entry of ⌈ **Tab** ⌉ the above line becomes:

```
/usr/src/linux> emacs Makefile
```

Makefile is the only file in this directory that begins with a capital M.

If an attempt to make the extension results in multiple alternatives, there is a warning sound, and, after the ⌈ **Tab** ⌉ key is pressed again, bash displays all possible variants.

variants

command history

The up and down scroll keys allow the user to move through the command history. In the above example, pressing the scroll up key once would yield the following on the command line:

```
/usr/src/linux> emacs Makefile
```

Pressing the scroll up again would display the following:

```
/usr/src/linux> cd /usr/src/linux/
```

environment variables

Environment variables enable the display of the host name and the current path in the prompt. To accomplish this, the following line is added to the file .bashrc in the respective home directory:

```
PS1='\h:$PWD>'
```

Bourne Again shell

The Bourne Again shell affords many other features that cannot be described here in detail. Please refer to the on-line Manual pages for more information on bash.

tcsh

C shell

command history

One alternative to the Bourne Again shell is tcsh, an extension of the C shell. Like bash it can automatically extend paths and commands when the ⌈ **Tab** ⌉ key is pressed, and the scroll keys allow moving through the command history and editing the command line. Furthermore, various additional functions can be activated, such as watch mode, where a message is output if a user logs in or out. The

display of all alternatives for automatic extension is invoked in tcsh `automatic extension`
with **Ctrl** + **D**, but all keys can be configured. The directory listing
of the directory /usr/src can be displayed without fully entering
the command cd:

```
linux1:/home/tul> cd /usr/src/ Ctrl + D
```

An interesting feature is the automatic correction of erroneously `correction`
entered commands or file names. Here tcsh attempts to use the next
closest command or file name. This feature is activated by entering
Meta + **s**.

rc files

The various UNIX shells each have their own *startup files* that they
execute when they are started. These files set environment variables
or display cute sayings (fortune). The shells behave differently
depending on whether they are a *login shell* and whether they are an
interactive shell (interactive: reading commands from the terminal `interactive shell`
instead of a script), in particular this determines which scripts they
execute at startup.

Overview of rc scripts:

File	Shell	Shell type	Scope
/etc/profile	bash, sh	login	systemwide
~/.bash_profile	bash	login	user-specific
~/.profile	bash, sh	login	user-specific
~/.bashrc	bash	interactive	user-specific
/etc/csh.login	csh, tcsh	login	systemwide
/etc/csh.cshrc	csh, tcsh	always	systemwide
~/.tcshrc	tcsh	always	user-specific
~/.cshrc	tcsh, csh	always*	user-specific
~/.login	tcsh, csh	login	user-specific

*tcsh: if .tcshrc does not exist

25

Environment

environment

Another way to transfer data to program is through the environment. Here a list of variables and their respective values is automatically passed to a program every time it is launched. In order to obtain a list of the currently defined environment variables, use the command set in the Bourne shell:

```
zeus:/home/uhl> set
PS1=$HOST:$PWD>
PS2=>
PATH
PATH=/bin:/usr/bin:/usr/local/bin:.
PWD=/home/uhl
TERM=vt100
UID=401
zeus:/home/uhl>
```

variables

These variables can be deleted and redefined as needed. For example, you can redefine a variable called AUTO as VW and pass it to another program as follows:

```
zeus:/home/uhl> export AUTO=VW
zeus:/home/uhl> set
PS1=$HOST:$PWD>
PS2=>
PATH=/bin:/usr/bin:/usr/local/bin:.
PWD=/home/uhl
TERM=vt100
UID=401
AUTO=VW
zeus:/home/uhl>
```

PATH, PS1

prompt

Environment variables are generally used to specify global system settings such as the access path for commands (PATH) or the nature of the prompt (PS1). A user can change or complement these settings in the startup scripts of the respective shell.

/etc/profile

/etc/csh.login

To make environment variables visible systemwide, they should be set in both /etc/profile (Bourne Shell) and in /etc/csh.login; otherwise users of the neglected shell cannot launch certain programs because of missing environment variables. It is even better to set systemwide environment variables on booting in a dedicated rc script; since processes inherit the environment of their parent process, this makes the environment variables accessible everywhere.

```
#
# Example of a .profile file
#
PATH=$PATH:/usr/local/bin
AUTO=vw
PS1='$HOST:$PWD>'
```

Redirection

The concept of standard input (`stdin`) and standard output (`stdout`) is basic for UNIX. This normally involves the keyboard and the console. Simple commands such as `ls` produce their results as standard output. A shell allows for the redirection of standard input or standard output in a file without involving the command. To do this, you use the operators > and <:

stdin, stdout

redirection

```
zeus:/home/uhl> ls > list.txt
zeus:/home/uhl>
```

As the above example shows, there is no console output in this case. The output is redirected to a file called `list.txt`, which can be displayed using `cat`:

file

```
zeus:/home/uhl> cat list.txt
Disktools
Documents
Help
Motif
News
UsrAdmin
demo.tex
demo.txt
zeus:/home/uhl>
```

Commands that expect data from standard input (e.g., `cat`) can also receive redirected input from a file:

```
zeus:/home/uhl> cat < list.txt
Disktools
Documents
Help
Motif
News
UsrAdmin
demo.tex
demo.txt
zeus:/home/uhl>
```

Aside from standard input and standard output, there is also a third channel that is linked to the console. Since it is used for the

stderr   output of error messages, it is called standard error channel (stderr). Even if the user redirects stdin and stdout, error messages will still be output to the console. The individual channels can be addressed through their file descriptors.

file	abbreviation	descriptor	default device
Standard input	stdin	0	keyboard
Standard output	stdout	1	console
Standard error	stderr	2	console

stderr   For instance, the following instruction is enough to redirect stderr to a file:

```
zeus:/home/uhl> cat list.txt 2>error.txt
```

stdout and stderr   Of course, stdout and stderr can both be redirected to a file:

```
zeus:/home/uhl> cat 2>&1 >output.txt
```

Here stderr is first redirected after stdout; then stdout is redirected to a file.

Often the existing contents of a file need to be retained when stdout is redirected. To achieve this, use the special operator >>, which appends the redirected output to an existing file rather than overwriting the file.

The possibility of using the standard output of one command as input for another one is even more interesting. This can be done with

pipe   the *pipe* operator ¦:

```
zeus:/home/uhl> ls ¦ wc
      8           8              63
zeus:/home/uhl>
```

Here the command wc counts the number of words, lines, and characters that it has received from the standard input, thus ascertaining the number of files in the current directory. The possibility of using links to form new commands out of a series of short commands makes the shell a very powerful tool.

linked commands

File name expansion

You may often find it more practical to transfer several files to a single command at once rather than entering each file name individually. This can be done using wildcards, which have a kind of joker function. If a transfer parameter contains a wildcard, the shell checks which file names in the appropriate directory match the search pattern and transfers these to the command:

wildcard

```
zeus:/home/uhl> cat *.txt
```

In this example, all the files ending with .txt are transferred to the command cat. The most important wildcards are the following:

Character	Function
*	replaces any characters (or none)
?	replaces any one character
[abc...]	replaces one character from a defined quantity
[a-z]	areas can be defined with a hyphen
[!abc...]	replaces all characters not contained in the defined quantity

Quoting

In addition to wildcards, the shell also recognizes a number of other metacharacters. These need to be *quoted*, however, to cancel the special meaning of these characters. You can do this by placing a backslash in front of the character:

metacharacters

```
zeus:/home/uhl> echo \?\?\?
???
zeus:/home/uhl>
```

To transfer a series of individual parameters to a command as a character string, enclose them in single quotes or double quotes:

single / double quotes

```
zeus:/home/uhl> echo "Hello World!"
Hello World!
zeus:/home/uhl> echo 'Hey "you" there!'
Hey "you" there!
zeus:/home/uhl>
```

As this example demonstrates, single quotes cancel the effect of double quotes.

Short commands

alias   Aliases can abbreviate frequently used commands. Create a new alias with the command of the same name:

```
zeus:/home/uhl> alias l='ls -l'
zeus:/home/uhl> l
total 1516
drwxr-xr-x        3 uhl        users        1024 May 14  1994  Disktools
drwxr-xr-x        2 uhl        users        1024 May  1  1994  Documents
drwxr-xr-x        2 uhl        users        1024 Aug  8 12:28  Help
drwxr-xr-x        2 uhl        users        1024 Dec 24 17:27  Motif
drwxr-xr-x        2 uhl        users        1024 Jul 31 12:56  News
drwxr-xr-x        3 uhl        users        1024 Mar 27  1994  UsrAdmin
-rw-r--r--        1 uhl        users     1474560 Dec 29 21:10  demo.tex
-rw-r--r--        1 uhl        users     1474560 Dec 29 21:10  demo.txt
zeus:/home/uhl>
```

In the Bourne shell you can get a list of the currently defined aliases by entering `alias` without parameters:

```
zeus:/home/uhl> alias
alias l='ls -l'
alias ll='ls -laF'
zeus:/home/uhl>
```

The construct **alias** *name=command* is permitted only in bash; in tcsh specify **alias** *name command* (also see Chapter 16).

To avoid repeatedly having to enter the same relatively long
shell script   command lines, create a shell script. A shell script can be executed like a normal UNIX command. Produce the shell script by creating a file with the desired name and containing the individual instructions:

```
#!/bin/sh
#
# filecount: shows number of files in current directory
#
ls | wc
```

The first line (/bin/sh) makes the above script run in a Bourne shell. The file's permissions have to be changed in order to allow execution of a shell script:

```
zeus:/home/uhl> chmod +x filecount
zeus:/home/uhl> filecount
        8       8       63
zeus:/home/uhl>
```

However, it is also possible to have instructions in a shell script that are considerably more complex than just calling up a few commands. The Bourne shell's script language also allows the construction of loops, tests, branches, and expressions. This means that you can program fairly complicated routines. Large parts of the UNIX system were developed on this basis. Particularly when the system is booted, it goes through a number of different shell scripts. The following provides a general overview of the development of such scripts.

programming

booting

Variables
Aside from the environment variables that are passed on to a program that is invoked, as mentioned above, there are also local variables within the shell. You can turn local variables into globally recognized environment variables by placing the key word export in front of them. Variables can accommodate any character string:

local variables

export

```
COMPUTER=IBM
```

In this example, the value IBM is assigned to the variable COMPUTER. Then if access to the contents of an (environment) variable is needed, a $ sign has to be put in front of the name:

access to variables

```
echo $COMPUTER
```

A series of special variables are already predefined within a shell script. These may contain, for example, the parameters from the command line:

command line

$#	number of transferred parameters
$0	name of the shell script
$n	nth parameter
$*	all parameters
$$	ID of the current process
$?	return value of the command last executed

double quotes

If the value of a variable within double quotes (") is accessed, then this value is replaced as usual by the current value. You can avoid this by using single quotes:

```
zeus:/home/uhl> echo "Terminal: $TERM"
Terminal: xterm
zeus:/home/uhl> echo 'Terminal: $TERM'
Terminal: $TERM
zeus:/home/uhl>
```

Backquote expansion

Within a command you can nest an additional command in
backquotes   *backquotes ' '.* The command in backquotes is evaluated first. The data that the command writes to the standard output are then inserted in place of the command in the enclosing command.

Example:

```
$ find -type f
./text1
./text2
./old/text3
./old/text5
$ grep John `find -type f`
...
```

find -type f searches the current directory and all its subdirectory and writes to standard output the names of all files it finds. grep then searches all these files for "John." The following entry is equivalent to the above grep:

```
$ grep John ./text1 ./text2 ./old/text3 ./old/text5
...
```

On decomposing a command into command names and arguments, the shell is not encumbered by ends-of-lines resulting from the output of a backquote-expanded command. They are treated like other *whitespace* (blanks or tabs).

whitespace

```
zeus:/home/uhl> cp `which ls` .
```

which ls determines where the program file for the UNIX command ls resides. The above entry copies ls into the working directory. We could have assigned the output of **which ls** to a variable:

```
zeus:/home/uhl> path=`which ls`
zeus:/home/uhl> echo $path
/bin/ls
zeus:/home/uhl> cp $path .
zeus:/home/uhl>
```

Arithmetic expansion

bash can also evaluate mathematical expressions with *arithmetic expansion*:

```
$[expression]
```

Here we have the four basic arithmetic operations with integers, integer division, logical operations such as And, Or, and Not, bit shifts, and relational operations. Within the arithmetic parentheses, you can nest other evaluations like backquote expansion.

Example:

```
golem:~> echo "$[453 < 857]"
1
golem:~> wc -c < bigfile
 341266
golem:~> echo "$[ ( `wc -c < bigfile` + 1023 ) / 1024 ] kilobytes"
334 kilobytes
```

Expressions enclosed in single quotes are not expanded, but are treated as pure text. Observe the output of the above command when the double quotes are replaced by single quotes:

33

```
golem:~> echo '$[ ( `wc -c < bigfile` + 1023 ) / 1024 ] kilobytes'
$[ ( `wc -c < bigfile` + 1023 ) / 1024 ] kilobytes
```

Keyboard input

read   The Bourne shell provides the instruction `read` for interactive data entry by the user. As a parameter, `read` expects the name of a shell variable under which the user's input is to be filed.

```
echo -n "Input: "
read line
echo $line
```

prompt   The program fragment above outputs a prompt, reads a line from the standard input, and files this under the variable `line`, which is output in the last command line.

Branches

if   The Bourne shell provides `if` for creating simple branches. Thus a routine can be made dependent on certain conditions. If the first condition is met, then only *commands1* executes. On *condition2*, *commands2* executes. *commands3* executes if neither of the conditions holds.

```
if condition1
then
        commands1
[ elif condition2
then
        commands2 ]
...
[ else
        commands3 ]
fi
```

     In general, a condition consists of calling up an external program.

test   If this returns zero, then the condition has been met. `test` is a special command for this purpose; it can also be accessed with `[`. A simple comparison of two character strings then looks like this:

```
if [ "$car" = "vw" ]
then
        echo "You have bought the right car!"
```

```
else
        echo "Buy a different car!"
fi
```

The test command also recognizes quite a few other arguments, which can be found in the reference (see Chapter 16). The case instruction provides another form of branching. Regular expressions (see Section 2.8) are used here to differentiate between the individual variations in a routine:

case

```
case value in
        expression1)
                commands1 ;;
        expression2)
                commands2 ;;
        ...
        *)
                commands3 ;;
esac
```

It is also possible to link several regular expressions with the | sign (OR):

OR

```
while true
do
        echo -n "* "
        read line
        case "$line" in
                monitor|bildschirm)
                        echo screen ;;
                auto)
                        echo car ;;
                haus)
                        echo house ;;
                ENDE)
                        exit 0 ;;
                *)
                        echo "Word unknown!" ;;
        esac
done
```

Loops

FOR loops provide the possibility of executing the same string of instructions several times for each parameter of the command line or for a password list.

FOR loop

The general syntax of a FOR loop looks like this:

```
for variable [in list]
do
        instructions
done
```

If no list is named, then the instructions are executed once for each

command line   parameter of the command line:

```
for i
do
        echo $i
done
```

This outputs the parameters of the command line successively.

```
for i in audi bmw mercedes volvo vw
do
        echo $i
done
```

extension   It is somewhat more practical, though, to use a script that adds the
extension .txt to all the files ending with .doc:

```
for i in *.doc
do
        echo $i
        tmp=`basename $i .doc`
        mv $i $tmp.txt
done
```

WHILE loops   WHILE loops keep repeating a block of instructions until the
passed condition is no longer met. Like the IF instruction, this type
of condition is an external command:

```
while condition
do
        commands
done
```

It could be used, for example, as follows:

```
while [ "$line" != "ENDE" ]
do
        echo -n "* "
        read line
        echo $line
done
```

The line that is read from the standard input is output repeatedly until
the user enters **DONE**.

2.8   Search patterns

Search patterns can be specified not only in the shells but also in the editors Emacs and vi and in search programs like grep. This is done using metacharacters, primarily ? and *. The meaning of these characters is different, however, for the shells and for other programs.

metacharacters

We need to differentiate between simple wildcards, as they are used to denote file names, and regular expressions. While the latter are more complicated, they do allow for the specification of more complex search patterns. The procedure for replacing these metacharacters is usually called *globbing* with shells and *pattern matching* with regular expressions.

regular expressions

globbing

pattern matching

We have already discussed how to work with wildcards in the shells above, so we will not go into that again here. At the moment, regular expressions are of greater interest. The following list provides an overview of the meanings of the metacharacters:

.   Any given character.

*   Any given number of the times that a preceding character or expression occurs. For example, a* would apply to any length of a series of the letter a, including no a.

+   The preceding character or expression must occur at least once. a+ means one or more a characters.

?   The last character or expression occurs exactly once or not at all.

^   Beginning of the line. This is used to create expressions that may occur only at the beginning of a line. For example, ^ab* represents an a at the beginning of a line, which may be followed by any number of occurrences of the letter b.

$ End of the line.

[]   Any of the characters inside the brackets. The characters ^ and - play a special role here. If the contents of the brackets begins with ^, then the statement is negated. All characters are permitted except for those stated. A range of characters can be defined with the character -. [A-Z] stands for any capital letters, and [^a-c] stands for any characters except a, b, and c. [123] stands for any of the characters 1, 2, or 3.

37

\ Cancels the special meaning of the subsequent character. This makes it possible to use metacharacters themselves in expressions. *+ means that * occurs at least once.

( ) Encloses a regular expression. This means, for example, that the characters * and + may also be used for other expressions.

variations

The meaning of these characters may vary slightly depending on the program, and additional metacharacters may be defined as well. When in doubt, check the manual. The following examples illustrate

grep

the use of regular expressions with the example of the command grep. This may need to be invoked with the option -E, allowing enhanced expressions. The relevant part of the output is printed here in bold type for easier understanding.

```
golem:/tmp# grep me testfile
meaning of these characters may vary slightly depending
on the program, and additional metacharacters may be defined
as well. When in

golem:/tmp# grep '^me' testfile
meaning of these characters may vary slightly depending

golem:/tmp# grep 'in$' testfile
on the program, and additional metacharacters may be defined
as well. When in

golem:/tmp# grep -E 'e+ ?c' testfile
meaning of these characters may vary slightly depending

golem:/tmp# grep -E 'en[^a-z]' testfile
on the program, and additional metacharacters may be defined
as well. When  in

golem:/tmp# grep 'a.*l' testfile
meaning of these characters may vary slightly depending
on the program, and additional metacharacters may be defined
as well. When in

golem:/tmp# grep 'a[^ ]*l' testfile
on the program, and additional metacharacters may be defined
as well. When in
```

The search pattern 1+ ?m stands for one or more occurrences of the letter 1, followed by an optional space and the letter m. (11)+[^$] means that the expression 11 occurs at least once, but it must not necessarily be followed by the end of the line. This expression must be enclosed in simple quotes, so that the shell does not attempt to process the expression, but rather passes it to the command grep directly.

2.9   Daemons

Daemons are special processes that run in the background and usually assume important tasks in a UNIX system. With daemons, large parts of the operating system run as independent programs. This keeps the operating system kernel relatively small. Furthermore, individual daemons can be activated, or restarted after a change in configuration, even during operation. Since daemons run as independent processes, they can run parallel to one another; thus, do not block other programs. The following sections illustrate some examples of daemons.

background

activate

Printer daemon (lpd)

At regular intervals the line printer daemon (lpd) checks the directory /usr/spool for new printing jobs and sends any such jobs to the respective printer. For outputting a file on a printer, Linux provides the lpr command known from BSD UNIX. New print jobs are normally appended to the end of the queue before they are sent by the printer daemon.

printer daemon

lpr

Cron daemon

If a user wants to execute a program at certain times or at regular intervals, the cron daemon makes this possible. For each user, this daemon manages a table in which the times are entered when the desired processes are to start. The output of an executed command or the respective error messages are sent to the user as e-mail. If a script is to be executed only once at a certain time, the command at does the job. Repeated execution of a process at regular intervals requires an entry in the user's cron daemon table crontab. A separate command named crontab serves this purpose.

e-mail

at

crontab

Syslog daemon

Since a daemon normally does not send output to the console, a separate protocol daemon was created to handle output and error messages from other daemons. This output can be displayed on the console, written to a file, or forwarded as e-mail to the system administrator.

protocol

39

2.10   Overview of commands

To help newcomers become familiar with Linux, we provide a collection of the most important UNIX commands, along with brief explanations. More detailed information is available in the standard UNIX literature or the On-Line Manual.

ls
outputs a list of files and directories. As an option, the file sizes, corresponding permissions, and file owners can be displayed. Recursive output of complete directory trees is also possible.

cd
if no parameter is specified, the current directory becomes the home directory.

cp
copies the specified files from one directory to another directory or to another file. As an option, a complete directory tree can be copied recursively.

mv
moves a file within a file system, or renames a file or a directory.

rm
removes a file. As an option, an entire file tree can be deleted recursively.

mkdir   creates a new directory.

rmdir   removes an empty directory.

exit   exits the current shell.

more
displays the contents of a text file page by page on the console. In addition, character strings can be searched for in the file.

man
displays the on-line documentation (Manual pages corresponding to a command.

cat
intended for the concatenation (appending) of text files, but can also be used to output a file.

grep   searches within the specified files for a certain pattern.

passwd   changes a user's password.

ps   lists all running processes with their process ID (see 16).

kill   terminates the process with the specified process ID.

su
temporarily changes the user ID, without having to repeat the login. If - is specified as an additional parameter, a renewed login is triggered.

## Chapter 3

Linux features

This chapter assumes that the reader already has a basic knowledge of UNIX or has read the previous chapters. Here we describe in more detail some of the important characteristics and features of Linux that distinguish this system from other UNIX variants and from other PC operating systems.

3.1   Virtual consoles

Many PC UNIX implementations support *virtual consoles*, which provide the capability to manage multiple independent login sessions on one console. Switching between the individual sessions usually occurs via a special key combination.

multiple logins

Under Linux the [Alt] key combined with a function key enables switching between virtual consoles. The maximum number of virtual consoles is determined in the kernel. The file /etc/inittab. establishes the configuration for which of these consoles is to display the login prompt.

kernel

Under the X11 System the [Alt] key is reserved for applications. The X Window System handles the switching to another virtual console with the three-way combination of [Ctrl] + [Alt] and the respective function key corresponding to the virtual console number. This allows the user to switch between the graphical interface of X Window System and the text-oriented interface of the virtual consoles.

X11

function keys

It is even possible to start multiple X servers. However, this is not recommended because there is seldom enough memory and thus performance suffers noticeably. Instead, use a virtual window manager under X Window System, such as `olvwm` or `fvwm`, which also offers multiple virtual consoles.

3.2 Linux file systems

file systems
The multitude of available file systems under Linux might seem confusing at first glance. The following subsections list these file systems and describe their most important features.

Linux disk file systems

first file system
MINIX file system The first Linux versions furnished only one type of file system, and it relied heavily on the MINIX file system. This circumvented the effort required for a completely new development. Furthermore, this provided a stable file system from the start, although the MINIX file system certainly has some significant drawbacks as well.

14 characters
64 MB partitions
File names cannot exceed14 characters in length and the size of a partition is restricted to 64 MB. Although newer versions of this Linux/MINIX file system permit longer file names (30 characters), this file system is meanwhile scarcely in use.

However, it is noteworthy that, in contrast to many proprietary System V implementations, even this first version of a Linux file
symbolic links
system also supported symbolic links.

Extended file system (ext) To overcome the above restrictions,
Remy Card
a Frenchman named Remy Card implemented the first alternative file system. His Extended File System (`ext`) for the first time supported files and partitions of up to 2 GB. He also raised the maximum length of file names to 255 characters.

i-nodes
But this system also has its weaknesses. Free blocks and i-nodes are not managed in a bit vector, but in a linked list. After
fragmentation
a longer period of operation, this leads to extensive fragmentation of the memory, which causes noticeably longer access times.

Extended-2 file system (ext2) From the Extended File System, the Extended-2 file system evolved after some time; this is currently
less fragmentation
the most widespread file system under Linux. The fragmentation

problems no longer occur in this system, and the limitation of 2 GB for file systems was canceled. Furthermore, Extended-2 supports a mechanism that saves lost sectors in a special directory (`lost+found`). A possible system crash and its resulting corrupt file system are recognized when the system is started, and the damage can be repaired with a special utility (`e2fsck`).

lost + found

In addition, Linux 2.0 now features quota support for the `ext2` file system. Here you also need the `quota` utilities.* Quotas are upper limits for the amount of data that an individual user or a user group can store in a file system. There is a soft quota, which can be exceeded for a limited time, and a hard quota, which is a fixed ceiling.

Xia file system The Extended-2 file system has not been the only attempt to establish a new, faster file system. At nearly the same time the Xia file system, named after its author, Frank Xia, appeared. This file system also increased the maximum partition size to 4 GB. File names can be up to 248 characters long. The size of a file is currently limited to 64 MB at this time.

Frank Xia

64 MB file size

UMSDOS The UMSDOS file system is a Linux file system in a normal DOS partition. It does not require repartitioning an existing DOS system; this makes UMSDOS ideal for trying out Linux. However, UMSDOS is significantly slower than the Extended-2 file system and so is not recommended for long-range use.

File systems of other operating systems

DOS file system The DOS file system permits Linux transparent access to DOS diskettes or partitions (and OS/2 FAT partitions). This permits access to preexisting data.

DOS & OS/2

VFAT file system (Windows 95/Windows NT) This file system accommodates the DOS file system extensions of Windows 95 and Windows NT (longer file names, etc.).

---

*Sunsite: `system/Admin/quotas-*`

Other file systems

OS/2 HPFS OS/2's file system is called *High Performance File System (HPFS)*. For diskettes, OS/2 employs the conventional MS-DOS file system; however, with HPFS file system support you can read OS/2 partitions with the same computer.

SCO
Xenix
Coherent

System V/Coherent file system This file system provides access to file systems of i386 UNIX System V derivates such as SCO, Xenix, and Coherent.

Amiga Fast File System

Amiga FFS The *Amiga Fast File System* (FFS) is relevant for the Amiga 68k port of Linux only; under PC Linux it is only used to mount file systems of a UNIX Amiga emulator since Amiga diskettes and PC floppy drives are incompatible.

UFS file system The UFS file system is used by FreeBSD, NetBSD, NeXTstep, SunOS, and Solaris.

Network file systems

NFS file system NFS enables accessing directories on other machines (*NFS servers*) as if they were a local hard disk. This is comparable to network drives under Novell. To configure Linux as an *NFS client* or server, see Section 9.14.

Root file system on NFS Linux 2.0 enables completely booting a computer via NFS. The kernel is loaded from floppy diskette; then the kernel mounts the root file system via NFS (IP address of the NFS server and the directories to be imported are passed as boot options). In this context you can determine your own IP address on

BOOTP
RARP

booting with one of the protocols BOOTP or RARP. To be able to use BOOTP or RARP, a BOOTP or RARP server must be running on the local network (i.e., on the same Ethernet cable!). BOOTP also allows determining the address of the NFS server and other information at boot time. By selecting the option CONFIG_INET_RARP, you can incorporate RARP support in the kernel. The utility rarp writes entries to the RARP tables.

First you need to specify the root file system /dev/nfs (this is only a code for the kernel; the device need not be created with mknod):

    root=/dev/nfs

The first important boot option is:

---

    nfsroot=[server-ip:]root-dir[,nfs-options]

---

server-ip

> The IP address of the NFS server: It can also be determined with BOOTP or specified in the second boot option.

root-dir

> The directory to be mounted by the server as the root file system.

nfs-options

> Several NFS mount options (NFS port on NFS server, ...).

The second boot option:

---

    nfaddrs=client-ip:server-ip:gw-ip:hostname:device:autoconf

---

client-ip

> Client's own IP address: It can also be determined with RARP or BOOTP, in which case this field can be left blank.

server-ip

> Address of the NFS server: It is returned by BOOTP servers and can then be omitted. If NFS and BOOTP servers are different, enter the address of the BOOTP server here and of the NFS server in the first option.

gw-ip

> Address of the gateway, if the NFS/BOOTP server is in a different network (corresponds to the default entry in the configuration of the routing tables).

hostname

> Client's own host name: It can also be determined with BOOTP.

45

device

> Network interface to which the RARP or BOOTP request is to be sent: If none is specified, requests are sent to all interfaces.

autoconf

> Here you can enter whether RARP, BOOTP, both, or neither is to be used to automatically determine the above information. If nothing is specified, RARP and BOOTP are used, inasmuch as the kernel supports them.

SMB file system   The SMB file system is new in Linux 2.0. SMB is a protocol that is used by Windows for Workgroups, Windows NT, LAN Manager, and OS/2. Similar to NFS, it supports mounting directories via a network. If Linux is also to be used as an SMB server, you can use the package Samba (see Section 9.15).

NCP file system   Likewise, the NCP file system is a new feature in Linux 2.0 (it was previously under development as kernel patches, but it has only now been integrated fully). NCP is also used for mounting directories via a network—here by a Netware file server. Using the NCP file system and providing your own Netware services is described in Section 9.18.

ISO 9660/HighSierra file system

CD-ROM
Rockridge Extensions
To provide access to CD-ROMs, Linux provides both ISO 9660 and High Sierra file systems. Likewise the Rockridge Extensions supporting longer file names have been implemented.

Proc file system

kernel data
process ID

ASCII
This process file system does not manage physical files, but enables access to data in the kernel and the currently running processes. On system startup the proc file system is normally mounted to the subdirectory /proc in the root directory. For every running process, this directory contains a subdirectory whose name is the respective process ID. The files that it contains provide a flexible interface to the actual process-specific information. In general these are virtual ASCII files whose contents can be output with the cat command. This allows the user to determine the contents of the command line or the environment variables of a process. Information about memory

requirements, the parent process, or the current process state can be extracted in this way. See the overview of the contents of the proc file system in Appendix 18.1.

3.3   Data exchange

Linux is seldom the sole operating system on a PC. More frequently another partition or hard disk contains DOS with MS-Windows, OS/2, or another PC UNIX variant. A user switching from DOS to Linux is seldom willing to sacrifice the old programs.

DOS, Windows

The following subsections show how Linux is able to work with other operating systems and exchange data and programs with them.

When using operating systems on one computer, a boot manager proves essential. At system startup, this utility enables the user to select the operating system to be booted. The Linux Loader (LILO) fulfills this function, among others. Chapter 5 describes the installation and operation of LILO.

boot manager

LILO

MTools

Since particularly the exchange of files with an DOS system is required nowadays of nearly all operating systems, for some time there have been freely available programs for processing DOS files under UNIX. As with many other UNIX systems, Linux provides the MTools for this purpose. These are commands like mdir and mcopy that support the reading of the directory of an DOS storage medium (typically a diskette) and the copying of files. The following is an example of accessing an DOS diskette with MTools:

DOS

mdir, mcopy

```
dirk1:/home/stefan# mdir a:
 Volume in drive A is dosdisk1
 Directory for A:/

COMMAND   COM     55591    3-10-93    6:00a
WINA20    386      9349    6-11-91   12:00p
AUTOEXEC  BAT       359    8-26-93    9:02p
CONFIG    SYS       377    5-23-93    2:48p
DOSKEY    COM      6012    6-11-91   12:00p
EDIT      COM       429    6-11-91   12:00p
FORMAT    COM     34223    6-11-91   12:00p
        9 file(s)     1270784 bytes free
dirk1:/home/stefan# mcopy -t a:autoexec.bat .
Copying AUTOEXEC.BAT
dirk1:/home/stefan# mdel a:autoexec.bat
dirk1:/home/stefan#
```

The disk drive device needs to be free, so that you can access the MTools on a diskette. This means that the diskette must not be mounted. The fastest way to format DOS diskettes is **mformat a:** under Linux.

DOS file system

In addition to MTools, Linux provides another method to access DOS

diskettes

DOS partitions

speed

cache

storage media, the DOS file system. This makes it possible to mount diskettes and DOS partitions of a hard disk in the same way as other file systems in the Linux directory tree. This provides completely transparent access to the contained files. Access is faster than with MTools because the input and output operation can now profit from the cache of the operating system. The following is an example of accessing an DOS partition with the DOS file system:

```
dirk1:/# cd msdos
dirk1:/msdos# ls -a
./   ../
dirk1:/msdos# cd ..
dirk1:/# mount -t msdos /dev/hda2 /msdos
dirk1:/# cd msdos
dirk1:/msdos# ls -a
./            command.com*    format.com*    tools/
../           config.sys*     io.sys*        wina20.386*
autoexec.bat* dos/            msdos.sys*     windows/
dirk1:/msdos# cd dos
dirk1:/msdos/dos#
```

mount and umount

However, the drawback of mounting diskettes is that they can no longer be inserted and removed at will; instead, the commands mount and umount must be invoked with each change of diskettes. If a diskette is removed while it is still mounted, then the diskette inserted subsequently is usually overwritten.

access privileges

user ID

Since DOS provides neither user IDs nor group IDs, the individual files of a mounted DOS file system cannot be assigned individual settings for access control. However, on mounting the volume, group and user IDs as well as access privileges for the overall file system can be specified as an option. This at least permits control of access to the file system as a whole.

A complete description of how the DOS file system functions under Linux and the available options can be found in the On-Line Manual page for mount and the file README.dosfs, which resides on ftp servers along with the source code of the file system. There are two On-Line Manual pages for mount, one for the command and one for the routine in the C library. To display the correct On-Line Manual page, the section must be specified in the invocation of the man command. The invocation for the man command would be:

section

```
man 8 mount
```

The most important options that can be specified in the invocation of the mount command for a DOS file system are:

- uid=*number*
- gid=*number*
- umask=*number*
- conv={binary|text|auto} (see next paragraph)

The following example shows the mounting of a DOS file system with the specification of options:

```
stef1:/# mount -t msdos -o umask=000 /dev/hda1 /dosc
```

The options can also be specified in the file /etc/fstab:

```
dev/hda3        none      swap      defaults
/dev/hda2       /         ext2      defaults
/dev/hda1       /dosc     msdos     rw,umask=000
none            /proc     proc      defaults
```

Text conversion

A fundamental problem in data exchange between DOS and UNIX is their different representations of new lines in text files with respect to carriage return (CR) and line feed (LF). In mcopy this has been solved with the command line option -t, which specifies whether to copy a file in binary mode or in text mode with conversion.

new line (CR/LF)

conversion

Since a mounted DOS file system allows access to many different files, there is no universal solution. Although there are options for the mount command that activate automatic conversion, this process

options

does not always function reliably. Whether a file is a text file or a binary file cannot always be decided with certainty.

3.4   Loadable Modules

monolithic kernels

Classical UNIX systems generally possess a monolithic kernel. The entire kernel needs to be newly linked if a new driver is to be integrated into the system. Although the architecture of the Linux kernel is very similar in principle, it does provide *loadable modules*. This term refers to object files that can be loaded or removed while the system is running. The iBCS2 emulator (see Section 4.3) is also integrated in this way. Numerous drivers and systems have been made module-capable under Linux 2.0. During kernel configuration this provides the choice of "No" (do not integrate in kernel), "Yes" (link into kernel) or "Module" (compile separately as a module).

loading while running

The following commands are used for the administration of modules:

insmod	Integrates the specified module into the system
depmod	Creates a list of dependencies between modules
modprobe	Loads the passed module and all modules that this module needs
rmmod	Removes the passed module
lsmod	Outputs a list of currently loaded modules
kerneld	Starts the kerneld, which loads and removes Kernel modules depending on demand

/etc/conf.modules

After kernel installation, specify in the file /etc/conf.modules the paths for the modules and which options are automatically given to a module. Then invoke **depmod -a** to determine mutual dependencies between modules.

kerneld

On booting, you should load the most important modules and also activate kerneld, which loads a module later if the kernel needs it—independently of the system administrator. kerneld was introduced with Linux 2.0. This makes working with modules quite transparent. However, kerneld cannot load all files independently.

Many file system modules must be loaded manually with `insmod` or (better) `modprobe`; the latter tests whether the module to be loaded requires additional modules and also loads these.

Additional details can be found in the Manual Pages `modules(2)`, `insmod(8)`, `rmmod(8)`, `lsmod(8)`, `modprobe(8)`, `kerneld(8)`, and `depmod(8)`.

3.5   Sound

Unlike a number of other PC-based UNIX systems, Linux supports all the common PC sound boards. The necessary drivers are available in the kernel code; however, they need to be configured (`make config`) before compilation. As soon as the appropriate driver is present in the kernel, a series of new devices become available:

PC sound boards

kernel

`/dev/mixer`	mixer for various audio channels
`/dev/audio`	Sun audio device (μ-law format)
`/dev/sequenzer`	sequencer device
`/dev/midi`	device for playing MIDI data
`/dev/sndstat`	status device for audio system
`/dev/dsp`	audio device (raw-format)

A series of programs exist for recording and playing audio data (`vrec` and `vplay`). In the simplest cases, however, the `cat` command is enough to record

recording and playing

```
zeus:/home/uhl> cat < /dev/audio > sound.au
```

or to play audio files:

```
zeus:/home/uhl> cat sound.au > /dev/audio
```

3.6   Extended commands

Many standard UNIX commands that Linux uses emerged from the GNU project and are extensions of the normal commands. For

GNU

options example, under Linux the command ls has more than 20 options with which the kind of display, sorting, or handling of symbolic notes can be modified as needed. Many distributions even contain color variants of the ls command that displays the lines of the directory listing by color according to the type of the directory element (link, executable file, tar file, subdirectory, etc.).

Here is an excerpt from the On-Line Manual page of the GNU ls command:

```
LS(1L)                                                            LS(1L)

NAME
       ls, dir, vdir, ll, lsf - list contents of directories

SYNOPSIS
       ls  [-abcdgiklmnpqrstuxABCFLNQRSUX1]  [-w  cols] [-T cols]
       [-I pattern]  [--all]  [--escape]  [--directory]  [--inode]
       [--kilobytes]  [--numeriC uid-gid]  [--hide-control-chars]
       [--reverse]   [--size]   [--width=cols]   [--tabsize=cols]
       [--almost-all]  [--ignore-backups]  [--classify]  [--file-
       type]   [--ignore=pattern]   [--dereference]   [--literal]
       [--quote-name]                                [--recursive]
       [--sort={none,time,size,extension}]                [--for-
       mat={long,verbose,commas,across,vertical,single-column}]
       [--time={atime,access,use,ctime,status}] [path...]
       ...
```

GNU tar

compression The GNU variant of the tar command has the option z for automatic
archive compression and decompression of tar archives, and the option M for establishing a multivolume archive (a single archive that is distributed on multiple storage media).

gzip

compress The command gzip replaces compress under Linux. This program is compatible with many other compression techniques and has a
efficiency significantly higher efficiency than compress. The command tar enables the combination of individual files and subdirectories into a single archive. A compressed tar archive that was compressed with the UNIX command compress had a size of 1.5 MB; gzip frequently requires only 900 KB.

source codes All these extended commands are naturally available in source code and can be compiled on other UNIX machines. The advantage
Linux of Linux is that these are used from the start and no additional effort

Figure 3.1. The Linux 2.0 logo

has to be invested in the configuration, compilation, and installation of these utilities.

The list of all enhanced commands and their options would certainly fill a book itself. The most important ones are listed in the Reference Section. Refer to the On-Line Manual pages and the individual commands there for more complete details.

reference

3.7 New features in Linux 2.0

After a long wait, since June 1996 the Linux community finally has a new series of stable kernels. The original target had been version number 1.4, but, due to the numerous, in part fundamental, modifications and extensions, originator Linus Torvalds considered incrementing the first version number to be appropriate.

What is new in Linux 2.0?

Porting to numerous other architectures

Originally Linux was an operating system tailored to Intel 386 compatible processors. Yet the lure of a powerful freeware operating system obviously proved so attractive that numerous volunteers and several commercial concerns (such as DEC with their high-end Alpha processor) became involved in porting Linux to various processors and computer architectures:

53

- DEC Alpha
- Motorola 68k
  - Amiga
  - Atari
  - Apple Macintosh (under development)
- PowerPC
- SPARC (Sun naturally; but also AP1000, a multicomputer)
- MIPS (Mips Magnum, DECstation, ...)

This support of numerous platforms gives reason to the hope that more companies will find it commercially attractive to port their software to Linux. If the simple **make config** has made you wonder where this multiplatform support is, try changing the command ARCH = i386 in /usr/src/linux/Makefile to ARCH=alpha, for example, and then repeat **make config**.

To compile a specific kernel, you need a corresponding gcc (or gcc as cross-compiler on a traditional 386 Linux machine). Likewise you need to use a different libc.

The American Linux distribution RedHat is already available in a DEC Alpha and a SPARC version; the Craftworks distribution also provides an Alpha version. There is also a distribution for Atari Linux named ALD.

SMP—symmetric multiprocessing

Although the development of microprocessors has not yet reached its absolute limits, the performance hunger of modern applications *multiprocessor boards* already makes the use of multiprocessor boards interesting. Instead of a single processor, these boards use multiple (maximum about *shared RAM* 16) processors that share the main memory and peripherals. Such systems are appearing on the market for various platforms such as Intel 80x86 and the PowerPC.

Linux SMP project Alan Cox's Linux SMP project seeks to secure Linux's future in this direction. Symmetric multiprocessing means that multiple *Symmetric* processors are connected to the same main memory and peripheral *multiprocessing* buses. The individual processors compute completely autonomously, but share access to common memory. To deliver speed advantages, the memory must be correspondingly fast: If the system has four processors that each transport three megabytes of data per second to and from memory, then memory must support reading/writing at least 12 megabytes of data per second in order to exploit the full computing power of the four processors. In practice these hard limits are softened somewhat by several tricks—all modern processors have more or less large on-chip or on-board caches, and a large part of all operations can be handled with data in cache without accessing main memory. Furthermore, additional hardware allows dividing main memory into banks that support parallel access.

Thus each processor can principally assume the same tasks because it accesses common memory—*symmetric multiprocessing*. A new process is assigned to the least busy processor. Customarily, load balancing the Linux scheduler executes multiple processes on one processor in separate time slices. Currently the kernel still operates with mutual exclusion, which means that at any time only one (active) process mutual exclusion can be in the kernel. However, plans are under way to incrementally reduce this mutual exclusion in the kernel to increasingly smaller regions to allow not only computationally intensive processes but also I/O-intensive processes to profit.

SMP support has already been provided with the 2.0 kernel, but it is still in an experimental stage and cannot simply be activated with a normal kernel configuration. In the mailing list `linux-smp@vger.rutgers.edu` Linux users discuss their experience with Linux SMP and various MP motherboards.

Modularization

Linux 1.2 already supported kernel modules; modules were required, e.g., in order to load MS-DOS and iBCS emulations. Now in Linux 2.0 many hardware drivers, file systems, and network engines have been modularized. This reduces kernel size and sometimes saves a whole kernel compilation since only a newly required module has to be generated.

Network support

For Version 2.0, Linux network support was fundamentally reworked and significantly accelerated. Also, numerous new extras were integrated. Likewise, the number of supported PC network adapters

ISDN support   grew significantly. In particular, ISDN support was integrated into the kernel sources, which enhances the attractiveness of Linux as a router operating system (see Section 9.8).

SMB and NCP   Linux 2.0 can mount volumes from SMB and Netware file servers; see Sections 9.15 and 9.18.

Appletalk DDP
PowerPC
AX.25
New protocols   Linux 2.0 supports Appletalk DDP, which is used by Apple computers, including the PowerPC. In addition, there is support for amateur radio protocol AX.25 with NET/ROM.

Ethernet bridge   A Linux 2.0 machine can be used as an Ethernet bridge. Two physically separate Ethernet cables combine to one logical Ethernet. The bridge forwards Ethernet frames from one network to recipients in the other.

Address aliasing   *Aliasing* is the assignment of multiple IP addresses to a single interface; see Section 9.4.

Multicasting   Multicasting means routing IP packets with multiple target addresses. If your Linux machine should also support
MBone
multimedia
communication
MBone (*M*ulticast back*Bone*, a protocol that is particularly interesting for multimedia communication such as audio/video transmission), you should activate this option.

Firewall features   Linux 1.2 already contained a simple IP packet
IP packet filter
filter. This has been greatly improved and extended; see Section 9.3. New firewall features include:

• IP masquerading: see Section 9.3.
• Transparent proxies: see Section 9.3.
• IP defragmentation: complete reassembly of IP fragments before routing; see Section 9.3.

IP tunneling   IP packets encapsulated in other IP packages are
IPIP
transmitted via a network (IPIP protocol). The purpose and details are given in Section 9.3.

Hardware

Linux 2.0 supports even more hardware than Linux 1.2. Refer to the list of available drivers in Section 5.3.

Watchdogs A watchdog is a software process or special hardware that periodically checks the computer for malfunctions and reboots or halts the machine as necessary; see Section 5.3.

Advanced power management This feature supports the energy-saving BIOS of various laptops; see Section 5.3.

Metadevices and RAID support A metadevice is a fusion of multiple hard disk partitions to a single logical block device. Among other things, this serves as the basis for RAID support (redundant storage of data in disk arrays to achieve greater data security and increased speed); see Section 6.6.

Code for Pentium and Pentium Pro In the realm of Intel architectures, Linux can be optimized for four processors: 80386, 80486, Pentium, and Pentium Pro. Pentium support is new in Linux 2.0. Select the kernel to be generated during kernel configuration. If you choose "Pentium," the C compiler generates code optimized for the Pentium, which somewhat improves execution speed.

Real-time clock support If you compile the kernel with the option CONFIG_RTC, you gain access to the AT real-time clock. The clock can be read via /proc/rtc: /proc/rtc

```
golem:~> cat /proc/rtc
rtc_time        : 10:52:23
rtc_date        : 1996-11-19
alarm           : 08:57:14
DST_enable      : no
BCD             : yes
24hr            : yes
square_wave     : no
alarm_IRQ       : no
update_IRQ      : no
periodic_IRQ    : no
periodic_freq   : 1024
batt_status     : okay
```

Other new features

Dynamic ramdisks While ramdisk support already existed under Linux 1.2, Linux 2.0 supports multiple ramdisks, and these can dynamically grow and shrink (depending on available memory) up to a size of 4 MB (even this ceiling can be raised in the kernel sources). This proves interesting, e.g., for the creation of packed boot disks; see Section 7.12.

Loop devices File systems normally reside on block devices such as hard disks or CDs, but it is possible in theory to mount a single file that contains the image of a file system. Linux 2.0 makes this possible in practice: Loop devices are interesting for the creation of boot disks (see Section 7.12), but also for checking an ISO-9660 file system before writing a CD, for preparing a boot file for DOSEmu, and many other small problems; see Section 7.12.

Java Support of Java as an executable format is something of a frill. The kernel recognizes Java bytecode and HTML files that contain an APPLET tag and executes them with the help of JDK.

Random number sources Various applications such as simulation, games, network protocols, and cryptography require preferably real random numbers rather than pseudorandom numbers as generated by the function rand(). Assuming good design, computers seldom offer sources of random numbers. The rotation of the hard disk or the time between keystrokes are random to some extent (these are *entropy sources*). The character devices /dev/random and /dev/urandom (major device number 1, minor device number 8 and 9, respectively) evaluate these random number sources and return random bytes. urandom returns characters faster, but they are less random.

3.8   The pros and cons of upgrading

After such a long list of new features, the question of upgrading seems rhetorical. The numerous new or improved hardware drivers in Linux 2.0 often leave you no choice, especially for new network and SCSI adapters, for more than two IDE devices, or for ISDN (some drivers were available for Linux 1.2, but only as separate kernel patches). Likewise, improved network performance and firewall support, a multitude of extras, and numerous small bug fixes make an upgrade attractive.

On the other hand, we have the old motto "never touch a running system." Upgrading to Linux 2.0 does cost some time and effort. After kernel compilation you should also install a new version of the C library. Likewise a whole row of programs require an upgrade; the specific programs are listed in `/usr/src/linux/Documentation/Changes` under "Current Releases":

- kernel modules: `modules-2.0.0.tar.gz`; resides in the same directory as the 2.0 kernels
- PPP daemon: Sunsite, `system/Network/serial/ppp/`
- procps: Sunsite, `system/Status/ps/procps*`
- gpm: Sunsite, `system/Daemons/gpm-*`
- System V `init`: Sunsite, `system/Daemons/init/sysvinit*`
- util-linux: Sunsite, `system/misc/util-linux*`
- mount: `ftp://ftp.win.tue.nl/pub/linux/util/mount-*`
- net-tools: `system/Network/sunacm/NetTools/net-tools-*`
- kbd: Sunsite, `system/Keyboards`
- Dynamic linker: Sunsite, `GCC/ld.so*`
- C compiler: Sunsite, `GCC/gcc-*.bin.tar.gz`
- Binutils: Sunsite, `GCC/binutils*`
- C library: Sunsite, `GCC/libc-*.bin.tar.gz`
- C++ library: Sunsite, `GCC/libg++-*.bin.tar.gz`
- termcap: Sunsite, `GCC/termcap-*`

The asterisk indicates the newest version. For the GCC packages (the last six) the same directory also contains the file `release.libc-*`, which contains other important information on compatible versions (also see Section 7.10).

Installing these packages might disable other programs or lead to unfamiliar error messages (`sendmail` or `vi`). As a whole, however, the upgrade to Linux 2.0 should not create other problems.

## Chapter 4

Emulators

The various emulators available to Linux users are increasing in importance. In the first edition of this book we described the DOS emulator within the chapter on Linux features. Meanwhile various other emulators have become available. Many such projects are no longer limited to Linux, but are being developed in parallel for other commercial and freeware UNIX variants such as FreeBSD.

4.1 DOS emulator

As for OS/2 and other newer operating systems, Linux has a DOS emulator that permits running DOS programs simultaneously with other Linux applications. However, this emulator does not emulate the DOS operating system, but only the rudimentary input/output routines (BIOS); it enables access to all important devices. With this system extension, DOS can be booted under the control of Linux. The particular DOS version is of subordinate importance.

DOS programs

BIOS
booting DOS

Overview

Although the emulator is still far from being able to run every DOS program without problems, the possibilities are quite impressive. Programs can run in graphic mode and with the support of high memory (HMA), upper memory blocks (UMB), and expanded memory (EMS). Support of the DOS protected mode interface (DPMI) and access to Novell servers within the emulator are also possible, but are still under development. DOS programs such as Norton Commander and the text editor QEdit work without problems, and even larger commercial products such as Turbo Pascal and WordPerfect can be used.

graphics
HMA, UMB
EMS
DPMI

Figure 4.1. DOS emulator under X11

X11

console

The emulator can run either under X11 as a separate window or in a virtual console in text mode (Figure 4.1). You can switch consoles within the emulator; as under X11, you simultaneously press ⎡Ctrl⎤ and ⎡Alt⎤ along with a function key.

image files

In addition to the normal diskettes and DOS partitions, the DOS emulator can also access the Linux file system and disk image files. DOS programs treat these files like real data media. They are used primarily for booting the DOS emulator.

To configure the DOS emulator, you edit the file /etc/ dosemu.conf. You also need a file named /etc/dosemu.users, which contains the names of all users with permission to use the emulator.

Disk image files are normally stored in the directory /usr/lib/dosemu or /var/lib/dosemu.

hardware

BIOS

The DOS emulator, as mentioned above, does not emulate the whole DOS operating system, but only the hardware and the BIOS of a PC. Thus, starting the emulator requires a DOS boot diskette, a hard disk partition with DOS installed, or a corresponding image file.

Direct access to a DOS partition of a hard disk and booting from this partition is one alternative. In this case, however, the partition must not be mounted in the Linux file system, since this can cause conflicts that can mean data loss.

conflicts

booting from

an image file

The alternative is booting from a diskette or a special image file, which the DOS emulator uses like a real diskette or hard disk.

Naturally, using a file in place of a boot disk affords an elegant and fast solution, but such a file must be created first.

Creating an image file for booting

Creating the boot image file for booting requires a normal bootable DOS diskette. Several special DOS programs that accompany the emulator also need to be copied onto this diskette. Alternatively, a ramdisk or a loop device file can be used instead of a slow floppy diskette (see p. 169). These programs allow access to the Linux file system from within the emulator and permit reading or modifying certain settings of the emulator. We also recommend copying a simple editor onto the diskette.

DOS diskette programs

editor

The following terminal capture shows the subdirectories of the DOS emulator distribution containing the driver and programs:

```
stef1:strobel/dosemu0.50p11/commands> ls
Makefile       dosdbg.c       exitemu.S      lredir.exe
vgaon.S
bootoff.S      dosdbg.exe     exitemu.com    lredir.readme
vgaon.com
bootoff.com    dosdbg.readme  lancheck.exe   pdipx.com
booton.S       dumpconf.asm   linpkt/        vgaoff.S
booton.com     dumpconf.exe   lredir.c       vgaoff.com
stef1:strobel/dosemu0.50p11/commands>
```

If these files are not included in the distribution, then the complete emulator distribution can be copied from one of the usual FTP servers. On the server sunsite.unc.edu, for example, the DOS emulator distribution resides in the directory /pub/Linux/system/emulators/dosemu. To copy the files from Linux to a DOS diskette, use MTools or mount the diskette.

FTP server

MTools

After all programs and files have been copied to the boot diskette, it can be copied to a file using the command dd, as in the following terminal capture. This file can be stored in any directory (bdisk in this example). If it is for personal use, employ the home directory; if multiple users will be using the DOS boot image, a system subdirectory should be created, such as /var/lib/dosemu.

dd

```
zeus:/home/strobel> dd if=/dev/fd0 of=bdisk bs=16k
```

The image `bdisk` can be mounted like an ordinardy MS-DOS disk partition or floppy using loop devices (see p. 169), and supplementary files can be copied into it—e.g., the utilities shipped with the DOSEmu package.

Now the configuration file for the DOS emulator must be modified so that this image file can be used for booting. The corresponding entries in the configuration file are:

```
boota
bootdisk {heads 2 sectors 18 tracks 80 threeinch file bdisk}
```

path

Unless the image file is located in the current directory, its complete path must be specified in the configuration file.

dos

Theoretically, you could start the DOS emulator now by entering `dos`. For practical use, however, you still need to make some settings.

Accessing DOS partitions

booting

After the boot disk image has been created as described above, the DOS emulator can be booted, but there is no access to the Linux file system or to a DOS partition on the hard disk.

emufs.sys

lredir

To access the Linux file system from within the emulator, use either the driver `emufs.sys` or the program `lredir`. The driver `emufs.sys` can map any directory of the Linux file system onto the next free drive letter. The redirector program `lredir` can replace already assigned drive letters. For example, `lredir` can be invoked as follows:

```
c:\> lredir c:\linux\fs/
```

path

The first parameter, in our example `c:`, specifies the drive letter to be replaced. The second parameter identifies the source, in our example the root directory of the Linux file system. `\linux\fs` represents the Linux file system and `/` specifies the path within the file system. The file `lredir.readme`, in the same directory as `lredir` program itself in the DOS emulator distribution, contains a detailed description of all the program's options.

There are many other ways to boot from a disk image, but they generally have negative consequences regarding subsequent access to floppy disk drives or other drive letters. We offer a brief overview of these approaches.

other ways to boot

Assume that the hard disk contains a DOS partition that was mounted under Linux as directory /dosc. There are several ways to access this partition under the DOS emulator:

- Boot from a diskette and invoke the driver emufs.sys in the file config.sys or the program lredir in the file autoexec.bat. This makes the directory /dosc under Linux the next alphabetical drive in the DOS emulator. In this case this would be C:. Since it is rather troublesome to always insert a diskette to boot the emulator, this method is used seldom, and usually only during installation.

- Boot from a hard disk image and use emufs.sys or lredir as above to access drive D:. The hard disk image file uses C: in this case.

- Boot from a hard disk image and use lredir in the file autoexec.bat to replace the drive letter C:. This makes the DOS partition accessible as C: and the floppy disk drives remain untouched. This provides the same environment as booting directly from DOS.

  The problem with this method is that the "hard disk" from which the file autoexec.bat is read is replaced by another while the file is still being read and executed. Thus this file needs to be identical in the hard disk image and on the real hard disk partition.

- Activate a disk image file as virtual drive A: and use the file config.sys or autoexec.bat as described above. Here the advantage is that you do not need a diskette to start the DOS emulator. The drawback is that the disk drive can no longer be used as drive A: because this letter is already occupied by the disk image.

- Use the special option bootdisk (see the start of this section) in the configuration file of the DOS emulator in order to boot from a disk image and switch this image off at the end of the file autoexec.bat. This is the most elegant method. Booting

65

produces a normal environment without image files, yet a disk image can be used for booting.

It is theoretically possible to access an DOS partition on a hard disk both directly via the DOS emulator and indirectly via the Linux file system, assuming that the DOS file system is mounted.

data loss

dual access

lredir

➡ **To prevent data loss, completely avoid this dual access**. To access a DOS partition from both Linux and the emulator, the emulator should access the DOS partition not directly, but via the device driver emufs.sys or lredir and the Linux file system.

Configuration

configuration file

The following example shows a complete configuration file for the DOS emulator in which the option bootdisk is used as described above. The example is divided into logical sections. Lines beginning with # are comments. The file is intended only as an example configuration, since it does not embrace all possible options.

```
# Example of a configuration file for the DOS emulator

# No debug messages
debug -a

# DOSemu Version message on startup
dosbanner on

# Enable access to video board ports
allowvideoportaccess on

# Keyboard and timer interrupts
keybint on
timint on

# Mouse options :
#      "microsoft"(default), "mousesystems3," "mousesystems5,"
#      "mmseries" or "logitech."
serial { mouse microsoft device /dev/cua0 }

#serial { mouse device /dev/cua0 }
#serial { mouse device /dev/cua1 }

# IPX in DOS-emulator (under development)
ipxsupport off

#video { vga console }
#video { vga console graphics chipset et4000 memsize 1024 }
#video { vga console graphics chipset trident memsize 1024 }
#video { vga console graphics chipset diamond }

# No special video supported, but graphic mode is  ok.
video { vga console graphics }

# Direct access to keyboard
RawKeyboard
```

```
mathco off            # on or off
cpu 80386
boota                 # booting from A:
xms 1024              # XMS size in K, or off
ems 1024              # EMS size in K, or off

# Here certain I/O ports can be allocated to the DOS-emulator
# ports { 0x388 0x389 }
# ports { 0x2f8 0x2f9 0x2fa 0x2fb 0x2fc 0x2fd 0x2fe }
# ports { 0x21e 0x22e 0x23e 0x24e 0x25e 0x26e 0x27e 0x28e
0x29e }

# Access to speaker
speaker native        # native, off or emulated

# Direct access to hard disks or hard disk  images is set.
# In our example we use lredir to access the partition
# /dev/hda1 --- no direct access

#disk { image "/usr/lib/dosemu/hdimage" }
#disk { partition "/dev/hda1" 1 readonly }
#disk { wholedisk "/dev/hda" }

# The file bdisk is used for booting. It is created from a
boot
# diskette with the following command:
# dd if=/dev/fd0 of=bdisk bs=16k
# At the end of the file autoexec.bat for this boot file,
# the file is disabled with the command bootoff and so access
# to drive A is restored.
bootdisk { heads 2 sectors 18 tracks 80 threeinch file bdisk }

# Direct access to floppy disk drives
floppy { device /dev/fd0 threeinch }
floppy { device /dev/fd1 fiveinch }

# This example uses no lasting disk image.
#floppy { heads 2 sectors 18 tracks 80 threeinch file bdisk }

#Printer access is not activated in this example.
#printer { options "%s" command "lpr" timeout 20 }
#printer { options "-p %s" command "lpr" timeout 10 }    # pr
format it
#printer { file "lpt3" }
```

The following debug settings are of interest only to developers and freaks. Normal users should set all debug options off. | Debug settings

```
debug {config  off      disk    off     warning off     hardware
off
       port    off      read    off     general off     IPC
off
       video   off      write   off     xms     off     ems
off
       serial  off      keyb    off     dpmi    off
       printer off      mouse   off
     }
```

The dosemu startup message and the timer interrupt can be toggled on and off: | startup message and timer

```
dosbanner on
#
# timint is necessary for many programs.
timint on
```

keyboard

The keyboard also needs to be defined.

```
# Possible values for keyboard layout:
#
#        finnish          us            dvorak      sf
#        finnish-latin1   uk            sg          sf-latin1
#        gr               dk            sg-latin1   es
#        gr-latin1        dk-latin1     fr          es-latin1
#        be               no            fr-latin1   portuguese
#
keyboard { layout de-latin1  keybint on  rawkeyboard on  }
# After how many keyboard polls is the CPU released?
# (0 turns this mechanismus completely off.)
HogThreshold 0
```

serial interfaces
and mouse

The settings for serial interfaces, a serial mouse, and a modem are optional. For a normal configuration, where the emulator runs under X11 and modem programs run directly under Linux, you can ignore these settings. To use the mouse under X11, you must not specify the mouse in the DOS emulation configuration file.

```
# activate one of the following settings as applicable:
#serial { com 1  device /dev/modem }
#serial { com 2  device /dev/modem }
#serial { com 3  device /dev/modem }
#serial { com 4  device /dev/modem }
#serial { com 3  base 0x03E8  irq 5  device /dev/cua2 }
#
# serial mouse:
#serial { mouse  com 1  device /dev/mouse }
#serial { mouse  com 2  device /dev/mouse }
#
# Type of mouse (do not use to run under X11!)
#mouse { microsoft }
#mouse { logitech }
#mouse { mmseries }
#mouse { mouseman }
#mouse { hitachi }
#mouse { mousesystems }
#mouse { busmouse }
#mouse { ps2  device /dev/mouse internaldriver }
```

dosemu on xterm

New versions of the DOS emulator can also be operated remotely. Output goes to a normal xterm or color-xterm. However, the type of terminal and character set need to be defined.

```
#*************************** TERMINALS ***************************
#
# IBM character set
#terminal { charset ibm  color on  method fast }
#
# color xterms or rxvt's without IBM font, 8 colors
#terminal { charset latin  color xterm  method fast }
#
# color xterms or rxvt's with IBM font, 8 colors
#terminal { charset ibm  color xterm  method fast }
#
# other terminals (not xterms or vt100)
#terminal { charset latin  color on  method ncurses }
#
# or further options ...
#terminal { charset latin  updatefreq 2  updatelines 25  color on
#           method fast  corner on }
```

If the DOS emulator is to run under X11, then screen update **X11** frequency can be adapted. Furthermore, the X11 options such as the name of the window and the icon can be defined.

```
# possible keywords:
#    "updatefreq" value                  (default 8)
#        Update frequency of screen output.
#        Smaller value = more frequent refreshes.
#
#    "updatelines" Wert                  (default 25)
#        How many lines are updated
#
#    "display" string                    (default ":0")
#        Display X server
#
#    "title" string
#        Title of window
#
#    "icon_name" string
#        Name of icon
#
X { updatefreq 8 updatelines 25 title "DOS in a BOX"
      icon_name "xdos" }
```

To run the DOS emulator on a console, you need to specify the video adapter. This setting determines whether graphic programs that **video adapter** directly access the video adapter will function. Incorrect settings here can result in a black screen and also the screen remaining black after ending the emulator or switching virtual consoles. The only remedial action then is restarting the computer. To do this, blindly switch to **reboot** another virtual console and shut down the computer with `shutdown -r now`.

```
#*********************** video adapter
#**********************************
# This sets the video adapter. This setting is critical.
# Careless settings can disable the system. ...
```

```
#
# Under X11 (with dos -x or xdos) these settings are irrelevant.
#
allowvideoportaccess on
#
# Standard VGA cards should function with this setting:
video { vga  console  graphics memsize 1024}
#
#video { vga   console   graphics   vbios_seg 0xe000 }
#video { vga   console   graphics   chipset trident   memsize 1024 }
#video { vga   console   graphics   chipset diamond }
#video { vga   console   graphics   chipset et4000   memsize 1024 }
#video { vga   console   graphics   chipset s3  memsize 1024 }
```

CPU

Additional settings inform DOS which processor and coprocessor are installed. Further, the drive letter of the boot drive should be set to either A or C; our example employs `BootA`.

```
# Math coprocessor (on / off)
mathco on
# CPU type (286 / 386 / 486)
cpu 80386
# Boot drive (BootA or BootC)
bootA
```

XMS, EMS, DPMI

Memory management within the emulator can be specified in relative detail. XMS, EMS, and DPMI, as well RAM for adapters, can be defined by size or switched off.

```
# XMS size in KB or off
xms 1024
# EMS size in KB or off
ems 1024
# For EMS, frame address can also be specified:
# ems { 1024 ems_frame 0xe000 }
# ems { ems_size 2048 emsframe 0xd000 }
#
# Where should RAM be merged?
# (Make changes here only if you know what you are doing!)
# hardware_ram { 0xc8000 range 0xcc000 0xcffff }
# DPMI size in KB or off
# DPMI might not be completely developed ...
dpmi off
```

I/O ports and interrupts

Managing interrupts and I/O ports is a critical matter. The options are intended primarily for developers and freaks who are familiar with the internal workings of DOS. Ordinary users should make no changes here.

```
sillyint off
#sillyint { 15 }
#sillyint { use_sigio 15 }
#sillyint { 10  use_sigio range 3 5 }

# ports { 0x388 0x389 }  # for SimEarth
```

Access to PC speakers can be either direct or converted to beeps.   speakers

```
# Access to PC speakers. Possible options are:
#  native      direct access
#  emulated    convert to beeps
#  off
#
speaker native
```

We do not recommend direct access to hard disks and partitions.   hard disk
However, if you have good reasons to do so, e.g., to access a partition
compressed with a stacker, this access can be enabled here.

```
# hard-disk image
#disk { image "/var/lib/dosemu/hdimage" }
#
# direct access to first partition of hda with option
# read-only for write protection
#disk { partition "/dev/hda1" 1 read-only }
#
# direct access to the entire first AT bus disk (hda)
#disk { wholedisk "/dev/hda" }
```

The following option specifies that booting will take place from
a disk image.   boot image

```
bootdisk { heads 2 sectors 18 tracks 80 threeinch
           file /var/lib/dosemu/bdisk }
```

Floppy disk drives need to be defined to allow access.   diskettes

```
# Type and device for floppy disk drives
floppy { device /dev/fd0 threeinch }
floppy { device /dev/fd1 fiveinch }
```

Access to the printer can be redirected from the DOS emulator   printer
to a corresponding device or even to a command under Linux.

71

```
#printer { options "%s"  command "lpr"  timeout 20 }
#printer { options "-p %s"  command "lpr"  timeout 10 }
#printer { file "lpt3" }
```

autoexec.bat

The `autoexec.bat` file which is used in the boot disk image could take the following form:

```
@echo off
lredir c: linux\fs/dosc
PATH C:\BAT;C:\TOOLS;C:\DOS;C:\EMU;C:\WINDOWS\WIN31;

lh DosKey
prompt $p$g
c:
bootoff
```

bootoff

changing boot
configuration

blank lines

After execution of the file `autoexec.bat`, the boot file can no longer be accessed because the command `bootoff` disables the disk image and restores access to the real disk drive. To make later changes in the boot configuration, enable the boot file again with the command `booton`.

Observe that the file `autoexec.bat` contains no blank lines after `bootoff`, since DOS would otherwise try to continue after the `bootoff` command. Since the file `autoexec.bat` no longer exists then, an error message would result.

Accessing Novell servers

IPX

The DOS emulator can also access Novell servers. Since this area is under continuous development, the procedure also changes rapidly. Principally you can either configure the emulator so that it already provides an IPX interface, or you can start an adapted version of the `pdipx` driver, contained in the DOS emulator package, from the DOS emulator. Both cases start exclusively a normal `netx` shell. This establishes the connection to the server and provides a new virtual (Novell) drive. Then it suffices to change to the Novell drive and to launch the server's `login` command command.

readme

Current information on this procedure should be included in the readme file of the respective DOS emulator package.

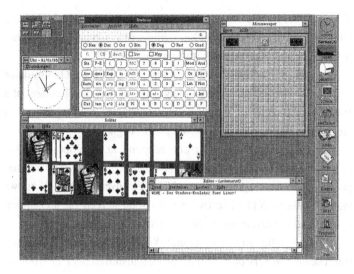

Figure 4.2. Solitaire under WINE

Starting and ending

Start the DOS emulator with the command dos or xdos. Here xdos is
only a reference to dos that launches the X11 version of the emulator.
Starting dos with the option -x has the same effect. Other possible
options generally serve to overwrite options in the configuration file
of the DOS emulator. Display these options by invoking dos -help.
Normally you will not need the other options.

dos

xdos

-x

-help

To terminate the DOS emulator, invoke the program exitemu,
press the key combination [Ctrl] + [Alt] + [PgDn], or simply end the
process of the DOS emulator from another virtual console with kill.

exitemu

4.2 WINE

A development that promises to have a significant influence on the
dissemination of UNIX on PCs both in the private and the commercial
sectors is the Windows Application Binary Interface (WABI).

WABI

This interface was developed by Sun Microsystems and licensed
by numerous UNIX producers, so that it will be available on all
common platforms. This interface makes it possible to run Microsoft
Windows programs directly under UNIX. The interface converts

Sun

MS-Windows

73

X11   Windows API calls to corresponding X11 calls, which has the interesting side effect that such programs can also be used by other X-servers due to the network transparency of X11.

DOS emulator   In early June 1993 the mailing list of the Linux DOS emulator began to host discussions about the porting or new development of a WABI for Linux. Within days a separate mailing list was set up for this project and the concrete development began.

First there were two relatively independent developments. One group developed a loader for MS-Windows programs, while another API group began development of an API for converting MS-Windows system calls to X11. The two groups soon agreed on a common WINE course, and the result was today's WINE.

FTP   Many smaller and several larger Windows applications already run. The newest version of WINE can be transferred per FTP from the directory `/pub/linux/ALPHA/Wine/development` of the server `tsx-11.mit.edu`.

4.3   iBCS2 emulator

iBCS2   Development has progressed farther on the iBCS2 emulator.* This emulator enables starting a number of commercial applications, such WordPerfect as WordPerfect, under Linux. The prerequisite is that the program must be available in one of the object formats employed by PC UNIX derivatives. UNIX System V Release 3 uses COFF; Release 4, ELF; SCO, COFF, ELF and SCO and interactive UNIX, a variant of COFF. Likewise Xenix V/386 and Wyse V/386 programs are in part executable under Linux.

SCO software packages are currently the most interesting because they are generally statically linked and thus require no shared libraries additional shared libraries.

Installation
Since the iBCS2 emulator is available as a loadable module (see section 3.4), installation proves relatively simple. All you need to do is change to the unpacked directory with the source code and enter `make`. After compilation you have a new object file named iBCS, insmod which you load with `insmod`:

*Source: `ftp://tsx-11.mit.edu/pub/linux/BETA/iBCS2`

```
zeus:/root# insmod iBCS
```

It makes sense to enter the emulator in one of the startup scripts (rc.local) so that it is loaded on booting.

rc.local

Complete installation requires you to create special device files. Observe the exact notation of the link /dev/null to /dev/X0R. (X [zero] R).

/dev/X0R

```
zeus:/root# mknod /dev/socksys c 30 0
zeus:/root# ln -s /dev/socksys /dev/nfsd
zeus:/root# ln -s /dev/null /dev/X0R
zeus:/root# mknod /dev/spx c 30 1
```

If you have a license for SCO shared libraries, copy these into a directory named /shlib. This permits execution of SCO programs that were not statically linked.

Applications

Thanks to the iBCS2 emulator, several interesting SCO applications can be used under Linux. The most prominent is certainly WordPerfect (version 5.1 or 6.0). (See Figure 4.3.)

WordPerfect

The Motif interface builder X-Designer has also been tested. (See Figure 4.4.)

X-Designer

If you have the SCO shared libraries, then SCO Open Desktop 3 and various associated utilities run with no problem under Linux. (See Figure 4.5.)

If you compare the performance of the applications under SCO and Linux, you will see that they run significantly faster under Linux. This is due to the more efficient implementation of the Linux kernel as well as the significantly faster X-server (XFree86). (See Figure 4.6.)

execution speed

4.4   HP48 emulator (X48)

Fans of the HP48 series will love the X48 emulator (Figure 4.7). It measures up to the original both optically and in functionality. For copyright reasons, operating the emulator additionally requires the contents of the original calculator's EPROMs. You can connect an external HP48 to the serial interface of the Linux computer. The main

HP48

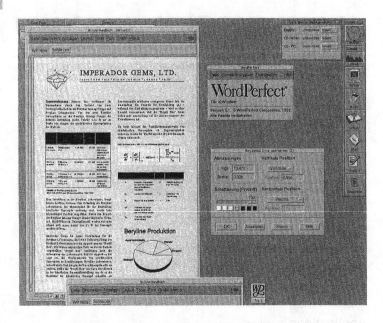

Figure 4.3. WordPerfect 5.1 under Linux

memory advantages of X48 over the original are significantly larger RAM and the possibility to cross-develop HP48 software. In addition to serious applications, this allows realization of computer games such as *Lemmings*.

4.5 IBM 3270 emulator

The X3270 emulator (Figure 4.8) allows Linux to connect to
mainframes IBM mainframes. However, connection requires the availability of a TCP/IP stack on the respective mainframe. To attain perfect emulation of a 3270 terminal, you also need to install special character sets.

4.6 Macintosh emulator

Apple Macintosh An Apple Macintosh emulator (Figure 4.9) has been presented by Abacus Research and Development. This is commercial software. Our impression from the demonstration version was quite positive.

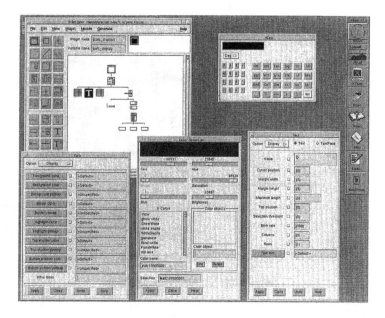

Figure 4.4. X-Designer

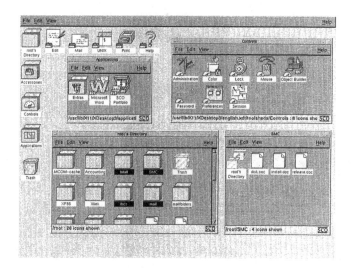

Figure 4.5. SCO's Open Desktop 3 under Linux

77

Figure 4.6. SCO ODT applications

Figure 4.7. HP48 emulator

Figure 4.8. IBM 3270 emulator under X11

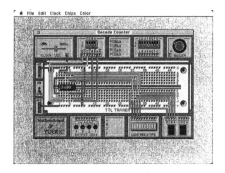

Figure 4.9. Apple Macintosh emulator

## Chapter 5

Installation

This chapter imparts the most important sources for Linux and describes its installation. First we cover general features that apply to almost all Linux distributions. Then we explain the particular installation of the Slackware distribution.

5.1 Linux distributions

Since Linux, as free software, consists of many components that were and are being developed by different people all over the world, there is no *official* Linux installation package encompassing all the programs available for Linux.

official package

However, various groups and individuals offer their own packages consisting of the Linux kernel along with many utilities, applications, and an installation program. Such a package is called a Linux distribution. Some producers of such distributions make it available on an FTP server package and also ship it on floppy disks or CD-ROMs for a fee. Linux distributions on FTP servers are normally spread over many subdirectories whose contents each fit nicely onto a floppy disk.

distribution
FTP server

Almost all such distributions include at least the kernel and all important utilities that you need for your initial installation. In addition, they usually include the GNU C compiler, the graphical user interface X11, and many other programs.

kernel

X11
installation program

Linux installation is normally guided by a menu-driven installation program that permits selective installation of subsets of the distribution. Most installation programs also offer interactive configuration of the system.

CD-ROM

NFS

In addition to installation from floppy disks, most distributions also support installation directly from CD, streamer tape, or NFS from another computer. Depending on your experience and the scope of the selected components, your installation time can range from one to several hours.

SLS

first large distribution

One of the first distributions to make a significant contribution to the propagation of Linux was SLS (Softlanding Systems) release by Peter MacDonald. For a long time it was the only distribution that enabled full installation with the C compiler and graphical user interface. With the appearance of other distributions such as

lost significance

Slackware, the SLS package declined in importance.

The current version used to reside in the directory `/pub/linux/`

tsx-11

`packages/SLS` on the FTP server `tsx-11.mit.edu`. Meanwhile it has become hard to find.

MCC Interim

Manchester

The University of Manchester assembled the MCC Interim release. Compared to other distributions, MCC is a lean package omitting

X11

less important programs such as X11 and TeX. The MCC distribution proves most suitable for users who want to install additional programs themselves and control exactly what is being deposited on their hard disks. However, we cannot recommend the package for novices.

Slackware

widespread

A newer distribution that enjoys relatively widespread propagation is the Slackware package. Originally based heavily on the SLS release,

color installation

Slackware meanwhile uses its own installation routines that give a very mature impression. Slackware's color windows, dialog boxes, and selection lists allow you at the beginning of the installation to specify the packages to be installed, the hard disk and partition to be used, and a country-specific keyboard table. The Slackware distribution permits installation from floppy disks, hard disk, or CD, or via NFS.

The scope of the Slackware distribution is quite extensive. In

many packages

addition to the base system, X11, XView, applications, TCP/IP,

UUCP, and network programs, Slackware offers a disk series with games and the newest GNU Emacs. Patrick Volkerding, manager of the Slackware package, assures that the package contains the current program versions, which certainly presents a challenge due to the rapid rate of development of the Linux system.

Patrick Volkerding

CD distributions

Many packages are now available on CD or as CD subscriptions. The subscriptions deliver a new CD several times a year with the newest version of the Linux kernel and several programs, or even a copy of a whole Linux directory tree from an FTP server. One well-known example is the CD from Yggdrasil Computing, which contains a bootable, installed Linux system as well as the source code of the MIT X11R6 system and many GNU utilities.

CD subscriptions

current programs

Yggdrasil
source codes

The CD distributions provide a simple and economical alternative for anyone who lacks an Internet connection. Some Linux CDs sell for under $30, and a CD-ROM drive has become standard equipment on high-end PCs.

economical prices

The problem that such CD distributions pose, akin to diskette distributions sold by mail order or in software stores, is that Linux continues to evolve on a daily basis; in the weeks or months between the assembly of the distribution and production of the CD to the actual shipment, a new version with numerous improvements could already be available on the network.

production delay

Unifix

The CD distribution from Unifix Software of Braunschweig, Germany, proves particularly interesting. In addition to the CD, the purchaser receives a small manual and a boot diskette that is used for the first system startup. After the installation of the 8 MB minimum configuration on an existing DOS partition or a new partition on the hard disk, the system is ready to use.

manual

All application programs can be started directly from the CD. If the computer has enough memory (8–16 MB), then the most important data on the CD are retained in memory, which naturally has a very positive effect on the access time. Changing the CD suffices

direct from CD

83

to make an update. The time-consuming installation of the complete Linux software becomes superfluous.

software list

quality

The Unifix distribution also distinguishes itself from other distributions through its content. A software list, which can be read with a WWW client, contains a classification and overview of all available programs. The configuration of the included utilities and applications is mature and well thought out. In addition, the Unifix distribution is the first and only Linux distribution conforming to POSIX.1 and so certified. Linus Torvalds has agreed to integrate the modificatins into the kernel as soon as possible. In the medium range, Unifix developers are striving for POSIX.2 and XPG4 conformity.

5.2   Sources

many sources

FTP servers

With the escalating popularity of Linux recently, there are meanwhile many sources from which to obtain the package and additional programs for Linux. The most direct and quickest way to procure individual programs and kernel versions is certainly tapping into an FTP server on the Internet.

FTP servers

Finland

tsx-11

C compiler

sunsite

The most important Linux FTP server in Europe is in Finland, which was the original Linux server. The newest version of the kernel as well as any alpha releases reside here. MIT's FTP server `tsx-11.mit.edu` contains the most recent GNU C compiler and the Linux C libraries.

By far the most important server is Sunsite (FTP address `sunsite.unc.edu`). It contains the Linux kernel, the C library, the C compiler, and practically all software packages available for Linux. Additionally, Sunsite contains the distributions RedHat, Debian, and Slackware. There are many mirror sites to Sunsite. A mirror is a second FTP server that has copied the contents of the first exactly and then regularly (every night or every weekend) makes contact with the original to update this copy. Appendix 18.5 contains a list of Sunsite mirrors. Since Sunsite mirrors are so widespread, most of our specifications for sources of Linux software in this book are given as a subdirectory of `sunsite.unc.edu:/pub/Linux/`.

FTP mail servers

If you lack direct access to the Internet but can send and receive electronic mail, you have the option of reaching the Internet FTP servers by way of an FTP mail server. An FTP mail server can send you programs from FTP servers via e-mail. You simply send an e-mail with the corresponding command to the mail server, which then accesses the FTP server, splits the program into smaller parts, and sends these encoded with the UNIX command uuencode as an e-mail reply.

To obtain a list of commands that such an FTP mail server understands, the user sends a message with the command help in the first line to the FTP mail server. Examples of such FTP mail servers include FTP-mailer@informatik.tu-muenchen.de and ftpmail@decwrl.dec.com.

Please note, however, that such a server is not suitable for transferring a complete Linux distribution. Such servers are generally limited to transferring small amounts of data.

Commercial distributors

Other sources of Linux and Linux programs are the various commercial dealers who offer Linux diskettes and CDs in software stores or by mail order. Their addresses can be located in computer industry periodicals. Some of these dealers even offer hard disks and even complete PCs with a running Linux system already installed.

Mailboxes

Meanwhile in many larger cities mailboxes have sprung up that have specialized in Linux or at least offer some Linux programs. Matthias Gmelch has assembled a list that contains an overview of such Linux mailboxes around the world. This list can be found in the directory /pub/linux/docs on the FTP server tsx-11.mit.edu and its many mirror servers.

5.3   Hardware

One of the most frequently asked questions regarding Linux is which hardware Linux supports and requires. The general prerequisite is a

---

e-mail

programs as mail

uuencode

help

mail servers

mail order

periodicals

hard disks

mailbox list

386 PC or better

PC-compatible computer with an 80386 or newer processor. Linux definitely does not run on old XTs or ATs with 80286 processors because Linux requires task-switching features that have only been available on PCs since the 80386.

RAM

The minimal hardware configuration for Linux is an 80386 SX computer with 2 MB of RAM. The installation can become difficult

2 MB low end
swap partition

because 2 MB of RAM is insufficient for installation programs. In this case a swap partition or a swap file must be created as soon as possible in order to allow launching programs and editors that are necessary for installation.

Normal work in text mode is possible starting at 4 MB of RAM. To be able to work with the X Window System in the normal version,

8 MB RAM or more

8 MB of RAM should be available. If the computer has 16 MB of RAM, this delivers a noticeable performance increase under X11.

Hard disk

By sacrificing the convenience of a graphical user interface in favor of a minimum hard disk installation, the storage requirements can be reduced to about 40 MB. However, for a full installation with X11, the

150 MB or more

C compiler, and all the tools and utilities, you need approximately 150 MB for Linux. There is hardly a ceiling on how much storage space a diligent network tapper can fill. With access to the Internet you will have no problem filling a 2 GB hard disk with free software. The supply of programming languages, utilities, libraries, and application programs has reached enormous proportions.

IDE hard disk
single-user mode

For an economical initial installation, we recommend using a hard disk with an IDE or EIDE interface. These are available in many versions up to 5 GB and afford adequate performance in single-user mode. However, rather than a larger IDE or enhanced IDE hard disk and for professional use, we suggest going to a SCSI system.

The IDE interface was supported from the beginning by the Linux kernel and needs no additional driver. With an additional kernel patch, Linux 1.2 supports two parallel IDE controllers and IDE/ATAPI CD-ROMs. However, Linux 2.0 provides a better alternative for IDE: it contains a greatly reworked and extended

EIDE driver supporting four controllers (if you have the spare change, you can operate eight IDE devices under Linux); in addition, the new driver adds support for IDE/ATAPI streamers, removable IDE devices (PCMCIA) and numerous workarounds intended to compensate for errors in various chipsets.

For larger and faster hard disks, the Small Computer System Interface (SCSI) is usually used. It permits operating up to seven devices in parallel. These devices can be hard disk drives, streamer tape drives, magneto-optical drives, CD-ROM drives, or scanners.

SCSI

hard disk, streamer,

CD-ROM

SCSI operation requires a special SCSI host adapter in the Linux kernel, but this is already contained in all current Linux distributions for the usual host adapters. Exotic host adapters should be avoided because drivers are seldom available. Drivers that are included with the device for DOS or other UNIX versions cannot be used with Linux.

avoid exotics

Controllers by well-known companies such as Adaptec, NCR, Future Domain, and Seagate pose no problems. In case of doubt, refer to the current list of supported hardware that is available on FTP servers under the title "Hardware HOWTO" (see Section 11.4).

supported controllers

HOWTO

Video boards

An uncomplicated solution for a video board is to use a simple board with an S3 chipset. The current X11 R6 package for Linux contains a special server optimized for this chipset. These boards are particularly fast in the 32-bit or 64-bit Local Bus or PCI variants of the S3 or Mach chipsets.

video board

with S3 chipset

Many chipsets from other manufacturers are also supported. The current list of supported hardware can be found on FTP servers along with the other HOWTOs under the name "XFree86 HOWTO."

XFree86 HOWTO

For an exotic video board or one equipped with little memory, the remaining option is the generic VGA server; however, it supports only 16 colors and a resolution of 640 by 480 pixels, or the mono server, which also supports Hercules graphics.

VGA

mono

Bus mice by all the familiar manufacturers, the usual serial mice, or a PS/2-compatible trackball can be used with Linux.

mouse

Bus system (ISA/EISA/PCI)

Linux supports mother boards with the old AT bus (ISA), with the more flexible and faster EISA bus, with Local Bus extensions, and with the newer PCI bus.

PCI bus

The PCI bus is processor-independent and significantly faster than the EISA system. It supports data transfer rates of up to 130 Mbytes/s in 32-bit mode. Several PCI mother boards have a very fast SCSI chip (NCR 53c810), for which the kernel contains a driver.

NCR SCSI chip

Although the specifications of the PCI standards were prepared with extreme care, some PCI components available today still deviate from it. This can cause compatibility problems between the mother board and peripheral boards. A dedicated PCI HOWTO provides more details on these difficulties as well as advice to potential purchasers of PCI hardware.

compatibility problems

Summary

Considering the continuing development on the hardware and software sectors, an 80486 computer with 33 MHz or higher and with 16 MB of RAM currently provides a reasonable and affordable configuration. The hard disk should have at least 200 MB of storage because a permanent shortage of storage precludes productive work. If you plan to use a CD-ROM drive or a streamer in addition to a hard disk, you should choose a SCSI configuration from the start.

recommended hardware

A 14-inch monitor is really too small for a multitasking environment where multiple windows are usually open simultaneously. The Linux X server is able to provide a larger virtual console, and most devices can display 800 by 600 pixels reasonably. Thus for a start, a 17-inch monitor is not absolutely necessary.

14" monitor too small

Network adapters

Linux 2.0 supports the following network adapters:

- Ethernet cards/adapters
  - 3COM 3c501, 3c503, 3c509, 3c523, 5c527, 3c579, 3c590, 3c592, 3c595, 3c597

- Cards with the following AMD chips: AMD 7990, 79C960, 79C961, 79C965 (includes Allied Telesis AT1500/AT1700/ AT2450, Boca BEN, HP-J2405A)
- AT-LAN-TEC/RealTek pocket adaptor
- Apricot Xen-II on-board Ethernet
- Boca-VLB/PCI
- Cabletron E21xx
- D-Link DE600 pocket adaptor
- D-Link DE620 pocket adaptor
- DE425, DE434, DE435, DE450, DE500
- DECchip Tulip (dc21x4x) PCI
- DEPCA, DE10x, DE200, DE201, DE202, DE422
- Digi Intl. RightSwitch SE-X
- EtherExpress 16
- EtherWORKS 3 (DE203, DE204, DE205)
- HP 10/100VG PCLAN (ISA, EISA, PCI)
- HP PCLAN (27245 and other 27xxx series)
- HP PCLAN+ (27247B and 27252A)
- NE 1000/1500/2000/2100
- Schneider & Koch G16
- SMC 9194
- SMC Ultra
- Western Digital WD80*3
• Ethernet (still unstable drivers)
- 3Com 3c505/3c507
- AT1700
- Ansel Communications EISA 3200
- EtherExpressPro
- FMV-181/182/183/184
- ICL EtherTeam 16i/32
- NI5210/NI6510
- SEEQ8005
- Zenith Z-Note

Look for additional information on supported Ethernet boards in the Ethernet HOWTO (see Section 11.4).
• IBM Token Ring adapters
• Arcnet cards

- ISDN cards
  - ICN 2B/4B
  - PCBit-D
  - Teles S0-16.0, S0-16.3 S0-8 and compatible (Niccy1016PC, Creatix)

Supported SCSI host adapters

- Adaptec AHA-1520, AHA-1522, AHA-1542, AHA-1740, AHA-2740, AHA-2840, AHA-2920 (see Future Domain), AHA-2940, and numerous others
- Advansys adapter
- Always IN2000
- AM53/79C974
- BusLogic (except FlashPoint)
- DTC3180/3280
- EATA ISA/EISA (DPT PM2011/021/012/022/122/322)
- EATA-DMA (DPT, NEC, AT&T, SNI, AST, Olivetti, Alphatronix)
- EATA-PIO (old DPT PM2001, PM2012A)
- Future Domain TMC-8xx/TMC-16xx
- NCR 5380/53c400/53c406a/53c7xx/53c8xx
- IOMEGA Zip Drive (parallel port)
- Pro Audio Spectrum/Studio PAS 16
- Qlogic FastSCSI!
- Quantum ISA-200S/-250MG (see Future Domain)
- Seagate ST-01/ST-02
- Trantor T128/T128F/T228
- UltraStor 14F/24F/34F
- Western Digital 7000

Operating the IOMEGA Zip Drive on a parallel port requires no hardware SCSI support. The ECP/EPP modes of the parallel port are not yet supported. To operate a printer simultaneously, compile both support for the Zip Drive and the previous parallel port driver (CONFIG_PRINTER for printers or PLIP) as modules and load and remove them as needed.

Nonstandard CD-ROM drives

Note that this section lists only non-IDE/ATAPI and non-SCSI CD-ROM drives (ones with their own CD-ROM controllers). If you have an IDE or SCSI CD-ROM, then you can skip this section when you compile the kernel.

- Aztech CDA268-01A
- CD-ROM-Interface on ISP16, MAD16, and Mozart sound cards (and any other with OPTi 82C928/82C929 chip)
- Conrad TXC
- CreaticeLabs CD200
- CyCDROM CR520/CR540
- Goldstar R420
- IBM External ISA CDROM
- Lasermate CR328A
- Longshine LCS-7260
- Mitsumi LU-005/FX-001/FX-001D (+ own driver for XA/multi-session)
- Matsushita CR-521/CR-522/CR-523/CR-562/CR-563
- Optics Storage DOLPHIN 8000AT
- Orchid CD-3110, Orchid/Wearnes CDD110
- Philips/LMS CM206
- Sanyo CDR-H94A
- Sony CDU31A/CDU33A (not automatically detected!*)
- Sony CDU-531/CDU-535
- TEAC CD-55A

Sound cards

- Audio Excell DSP16
- Crystal CS4232-based cards (AcerMagic S23, TB Tropez Plus, many PC motherboards [Compaq, HP, Intel, . . .])
- Ensoniq SoundScape and compatible
- Gravis Ultrasound GUS, GUS+16, GUS MAX, GUS ACE, GUS PnP
- cards with 6850 UART MIDI chip

*See /usr/src/linux/Documentation/cdrom/cdu31a

91

- Logitech SoundMan Wave
- Logitech Sound Man 16
- MAD16- and Mozart-based cards
- MediaTriX AudioTriX Pro
- Media Vision Jazz16-based cards
- MPU-401 and compatible
- Pro Audio Spectrum 16
- Pro Audio Studio 16
- Pro Sonic 16
- PSS-based cards (AD1848 + ADSP-2115 + Echo ESC614 ASIC)
- Soundblaster SB 1.0 to 2.0, SB Pro, SB 16, SB16ASP, AWE32
- Turtle Beach Maui and Tropez
- Windows Sound System (MSS/WSS)
- Yamaha FM synthesizers (OPL2, OPL3 and OPL4)

Multiple serial port cards

- Cyclades Cyclom-Y
- DigiBoard PC/Xe, PC/Xi, PC/Xeve
- SDL RISCom/8
- Stallion EasyIO, EC8/32, EC8/64, ONboard, Brumby

Non-serial mice

- ATIXL busmouse
- C&T 82C710 mouse
- Logitech busmouse
- Microsoft busmouse
- PS/2 mouse

Non-IDE/SCSI streamer

Note the important information in the Ftape-HOWTO (see Section 11.4).

- QIC-02
- QIC-10
- Travan

Advanced Power Management

Some BIOS provide an APM interface (Advanced Power Management). If you run Linux on a notebook, you should select this option. The APM driver saves the battery when no processes are running by reducing the clock rate of the CPU and shutting off the background illumination of the LCD. Shutting off hard-disk motors is not supported yet.

Watchdog support

The Linux watchdog driver provides not only a software watchdog but also support for watchdog hardware. Depending on their level of refinement, hardware watchdogs include features such as monitoring the processor temperature, ventilator, and operating voltage, and automatically rebooting the computer if a hardware timer is not reset at least once per minute. This proves interesting for servers intended to reboot on any kind of error to put them back into commission quickly. With a software watchdog, rebooting is not triggered in some cases.

Other drivers

The list of supported hardware is by no means complete. On the one hand numerous sound cards, CD-ROMs, etc., are compatible to one of the listed devices and thus supported. On the other hand, many hardware drivers are not initially integrated in the kernel sources because they are still being developed or tested or because Linus Torvalds has not found time to integrate them. Many of the drivers included in Linux 2.0 were once kernel patches or modules for Linux 1.2 (e.g., ISDN support).

5.4   Installation

This section explains the Installation procedure in more detail using the Slackware distribution. This distribution seems to be the most widespread because it can be copied freely and is contained on many CDs from various vendors. With small deviations, this procedure applies to other distributions as well. The following examples refer

Slackware

to the Slackware 2.1.0 distribution (installation of newer versions is identical).

installation procedure
The basic steps of a Linux installation are:

- Booting of a minimum Linux system from a boot (and possibly root) diskette
- Creation of partitions for Linux
- Creating file systems and swap regions
- Copying the system to the hard disk
- Configuration of the most important system files
- Installation of a boot manager
- Configuration of the graphical user interface
- Creating the users

Boot diskette

booting from floppy disk
The installation procedure begins with the booting of a minimum Linux system that contains only the kernel and only the most important utilities and the installation program. The Slackware distribution contains two diskettes for this purpose, called the boot
boot and root disk
and the root diskette.

Diskettes are provided in 3¼-inch or 5½-inch versions. Both the
different versions
boot diskette and the root diskette are available in various versions.
drivers
The boot diskettes differ in the drivers that they contain in the kernel; the root diskette contains a minimal file system with the most important utilities and the installation script.

If the distribution was purchased as a diskette package, then the diskettes are preconfigured in a bootable version. Otherwise the
image files
installation diskettes contain image files. To create a bootable diskette or one with a Linux file system from such an image file, it must be transferred to the diskette with a special utility as described below. The images for boot and root diskettes are usually in the following directories of the Slackware distribution:

- `bootdsks.12`
- `bootdsks.144`
- `rootdsks.12`
- `rootdsks.144`

The directory `bootdsks.144` contains the following files:

```
README   cdu535.gz      old1118.gz
WHICH.ONE     loaded.gz       sbpcd.gz
alpha.gz      mitsumi.gz      scsi.gz
bare.gz nec260.gz      scsinet.gz
cdu31a.gz     net.gz    xt.gz
```

For a 3¼-inch floppy disk as DOS drive A is the boot drive, and the directories `install/1.44meg/bootdisks` and `install/1.44meg/rootdisks` contain the correct data. The files for a 5½-inch floppy disk drive are found in the directory `install/1.2meg`.

3¼ or 5½ inch

For remote installation of Linux via NFS, the kernel must contain a driver for the network board in the file for the boot diskette. If the computer has a network board for which the kernel on the boot diskette has no driver, you can create a custom boot diskette (see Section 7.12).

remote installation drivers

The same applies to a system with a SCSI hard disk and an exotic SCSI host adapter for which none of the boot diskettes has the proper driver. In case of doubt, read the README file contained in the same directory as the disk image files, to determine which files are suitable for which hardware configurations.

SCSI host adapter README

There are also different files for the root diskette, although here the distinction is only between a diskette with color support and a monochrome installation program. In most cases the file for the color installation program can be used: for a 3¼-inch drive, the file `rootdsks.144/color144.gz`. The other directories contain files for creating custom boot diskettes or additional tools and information.

root disk

After you have selected the correct files for the boot and root diskettes, you need to transfer them onto formatted diskettes either under DOS with `rawrite.exe` or under UNIX with the `dd` command. First, decompress the source files with `gzip`. The following example demonstrates this procedure.

creating floppy disks
rawrite.exe
gzip

```
stef1:/tmp> gzip -d bare.gz
stef1:/tmp> dd if=bare of=/dev/fd0 bs=8k
180+0 records in
180+0 records out
stef1:/tmp>
```

booting

LILO

After you have created the diskettes, insert the boot diskette in the boot drive and reboot the computer. The first message to be displayed comes from LILO, the Linux boot manager and loader, which is installed on the boot diskette. The following example shows the first message during booting.

```
Welcome to the Slackware Linux 2.1.0 bootkernel disk!

If you have any extra parameters to pass to the kernel, enter them at the
prompt below after one of the valid configuration names (ramdisk, mount, drive2)

Here are some examples:

ramdisk hd=cyl,hds,secs    (Where "cyl," "hds," and "secs" are the number of
                            cylinders, sectors, and heads on the drive.  Most
                            machines won't need this.)

In a pinch, you can boot your system with a command like:
mount root=/dev/hda1

On machines with little memory, you can use mount root=/dev/fd1 or
mount root=/dev/fd0 to install without a ramdisk.  See LOWMEM.TXT for details.

If you would rather load the root/install disk from your second floppy drive:
drive2 (or even this:  ramdisk root=/dev/fd1)

DON'T SWITCH ANY DISKS YET! This prompt is just for entering extra parameters.
If you don't need to enter any parameters, hit ENTER to continue.

boot:
```

The Linux Loader now waits for input. For a normal installation in which the boot drive is also used for the root diskette, it suffices to press 〔 **Return** 〕.

parameters

In some cases, such as if a CD-ROM drive, a hard disk, or a network board is not correctly recognized, special parameters have to be passed to the kernel. These parameters are listed after the specification of the boot option. An entry after the boot prompt has the following structure:

```
Boot choice Parameter=Value,Value,..  Parameter=Value,Value,...
```

example network board

An example was shown in the above Linux Loader message. The following is another example:

```
ramdisk ether=5,0x320
```

This tells the driver for the Ethernet board in the kernel that the board is using interrupt 5 and I/O address 0x320.

If the choices are correct and any necessary options have been passed, then the Linux Loader loads the kernel. The kernel first decompresses itself and then initializes its individual components, displaying corresponding messages all the while. The messages of the device drivers indicate which devices were recognized and successfully initialized. The sequence of displays during the boot process could look like this:

interrupt and IO address

kernel starts

device drivers

```
Loading ramdisk ........
Uncompressing linux...memory is tight...done.
Console: colour EGA+ 80x25, 1 virtual console (max 63)
bios32_init : BIOS32 Service Directory structure at 0x000fc300
bios32_init : BIOS32 Service Directory entry at 0xfc580
pcibios_init : PCI BIOS revision 2.00 entry at 0xfc5b0
Serial driver version 4.00 with no serial options enabled
tty00 at 0x03f8 (irq = 4) is a 16550A
tty01 at 0x02f8 (irq = 3) is a 16550A
lp_init: lp2 exists, using polling driver
Calibrating delay loop.. ok - 36.08 BogoMips
scsi-ncr53c7,8xx : at PCI bus 0, device 4, function 0
scsi-ncr53c7,8xx : NCR53c810 at memory 0xfc800000, io 0xd000, irq 11
scsi0 : using io mapped access
scsi0 : using initiator ID 7
scsi0 : using level active interrupts.
scsi0 : burst length 8
scsi0 : using 40MHz SCSI clock
scsi0 : m_to_n = 0x90, n_to_m = 0xa0, n_to_n = 0xb0
scsi0 : NCR code relocated to 0x383b10
scsi0 : testing
scsi0 : test 1 started
scsi0 : tests complete.
scsi0 : NCR53c(7,8)xx (rel 3)
scsi : 1 hosts.
Vendor: TOSHIBA    Model: CD-ROM XM-3401TA  Rev: 2873
Type:   CD-ROM                        ANSI SCSI revision: 02
scsi : detected total.
Memory: 29780k/32768k available (868k kernel code, 384k reserved, 1736k data)
This processor honors the WP bit even when in supervisor mode.  Good.
This processor honors the WP bit even when in supervisor mode.  Good.
Floppy drive(s): fd0 is 1.44M
FDC 0 is a post-1991 82077
Swansea University Computer Society NET3.017
Swansea University Computer Society TCP/IP for NET3.017
IP Protocols: ICMP, UDP, TCP
eth0: SMC Ultra at 0x240, 00 00 C0 16 02 A0, IRQ 5 memory 0xe0000-0xe3fff.
smc-ultra.c:v1.10 9/23/94 Donald Becker (becker@cesdis.gsfc.nasa.gov)
Checking 386/387 coupling... Ok, fpu using exception 16 error reporting.
Checking 'hlt' instruction... Ok.
Linux version 1.1.59 (root@fuzzy) (gcc version 2.5.8) #6 Sat Oct 29 1994
RAMDISK: 1474560 bytes, starting at 0x21b850
```

After the kernel has been successfully loaded and started, a message appears on the screen that prompts the user to replace the boot diskette with a root diskette containing the basic file system.

switch floppy disk

```
Please remove the boot kernel disk from your floppy drive, insert a
root/install disk (such as one of the Slackware color144, colrlite,
tty144, or tty12 disks) or some other disk you wish to load into a
ramdisk and boot, and then press ENTER to continue.
```

ramdisk   When the root diskette is ready, its contents are read into a RAM-
disk, thus completely loading the root file system and the installation
program into memory and freeing the floppy disk drive for other
diskettes.

```
VFS: Disk change detected on device 2/28
RAMDISK: Minix filesystem found at block 0
RAMDISK: Loading 1440 blocks into RAM disk
done
```

welcome   On completion of booting, a welcome message appears on the
screen that explains subsequent steps.

```
Welcome to the Slackware Linux installation disk, (v. 2.1.0)

###### IMPORTANT! READ THE INFORMATION BELOW CAREFULLY. ######
- You will need one or more partitions of type "Linux native" prepared. It is
  also recommended that you create a swap partition (type "Linux swap") prior
  to installation. Most users can use the Linux "fdisk" utility to create and
  tag the types of all these partitions. OS/2 Boot Manager users, however,
  should create their Linux partitions with OS/2 "fdisk," add the bootable
  (root) partition to the Boot Manager menu, and then use the Linux "fdisk" to
  tag the partitions as type "Linux native".
- If you have 4 megabytes or less of RAM, you MUST activate a swap partition
  before running setup. After making the partition with fdisk, use:
  mkswap /dev/<partition> <number of blocks> ; swapon /dev/<partition>
- Once you have prepared the disk partitions for Linux, and activated a swap
  partition if you need one, type "setup" to begin the installation process.
- If you want the install program to use monochrome displays, type:
  TERM=vt100
  before you start "setup".

You may now login as "root".
slackware login:
```

login   To continue, enter the user name root at the login prompt. This
brings another message:

```
Linux 1.1.59. (Posix).

If you're upgrading an existing Slackware system, you might want to
remove old packages before you run 'setup' to install the new ones. If
you don't, your system will still work but there might be some old files
left laying around on your drive.

Just mount your Linux partitions under /mnt and type 'pkgtool'. If you
don't know how to mount your partitions, type 'pkgtool' and it will tell
```

```
you how it's done.

To start the main installation, type 'setup'.
```

All subsequent steps take place under Linux.

Partitioning

Installing Linux requires at least one free partition. However, it makes sense to create three partitions: one for the root file system, one for the home file system, and one as a swap partition. Then a new installation of the system can leave the /home partition unscathed and ready for remounting after the installation. This also retains all user files.

multiple partitions
/home separate

If the hard disk does not contain any partitions that can be used for Linux, then the partitions must be created first with the Linux command fdisk. The following example demonstrates the creation of partitions for Linux. Assume that one partition for DOS already exists on the hard disk.

fdisk

The partition type that is specified for a new partition is 83 (Linux native). The intended swap partition is set to type 82 (Linux swap).

A partition's type is read by the installation program, which thus recognizes which partitions can be used for the installation. If partitions for Linux already exist, for example, which were created under DOS with fdisk, then the type of any partition to be used for a Linux file system should be set to 83 with the fdisk command under Linux.

Type of a partition

DOS-fdisk

The following terminal capture reflects the execution of fdisk under Linux:

fdisk under Linux

```
# fdisk
Using /dev/hda as default device!
Command (m for help): p
Disk /dev/hda: 14 heads, 35 sectors, 978 cylinders
Units = cylinders of 490 * 512 bytes

   Device Boot  Begin     Start    End  Blocks  Id  system
/dev/hda1          1         1     418  102392+   6  DOS 16-bit >=32M

Command (m for help): n
Command action
   e   extended
   p   primary partition (1-4)
p
Partition number (1-4): 2
First cylinder (419-978): 419
Last cylinder or +size or +sizeM or +sizeK (419-978): +100M

Command (m for help): p
```

```
Disk /dev/hda: 14 heads, 35 sectors, 978 cylinders
Units = cylinders of 490 * 512 bytes
 Device Boot   Begin      Start    End  Blocks  Id  system
/dev/hda1          1          1    418  102392+  6  DOS 16-bit >=32M
/dev/hda2        419        419    836  102410  83  Linux native

Command (m for help): n
Command action
  e   extended
  p   primary partition (1-4)
p
Partition number (1-4): 3
First cylinder (837-978): 837
Last cylinder or +size or +sizeM or +sizeK (837-978): +8M

Command (m for help): p
Disk /dev/hda: 14 heads, 35 sectors, 978 cylinders
Units = cylinders of 490 * 512 bytes
 Device Boot  Begin      Start    End  Blocks  Id  system
/dev/hda1          1          1    418  102392+  6  DOS 16-bit >=32M
/dev/hda2        419        419    836  102410  83  Linux native
/dev/hda3        837        837    870    8330  83  Linux native

Command (m for help): n
Command action
  e   extended
  p   primary partition (1-4)
p
Partition number (1-4): 4
First cylinder (871-978): 871
Last cylinder or +size or +sizeM or +sizeK (871-978): 978

Command (m for help): p
Disk /dev/hda: 14 heads, 35 sectors, 978 cylinders
Units = cylinders of 490 * 512 bytes
 Device Boot  Begin      Start    End  Blocks  Id  system
/dev/hda1          1          1    418  102392+  6  DOS 16-bit >=32M
/dev/hda2        419        419    836  102410  83  Linux native
/dev/hda3        837        837    870    8330  83  Linux native
/dev/hda4        871        871    978   26460  83  Linux native

Command (m for help): t
Partition number (1-4): 3
Hex code (type L to list codes): L
0   Empty         8  AIX          75  PC/IX         b8  BSDI swap
1   DOS 12-bit FAT 9  AIX bootable 80  Old MINIX     c7  Syrinx
2   XENIX root    a  OPUS         81  Linux/MINIX   db  CP/M
3   XENIX usr     40 Venix 80286  82  Linux swap    e1  DOS access
4   DOS 16-bit <32M 51 Novell?    83  Linux native  e3  DOS R/O
5   Extended      52 Microport    93  Amoeba        f2  DOS secondary
6   DOS 16-bit >=32 63 GNU HURD    94  Amoeba BBT    ff  BBT
7   OS/2 HPFS     64 Novell       b7  BSDI fs
Hex code (type L to list codes): 82
Changed system type of partition 3 to 82 (Linux swap)

Command (m for help): p
Disk /dev/hda: 14 heads, 35 sectors, 978 cylinders
Units = cylinders of 490 * 512 bytes

   Device Boot  Begin   Start    End  Blocks  Id  system
/dev/hda1          1          1    418  102392+  6  DOS 16-bit >=32M
/dev/hda2        419        419    836  102410  83  Linux native
/dev/hda3        837        837    870    8330  82  Linux swap
/dev/hda4        871        871    978   26460  83  Linux native

Command (m for help): w
The partition table has been altered!
Calling BLKRRPART ioctl() to re-read partition table
Syncing disks
Reboot your system to ensure partition table is updated
#
```

All partitions, including the logical drives of an extended partition, are simply numbered sequentially under Linux and can be used like a primary partition. All partitions are mapped onto files in the directory /dev, their names beginning with hd for normal hard disks or sd for SCSI hard disks. More detailed information can be found in Section 5.3.

Creating file systems

Before a partition is capable of storing files, a file system must be created on it. In general this is done by selecting the respective menu item in the installation script.   *menu*

Alternatively, a file system can be created manually with the command mkfs. This command is only a front end that invokes the respective program to create the selected file system according to the file system type parameter (option -t) that is passed to it. For an Extended-2 file system, for example, this is the command mke2fs.   *mkfs*

```
# mkfs -t ext2 -c /dev/hda4
```

The parameter -c activates the verification of the blocks on the hard disk that are used for the file system.   *verify*

Creating a swap partition

Similarly, a swap partition is created with the command mkswap. In addition to the device, the number of blocks in the partition must be specified. This can be obtained easily by invoking the program fdisk with the option -s, which specifies the size of a partition in blocks.   *mkswap*

```
# fdisk -s /dev/hda3 8330
# mkswap /dev/hda3 8330
Setting up swapspace, size = 8523776 bytes
#
```

To activate the new swap partition, enter the command swapon followed by a partition parameter. Display the current state of main memory with the command free.   *swapon*

101

Figure 5.1. The main menu of the installation program

```
# swapon /dev/hda3
# free
            total     used      free    shared   buffers
Mem:         7060     5248      1812       888     2300
Swap:        8324        0      8324
#
```

RAM For a machine with 8 MB of RAM or more, the swap partition, like the file system, could be created and activated in the installation program. If you select the menu item ADDSWAP, the hard disk is

type Linux swap searched for a partition of type Linux swap. If such a partition is found, the user can register it as the swap partition. Then this partition can be initialized with mkswap and activated with swapon.

4 MB or less If the machine has 4 MB of less RAM, then a swap partition has to be created and activated before the invocation of the installation program. The available memory will not suffice otherwise.

Copying to the hard disk

setup Once the swap partition and the file system are set up, the Linux system can be copied onto the hard disk by invoking the installation program via the command setup.

The most important items in the main menu are the selection of

source medium the source medium, the selection of the target partition, the choice of

target partition the components to be installed, and the start of the actual installation. These menu items are automatically linked; that is, if the first point

installation program is selected, the installation program automatically moves to the next item when the first item is complete. The choice of installation mode

packages between quick mode and verbose mode should be left at verbose.

Figure 5.2. Selecting the source medium

The source medium could be the hard disk if the files from the diskettes were copied there beforehand, the disk ettes themselves, another computer on the network mounted with NFS, a CD-ROM, or a streamer tape. Installation from a streamer tape is somewhat more tedious than the other possibilities and is explained in a separate README file.

hard disk, floppies, CD-ROM, NFS, or streamer

An installation via NFS requires entering several network parameters such as the IP address of the target computer and that of the NFS server, the network mask, the broadcast and network address, and the path of the distribution on the NFS server. These terms are explained in Chapter 9. In case of doubt, call on the network administrator who knows the local setup for advice.

NFS parameters

network administrator

The selection of the target partition is also menu-driven. The installation program independently searches the system for all partitions of type Linux native and displays these for selection:

target partition

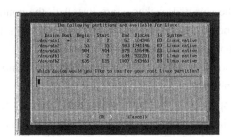

Figure 5.3. Selecting the target partition

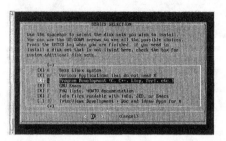

Figure 5.4. Selecting packages

additional partitions

/home

After the root partition has been created, the installation program asks whether additional partitions are to be mounted. If you want to install /home and possibly /usr on separate file systems, you need to specify these here.

packages

Likewise you select the packages you want to install from a list of all possible packages of the distribution, accompanied by short descriptions.

INSTALL

descriptions

configuations

Next you invoke the menu item INSTALL mode. You will be presented with a selection of modes in which the copying procedure can be carried out. For an initial installation we recommend the NORMAL mode as the best choice. This mode installs the fundamental system components automatically and asks the user about optional elements. Before each copying step the installation program displays information about the subpackage being installed or the option for selection, which eases deciding about optional components.

Once the selected packages are installed, the configuration of the system begins. Here various parameters and links are set, such as for the connection of a modem or a mouse.

LILO

You also have the option of installing the Linux Loader in menu-driven mode.

On completion of the installation, the program automatically returns to the main menu, where you can quit. This ends the installation of the Slackware distribution and the computer can be rebooted.

Figure 5.5. Mouse configuration

5.5 Boot manager

The Linux Loader (LILO) permits loading Linux immediately on booting. If there are multiple operating systems on the hard disk, then LILO can manage the selection of the system to be started. Besides Linux, LILO can load DOS, OS/2, or a different PC-UNIX variant, and can even boot these from a second hard disk.

Linux Loader

selecting the OS

The operating principle resembles that of the OS/2 boot manager. Instead of loading an operating system immediately, LILO starts first and lets you choose from among all registered operating systems and configurations.

boot manager

Operation

The loader first presents itself with the word "LILO" across the screen. Then you have a configurable amount of time to press one of the keys **Alt**, **Ctrl**, or **AltGr** to not boot the standard configuration, but to select another partition or configuration. Then the loader prompts you with the configurable boot: message to enter a boot variant.

As soon as the boot prompt appears, you can press the tabulator key to display a list of available alternatives.

Tab

```
LILO boot: Tab
linux        linux-old       dos
boot: linux
Loading linux
```

If one of the above keys is not pressed during the preset time, then the first selection is made automatically and the first defined operating system is loaded.

automatic selection

Configuration

We describe a typical installation for a system with an (E)IDE hard disk drive with the Linux root file system installed on the second partition (Figure 5.6). First adapt the file /etc/lilo.conf:

/etc/lilo.conf

```
boot = /dev/hda2
root = /dev/hda2
install = /boot/boot.b
message = /boot/message
map   = /boot/map
delay = 100
compact
image = /vmlinuz
        label = linux
        read-only
image = /vmlinuz.old
        label = linux-old
other = /dev/hda1
        label = DOS
```

The first line specifies where LILO will be installed. The choices are at the start of a hard disk drive and thus in the master boot record (MBR), or at the start of a partition. The securest solution is to install LILO at the start of the Linux root file system and to activate this partition (see below). The specification **boot=/dev/sda** or **boot=/dev/hda** installs LILO in the MBR. **boot=/dev/sda1**, e.g., installs LILO in the first partition of the first SCSI disk; in this case another boot manager must be in the MBR (see below).

MBR or start of a partition

Installing LILO in the master boot record (MBR) means overwriting the original DOS MBR. However, this can be restored with **fdisk ~/mbr** under DOS (or inadvertently with some virus programs).

root = /dev/hda2 specifies where the kernel should attempt to mount the root file system.

root file system

compact optimizes LILO to prevent reading each sector individually.

install = /boot/boot.b is an optional setting that specifies the boot sector to be installed. The default setting is /boot/boot.b.

boot sector

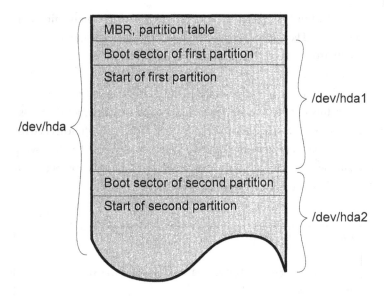

Figure 5.6. Logical structure of a hard disk

message = /boot/message is likewise optional and speci- message
fies the name of the text file that is displayed on booting before the
prompt. This file normally contains notes on the possible boot options
and image files.

You can define map = /boot/map to specify another map file. map file
Here during installation LILO stores information about the possible
image files and options. The default value is /boot/map.

delay specifies the time interval in tenths of seconds that LILO delay
should wait for a key to be pressed before automatically selecting
the first boot alternative.

The entry image = /vmlinuz and the subsequent indented
lines describe the first boot alternative. The kernel image file to be kernel image files
booted is vmlinuz and resides in the root directory. The designation
that you need to enter to boot is linux. read-only overwrites the read-only
kernel settings that specify whether the root file system is mounted
read/write or read-only.

The second boot alternative is the file /vmlinuz.old. This is
an older kernel image file that has been saved for the event that the other image files
current kernel might cease to function.

107

DOS The third boot alternative is the DOS partition on the first IDE hard disk. The tag other assures that LILO does not attempt to start Linux from this partition, but instead the loader of another operating system.

A quite useful option in the LILO configuration file is append. After this option, as with the boot prompt of LILO, you can pass parameters for the kernel or the init process. This is often needed for sound boards or systems with two Ethernet adapters. The following example shows the file /etc/lilo.conf of a Linux computer that is used as a router and thus has two Ethernet boards.

parameters for kernel or init

```
boot    = /dev/sda1
root    = /dev/sda1
compact
delay   = 50
append  = "ether=10,0x280,eth0 ether=5,0x340,eth1"

image = /vmlinuz
        read-only
        label = linux

image = /vmlinuz.fw
        label = firewall
```

eth0 and eth1 The append line establishes the mapping of the Ethernet boards to the devices eth0 and eth1 as well as their interrupt and I/O port settings. See Section 6.2 for an overview of possible kernel parameters.

Kernel image files

A kernel image is a file that contains the actual kernel of the operating system along with an initialization program and loader. This file is created on compilation of the kernel whose source code resides in /usr/src/linux (see Section 6.2).

compiled kernel

LILO To be able to boot from a kernel image file, you need to enter its name in the LILO configuration file and reinstall the loader.

old kernel image After compiling a new kernel, you should also enter the old version of the kernel image in the configuration file. In case you made an error in the compilation or configuration of the kernel and the system does not boot with the new kernel, you can boot with the old kernel and correct the error.

This backup approach is already supported by the makefile of the kernel. On invocation of **make zlilo** in the kernel source code directory /usr/src/linux, after compilation the new kernel image file is copied to /vmlinuz and the old one is renamed to /vmlinuz.old.

make zlilo

Activating the loader

To activate the entries in the configuration files, LILO must be reinstalled. Invoke the script install in directory /etc/lilo, which writes the actual loader with its current configuration to a boot sector or the MBR.

LILO

```
dirk1:/root# lilo
Added linux
Added linux-old
Added DOS
dirk1:/root#
```

Removing LILO

If LILO was installed as described above in the partition of the Linux root file system, then reactivating the previously active partition fdisk, e.g., to boot DOS directly, suffices to uninstall LILO.

activate old partition

If LILO was installed in the MBR and should now be removed for whatever reason, then the previous contents of the MBR must be restored. If DOS is available on another hard disk or partition, then the simplest solution is to invoke the DOS fdisk program with the option /mbr. This installs a new master boot record and overwrites LILO.

fdisk /mbr

LILO Options

-R *directory*

First of all, LILO changes to the specified directory and treats it as the root directory. This makes sense if you boot from a non-boot diskette and you want to restore the boot sector of the hard disk. Without -R **the boot diskette can unintentionally be rendered unusable**.

◄

109

-q

Nothing is installed; LILO simply displays the current bootable configurations. For the above example this would be:

```
> lilo -q
linux           *
linux-old
dos
```

The asterisk marks the default configuration if no other is specified.

-C *file*

LILO uses a configuration file other than /etc/lilo.conf.

Alternative boot manager

OS/2 boot manager

To install a boot manager other than LILO, such as the OS/2 boot manager, LILO must not be installed in the MBR; otherwise it will definitely be started as the first boot alternative.

OS/2 fdisk

The OS/2 version of fdisk should be used to set up the partitions. Afterwards the OS/2 boot manager can be initialized and the boot partition can be activated. Then the Linux partition where the Linux loader was installed should be registered as well. On booting the OS/2 boot manager is activated; from here the user can either select OS/2 or, via LILO, start the Linux system. Check the LILO User's Guide or the LILO FAQ for more information on the Linux loader, or other FAQs and HOWTOs (see Section 11.4) that are available on various FTP servers.

## Chapter 6

Configuration

O nce the system files have been copied onto the hard disk and   files
the Linux loader has been installed, some of the configuration
files need to be adapted. This fine-tunes the operating system to the
available hardware.

6.1   General configuration

Most configuration files belong in the directory /etc. Many of these   /etc
files are fixed in content and normally need not be changed. The
appendix to this book contains a brief description of the files. This
chapter discusses the configuration modifications that have to be
carried out after the Linux loader is installed on normal PC hardware.

File systems

When the system starts up, one of the rc scripts (see Section 7.2)
invokes the command mount, which mounts all file systems. The   mount
command is usually invoked with the option -a, which automatically
mounts all file systems specified in the file /etc/fstab into the   /etc/fstab
directory tree. This file should list all available file systems, including
those that are not intended for automatic mounting. Files that are not
to be automatically mounted are listed with the option noauto, which   noauto
overrides automatic mounting with **mount -a**. This permits global
specification of mount options for all file systems.

The following example (excerpt from the file /etc/fstab)
shows these entries for a computer on which not only /home but
also /usr and /var were installed on separate partitions:

111

/dev/sda1	/	ext2	defaults
/dev/sda2	/usr	ext2	defaults
/dev/sda3	/var	ext2	defaults
/dev/sda5	/home	ext2	defaults
/dev/sda6	none	swap	
none	/proc	proc	defaults
/dev/scd0	/cdrom	iso9660	defaults,user,noauto,ro
zeus:/usr/src	/usr/src	nfs	defaults

device

The entries correspond largely to the parameters of the `mount` command. The first column identifies the device to be mounted. For an NFS mount, this is the host followed by a colon and the corresponding directory. The second column identifies the path of the *mountpoint*, the existing directory to which the new file system is to be mounted. The third column specifies the type of the file system.

mountpoint

options

Most file systems permit the specification of additional options that are passed via the last column. If you do not want any particular parameters, you should enter `defaults` here to activate the standard options.

defaults

proc

The entry that mounts the `proc` file system is important because several commands, such as a variant of `ps`, are dependent on this directory. System information is represented here in the form of files and subdirectories.

Swap space

RAM

If the target computer has 8 MB or less of RAM, it is necessary to create a swap partition or a swap file if this was not already done during installation. Otherwise the machine will not have enough memory to execute multiple programs simultaneously under the graphical user interface. Four MB of memory does not even suffice to recompile the kernel while running an editor at the same time. Even with 16 MB we recommend extending virtual memory with a swap partition.

swapon

The command `swapon` activates the swap space (see Section 5.4). Entering the swap partition in the file `/etc/fstab` like a file system affects its automatic activation on system startup. The preceding example contains such an entry.

In some cases it makes sense to use a swap file instead of a swap   swap file
partition. Such a file must first be created in the desired size using
the command `dd`. The following example demonstrates creating and
activating a swap file:

```
hermes:/# free
            total      used      free     shared    buffers
Mem:        31380     29476      1904      17260     10092
Swap:           0         0         0
hermes:/# dd if=/dev/zero of=/swapfile bs=1k count=8192
8192+0 records in
8192+0 records out
hermes:/# mkswap /swapfile 8192
Setting up swapspace, size = 8384512 bytes
hermes:/# sync
hermes:/# swapon /swapfile
hermes:/# free
            total      used      free     shared    buffers
Mem:        31380     29484      1896      17260     10092
Swap:        8188         0      8188
hermes:/#
```

Swap files are also entered in the file `/etc/fstab` so that they   /etc/fstab
can be automatically activated with the command `swapon -a`. Here
the swap file is entered in place of the device:

```
/swapfile       none        swap
```

Login

If the shadow password package included in many distributions has   shadow password
been installed, the many options concerning user login are set in
the file `login.defs` in the `/etc` directory. For example, this file
specifies how long the login prompt is disabled (the delay) after the
entry of an incorrect password and lists the devices from which the
user `root` can log in.

Corresponding notes can be found in the file `/etc/login.defs`   /etc/login.defs
itself or in the corresponding On-Line Manual page. Figure 6.1 is a
small excerpt from this file.

```
# Delay in seconds for which the login prompt is disabled
# after entry of a wrong password.
FAIL_DELAY 2

# Devices from which a login as root is permissible
#CONSOLE     /etc/consoles
#CONSOLE     console:tty01:tty02:tty03:tty04
CONSOLE      tty1:tty2:tty3:tty4:tty5:tty6:tty8
```

113

```
# Files to be output after a login
MOTD_FILE   /etc/motd
```

Figure 6.1. Excerpt from the file /etc/login.defs

other login packages

Alternative login packages that do not support shadow passwords normally do not include this file. They set the corresponding parameters at compilation.

Keyboard layout configuration

As of version 0.99.10 of the Linux kernel, keyboard settings are no longer bound to the compilation of the kernel; they can be changed at

loadkeys

run time. The command loadkeys serves this purpose by loading a table containing a keyboard layout. On system startup, this command should be invoked from one of the rc files. For example, German-

de-latin1.map

speaking users would use the file de-latin1.map as their keyboard layout; it provides a normal German keyboard with umlauts as defined by ISO Latin-1. Similar keyboard maps exist for Spanish, French, and other languages.

To ensure comfortable operation under Linux, the appropriate country-specific keyboard map file needs to be chosen from

/usr/lib/kbd/keymaps

the directory /usr/lib/keymaps, /usr/lib/kbd/keymaps, or /etc/keymaps, depending on the distribution. To load the correct keyboard layout on booting, invoke the command loadkeys in one of the rc files. The following excerpt from the file /etc/rc.d/rc.local demonstrates loading the German keyboard layout:

```
# loading country-specific keyboard layout for German
/usr/bin/loadkeys /usr/lib/keymaps/gr-latin1.map
```

6.2   Kernel

Like the commands, utilities, and all other Linux programs, the

source code

kernel—the actual heart of Linux—is available as source code for free. The kernel was written primarily in C, with some small parts in Assembler. In addition to the scheduler, which manages the

switching between running process es, the kernel contains the drivers
for peripheral devices and the routines for managing the file systems.

Configuration of the kernel

Another step after the base installation of the operating system is
the configuration and compilation of the kernel. However, in many
cases this can be omitted. In order to achieve optimal fine-tuning
to the available hardware, compilation is absolutely recommended.
This allows the administrator to dispense with drivers that are not
needed, to add new drivers, and to modify settings of drivers. This
customizing reduces the memory requirements of the kernel and
accelerates booting.

In the sources for Linux 2.0 you will now find the directory
Documentation/. If you want to compile a new kernel, this
directory often provides important information on which kernel
options you need in order to use available hardware and which boot
options to specify later.

Normally the source code of the kernel is located in the directory
/usr/src/linux. This directory also contains a configuration
script that is invoked by the makefile and significantly simplifies
the customizing of the kernel. This script is activated with make
config and permits setting the following options:

- Settings for kernel modules
- General kernel settings
- Block devices: floppy, IDE disk drives/CD-ROM drives/..., ramdisks, metadevices
- Network support: features (firewall, routing, ...), supported network layer protocols (TCP/IP, IPX, Appletalk, ...), hardware (Ethernet boards, ...), ISDN support
- SCSI support and SCSI host adapters
- Nonstandard CD-ROM drives (neither IDE/ATAPI nor SCSI)
- File systems (Extended-2, DOS file system, ISO-9660 [CD-ROM], ...)
- Character devices (printer port, serial port, real-time clock, power management, ...), nonserial mice
- Sound cards

You can configure the 2.0 kernel much more comfortably with **make menuconfig** (console) or **make xconfig** (under X-Windows; requires Tcl/Tk). A full overview of Linux 2.0 kernel options can be found in Section 6.2.

I/O address

interrupt

If the kernel fails to recognize special parameters such as the I/O address or interrupt number of a board and these need to be specified, it sometimes does not make sense to change these in the source code of the respective driver. Instead, they should be passed to the kernel on booting. Such parameters can be entered in LILO manually or

append

as an append instruction in the file /etc/lilo.conf (see Section 5.5). For example, a computer equipped with two Ethernet boards for use as a router or gateway must have the specifications of the boards entered, since the kernel normally expects only one network board.

Compilation

Once all necessary specifications have been made, the dependencies of the kernel among the individual parts of the source code have to be determined anew. This process is started with the invocation of

make dep

make dep. This requires being in the main directory of the kernel source code (/usr/src/linux). Since old object files could still be present when the configuration is modified, these should first be

make clean

removed with make clean.

At this point the actual compilation process can start. Here the makefile plays a central role, as during installation and compilation of

dependency

most other programs: it contains the dependency information on the individual source code files and helps to coordinate various scripts for configuration and installation of the kernel.

compressed kernel

Normally a compressed kernel is generated; then an integrated routine decompresses the kernel during booting. This feature of the Linux kernel makes it possible to put a minimal but complete Linux system that supports all hardware (network, streamer, SCSI devices, CD-ROM) onto a single boot disk. The time lost in decompression is insignificant.

The following lists the most important variants in the invocation of the make command:

`make dep`

> Determines anew the dependencies among source code files, which should be done after any modification in the configuration of the kernel.

dependencies

`make clean`

> Deletes all object files. On the next compilation, all source code files are compiled from scratch.

deleting

`make`

> Compiles kernel only; no kernel image is created.

compilation

`make zImage`

> Compiles the kernel and creates a compressed, bootable kernel image in the directory `/usr/src/linux/arch/i386/boot`. Here 508 KB is the upper limit for kernel size. If you really need a larger kernel, you should user the targets `bzImage` or `bzlilo` (maximum: 1 MB).

kernel image

`make zlilo`

> Creates a new kernel image as above and copies it to `/vmlinuz`. If an old file of the same name is present, it is stored to `/vmlinuz.old`. Then the installation script of the Linux loader. is invoked, so that with the next system startup the new kernel can be booted.

old image
/vmlinuz

`make bzImage`

> Like **zImage**, but here you can compile very large kernels as well.

`make bzlilo`

> Like **zlilo**, but also intended for very large kernels.

`make disk`

> Writes the image file directly to the disk currently in drive `/dev/fd0` (MS-DOS: `A:`) on completion of compilation. Before this command is invoked, an empty, formatted diskette should be placed in drive `/dev/fd0`.

boot disk

`rdev -v image videomode`

> e.g., **rdev -v /vmlinuz -1**. This sets the video mode with which the kernel initializes the video board. `-1` represents normal resolution; with `-3` the kernel prompts the user for the resolution on startup.

video mode

Passing parameters to the kernel

The options of the various drivers can be passed to the kernel on
booting. These parameters must be either entered manually after the
boot prompt or specified in the configuration file of the Linux loader
append   in an append line (see Section 5.5). The most important parameters
are listed in the following overview:

advansys=*ports*

> The Advansys SCSI driver should probe for the adapter only
> on the specified ports (without this option a series of ports is
> probed)

aha152x=*IO-addr*, *IRQ*, *SCSI-Id*, *Reconnect*, *Parity*, *Debug*

> Sets parameters for Adaptec 152x controller

aha1542=*port*[, *bus-on*, *bus-off*[, *dma-speed*]]

> Adaptec AHA1542 configuration

aic7xxx=[extended] [no-reset]

> Configuration of AIC7xxx chip based SCSI host adap-
> tors (e.g., Adaptec AHA2940); extended = "Extended
> translation," no-reset = "no SCSI bus reset on booting"

AM53C974=*host-scsi-id*, *target-scsi-id*, *max-rate*,
max-rate

> Configuration of Am53/79C974 drivers

aztcd=*port*[, 0x79]

> Configuration of Aztech CDA268-01A; if the kernel still does
> not recognize it with a port specification, additionally specify
> 0x79

baycom={*modem*| *port*| *irq*| *options*}

> Configuration of Baycom amateur radio modem

bmouse=*IRQ*

> Sets the IRQ for the bus mouse.

buff=*param*

> Passes parameters that influence the behavior of the swap
> routines

BusLogic=...

> Configuration of driver for BusLogic MultiMaster SCSI
> adapter

`cdu31a=`*`port,IRQ`*

    Sets parameters for Sony CDU-31A CD-ROM driver

`cm206={auto|{`*`port`*`|`*`irq`*`}*}`

    Configuration of Philips/LMS CM206; if `auto` is specified, the driver attempts to autonomously find the drive; otherwise ports and IRQs to be probed can be specified (in any order)

`debug`

    Sets the debug level within the kernel to 10 ("log everything").

`digi=...`

    Configuration of DigiBoard cards (multiple serial ports)

`ether=`*`IRQ,port,P1,P2,device`*

    Passes parameters of the installed Ethernet boards to the corresponding drivers in the kernel; the meaning of *P1* and *P2* depends on the respective driver; usually 0 is specified here; *device* contains the name of the Ethernet device to which the parameters apply; the default is `eth0`

`fdomain=`*`port`*`[,`*`irq`*`[,`*`adapter-id`*`]]`

    Future Domain driver configuration

`floppy=...`

    Parameter for configuration of floppy disk drives and controllers; see `/usr/src/linux/drivers/block/floppy.c`

`gscd=`*`port`*

    Goldstar R420 configuration

`hd=`*`cylinders,heads,sectors`*

    Defines the geometry of the hard disk; this option is only required if a hard disk is not recognized

`icn=`*`port`*`[,`*`mem`*`]`

    Configuration of the ICN ISDN card; since it uses memory-mapped I/O, you might have to specify a memory region to avoid conflicts with Ethernet cards or others

`in2000=...`

    Configuration of SCSI driver for Always IN2000 ISA

`isp16=[`*`port`*`[,`*`irq`*`[,`*`dma`*`]]][[,]`*`type`*`]`

    Configuration for ISP16, MAD16 or Mozart sound card (with CD-ROM interface); *type* can be `sanyo`, `sony`, or `mitsumi`

`load_ramdisk={0|1}`

    1 = load ramdisk image from boot diskette; see Section 7.12

`max_scsi_luns=`*No*

> Sets the highest logical unit number for SCSI devices

`mcd=`*IO-addr*`,`*IRQ*`,`*Mitsumi_Bug_Wait*

> Sets parameters for Mitsumi CD-ROM drive

`mcdx=[`*port*`[,`*irq*`]]`

> Configuration of Mitsumi CD-ROMs

`mem=`

> Specifies the amount of installed main memory; Linux normally determines this with a BIOS invocation, but this does not work for machines with more than 64 MB RAM; in this case you need to specify `mem=`*megabytes*

`msmouse=`*irq*

> Specifies IRQ of Microsoft bus mouse

`ncr5380=`*IO-addr*`,`*IRQ*`,`*DMA*

> Defines parameters for a SCSI-host adapter with NCR 5380 chip

`ncr53c400=`*port*`,`*irq*`,`*dma*

> NCR53C400 configuration

`ncr53c406a=`*port*`[,`*irq*`[,`*fastpio*`]]`

> NCR53c406a configuration

`no-hlt`

> Switches off the invocation of the `hlt` statement in the kernel's idle loop

`noinitrd`

> (Only for debugging purposes)

`no-scroll`

> Suppresses scroll up with (**Shift**) + (**PgUp**); this option is important for the Braille output device Braillex "ib80-piezo" (manufacturer: F.H. Papenmeier, Germany)

`no387`

> Specifies that the kernel should not use the arithmetic coprocessor but its own emulation, which must be compiled in the kernel

`optcd=`*port*

> Configuration of Optics Storage 8000 AT

`panic=`*timeout*

> If a timeout value (in seconds) is specified here, then the kernel reboots after this number of seconds when a *kernel panic* occurs (something drastic has occurred and the system cannot continue; usually a `panic` message is displayed)

`pas16=`*IO-addr, IRQ*

> Sets parameters for the PAS 16 host adapter

`pcbit=`*mem[, irq[, mem...]]*

> Configuration of PCBit ISDN card

`ppa=`*port[, speed-max[, speed-min[, nybble]]]*

> Configuration of pseudo-SCSI driver for IoMega Zip drive

`profile=`*shift*

> Kernel profiling: at regular intervals (*shift*), records which code the kernel is currently executing; serves to detect speed-critical code positions

`prompt_ramdisk={0|1}`

> Allows the user to change disks between booting and mounting the root file system

`ramdisk=`*kilobytes*

> Under Linux 1.2, the size of the ramdisk is set to the specified value (in KB); the equivalent under Linux 2.0 is `ramdisk_size`

`ramdisk_size=`*size*

> Maximum size of a ramdisk

`ramdisk_start=`*block*

> Start of ramdisk image; see Section 7.12

`reserve=`*port, length{, port, length...}*

> Prevents device drivers from accessing the specified range of I/O ports to independently find supported adapters on booting

`riscom8=`*port[, port[,...]]*

> Configuration of SDL Communications RISCom/8 card (multiple serial ports)

`ro`

> Defines that the root file system is to be mounted read-only

`root=`*device*

> Specifies from which device the kernel mounts the root file system

rw

> Defines that the root file system is to be mounted read/write

sbpcd=*port*,*type*

> Sets parameters for Soundblaster / Panasonic CD-ROM driver

sjcd=*port*

> Specifies I/O port of Sanyo CDR-H94A adapter

sonycd535=*port*

> Configuration of Sony CDU-531/-535

sound=0x*TaaaId*

> Sets parameters for sound boards. The parameters are specified in a single hexadecimal number. The individual digits have the following meanings:
>
> *T*
>> type of board, where T can assume the following values:
>> 1. FM Synth (YM3812 or OPL3)
>> 2. Soundblaster 1.0 to 2.0, Soundblaster Pro and 16
>> 3. Pro Audio Spectrum 16
>> 4. Gravis UltraSound
>> 5. MPU-401 UART Midi
>> 6. SB16 with 16-Bit DMA number
>> 7. SB16 Midi (in MPU-401 emulation)
>
> *aaa*
>> I/O-address
>
> *I*
>> IRQ
>
> *d*
>> DMA channel (0, 1, 3, 5, 6, or 7)

st=*bufferSize*,*WT*,*MaxTapeBuffer*

> Sets parameters for a SCSI tape drive; the exact meaning of the parameters can be found in the README.st file in directory drivers/scsi of the kernel source code

st0x=*ROM-address*,*IRQ*

> Sets parameters for Seagate st01 and st02 host adapters

swap=*param*

> Passes parameters that influence the behavior of the swap routines

teles=*port*[,*irq*[,*mem*[,*protocol*[,*port*...]]]]

> Configuration of Teles ISDN card

tmc8xx=*ROM-addr*,*IRQ*

> Sets parameters for Future Domain TMC8xx host adapter

t128=*ROM-addr*,*IRQ*

> Sets parameters for T128 host adapter

xd=...

> Configuration for old XT hard disk drives

6.3 Daemons

Daemons are server programs that handle various background tasks independently of the user. They provide Internet services, execute commands at specified times, or handle writing the I/O buffers to disk at regular intervals. Most daemons have no interactive command interface. Instead, you must modify their configuration files and send the signal HUP (**kill -HUP** *daemon-PID*) to cause the daemon to reload its configuration file. **Some versions of** nfsd **and** mountd **do not react to** HUP; **they must be terminated and restarted.**

syslogd

Since no terminal is assigned to daemons, they normally do not output error messages but send all error messages and other reports to the syslog daemon. To simplify the detection of errors in the configuration of daemons and other programs, configure the syslog daemon next.

error messages

syslog

As usual, there are several versions of this daemon under Linux. In the following description we describe the syslogd / klogd combination by Dr. G. Wettstein, which is more readily configurable compared to the normal BSD syslogd.

syslogd / klogd

The syslog daemon syslogd can write a message that it receives from another daemon to a log file, send it by e-mail to certain users, or display it directly on the console. Settings can be made individually to determine where the message is output for each unit that sends syslog

log file, e-mail, console

123

a message and for the priority of such a message. These settings are specified in the file /etc/syslog.conf.

/etc/syslog.conf

One solution that usually suffices is to output especially important messages on the console and to collect all other messages according to priority in a log file. The entries necessary in /etc/syslog.conf to achieve this are as follows:

priority

```
*.alert                 /dev/console
*.crit                  /dev/console
kern.*                  /dev/console

*.debug                 /var/adm/debug
*.=info;*.=notice       /var/adm/messages
*.warn                  /var/adm/syslog
```

All entries consist of the specification of a unit and a priority and the target of the messages. An overview of all defined units and priorities can be found on the On-Line Manual page for syslogd or for the file syslog.conf. The extensions in the version by Dr. Wettstein are described on the Manual page syslogd(8).

unit and priority

The files in the directory /var/log must already exist when the syslog daemon starts. To create an empty file, it is simplest to use the command touch with the respective file as the parameter.

files must exist

To check whether the settings in the configuration file are correct, terminate the syslog daemon with the kill command and then restart it with the option -d. This starts the daemon in debug mode; syslog then displays a matrix showing which messages are written to which files or sent to which users.

option -d

matrix

Since in the above configuration all messages are appended to files, the administrator should ensure that the log files do not grow out of proportion. We suggest using a script that crond executes regularly to move the log files to another directory and then create them anew. Afterwards the syslog daemon must be notified by means of /etc/syslogd.reload to reopen its log files. If problems arise later, the old log files can still be referenced.

log files

Printer daemon

The general definition and configuration of printers takes place in the file /etc/printcap. This file specifies, for example, whether to include a cover sheet with each new print job or whether a form

/etc/printcap

feed should follow a print job. Furthermore, multiple printer queues can be created, each with its own filter program.

In order to enable a computer to access print servers, which provide printers via the network, the client machine must be entered in the file /etc/hosts.lpd of the print server. This file contains the names of all computers that have access to the printer. The following example shows the file /etc/printcap of a Linux machine that does not possess its own printer, but has access to a printer on a workstation:

```
#
# /etc/hosts.lpd
#
hades.demo.de
hermes.demo.de
jupiter.demo.de
```

The following example shows the file /etc/printcap of a Linux machine that does not possess its own printer, but has access to a printer on a workstation named zeus:

```
#
# /etc/printcap: configuration of a remote printer (zeus)
#
lp:lp=:rm=zeus.demo.de:sd=/usr/spool/lp:mx#0
```

Every line of the printcap file defines a printer queue. The individual options are delimited by colons, whereby the first attribute specifies the name of the queue (lp). If an entry extends beyond a single line, the end of a continued line is marked with a backslash (\).

lp=

> designates printer interface (default is /dev/lp)

rm=

> name of remote host that is printer server

rp=

> name of remote printer queue (default is lp)

sd=

> name of local spool directory

`if=`

name of input filter

`of=`

name of output filter

`mc#`

max. number of possible copies of a document

`mx#`

max. size of a job in blocks; `mx#` permits jobs of any size

`sc`

suppresses multiple output of a document

`sf`

suppresses output of page feed after every print job

`sh`

suppresses output of a title page before every print job

options   The list above gives the most important options. More detailed information can be found in the corresponding On-Line Manual page. Text options end with an equal sign (=), numeric ones with a pound sign (#).

international
character sets   International character sets (e.g., French, Spanish, German) pose a problem in outputting text files to a printer. For German, this includes the umlauts. The installation of a corresponding filter can deliver satisfactory results here. Such a filter can be realized in various

C program   ways. The following example for German lists a simple C program that converts umlauts and sends the printer a carriage return (CR)

tr   after each line. Alternatively, the UNIX command `tr` for character conversion could serve this purpose.

```
/******************************************************
 * Umlaut conversion for EPSON printer
 ******************************************************/

#include <stdio.h>

main (int argc, char *argv[])
{
    int ch;

    while ((ch = getchar ()) != EOF)
    {
        /* printer needs CR+LF */
        if (ch == '\n')
          putchar ('\r');

        /* convert ISO to PC */
```

```
    switch (ch)
    {
       case 228: /* "a */
          ch = 132;
          break;
       case 246: /* "o */
          ch = 148;
          break;
       case 252: /* "u */
          ch = 129;
          break;
       case 196: /* "A */
          ch = 142;
          break;
       case 214: /* "O */
          ch = 153;
          break;
       case 220: /* "U */
          ch = 154;
          break;
       case 223: /* sz */
          ch = 225;
          break;
       case 167: /* paragraph */
          ch = 21;
          break;
       default:
          break;
    }
    putchar (ch);
}
}
```

Such a filter is linked via the option if (input filter) or of (output filter) in the /etc/printcap file. An output filter is initialized only once for multiple waiting print jobs; an input filter is restarted for each print job.

/etc/printcap

```
#
# /etc/printcap: printer configuration
#
lp:lp=/dev/lp1:sf:sd=/usr/spool/lp:mx#0:sh

# text queue
txt:lp=/dev/lp1:sd=/usr/spool/txt:\
      if=/usr/spool/lp/epson:mx#0:sh:sf

# PostScript queue
ps:lp=/dev/lp1:sd=/usr/spool/ps:\
      if=/usr/spool/lp/Postscript:mx#0:sh:sf
```

Registering multiple printer queues enables switching between filters as needed. The choice of the correct queue is specified in a parameter of the lpr command. The following allows printing a text with umlauts:

multiple queues

```
linux1:/home/tul> lpr -Ptxt Umlaut.txt
```

With the right filter an ordinary matrix, ink jet, or laser printer can easily be converted to a full-scale PostScript printer. The following shell script should be registered as a filter:

```
#!/bin/sh
#
# PostScript printer filter
#

DEVICE=epson

exec /usr/bin/gs -q -sPAPERSIZE=a4 -dSAFER\
    -sDEVICE=$DEVICE -sOutputFile=- -
```

The above example assumes that the printer is an Epson-compatible device. Another type of printer could be substituted by adjusting the sDevice parameter. Ghostscript provides a list of possible options:

```
hermes:/home/uhl> gs -help
Ghostscript version 2.6.1 (5/28/93)
Copyright (C) 1990-1993 Aladdin Enterprises, Menlo Park, CA.
Usage: gs [switches] [file1.ps file2.ps ...]
Available devices:
    x11 dmp bj10e bj200 cdeskjet cdjcolor cdjmono cdj500
    cdj550 declj250 deskjet dfaxhigh dfaxlow djet500 djet500c
epson
    eps9high epsonc escp2 ibmpro jetp3852 laserjet la50 la75
    lbp8 ln03 lj250 ljet2p ljet3 ljet4 ljetplus m8510
    necp6 oki182 paintjet pj pjxl pjxl300 r4081 t4693d2
    t4693d4 t4693d8 tek4696 bmpmono bmp16 bmp256 bmp16m
gifmono
    gif8 pcxmono pcx16 pcx256 tiffg3 pbm pbmraw pgm
    pgmraw ppm ppmraw bit

    . . .

hermes:/home/uhl>
```

The apsfilter package poses an interesting alternative to creating multiple queues. Here it suffices to register a single filter script, which then automatically recognizes the type of the document to be printed and activates the appropriate filter; thus, you can output any kind of data via a single queue:

```
zeus:/home/uhl> lpr postscript.ps tex.dvi text.txt
```

The printcap file for the aps filter and an HP Deskjet looks like this:

```
#
# /etc/printcap: Printer configuration for aps filter
#
# apsfilter setup Wed Oct 5 17:24:41 MET 1994
#
# APS_BASEDIR:/usr/local/apsfilter
#
#
lp|lp2|djet500-a4-auto-mono|djet500 auto mono:\
        :lp=/dev/lp1:\
        :sd=/usr/spool/djet500:\
:if=/usr/local/apsfilter/filter/aps-djet500-a4-auto-mono:\
        :mx#0:\
        :sh:

ascii|lp1|djet500-a4-ascii-mono|djet500 ascii mono:\
        :lp=/dev/lp1:\
        :sd=/usr/spool/djet500:\
:if=/usr/local/apsfilter/filter/aps-djet500-a4-ascii-mono:\
        :mx#0:\
        :sh:

raw|lp3|djet500-a4-raw|djet500 auto raw:\
        :lp=/dev/lp1:\
        :sd=/usr/spool/djet500:\
        :if=/usr/local/apsfilter/filter/aps-djet500-a4-raw:\
        :mx#0:\
        :sh:
```

6.4   Serial login

To configure a login via a serial interface, instead of the normal getty
command, use the mgetty package by Gert Döring. mgetty makes it   mgetty
possible to operate multiple services on a single port simultaneously.
In addition to normal login, faxes can be sent and received. An
extended version named vgetty makes it possible to connect a Zyxel   vgetty
modem as an answering machine.

mgetty is normally started by the init process during booting.
This requires an entry in the file /etc/inittab:

```
#
# Start mgetty on port /dev/ttyS0
#
S1:45:respawn:/usr/sbin/mgetty ttyS0
```

6.5   Fax

Sending and receiving faxes can be configured with the mgetty/
sendfax package.   sendfax

Receiving

G3 format

mgetty automatically saves an incoming fax in the directory /var/spool/fax/incoming as a G3 file, then sends an e-mail message to the user faxadmin to report the fax arrival (Figure 6.2).

```
Date: Wed, 11 Jan 95 14:24 MET
From: Fax Getty <root@hn-net.de>
To: faxadmin@hn-net.de
Subject: fax from " +49 9344 1636"

A fax has arrived:
Sender ID: " +49 9344 1636"
Pages received: 1

Communication parameters: +FCS:0,3,0,2,0,0,0,0
    Resolution : normal
    Bit Rate : 9600
    Page Width : 1728 pixels
    Page Length: unlimited
    compression: 0 (1d mod Huffman)
    Error Corr.: none
    Scan Time : 0

Reception Time : 0:46

Spooled G3 fax files:

   /usr/spool/fax/incoming/fnf13dbfcS0-+49-9344-1636.01

regards, your modem subsystem.
```

Figure 6.2. Message from mgetty to faxadmin

new_fax

If the directory /usr/local/bin contains a script named new_fax, then it is executed after the successful receipt of a fax. Here other actions, such as conversion to another graphic format or printing, can be realized. For example, the pnm tools can be used for converting a G3 file to other formats.

pnm tools

```
#!/bin/sh
#
# new_fax: convert incoming g3 faxes to GIF.
#

shift 3

for i in $*
do
      /usr/local/netpbm/g3topbm $i | /usr/local/netpbm/ppmtogif > $i.gif
      rm $i
done
```

A script to display all received faxes could look like this:

```
#!/bin/sh
#
# faxview - displays incoming faxes
#
xloadimage -geometry 1000x720+10+10 -xzoom 50 /var/spool/fax/incoming/*.gif
```

Sending

Faxes are sent with `sendfax`. The file to be sent must be in G3
format. A PostScript file can be converted easily with Ghostscript:

sendfax

```
#!/bin/sh
#
# psfax - Sends a PostScript file as a fax.
#
echo 'Converting PS to G3 fax ...'

gs -q -sPAPERSIZE=a4 -sDEVICE=dfaxhigh -sOutputFile=/tmp/$2.fax - <$2

echo 'Sending fax to' $1

sendfax $1 /tmp/$2.fax

rm /tmp/$2.fax
```

In the event of any problems, refer to the log file `/var/spool/`
`fax/Faxlog`, which gives the protocol for all actions of the `sendfax`
command.

log file

6.6   Metadevices and RAID

Hardly any PC user has never cursed the possibilities of hard disk
partitioning. Beyond the distribution of data on various physical hard
disks, an antiquated BIOS or controller often forces further splitting
into many small partitions. At least under Linux, the unpleasant
question of "What is to be put in which partition and how much
space will it require?" seems to be a thing of the past: the new 2.0
kernel supports metadevices, which consist of any conglomeration
of hard disk partitions, over which the contents of a single file
system are distributed. Such a metadevice can then be mounted like a
single block device. This enables packing one or two other operating
systems each onto a drive and leaving the remaining partitions to
Linux without any inconvenience. However, there is one important
restriction: once a metadevice is constructed, new partitions cannot
be appended and no partition can be decoupled. Metadevices also

impose additional risks: A single failed disk corrupts the whole file system. Metadevices also provide the basis for Linux's RAID support (RAID: "Redundant Array of Independent Disks"). Linux 2.0.25

RAID Mode 0   supports RAID Mode 0. Mode 0 by itself is not used for fail-safe disk arrays, but for maximizing throughput by optimal distribution of data over different physical disks ("striped mode"). Mode 1 and others will be supported soon.

The kernel must be compiled with the option CONFIG_MD. Furthermore, you need at least one of the options CONFIG_MD_LINEAR or CONFIG_MD_STRIPED (the latter corresponds to RAID Mode 0). In addition, you need the md utilities.*

Metadevices are referenced as /dev/md * (major device number 9, minor number starting at 0). The following combines the three partitions /dev/sda1, /dev/sdb2, and /dev/sdb3 to a metadevice :

```
golem:~> mdadd /dev/md0 /dev/sda1 /dev/sdb2 /dev/sdb3
```

/dev/md0 is activated as follows:

```
golem:~> mdrun /dev/md0
```

Then it can be mounted normally, assuming that a file system was created the first time:

```
golem:~> mke2fs /dev/md0
```

On system shutdown, after umount the metadevice is decomposed again:

```
golem:~> mdstop /dev/md0
```

You can combine the metadevices you use in the configuration

/etc/mdtab   file /etc/mdtab (Figure 6.3):

*ftp://sweet-smoke.ufr-info-p7.ibp.fr/public/Linux/md034.tar.gz

```
# Metadevices configuration file
/dev/md0        linear  /dev/sda1 /dev/sdb2 /dev/sdb3
/dev/md1        raid0   /dev/sdc1 /dev/sdd1
```

Figure 6.3. Example of /etc/mdtab

The metadevices entered in this file can be activated simply with

```
golem:~> mdadd -ar
```

and decomposed with

```
golem:~> mdstop -a
```

These two commands should be entered in appropriate boot scripts (for Slackware boot scripts: rc.S or rc.6 and rc.K) before mounting and after unmounting.

For further details, see mdadd(8), mdrun(8), mdstop(8), mdop(8), and mdtab(5).

6.7   Streamers and CD-ROM drives

Many PC configurations today include a streamer and/or a CD-ROM drive. Linux supports such mass storage media, too. If purchasing a new streamer or CD-ROM drive, choosing a SCSI device simplifies Linux installation. Due to the standardization of the command set for SCSI devices, configuration proves quite easy. If the SCSI driver has already been compiled into the kernel, it suffices to make the appropriate entries in the /dev directory via the command mknod. Most Linux distributions create these device files automatically during installation. For example, to configure CD-ROM drives (scd?) and SCSI streamers (rmt?), the following entries must exist:

```
linux1:/dev> ls scd* rmt*
crw-rw-rw-  1 root    root      9,    0 Jan 23 1993    rmt0
crw-rw-rw-  1 root    root      9,    1 Jan 23 1993    rmt1
brw-rw-rw-  1 root    root     11,    0 Jan 23 1993    scd0
brw-rw-rw-  1 root    root     11,    1 Jan 23 1993    scd1
linux1:/dev>
```

SCSI

133

device-specific files

If these entries do not exist, the system administrator can generate them with the following commands:

```
linux1:/dev> mknod /dev/rmt0 c 9 0
linux1:/dev> mknod /dev/scd0 b 11 0
```

floppy streamer

Because of the lack of standards for other drivers, the configuration of a floppy streamer or a CD-ROM drive with its own AT bus controller can prove significantly more problematic. Meanwhile, however, corresponding drivers for the most common models have become available under Linux; in order to be used, these also must be compiled into the kernel.

## Chapter 7

Administration

U pon completion of the installation of the Linux system and
the most important aspects of configuration, it is time to enable
users to access the system. In addition, there will soon be requests for
applications that are not contained in the installation packages. After
some time new versions of some system components will appear
and need to be installed to keep pace with continuing development.
These kinds of jobs are collectively termed *system administration*.
Since system administration tasks on all UNIX systems are very
similar, we refer the reader to the standard literature and here only
share some tips and notes to Linux-specific details.

users

upgrades

system administration

7.1 The administrator

Only the superuser `root`, that is, the system administrator, can
modify the configuration files of the system. The corresponding
access privileges of these files guard them against unauthorized use.
The system administrator generally has access to all files and can
modify them at will.

root

access

This also means that the administrator could crash or erase
the entire system. For example, imagine that an administrator were
carelessly to enter the following command to delete all files in a
directory (with options set to remove all subdirectories recursively
and without confirmation) and do so from the root directory (/):

```
linux1:/> rm -rf *
```

This would immediately delete the entire system. If this command
were to be executed without `root` permissions, then the access

delete all

permissions

privileges of the system files and directories would guarantee that at worst all the user's own files would be deleted. However, this would have no influence on other users or the overall system.

caution   Thus, a system administrator must proceed with extreme caution and only log in as root to modify a system file or to install a new program.

7.2   Booting

booting   To facilitate understanding of the system, we next describe how a Linux system boots and which programs and scripts are processed during booting. Independent of the operating system, the *master boot*

MBR   *record* (MBR) is loaded first during booting. The partition tables and the loader program that loads the boot sector of the active partition are located here.

LILO   If the Linux loader (LILO) is installed at the beginning of the active partition, then it starts first and presents a choice of

selection   various Linux kernels and DOS. If the user selects a Linux kernel, the respective kernel image is loaded and started. Optionally, after

parameters   specification of the image, parameters can be passed to the kernel itself or to the initialization process.

First the kernel initializes the video board and possibly prompts

resolution   for the desired screen resolution. Then it installs the various device

drivers   drivers, which usually each display a comment. Then the kernel mounts the root file system and starts the process init.

run levels   Like UNIX System V, Linux has various run levels, which are specified in the file /etc/inittab. These are various configurations in which only certain system components are activated. Normally the

multi-user   system starts in multi-user operation. This means that multiple getty

getty   processes are started for the console and optionally for the serial ports. In addition, in this mode all network daemons are activated.

single-user mode   Single-user mode provides an alternative that is intended primarily for system administration. This mode is activated when the option single is specified during booting. This option is not evaluated either by LILO or the kernel, but passed to the init process after the kernel starts. Another run level might start a graphic login prompt (xdm) instead of the usual terminal login, for example.

Because `init` is the first process that the kernel starts, it is *init* always assigned process number 1 and is the parent of all further processes. The `init` process also executes various scripts in the directory `/etc/rc.d`, which usually begin with `rc`. These scripts */etc/rc.d* reinitialize various system files and mount the local file systems. NFS file systems are not mounted yet, because the network and the respective daemons have not been started. The exact sequence and ordering of the various scripts can vary from system to system. In *scripts* the Slackware distribution, the following files reside in the directory `/etc/rc.d`:

```
/etc/rc.d> ls
rc.0*      rc.K*    rc.S*      rc.inet1*    rc.local*
rc.6*      rc.M*    rc.font*   rc.inet2*    rc.serial*
```

`rc.S`

> initializes the system. This script is invoked first on booting.

`rc.serial`

> initializes the serial connections. This script can be invoked optionally from the script `rc.S`.

`rc.M`

> multi-user setup. Here the most important daemons are launched.

`rc.font`

> optionally activates a different font for the console.

`rc.inet1`

> initializes the lower layers of the TCP/IP system. Here the IP address, the host name, and the routing table are set.

`rc.inet2`

> starts the network daemons.

`rc.0`

> invoked when the system is halted.

`rc.6`

> invoked when the system is rebooted.

`rc.K`

> invoked on switching from multi-user mode to single-user mode.

The following example shows a slightly cropped version of an
rc.S script:

```
#!/bin/sh

PATH=/sbin:/usr/sbin:/bin:/usr/bin

# enable swapping
/sbin/swapon -a

# Start update.
/sbin/update &

# Test to see if the root partition is read-only, like it
ought to be.
READWRITE=no
if echo -n >> "Testing filesystem status"; then
rm -f "Testing filesystem status"
READWRITE=yes
fi

# Check the integrity of all filesystems
if [ ! $READWRITE = yes ]; then
/sbin/fsck -A -a
# If there was a failure, drop into single-user mode.
if [ $? -gt 1 ] ; then
echo "*****************************************"
echo "fsck returned error code - REBOOT NOW!"
echo "*****************************************"
/bin/login
fi
# Remount the root filesystem in read-write mode
echo "Remounting root device with read-write enabled."
/sbin/mount -w -n -o remount /
if [ $? -gt 0 ] ; then
echo "Attempt to remount root device as read-write failed!
This is going to"
echo "cause serious problems...  "
read junk;
fi
else
echo "Testing filesystem status: read-write filesystem"
if [ -d /DOS/linux/etc -a -d /DOS/linux/dev ]; then # no warn
for UMSDOS
cat << EOF

*** ERROR: Root partition has already been mounted read-write.
Cannot check!

For file system checking to work properly, your system must
initially mount
the root partition as read only.  Please modify your kernel
with 'rdev' so that
it does this.

EOF
echo -n "Press ENTER to continue. "
read junk;
fi
fi

# remove /etc/mtab* so that mount will create it with a root
entry
/bin/rm -f /etc/mtab* /etc/nologin /var/adm/utmp

# Looks like we have to create this.
cat /dev/null >> /var/adm/utmp

# mount file systems in fstab (and create an entry for /)
```

```
# but not NFS because TCP/IP is not yet configured
/sbin/mount -avt nonfs

# Configure the system clock.
# This can be changed if your system keeps GMT.
if [ -x /sbin/clock ]; then
/sbin/clock -s
fi

# Run serial port setup script:
# (CAREFUL! This can make some systems hang if the rc.serial
script isn't
# set up correctly.  If this happens, you may have to edit the
file from a
# boot disk)
#
#/bin/sh /etc/rc.d/rc.serial
```

After rc.S, for multi-user mode the script rc.M executes. This script starts the most important daemons. If a network is present, the scripts rc.inet1 and rc.inet2 are invoked here.

network

It might make sense to complement the boot scripts with your own commands. **Be careful: an error might render your computer unbootable.** Thus always keep a complete kernel and root file system at hand (see Section 7.12). Many distributions go beyond the Slackware boot scripts and work with a series of configuration files that are read by their boot scripts. Whenever possible, make your changes in configuration files rather than in the boot scripts themselves.

7.3   Shutdown

As with all UNIX systems, one should avoid simply turning off a Linux computer. Instead, the system must be shut down properly with the command shutdown. The reason for the necessity of the shutdown procedure is that, due to the internal cache of the kernel, usually all data that were written by programs to the hard disk interface have not yet physically been stored on the hard disk. Furthermore, frequently needed information, such as the i-node table and the superblock of the file system, are likewise held in RAM. Turning off the computer without using the command shutdown can lead to inconsistencies on the hard disk and resulting data loss.

shutdown

cache

i-node tables

The command shutdown ensures that all buffers have been transferred to the storage media and that all processes are terminated

shutdown

sync   properly. The command `sync` writes buffers to the hard disk without shutting down the system. This command is seldom used, however.

7.4   The Linux directory tree

orientation

file system standard

distributions

To assist new Linux users and inexperienced system administrators in gaining an orientation in the system, this section describes the most important directories of a typical Linux installation. The organization of the Linux file system has been determined in the Linux File System Standard, which resides as a PostScript file on the usual FTP servers along with other documents. This standard has been recognized by most of the producers of distributions and packages, and the following description assumes a typical distribution.

root directory

image files

home directory

/root

/etc/passwd

The directory / is the root of a Linux directory tree. It is thus called the root directory. Beyond the Linux kernel image files that are needed for booting and the most important subdirectories, it should contain no other files. System administrators frequently use the root directory as their home directory. However, we recommend creating a separate directory for this purpose, e.g., `/root`. This makes it easier to distinguish the administrator's configuration files from system files. To create a new home directory, use an editor to modify the respective entry in the file `/etc/passwd`.

Directories in the root directory
`/bin`

programs

    The most important programs that need to be available even if `/usr` is inaccessible reside in this directory. These include, e.g., the commands `mv`, `cp`, `cat`, and `rm`. Contrary to `/sbin`, which contains only programs for booting and system administration, the programs in `/bin` are intended for all users. All other commands that are not essential in case of emergency reside in `/usr/bin` (also see `/usr`).

`/boot`

LILO

    This directory contains the map files of the Linux loader and backups of the old boot sector and partition table. These files are normally used only by LILO or created automatically by LILO.

`/conf`

> If this directory exists, it contains exclusively configuration
> files, which otherwise reside in `/etc` or other directories. In
> this case, rather than actual files, the directory `/etc` contains
> only symbolic links to the files in `/conf` or its subdirectories,
> such as `/conf/net`. However, the simplest installations get
> by without `/conf`.

configuration

`/dev`

> As the name `/dev` suggests, this directory contains all device
> files, which are special files assigned to I/O drivers.

devices

`/dist`

> This is where the Unifix and Linux Universe distributions
> mount their CD. Packages and programs that were not
> installed on the hard disk exist on the hard disk as links to
> files in subdirectories of `/dist`.

CD drive

`/etc`

> The `/etc` directory contains configuration files. These
> include the files `passwd` and `group`, which contain user and
> group information, respectively, and the configuration files
> of the TCP/IP daemons such as `services`, `inetd.conf`,
> and `exports`. Before the file system standard, this directory
> frequently contained daemons and system programs such
> as `init` and `update`; these have now been moved to the
> directory `/sbin` or `/usr/sbin`.

configuration files

`/etc/init.d`

> In some distributions this directory contains the actual `rc`
> scripts used by the system during booting and shutdown.
> These scripts are invoked by System V systems via symbolic
> links in the directories `/etc/rc0.d` to `/etc/rc6.d`.

rc scripts for booting
and shutdown

`/etc/Isode`

> This directory contains configuration files for the Isode
> package.

Isode

`/etc/keytables`

> The file system standard provides this directory for the
> keyboard layout maps, which can be loaded on booting.
> American distributions sometimes use `/usr/lib/key-`
> `tables` or `/usr/lib/kbd/keytables`.

keyboard layout

141

`/etc/ppp`

PPP   The PPP configuration files reside in this directory.

`/etc/rc.d`

             Instead of in `/etc/init.d`, the scripts that are invoked on
system startup   system startup by `init` can also reside directly in `/etc/rc.d`
             or `/etc`.

`/etc/rc0.d` to `/etc/rc6.d`

             These directories are used by distributions where the
scripts   startup scripts reside in `/etc/init.d`. The scripts in these
run level   directories are executed by `init` on a change of the run level.
             The directories `/etc/rc?.d` contain only link to files in
             `/etc/init.d`.

`/etc/skel`

             The files in this directory are automatically copied into
new user   the home directory of the user on creation of a new
             user with `useradd -m`. The directory normally contains
             examples of configuration files, including `.cshrc`, `.bashrc`,
             `.Xdefaults`, and `.emacs`.

`/etc/X11`

X11   The file system standard assigns this directory for local X11
             configuration files. These include `XF86Config` with general
             settings for the server and the monitor, `Xmodmap` with the
             keyboard layout under X11, `xinitrc`, and the files for `xdm`.

`/FTP`

             In some distributions this directory is used by the FTP server
ftp or anonymous   daemon. Users logging into the server as `ftp` or `anonymous`
             can access only subdirectories of `/FTP`. Other distributions
             use the directory `/home/FTP` for this purpose.

`/home`

home directories   This directory encompasses a home directory for each user
             except `root`. Each such subdirectory holds user-specific
             configuration files. Aside from these personal files of the user,
             no programs should be installed here. Since this directory
             usually resides on a separate partition, we do not advise
             putting the home directory of `root` in this directory as well.
             If this file system should not be mountable due to an error,

then even the administrator might not be able to log into the
system to correct the error.

/install

The installation program of some distributions employs this
subdirectory to store information on installed packages.   installed packages
Other distributions use special directories under /var or
/usr.

/lib

The images of the most important shared libraries of the   libraries
system reside in directory /lib. These images are the parts
of the shared libraries that contain the actual routines. They
are loaded with the programs using them. The other parts
(.a library files), called *stubs*, are stored in the directory
/usr/lib. They are linked to the programs and contain
only links to the actual routines. Shared libraries that are
not absolutely necessary for booting and administration,
such as the libraries of the X Window System, should be
stored in another directory under /usr. For X11 this is
/usr/X11R6/lib. /lib contains only symbolic links to
these libraries.

/local

In some CD distributions a symbolic link from /usr/local
points to this directory. Local programs that are not contained   local programs
on the CD should be installed here.

/lost+found

This directory is created automatically with the creation of a
file system of type ext2 and is used by utilities such as fsck.   ext2

/mnt

This directory should be empty and is often used to
temporarily mount diskettes or file systems of other   mounting
computers via NFS.

/proc

Normally the proc file system is mounted here. The proc
file system is a special file system that stores information on
the kernel and running processes as subdirectories and files.   kernel info
These files can be read as text, thus permitting easy access to
this information (also see Section 18.1).

143

/root

superuser's home

Although this directory is optional, most Linux distributions create it. This is the superuser's home directory (root). Normally this directory is not on the same partition as the home directories of normal users.

/sbin

system programs

This directory contains only the most important programs and commands required for booting the system and for basic system administration. These include getty, init, update, fdisk, fsck, ifconfig, ping, and lilo. Programs that are needed by users other than root reside in /bin or in /usr/bin if they are not absolutely necessary in the event of an emergency.

/shlib

shared

Shared libraries for the iBCS2 emulation are stored here.

/tftpboot

tftp daemon

Some distributions use this directory for the tftp daemon. If so, then access per tftp can be restricted to this directory.

/tmp

temporary files

This directory is used by many programs for temporary files. All users have read/write access to /tmp. Files in this directory can normally be deleted when no processes are running. Except for the administrator, no other user should be logged in while these files are being deleted. Often the files in the /tmp directory are deleted automatically on system startup by means of an entry in the file /etc/rc.d/rc.local.

/user

mounting

This directory, inasmuch as it exists, is normally empty and is used for mounting.

/usr

user programs, libraries, Manual pages, and configuration

This directory contains almost all other important subdirectories that are not directly needed for booting the system. Separating machine-specific configuration, essential programs for the system administration, and log or spool files from the programs in /usr enables using /usr from a CD or for multiple machines from a common NFS server. In this

case the /usr directory must be mounted write-protected.
The most important programs for system administration and
the necessary libraries must reside in the root file system so
that in the event of a system error where the CD or the NFS
server becomes inaccessible, the error can be corrected. The
root file system should be as small as possible to allow shared
utilization of as many programs and as much disk space as
possible.

/var

This directory includes all files that are written to frequently
and whose size changes often. These include especially log
and spool files. Many of the subdirectories under /var   log and spool files
were previously under /usr. To be able to mount /usr
for simultaneous read-only access per NFS, these dynamic
subdirectories were transferred to the directory /var. They
include /var/spool with the subdirectories for mail and
the printer queues, /var/adm with the system log files, and
/var/lock with the lock files.

Subdirectories under /usr

/usr/X11R6

This is the directory of the X Window System since Release   X11R6
6. The directories /usr/lib/X11 and /usr/bin/X11 are
links to this directory tree.

/usr/X386

This is the start of the directory tree of older versions of X11   X11R5
packages. As of Release 6 the subdirectory /usr/X11R6 is
used instead.

/usr/adainclude

The include files of the GNU Ada compiler reside here.   GNU Ada

/usr/adm

This directory is a link to /var/adm.

/usr/bin

Most system programs and UNIX commands for users, as   programs and
well as those for the administrator that are not absolutely   commands
needed in case /usr cannot be mounted, reside here. This
separation of UNIX commands into those stored in /bin or

145

/sbin and those stored in /usr/bin is not always handled consistently. In case of doubt when looking for a command, it pays to look in both directories. Both /bin and /usr/bin should always be included in the environment variable for the path (PATH).

/usr/bin/X11

X11   X11 programs are normally installed in this directory. However, this is usually a symbolic link to /usr/X386/bin or /usr/X11R6/bin in the newer X11 releases. This directory should be contained in the PATH environment variable.

/usr/dict

dictionary   This directory originally contained an English dictionary for the look command and other programs for spell checking.

/usr/doc

documentation   Documentation that is not available as a Manual page or in Info format is stored in this directory.

/usr/etc

configuration   This directory should contain configuration files that are shared by multiple machines. Often this is only a symbolic link to the directory /etc.

/usr/g++-include

This directory contains header files for the GNU C++ compiler.

/usr/games

games   Here we have games and other entertainment programs that are of subordinate importance for serious application.

/usr/include

include files   This is the directory for include files of the C library. This directory contains the subdirectories sys and linux, whereby linux is a link to a subdirectory of /usr/src/linux.

/usr/info

GNU Info files   This directory is used for the GNU Info system. The files in this directory can be viewed in info mode in the Emacs editor or with programs like tkinfo; they provide the primary documentation of GNU programs.

/usr/lib

> The static libraries for various programming languages and
> the stubs for shared libraries are stored here. In addition, this
> directory contains subdirectories that usually contain help
> and configuration files of other programs.

libraries

/usr/lib/X11

> Here we find the configuration data, character sets, color
> tables, and other files of the X Window System. This
> directory is usually a link to /usr/X11R6/lib/X11.
> Files associated with the local configuration of X servers,
> such as XF86Config, should actually be stored under
> /etc/X11 according to the file system standard. However,
> few distributions abide by this point.

X11 configuration

/usr/local

> This directory should contain all additional programs that
> were not contained in the installation package. Usually this
> directory contains a complete subdirectory tree consisting
> of bin, lib, etc, include, and man directories. As a
> rule, /usr/local/bin is included in the path for programs
> (PATH) and /usr/local/man in the path for Manual pages
> (MANPATH).

additional packages

/usr/man

> The Manual pages are located in subdirectories of /usr/man.

Manual pages

/usr/openwin

> In the subdirectories of /usr/openwin we find pro-
> grams and data of the XView package from Sun. The
> libraries and configuration files are usually in the directory
> /usr/openwin/lib. The most interesting of these files
> are the definition files of the menu for the OpenLook win-
> dow manager (olwm and olvwm). The file names all begin
> with openwin-menu. The window manager itself and other
> programs reside in /usr/openwin/bin.

OpenWindows/XView

/usr/pkg

> Some CD distributions use this directory to enable separate
> installation of individual program packages. From here the
> programs can be installed on the hard disk with an installation
> program.

installation

/usr/sbin

As in the directory /sbin, here we find primarily programs
for system administration, although only ones that are not
system programs | essential for booting the system. In addition, this directory
network daemons | contains network daemons.

/usr/share

shared programs | This directory contains files that are machine-independent.
The contents of the directory can then be mounted on various
machines with different architectures per NFS. Examples
of such files include the Manual pages and the terminfo
database.

/usr/src

source code | The subdirectories under /usr/src contain the source
code of system programs. The most important of these
subdirectories is /usr/src/linux, where the source code
of the Linux kernel is located.

/usr/TeX

T_EX | The T_EX package is installed in this directory. In accordance
with the file system standard, T_EX data files should reside
under /usr/lib/TeX.

7.5 Users and groups

As described in Section 2.1, every user has an unambiguous login
name and a unique UID and belongs to one or more user groups. This
information is stored in the files /etc/passwd and /etc/group.
To create a new user, these files are usually not modified with a text
useradd | editor. Instead, the program useradd is used. This program collects
all the important information via the command line. Then it modifies
shadow files | the files /etc/passwd and /etc/group as well as the respective
shadow files, which contain the encrypted user and group passwords
and, for security reasons, can only be read by the superuser.

The administrator can simplify the task of managing users and
default values | groups by entering the -D option with useradd once to set default
values for the group, the longevity of passwords, and the directory
for the home directories of users.

Furthermore, user-specific configuration files, such as .pro-
file, .bashrc, and .openwin-menu can be stored in the directory
/etc/skel. When a new user is created, these files are automatically
copied into the user's home directory.

/etc/skel

If default values have been defined and the correct files have been
stored in /etc/skel, then a new user can be created by invoking
the following:

new user

```
linux1:/> useradd -m username
```

The user ID will automatically be the next free number. Next, a
password has to be assigned with **passwd** *username*, since the new
account would otherwise remain disabled.

user ID and password

In addition to useradd, there are commands to modify the
settings (usermod) and to delete a user (userdel). chsh sets the
login shell and chfn the full name of a user. The Manual pages
provide more information on useradd and other commands.

modifications

The following example shows the specification of default values
and the adding of a new user:

```
dirk1:/etc# useradd -D -g 6 -b /home -f 3 -e 999
dirk1:/etc# useradd -m peter
dirk1:/etc# passwd peter
Changing password for peter
Enter the new password (minimum of 5 characters)
Please use a combination of upper and lower case letters and
numbers.
New Password:
Re-enter new password:
dirk1:/etc#
```

Groups are managed with the commands groupadd, group-
mod, and groupdel. To assign a user to another group, the command
usermod with the option -G is used.

groups

usermod

Anonymous FTP

In addition to root, the user ftp (user) plays a special role. If this
user exists, any user can log in to the computer with the ftp command
without needing to have an account. The user simply assumes the
identity of user ftp or anonymous, and the system prompts for the

ftp

anonymous

user ftp   user's e-mail address as password. The home directory of user `ftp` is then used as the root directory, so that a user who gains access in this way has access only to certain files.

However, this requires the presence of the subdirectories `dev`, `bin`, and `usr` with their corresponding files in the home directory

ftp directories   of user `ftp`. The exact structure of this file tree is explained in the On-Line Manual page for `ftpd`.

7.6   Shells

/etc/shells   To allow users to change their shells themselves, the file `/etc/shells` must list every available shell with its path. This is often forgotten when a shell is installed later.

If there is no entry for a shell in the file `/etc/shells`, the

login shell   shell cannot be used by users as a login shell and there are problems with various TCP/IP programs. The following example shows the contents of such an `/etc/shells` file.

```
/bin/sh
/bin/bash
/bin/ksh
/bin/tcsh
```

chsh   The command `chsh` permits users to change their login shells. The administrator should also use this command in the configuration of an account. In this case the respective user name must be passed as a parameter.

```
dirk1:/home/stefan# chsh
Changing the login shell for stefan
Enter the new value, or press return for the default
Login Shell [/bin/sh]: /bin/bash
dirk1:/home/stefan#
```

7.7   User information

The message that is displayed before the login prompt appears is

/etc/issue   located in the file `/etc/issue`. This file normally contains entries with a greeting message, the name of the computer, and instructions for users.

After a user has logged in, usually the message from the file /etc/motd is displayed. For some systems that use corresponding login program shadow passwords, this can be configured in the file /etc/login.defs.motd. The acronym motd stands for "message of the day," and this file should also be used as such.

Some distributions, including Slackware, overwrite the files /etc/issue and /etc/motd in the startup scripts of the system. To allow the user to customize these files, the commands that overwrite them must be removed from the scripts. In the Slackware distribution this occurs in /etc/rc.d/rc.S.

7.8   Backups

The tar command affords a relatively simple way to make backups of important files. tar is one of the standard UNIX commands available under Linux, but in its enhanced form from FSF.

tar

For example, to back up all data in the directory /home/stefan onto diskettes, the tar command can be invoked with option M (multivolume mode). When one diskette is full, tar prompts for the next. The following example shows the creation of a tar archive on diskette:

floppy disk

```
dirk1:/root# cd /home/stefan
dirk1:/home/stefan# tar cvfM /dev/fd0 *
```

Subdirectories are automatically included in this archiving. To restore such a backup onto the hard disk, the tar command is invoked again with option M (otherwise it would terminate after the first diskette). The following example restores a tar archive from diskettes:

subdirectories

```
dirk1:/root# cd /home/stefan
dirk1:/home/stefan# tar xvfM /dev/fd0
```

Larger backups can be made onto a streamer in the same manner. Instead of /dev/fd0, the device driver of the streamer (/dev/rmt0) is specified.

streamer

GNU tar The M option is not available on other UNIX systems that do not use the GNU `tar` command. Therefore, for backups that might be transferred to other UNIX machines, this option should be avoided.

The `tar` command assumes, as does MTools, that the diskettes it uses are already low-level formatted. Likewise the command `mformat` writes a DOS file system only onto a formatted diskette. fdformat For actual low-level formatting, use the command `fdformat`.

7.9   File system management

Another responsibility of the system administrator is managing the file system. In normal operation this task is restricted to checking free memory at regular intervals, monitoring the log files, and from time to time deleting the contents of the /tmp directories.

crash In the event of a system crash, however, the administrator must carry out a consistency check of the file system. Most distributions booting execute a consistency check on each booting. Here, during booting of the kernel, the file system is first mounted as read-only and checked. Then it is mounted again in an `rc` script as read/write. If problems arise, the consistency check needs to be carried out manually.

For this purpose the individual Linux file systems provide a file system check special tool named `fsck` (file system check). The administrator must ensure that the file system to be checked is not mounted and that the appropriate check program is used. For the currently most popular e2fsck ext2 file system, the corresponding tool is `e2fsck`. The following example demonstrates a consistency check for an ext2 file system:

```
hermes:/root# mount
/dev/sda1 on / type ext2 (defaults)
/proc on /proc type proc (rw)
/dev/sda2 on /usr type ext2 (rw)
/dev/sda5 on /var type ext2 (rw)
/dev/sda6 on /www type ext2 (rw)
/dev/sda7 on /FTP type ext2 (rw)
hermes:/root# umount /FTP
hermes:/root# e2fsck /dev/sda7 fsck.ext2
0.5a, 5-Apr-94 for EXT2 FS 0.5, 94/03/10
Pass 1: Checking inodes, blocks, and sizes
Pass 2: Checking directory structure
Pass 3: Checking directory connectivity
Pass 4: Checking reference counts
Pass 5: Checking group summary information
/dev/sda7: 9094/212160 files, 750177/845401 blocks
hermes:/root# mount -text2 /dev/sda7 /FTP
hermes:/root#
```

fsck is invoked with the partition or file system as a parameter. Normally the program displays any inconsistencies on the console. If no error messages appear, the file system has not been corrupted.

Special options permit automatic error correction. However, fsck program authors usually recommend repairing a damaged file system interactively.

7.10   Upgrades

Because, particularly with Linux, new versions of the kernel, the C library, or the C compiler are released almost every month, one of the tasks of the system administrator is to install these updates in the system. This section explains how to incorporate such updates.

GCC

The newest version of the GNU C compiler (GCC) for Linux can be downloaded from the FTP server tsx-11.mit.edu. It usually encompasses several files compressed with tar and gzip and containing compiled programs (binaries) for Linux.

To replace the old C compiler with the new version, it usually suffices to unpack the tar files in the root directory. The older version is overwritten in the process. To save storage space, the directories of the old version under /usr/lib/gcc-lib can be deleted.

More detailed instructions for updating are included in the corresponding README or RELEASE files found in the same tar archive.

Shared libraries

Purpose and mechanisms   Many UNIX programs share various elementary program components such as file operations that can make up a large proportion of the overall program. To save main memory and disk space, shared libraries were designed .so to contain such common code. When a program is launched, the required shared libraries are loaded automatically. If another program is already using a given shared library, its code in main memory is used by the new program also, resulting in the memory-

saving memory   saving effect. Another advantage of shared libraries is that they make programs more independent of the Linux version and installation currently running because many system-dependent tasks are assumed

portability   by functions in the shared libraries.

Shared libraries are designated by the .so extension in the file name; in addition, as with normal libraries, they usually have a leading lib.

version numbers   Almost all shared libraries have version numbers consisting of two parts, the major version (first number) and the minor version (remaining numbers). Libraries with the same major version should be mutually compatible.

Practically all Linux distributions and software packages have

ELF   meanwhile been changed to the binary format *ELF*. ELF is a standard format for executable files, shared libraries, and object

a.out   files. Advantages of ELF over its predecessor a.out include its simpler programming and its use of shared libraries. In ELF program files only a single shared library is specified explicitly: /lib/ld-

ld-linux   linux.so.1. On program start, ld-linux handles loading other required shared libraries and linking them to the program code. ld-

ld.so.cache   linux employs the file /etc/ld.so.cache, where the paths of all shared libraries in the system are stored. This file is created and

ldconfig   updated with the command ldconfig, which searches all directories

ld.so.conf   specified in /etc/ld.so.conf for shared libraries and writes the search results to /etc/ld.so.cache.

symbolic links   In addition, ldconfig creates symbolic links in the individual directories. For example, if /lib contains the three shared libraries libc.so.5.0.9, libc.so.5.2.16, and libc.5.2.18, then ldconfig creates a symbolic link named libc.so.5, which points to the latter: With the same major version numbers, this file has the highest minor version number. If the directory /lib also contains older libcs with major number 4, the link libc.so.4 is created to

➡   the newest of these. **Do not change these symbolic links manually!** For example, if you delete the link /lib/libc.so.5, then on attempting to create it anew with ln you would find that ln is dynamically linked and needs precisely this link to execute (whether a libc with the exact version number exist in /lib is not relevant).

In general, you should invoke `ldconfig` after each new installation of program packages. In many Linux distributions `ldconfig` is automatically invoked on booting. You should also observe the README files in program packages and enter new directories with shared libraries in `/etc/ld.so.conf`. By default, `ldconfig` searches only the directories `/lib` and `/usr/lib`.

new installation of program packages

The C library The most important shared library is the C library `libc`. In addition to standard C functions, it also contains UNIX functions that largely coincide with those of other UNIX sysems, as well as network functions and more. The current major version is 5. As with Linux, there are different version numbers that indicate whether the version is stable or still under development. If the second number in the version is even (e.g., 5.2.16), it is stable code, otherwise a "hacker"-libc (e.g., `libc-5.3.12`).

version numbers

The current C library resides at Sunsite under `GCC/libc*`. In addition to the precompiled `libc`, the source code is also available, although you do not need it. For every `libc` version there is a file `release.libc` in the same directory; it contains important information and should certainly be loaded as well. Usually a new `libc` version also requires upgrading several other libraries. The minimum versions of these libraries (i.e., these or newer ones) are also listed in the `release.libc` file. Now and then a program might no longer function after an upgrade; in this case you will find patches at the end of the `release` files.

release.libc

patches

Installation is likewise described exactly in `release.libc`. First you need to remove a number of symbolic links. Then unpack `libc-*.bin.tar.gz`:

```
> tar xzvf libc-5.2.18.bin.tar.gz -C /
-rw-r--r-- bin/bin       3669 Feb 18 06:34 1995 usr/include/arpa/ftp.h
-rw-r--r-- bin/bin       3668 Feb 18 06:34 1995 usr/include/arpa/inet.h
-rw-r--r-- bin/bin      12462 Dec 22 22:48 1995
usr/include/arpa/nameser.h
-rw-r--r-- bin/bin      10498 Feb 18 06:34 1995
usr/include/arpa/telnet.h
-rw-r--r-- bin/bin       2982 Feb 18 06:34 1995 usr/include/arpa/tftp.h
-rw-r--r-- bin/bin         90 Feb 18 06:34 1995
usr/include/bsd/sys/ttychars.h
-rw-r--r-- bin/bin        998 Jun 11 02:25 1995 usr/include/bsd/bsd.h
-rw-r--r-- bin/bin         44 Aug 25 05:35 1995 usr/include/bsd/curses.h
-rw-r--r-- bin/bin        188 Feb 18 06:34 1995 usr/include/bsd/errno.h
-rw-r--r-- bin/bin       2273 Feb 18 06:34 1995 usr/include/bsd/sgtty.h
```

155

```
-rw-r--r-- bin/bin        603 Feb 18 06:34 1995 usr/include/bsd/signal.h
-rw-r--r-- bin/bin        247 Feb 18 06:34 1995 usr/include/bsd/stdlib.h
...
```

After unpacking, invoke `ldconfig`.

Kernel

source code

Finnish FTP server

delete

unpack

The source code of the newest kernel can be downloaded from most Linux FTP servers. However, it first appears on Finland's `nic.funet.fi`. To install the newest version of the kernel, we recommend first completely deleting the directory `/usr/src/linux` and then unpacking the `tar` archive with the kernel source code into the directory `/usr/src`. In the process the subdirectory `linux` is re-created.

compilation

Then, as described in the section on configuration and compilation of the kernel (see Section 6.2), the drivers to be used can be defined with `make config` and the new kernel can be compiled.

7.11   Installation of software packages

The programs contained in Linux distributions come from diverse sources. Some packages were developed exclusively for Linux, while others were originally software for BSD UNIX. This thus precludes uniformity of installation. Newer programs are usually easier to install. This section introduces the most important alternatives and conventions.

source code

or precompiled

package contents

Software packages for Linux are distributed either as (C) source code or (as is usual for commercial systems) precompiled. They reside on FTP servers as `.tar.gz`, `.tgz`, `.tar.Z`, or `.zip` files (and sometimes less common formats). You can unpack these files with `tar` or (for `.zip`) `unzip`. First you should view the contents of the archive with **tar tzvf** *package*. At the end of each display line is the name of the individual files in the archive. Often the first directory in the path is named similar to the name of the package. If this is not the case (i.e., there are numerous directories), you should unpack the archive into its own directory to avoid unpacking a huge number of subdirectories and files into the current directory, where

you would otherwise be unable to distinguish the new contents from
the original contents. Unpack an archive with

```
golem:~> tar xzvf package -C destination-directory
```

Documentation

After unpacking an archive, **the user should definitely read
any included** README **or** INSTALL **files**, which contain important
instructions for compilation. These usually address the supported
platforms and any problems that might arise. Furthermore, these
files tell you in advance whether the package is suitable for your
system at all and whether additional packages have to be installed.
In case you need a certain version of another package, note that most
programs display their version number when they are invoked with
-v, -V, -version, or --version (also see the Manual pages). All
of the following notes serve only an explanatory and orientation role
when problems occur; directions in the documentation to a specific
package take priority.

Packages often contain extensive user documentation in the form
of a PostScript or TEX file. At least a UNIX On-Line Reference
Manual page should be included in any case.

Installation

Precompiled software packages These packages are generally easier to install than source-code versions. If you have a choice
between these two alternatives, install the precompiled version. Much
of the Linux software in various distributions is already in precompiled form. If an archive file on an FTP server is not already in a
Linux directory (e.g., in a Sunsite or TSX-11 mirror), its name generally contains linux, linuxelf, i486-linuxelf, or the like.
aout might also appear in the name; in this case you should look for
the package in ELF format.

In the same directory as the archive file you will generally find
README, .lsm, or .doc files with analogous names. Download these
as well; they are not large and often contain important information

patch
diff

for installation. You should also download files with similar names that contain `patch` or `diff`.

unpacking

Precompiled packages are generally assembled so that you can unpack them at a given location in the Linux directory tree—usually `/`, `/usr`, or `/usr/local`. However, first scan the README files for installation directions—a package unpacked at the wrong location is troublesome to delete and often overwrites older files. If the archive file contains `README` or `INSTALL` files, unpack* them separately and read them first.

Software as source code   Software as source code need not be difficult to install. Some poorly maintained packages pose the problem that they cannot be compiled without modifications of `Makefiles` or of even the source code. In this case, observe Section 7.11 or look again for the precompiled version. Many FTP servers provide the contents of various Linux distributions and just might offer what you are looking for.

corrections

Fortunately, these comments for emergencies do not apply to most packages. In the following we explain the most frequent installation methods.

make

Practically all source-code versions require that the programs be compiled with **make** (frequently with parameters). Often you first need to invoke an automatic configuration tool:

configure

configure script

Many newer programs, especially those of the Free Software Foundation, contain a `configure` script. **configure --help** displays options with which the `configure` script can be invoked. **configure** analyzes the computer, operating system, libraries, and available UNIX commands and generates an appropriate **Makefile**. `configure` scripts are created with the GNU utility `autoconf` from the file `configure.in`. Installing such software packages is quite simple.

*Extracting individual files: **tar xzvf** *archive filename*

Imakefile

Imakefile

imake

xmkmf

Here **xmkmf -a** must be specified first, then **make**. Here, too, there are seldom problems.

Other cases require editing the Makefile or some header files (often called `config.h`) before compilation. Even if the documentation does not specifically call for it, it makes sense to examine the Makefile and to modify the correspondingly marked sections. For safety's sake, make a copy of any file before modifying it.

modifications

After successful compilation, the programs and files need to be copied to various positions in the Linux directory tree. Many **Makefiles** already contain the corresponding files, so that you only have to invoke **make install**.

make install

Patches Some packages assume that you will *patch* other source codes for compilation (e.g., the Linux kernel) and then compile again. Patching means that some small modifications are made that are specified in a patch (`.diff` or `.patch` files or others). After you have unpacked the other package, you should invoke **patch <** *patchfile* in its root directory or in a higher directory (note the file names in the patch file and use the option -p0 as needed; see patch(1)). If there are multiple patch files, then patch must be executed for each and in the correct order (the patches are generally numbered). If some of the "hunks" (single modifications) fail, then the patch file and the package are not exactly compatible—you need another version of the package or you must manually apply the "hunks" (which requires familiarity with C and the respective program). If all hunks are rejected, try the option -p0.

`.diff`

`.patch`

multiple patch files

Failed installation Here are a number of possibilities:

- The package is not compatible with your current Linux kernel version (often indicated by the message *symbol-name* undeclared during compilation).
- The package is not compatible with your libc version or another shared library (usually indicated by the message can't resolve symbol: *name*).

- You have not given the README files their deserved attention. This is not so bad, as you can try again.
- The package is defective. You can try to fix the errors manually (see Section 7.11), or you can double-check whether the package should be executable on your computer and with your Linux version, whether all other prerequisites are fulfilled, and whether your Linux installation is free of errors. Then you should describe your problem in a dedicated Linux newsgroups or in a mailing list (see Sections 11.3 and 11.6) and, if you fail to get advice there, ask the maintainer or the author of the packages. For news postings or mail, always mention your Linux and libc versions, the source of the package (FTP server, directory, and file name), and the version of the packages.

Configuration

environment variables

After installing a package, you often need to edit some configuration files and adapt them to your own computer. Likewise you might need to set new environment variables in startup scripts of various shells (see Section 2.7).

Manual adaptation

error

If the compiler terminates the make procedure with an error message, then the user must make some manual adaptations. This occurs frequently with programs that do not use the configure script. With a little practice, such adaptations are easy to carry out. The following is a potential error message:

```
linux2:/home/tul/tmp> gcc bsp.c
bsp.c: In function 'main':
bsp.c:3: 'errno' undeclared (first use this function)
bsp.c:3: (Each undeclared identifier is reported only once
bsp.c:3: for each function it appears in.)
linux2:/home/tul/tmp>
```

unknown symbol

Here the compiler did not know the definition of a symbol. This can have several causes. If the symbol is a constant or a macro, then either it is not available under Linux or the header file containing the declaration was not included with #include. The same applies to C functions whose prototypes are in header files. The user should

first gain an overview of this function and its parameters from the
On-Line Reference Manual page.

To determine whether a function or another symbol exists under
Linux, the system include files, i.e., the C header files of the Linux C   search in header file
library, can be searched. These header files are located in the directory
/usr/include and can be searched with the following command:

```
find /usr/include -name "*.h" -exec grep "symbol" {} \; -print
```

The find command seeks all header files in the directory   /usr/include
/usr/include and all its subdirectories; then find invokes the
grep command, which searches each found file for the symbol.
If the undefined symbol is a function that differs on many UNIX
systems, then the source code frequently contains alternatives that
can be activated with a compiler option such as -DSYSV or -DBSD.   System V and BSD
In the source code this could take the following form:

```
#ifdef SYSV
        function_a (x, y, z);
#else
        function_b (x, y, z);
#endif
```

If the user needs to make modifications in the source code, they
should be embedded in #ifdef. or #ifndef linux commands.   #ifdef
Here linux is a symbol that is automatically declared by the
compiler when it is invoked under Linux.

```
#ifdef linux
        changes
#else
        old code
#endif
```

If the compiler does not report error messages, but the linker
displays error messages on undefined symbols, then the program nm   nm
provides a valuable aid. It outputs a list of symbols declared and
used in object files and libraries. In combination with using grep   grep
for searching the list of undefined symbols, this makes it possible to
determine where a symbol is used and which library contains it:

161

```
linux1:/home/tul> nm prog1.o | grep "symbol"
```

With a little practice, the user will be able to adapt smaller programs in only a few minutes so that they can be compiled under Linux.

Archiving

After modifications have been made on the source code of a program, the modifications should be stored in a file with the help of the `diff` (difference) command. Then the modifications can be applied at any time to the original program with the. `patch` command, and these modifications also can be made available to other users.

diff

patch

The following example shows how to use `diff`:

```
hermes:/usr/src# diff -Nrc tcsh-6.05 tcsh-6.05.patched > tcsh.patch
```

To apply the changes in the `patch`/`diff` file to the unchanged source code, invoke `patch` as follows:

```
hermes:/usr/src# patch < tcsh.patch
Hmm... Looks like a new-style context diff to me...
The text leading up to this was:
--------------------------
|diff -Nrc tcsh-6.05/Makefile tcsh-6.05.patched/Makefile
|*** tcsh-6.05/Makefile Thu Jan  1 01:00:00 1970
|--- tcsh-6.05.patched/Makefile Thu Dec 15 13:10:57 1994
--------------------------
(Creating file tcsh-6.05/Makefile...)
Patching file tcsh-6.05/Makefile using Plan A...
Hunk #1 succeeded at 1.
Hmm... The next patch looks like a new-style context diff to me...
The text leading up to this was:
--------------------------
|diff -Nrc tcsh-6.05/tc.func.c tcsh-6.05.patched/tc.func.c
|*** tcsh-6.05/tc.func.c        Sun Jun 26 00:02:54 1994
|--- tcsh-6.05.patched/tc.func.c        Wed Dec 14 00:03:25 1994
--------------------------
Patching file tcsh-6.05/tc.func.c using Plan A...
Hunk #1 succeeded at 1858.
Hunk #2 succeeded at 1872.
Hmm... The next patch looks like a new-style context diff to me...
The text leading up to this was:
--------------------------
|diff -Nrc tcsh-6.05/tc.who.c tcsh-6.05.patched/tc.who.c
|*** tcsh-6.05/tc.who.c Sun Jun 26 00:02:55 1994
|--- tcsh-6.05.patched/tc.who.c Thu Dec 15 13:10:47 1994
--------------------------
Patching file tcsh-6.05/tc.who.c using Plan A...
Hunk #1 succeeded at 250.
Hunk #2 succeeded at 589.
done
```

7.12   Creating boot diskettes

Not only novices accidentally delete important files and make the   important files
system unbootable. Such files primarily include kernel images that
are loaded by LILO, shells, and files in the /etc directory. In such   /etc
a case there are several approaches to repairing the system.

If the system refuses to start even in single-user mode (see   single-user mode
Section 7.2), the situation requires a boot diskette. If the installation   installation disks
diskettes or CD of a distribution such as Slackware, Universe, LST,
or SLS is available, a Linux system can be booted from it. Instead
of launching the installation program, mount the root partition of the
hard disk and reconstruct or copy the missing files. A diskette or
streamer backup of important files is quite helpful at such a time.

If only the boot kernel on the hard disk is corrupted, a functioning   kernel on disk
kernel from another system can be copied directly onto a diskette.
This contains only the kernel and no file system or additional files.
You can boot from this diskette. After booting, the kernel will attempt
to mount the root file system. The device or partition that the kernel   mount root file system
should attempt to mount can be specified with the program rdev (see
Section 7.12).

If important files in the /etc directory have been damaged and   /etc
booting with the root partition proves impossible, then this requires
a diskette with its own root file system. The boot kernel can reside   own file system
either on the same or on a second diskette. The more elegant variant
is certainly with a single boot diskette containing both the boot kernel   boot/root disk
and the root file system. Such a diskette allows booting of a minimum
but independent Linux system from which the partitions of the hard   mount hard disk
disk can be mounted to correct the error.

If a diskette is used as the root file system, it must not be removed
from the drive. This proves quite impractical if you need to read other
disks. Here a ramdisk comes to the rescue; on booting, the diskette is   ramdisk
copied onto it. This permits using a ramdisk as the root file system,
and the floppy disk drive is freed for other diskettes.

Creating such a boot/root diskette is not particularly difficult.   creating a boot/root disk
First you need a formatted diskette. Here you can use the DOS
program format, the Linux program fdformat, or a preformatted   fdformat
disk. Normally a MINIX file system is created on this diskette.

The following tips refer to Linux 2.0.

The boot disk kernel

Naturally the boot disk must contain a kernel. Due to a shortage of
space, this kernel must be lean and contain no extraneous drivers. The
options CONFIG_NET and CONFIG_INET should be used anyway,
however, since otherwise the kernel might not be compilable.

Booting requires ramdisk support (see below) as well as Minix
and Extended-2 file system support. Since a boot disk is intended not
only for booting but also for repairing a hard disk, the kernel needs
drivers for this purpose—IDE or SCSI support.

The root file system

For the following steps, create a new directory for setting up the root
file system for the boot disk (called /rootimg below).

After initialization, the kernel mounts a root file system and
invokes the UNIX command init. To conserve space, instead of
init you can use the script /etc/rc (which the kernel invokes if
it does not find init). For the contents of /etc/rc, see the script
below between cat > /etc/rc <<EOF and EOF.

➥ Because init is not used, the key combination [Ctrl] + [Alt] +
[Del] **causes an immediate reboot**. Any file systems still mounted
are not shut down cleanly; this must be done manually before the
"three-finger salute": **umount -a**.

Naturally booting also requires the above utilities; to be able
to work with the boot disk at all, you also need the most important
UNIX commands such as ls, mv, cp, fsck... You should also have
an editor (e.g., vi) at your disposal, since you sometimes need to
correct errors in configuration files.

Creating a packed root file system image

The Linux kernel recognizes whether the root file system to be
mounted is a normal one or an image packed with gzip. In the
latter case the packed image is unpacked to the ramdisk and then the
ramdisk is mounted (the kernel must have ramdisk support, and the
loading of the ramdisk must be activated with rdev [see below]).
The advantage of packed images is that they boot faster (because

Margin notes:
lean
ramdisk support
IDE or SCSI support
/etc/rc
utilities
faster booting

less must be loaded from the floppy disk) and the prospect of getting
everything on one disk.

There are various ways to create a packed image. All the methods
create the root partition on a floppy disk, a ramdisk, or a loop
device (see Section 7.12) and then sequentially pack the image of
the contents of the floppy, ramdisk, or loop device with `gzip`. Here
image does *not* mean the individual files and directories, but the entire   image
block device, track by track, sector by sector.

A script to automatically create a boot disk

The following script automatically creates a boot disk. It assumes that
the already compiled kernel is in the current directory as `zImage`.

```
#!/bin/bash

mkdir rootfs
if [ -e /dev/loop1 ]; then
        # loop-Devices supported
        ROOTIMG=rootimg
        MNTOPT="loop=/dev/loop1"
        SIZE=4096
elif [ -e /dev/ram1 ]; then
        # Linux 2.0 ramdisks supported
        ROOTIMG=/dev/ram1
        MNTOPT=defaults
        SIZE=4096
else
        # Slow floppy method
        ROOTIMG=/dev/fd0
        MNTOPT=defaults
        SIZE=1440
fi

dd if=/dev/zero bs=1k count=$SIZE of=$ROOTIMG
mkfs -t minix $ROOTIMG $SIZE
mount $ROOTIMG rootfs -o $MNTOPT

# Fill the root file system with necessary and useful stuff
cd rootfs
mkdir etc bin sbin dev lib mnt proc
cp -a /dev/fd0 /dev/console /dev/tty* /dev/hd* /dev/sd* /dev/zero /dev/null dev
mknod dev/rootram b 1 0
for a in bash cat ln ls mkdir rmdir rm bash mknod; do
        cp /bin/$a bin
done
ln -s /bin/bash bin/sh
for a in ldconfig fdisk mke2fs e2fsck mkswap mount umount update; do
        cp /sbin/$a sbin
done
for a in ldd vi elvis; do cp /usr/bin/$a bin; done
cp -v /lib/ld-linux.so.1 /lib/libc.so.5 /lib/libm.so.5 /lib/libtermcap.so.2 lib/
chroot . /sbin/ldconfig

cat > etc/rc <<EOF
export PATH=/sbin:/bin
update &
mount -av
# Loading keytable for foreign keyboard (e.g., German)
loadkeys /etc/de-latin1-nodeadkeys.map
EOF
```

```
chmod +x etc/rc

cat > etc/fstab <<EOF
/dev/rootram     /                ext2    defaults   0   1
none             /proc            proc    defaults   0   2
EOF

# If you need more utilities, add some "cp" here:

# Please comment out if you use US keyboard layout
cp /usr/bin/loadkeys bin
cp /usr/lib/kbd/keytables/de-latin1-nodeadkeys.map etc

# Unmount and generate packed image
cd ..
umount rootimg
rmdir rootfs
dd if=$ROOTIMG bs=1k count=$SIZE | gzip -v9 > rootimg.gz

KSIZE=$[(`wc -c < zImage`+1023)/1024]
RSIZE=$[(`wc -c < rootimg.gz`+1023)/1024]
TOTAL=$[$KSIZE+$RSIZE]

if [ $TOTAL -gt 1440 ]; then
        echo "Insert floppy disk 1 and press <return>"
        read
        dd if=zImage bs=1k of=/dev/fd0
        rdev -r /dev/fd0 49152
        echo "Insert floppy disk 2 and press <return>"
        read
        dd if=rootimg.gz bs=1k of=/dev/fd0
else
        echo "Insert floppy disk and press <return>"
        read
        dd if=zImage bs=1k of=/dev/fd0
        dd if=rootimg.gz bs=1k of=/dev/fd0 seek=$KSIZE
        rdev -r /dev/fd0 $[16384+KSIZE]
fi

rdev /dev/fd0 /dev/fd0
rdev -R /dev/fd0 0

echo -e "\adone"
```

The following sections explain this script in order to help the reader make modifications and extensions. You should be familiar with fundamentals of shell script programming (also see Section 2.7).

Configuration with rdev

The kernel freshly written onto diskette still needs quite a bit of information for its work. After initialization it must know on which root partition block device the root partition to be mounted resides. When installing with LILO, you specify the device with root=. However, LILO cannot be used because no boot loader should be written at the start of the diskette. You do not always need a boot loader because the Linux kernel contains code to boot itself. Here the kernel must reside exactly at the start of the diskette or hard disk partition. In this case using LILO would even be dangerous, since the boot loader code

would overwrite the first part of the kernel (this is the sole purpose
of `rdev`; in all other cases LILO is more powerful because of the
possibility to pass boot options to the kernel).

The `rdev` options are:

`rdev` *kernel image root-dev*

Determines major and minor device numbers of *root dev*
and writes them to the *kernel image*. After initialization,
this kernel will mount the specified device. If you boot
from diskette by loading to ramdisk (see below), you should
specify `/dev/fd0`.

`rdev -r` *kernel-image code*

This determines the size of the ramdisk under Linux 1.2. **This
is no longer valid under Linux 2.0!** *code* is now structured
as follows:

Bit	meaning
0-13	Specify the position of the root file system image on the diskette; the units are 1 KB blocks.
14	1 = Copy the root file system from diskette to ramdisk and boot from ramdisk. The advantage is that the ramdisk is faster, and the diskette can be removed from the drive after booting.
15	1 = Allows changing disks after the kernel is loaded. If the kernel and the root file system image do not fit on a single diskette, they must be put on two diskettes and this bit must be set in the kernel image. In this case bits 0-13 naturally refer to the second diskette.

The size of the ramdisk is no longer relevant since it is
flexible in the 2.0 kernel.

`rdev -R` *kernel-image read-only?*

If *read-only?* is not 0, then the kernel mounts the root file
system for booting as read-only. This is the normal approach:
After booting, the root file system is checked for errors
(`fsck`) and then is mounted as read/write. A file system

mounting the
root file system

mounted initially as read/write cannot be checked for errors (there is a danger that a modification during the check could confuse fsck, so fsck refuses to check if the file system is read/write). The boot disk created by the above script does not carry out a file system check and immediately mounts as read/write.

rdev -v *kernel-image mode*

Determines the mode that the kernel is to initially set for the graphic adapter. For the individual codes see rdev(8).

There are three methods for creating the root file system image, although they are essentially the same: a file system is created on a

diskette, ramdisk, loop device

floppy disk, on a ramdisk, or in a file (loop device). The file system is mounted and the most important files are copied to it or created. After unmounting, an image is created from the diskette, ramdisk, or file (for the diskette, reading is track by track, sector by sector, and similarly for a ramdisk or file). This image is then compressed

compression

with gzip. gzip is invoked in the above script with the option -9 for maximum compression. The root file system might occupy significantly less space than is available on the diskette, ramdisk, or file. The parts of the diskette, ramdisk, or file that are not used by the file system still contain the zeros that were written at the start—

zero blocks

these large zero blocks are extremely redundant and are compressed (almost completely) away by gzip.

shared libraries

In the above example, the most important shared libraries are packed onto the boot disk. The version numbers naturally depend on the Linux version used; the above example assumes Linux 2.0 or newer, as well as libc and libm version 5, ld-linux version 1, and libtermcap version 2. Incrementation of these version numbers is currently not anticipated soon; as necessary, these version numbers will need to be changed in the script.

As mentioned, after booting the kernel first looks in /etc, /bin, and /sbin for the program init. If it is not found (as with our boot disk), the kernel executes /etc/rc. In our shell script this file is created in somewhat hidden form. cat > /etc/rc <<EOF means that beginning at this line characters are written from the script to the file /etc/rc until it reads the string EOF. After EOF the execution

of the shell script continues normally. After booting, the shell script
looks like this:

```
export PATH=/sbin:/bin
update &
mount -av
# Loading keytable for foreign keyboard (e.g., German)
loadkeys /etc/de-latin1-nodeadkeys.map
```

The file /etc/fstab was likewise created in somewhat hidden
form. mount -av in /etc/rc mounts all file systems that are
specified in /etc/fstab (assuming that they are not already
mounted). The file on diskette looks like this:

```
/dev/rootram     /              ext2    defaults    0   1
none             /proc          proc    defaults    0   2
```

Why is there no /etc/passwd? It is simply not needed because   /etc/passwd
root is the only user that must work with the system booted from
diskette, so there is no login.

Loop devices

Loop devices enable mounting file systems that are not on a block
device, but stored in a normal file. Loop devices derive their name
from the (finite, yet noteworthy) recursion: a file system contains a
file that contains a file system, which contains files... Your mount
must be version 2.5 or newer!

The actual purpose of loop devices is also to encrypt the file
system stored in the file—but for this you need additional utilities.*   encryption
There are three modes: none (no encryption), XOR (simple XOR
with a key), and DES (most secure).

Loop devices are block devices with major device number 7. To
mount a file, you first have to create a file system on it. mkfs has
never cared whether it creates a file system on a block device or in a
file:

*ftp://ftp.funet.fi:/pub/OS/Linux/BETA/loop/

169

```
golem:~> dd if=/dev/zero bs=1k count=1000 out=testfile
1000+0 records in
1000+0 records out
golem:~> mkfs -t ext2 testfile 1000
mke2fs 0.5b, 14-Feb-95 for EXT2 FS 0.5a, 95/03/19
256 inodes, 1000 blocks
50 blocks (5.00%) reserved for the superuser
First data block=1
Block size=1024 (log=0)
Fragment size=1024 (log=0)
1 block group
8192 blocks per group, 8192 fragments per group
256 inodes per group

Writing inode tables: done
Writing superblocks and filesystem accounting information:
done
```

Now the file can be mounted:

```
golem:~> mount -v testfile /mnt -o loop=/dev/loop1
```

Thereafter, the loop device /dev/loop1 belongs to testfile. For other files, you need to use another loopback device.

## Chapter 8

X Window System

As the propagation of graphical workstations began, there were scarcely any standards for programming graphical user interfaces (GUIs). Most manufacturers provided their own GUIs with their machines. If an application that was intended to exploit the graphical possibilities of the new machines was to run on different platforms, it had to be developed and maintained in multiple variants. Large institutions that worked with systems from various manufacturers particularly felt the brunt of these problems.

GUIs

platforms

This prompted the Athena Project at the Massachusetts Institute of Technology (MIT) to develop a platform-independent, uniform environment for the development of graphical applications. At first the development of the X Window System received financial support only from DEC and IBM.

MIT Athena Project

In January 1987 12 renowned workstation producers joined to form the X Consortium. The goal of this institution was to promote the further development and standardization of the X Window System and to enable commercial utilization. In the same year the X Window System Version 11 Release 1 (X11 R1, or X11) appeared. Contrary to previous versions, version 11 had outgrown the research stage. Although the new release was no longer compatible to version 10, it afforded much greater flexibility and performance. Version X11 achieved commercial breakthrough and quickly developed into the standard graphical user interface for UNIX systems from a broad range of manufacturers.

X Consortium

X11 R1

8.1   Features

superior GUI

The X Window System boasts features that distinguish it from conventional graphical user interfaces such as Apple Finder and MS-Windows. The following subsections describe the most important concepts of this powerful system.

Openness

Contrary to most other GUIs, the X Window System was conceived from the start as an open system. This means that the developers

manufacturer-independent

maintained independence from any manufacturer-specific policy and also that the complete source code is available for free.

hardware-independent

The X Window System supports comfortable development of portable and hardware-independent software. The programmer need not worry about the underlying hardware platform. The system supports numerous input and output devices. Interfaces for manufacturer-specific extensions allow connection of specialized hardware.

X11 acceptance

The manufacturer independence and the extreme portability of the X Window System have won it a high level of acceptance from the workstation sector. Today there is hardly a hardware platform, from PC to mainframe, for which the system is not available. This general availability also proves to be an advantage for Linux users. The

XFree86 server

X Window System server XFree86 that runs under Linux displays extremely high performance on normal PC hardware. In any case, X11 is equal to commercial X servers, and in many areas it even proves superior.

Client/server architecture

Due to its internal structure, the X Window System distinguishes

X server and client

between the *X server* and the *X client*. The server program is responsible for managing local hardware such as monitor, keyboard, and mouse, and provides the interface between the user and the individual X applications, which are the X clients.

In general, a workstation runs only one server, which provides any number of clients with input and handles screen output requested by these clients. However, it is quite possible that one server might manage multiple monitors that are connected to a single workstation, which is particularly interesting for CAD systems.

CAD

X protocol

The X protocol provides the only connection between the server and the X clients. Due to this standard protocol, the clients could even be running on other computers on the network (see "Network Transparency" below).

network transparency

The reader needs to be clear that the designations X server and X client deviate from the accustomed terminology. Normally, a *server* is a machine that is superior to its clients in terms of hardware and processes data queries or computations of these clients. Under the X Window System this is usually inverted: the server runs the front end (a normal workstation), while the *client*, a more powerful machine, runs the back end. Often this distinction disappears because the server and the client are running on the same machine.

server and client

This distinction between client and server has some consequences for both the programmer and the user. For example, the programmer has to transfer a graphic that the client has in bitmap form over the network to the server before it can be displayed. These interrelationships need to be considered in the development of X11 applications to avoid creating unnecessary network traffic and thus provoking the resulting loss in execution speed.

bitmap

network traffic

Since an X client is relatively loosely coupled to the server, the inexperienced user can encounter some surprises from time to time. For example, if a client does not respond immediately to user input because of high network or CPU load, many users tend to repeat the input. However, since the X server records every event and definitely sends it to the client, the action could be executed repeatedly, which only very rarely satisfies the intentions of the user.

loose coupling

response time

Network transparency

An important feature of the X Window System is its network transparency. Most workstations on the UNIX sector are connected via network to one another. The X Window System provides a mechanism for redirecting the graphical output of an application to any workstation on the network. This feature permits running

redirecting output

173

computation-intensive programs on the most powerful CPU while the input and output are handled by a smaller workstation on the network.

If a commensurately fast network connection is available, the two machines could even be located thousands of miles apart.

TCP/IP, DECnet   Although it currently supports only TCP/IP and DECnet, the X Window System is principally not bound to a specific network protocol.

performance   Surprisingly, this network transparency hardly leads to a loss in execution speed compared to conventional graphic systems. The X Window System also supports the display of local applications as well as programs running on remote machines on the network all on one monitor. Therefore, the X Window System provides an ideal

integration   basis for integration in all possible application domains.

8.2   Structure

The structure of the X Window System reflects several layers (Figure

layers   8.1). Although the user normally does not perceive these layers, understanding this structure should help to clarify some of the phenomena that the X Window System user experiences.

Xlib and X protocol

A very extensive graphics library with a standardized C interface named Xlib provides the basis of the X Window System. Every invocation of an Xlib routine is translated to a corresponding

protocol layer   data stream that is then transferred via the network (X protocol layer) and can be interpreted on another workstation. This also guarantees problem-free communication between workstations of different manufacturers.

video hardware   X11 does not permit any kind of direct access to the video hardware and does not provide any means for circumventing its standardized interface.

Intrinsics

Since Xlib permits only rudimentary graphic operations such as drawing lines and circles and filling surfaces, higher layers were

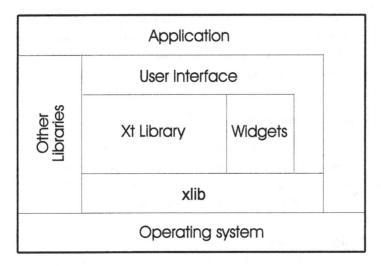

Figure 8.1. Structure of an X11 application

introduced. With the X Toolkit, MIT made a highly mature proposal
for the implementation of such libraries. For creating graphical user
interfaces, the developer normally uses objects on the toolkit level. If
an application needs additional primitive graphical output operations,
these are realized with direct Xlib invocations.

  The X Toolkit Intrinsics Library (Xt Library) supports the
development and use of complex graphical objects such as buttons,
text input fields, and selection menus. These objects are collectively
called *widgets*.

X Toolkit

Xt Library

widgets

Widgets

The actual look and feel of such objects is not determined further
by the intrinsics library. A design goal in the development of the X
Window System was not to prescribe the look of applications that
build on it, but only to provide interfaces for the implementation and
use of such widget sets. Thus, over time, various sources produced
such widget libraries, sometimes with significant deviations in look
and feel. However, this multiplicity seems to have tended to confuse
users.

look and feel

175

OSF/Motif Very recent developments show that most manufacturers have agreed on the Motif widget set of the Open Software Foundation as the de facto standard. This suggests that the future will likely see a uniform concept for graphical user interfaces under X11.

8.3   X resources

flexibility
object-oriented

In their design, the developers of the X Window System created an unusually flexible interface for the configuration of various parameters of the system. The basis was the object-oriented approach of the X Toolkit and the widget sets building on it.

Widget attributes

default settings

Each widget has a number of specific attributes such as position, size, shape, and color. These attributes can be influenced by the programmer as well as later by the user. Every graphical object has internal default settings as determined by the widget developers. The programmer of an X application normally modifies these settings only as much as necessary for the specific requirements.

Resource files

resource manager

When an X application starts, the resource manager loads any new data from the X resource database, whose contents the user can modify in several stages.

8.4   Window managers

window decoration

The window manager is a special client that usually exists only once per workstation. Its job is managing the various windows of a display to allow the user to modify the position and size of windows. The window manager also handles the window decoration, which designates the peripheral regions of a window and its various control elements. Naturally, the respective X client is responsible for the contents of a window.

The X Window System likewise does not prescribe the look and feel of the window manager. To assure problem-free communication between a given window manager and the clients running under

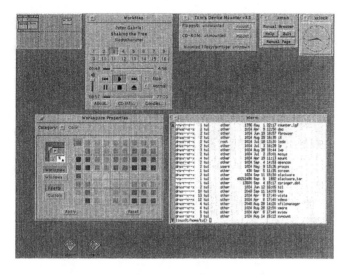

Figure 8.2. The olvwm window manager

its control, the X Consortium passed the ICCC (Inter-Client   ICCC
Communications Conventions).

Users have a broad choice of different window managers, each
having its advantages and drawbacks. The standard X distribution,
for example, contains the twm (Tab Window Manager), which affords
little in the way of comfortable operation. The Open Software
Foundation (OSF) created the Motif window manager (mwm), whose   OSF Motif
look and feel matches the Motif widget set. Sun Microsystems'   OpenLook
OpenLook Window Manager (olwm) is available free as source
code. olwm was extended by a third party to the OpenLook Virtual
Window Manager (olvwm), which provides almost any number of
virtual screens and allows switching between them with the desktop
manager (Figure 8.2).

However, most Linux distributions favor fvwm by Robert Nation   fvwm
(Figure 8.3). This window manager is also based on twm but
consumes significantly less memory than the original. By using a
configuration file (.fvwmrc) and by setting numerous parameters,
the user can exert significant influence on the look and feel of fvwm.
This allows the user to mimic the look and feel of mwm or the window

177

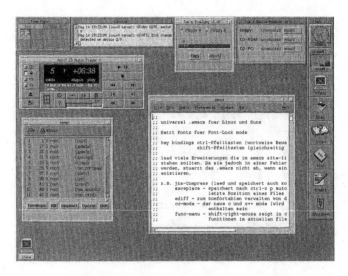

Figure 8.3. The fvwm window manager

virtual desktop   manager by Silicon Graphics. A virtual desktop supports multiple screens, similar to olvwm.

Especially noteworthy is the feature allowing the linking of external modules, which can then communicate with the window

GoodStuff   manager via a defined interface. One such module is GoodStuff, an icon bar on which the user can place icons for the most frequently used applications on the desktop and from which they can be launched. Another module permits the coupling of sounds to certain user actions such as opening and closing a window. Another option

gwm   is the generic window manager (gwm), whose look and feel the user can adapt to either of the two standards (OpenLook or Motif) using a built-in Lisp interpreter.

ctwm   ctwm is another offspring of twm, but it offers a more pleasing look and feel and is more configurable than its predecessor.

8.5   Toolkits

This section introduces the most important libraries (toolkits) for the production of graphical user interfaces under the X Window System.

Athena widget set

The first available widget set for the X Window System was the Athena widget set, which remains its standard and is included in the MIT distribution. Many early X applications used the Athena widgets. Even today many freeware programs continue to use these widgets.

Athena

MIT

Unfortunately, the somewhat antiquated look and feel of some of its elements has led manufacturers of commercial applications to adopt more modern toolkits. Due to the similarities between intrinsics-based toolkits, this certainly posed no great problem. However, the look and feel of the Athena widgets has recently received a face lifting. The free availability of Athena's source code made it possible to exchange drawing routines. The modifications led to a Motif-like three-dimensional look. Interestingly, in Linux the new library (`libXaw3D`) can simply replace the old one (`libXaw`).

intrinsics

source code

libXaw3D

OpenLook

OpenLook itself represents only a detailed specification of the look and feel for graphical user interfaces. After several years of development, it was released by AT&T and Sun Microsystems with the goal of setting a standard for graphical user interfaces under X11.

AT&T, Sun

On the basis of the OpenLook specification, Sun developed a toolkit for the X Window System (`XView`) that is nearly compatible to Sun's previous graphic system, SunView. This toolkit was included in release 4 of the MIT distribution of X11, making it public domain. Unfortunately, XView builds directly on Xlib, which means that it is not a true widget set. Sun used this toolkit to implement a series of standard applications that are delivered with every Sun workstation (OpenWindows Deskset).

XView

By delivering OpenLook with its UNIX System V systems, AT&T contributed to OpenLook's wide propagation. As an alternative to XView, an X Toolkit-based widget set that likewise met the OpenLook specifications was developed primarily by AT&T.

System V

OSF/Motif

To spur the development of new technologies and standards, especially for UNIX systems, most of the renowned UNIX

manufacturers (including Hewlett Packard, IBM, and DEC, but not
Sun and AT&T) joined forces in the Open Software Foundation
(OSF). This group also recognized the need for a uniform user
interface for X11 and initiated the development of OSF/Motif.
Especially DEC and HP were involved substantially in the design
and implementation.

OSF

Within a few months a user interface emerged that had
been adapted to the look of common GUIs on the PC sector.
Its main components were the Motif window manger (mwm) and
the X intrinsics-based Motif widget set. In addition, the formal
User Interface Language (UIL) was defined that enabled simple
description of Motif-based graphical user interfaces. This description
can be translated to a binary format with a special compiler and
interpreted with the help of a library. Numerous third parties
offer programs for the interactive creation of Motif graphical user
interfaces.

mwm

UIL

Due to the large number of companies involved in OSF, Motif
soon became the de facto standard of the UNIX world. OpenLook
developers Sun Microsystems and AT&T (later transferring to UNIX
System Laboratories and Novell) merged with the Motif interface
trend in the spring of 1993 with the COSE Initiative (Common
Open Software Environment). This delivered the coup de grace for
OpenLook, at least on the commercial sector. The primary goal of
COSE is the standardization of the Motif-based desktop environment
CDE (Common Desktop Environment).

de facto standard

COSE

Since OSF did not make the source code of Motif available
for free, users have to pay fees for each run-time license. For this
reason, Motif was not available for Linux from the start. Meanwhile,
however, there are commercial Linux versions of OSF/Motif at
reasonable prices. Universities can purchase the source code directly
from the OSF and compile it on their workstations, which was done
at various sites for Linux systems.

license

SUIT

SUIT (Simple User Interface Toolkit) was developed at the
University of Virginia. Contrary to most X toolkits, this toolkit is also
available for other common user interfaces such as MS-Windows and

University of Virginia

Apple Finder. SUIT enables the development of applications that are across platforms
portable between these operating systems. Its look and feel strongly
resembles OSF/Motif, which should help its user acceptance.

    A particular feature of this library is its integrated interface interface editor
editor, which enables the user to manipulate the interface easily and
interactively. For example, the user can modify the position and form
of objects without needing to recompile the application. When the
user quits the application, all modifications are automatically written
to a file.

InterViews and Fresco

InterViews is an extensive graphical environment that was developed
at Stanford University. In contrast to X Toolkit and its widget sets,
InterViews has a C++ interface and thus incorporates object-oriented C++ toolkit
concepts. In addition to its graphics library, the InterViews system
provides an interactive interface editor (ibuild), a WYSIWYG
(what you see is what you get) text editor (doc), a C++ class
browser (iclass), and a powerful, vector-oriented drawing program
(idraw). Due to the quite substantial overhead, InterViews also puts
significant demands on the hardware.

    Version 6 of X11 included the new toolkit Fresco, which Fresco
represents a further development of InterViews. Fresco enables
embedding graphical objects from other programs, which can be
running on arbitrary computers on the network. The interface is
specified with a language conforming to CORBA (IDL). CORBA, IDL

XView, Slingshot, and UIT

XView is an independent toolkit that is not based on Xt intrinsics.
The Sun Microsystems product was delivered with Release 4 of the
X Window System. The programming interface depends strongly
on the antiquated SunView, the non–network-transparent, highly SunView
kernel-dependent graphical user interface on older Sun workstations. Xview
XView implemented the look and feel of OpenLook and, because of
the object-oriented approach of its not overly complex structure, was
relatively easy to program.

    To extend the features of XView, a Sun Microsystems employee
in England developed the Slingshot extensions. This package offers Slingshot

181

numerous new graphical objects that harmoniously integrate into the base system. Slingshot extends the object-oriented approach with rudimentary graphical figures such as lines and rectangles. The Slingshot extensions also simplify the programming of the drag-and-drop functionality that was already relatively mature in OpenLook.

UIC

To adapt XView (and Slingshot) to the newest developments in the field of programming languages, another Sun employee developed a C++ class hierarchy, UIC, which permits the utilization of all XView objects and simplifies using them. Unfortunately, the integration of functions in derived C++ classes can pose some problems.

8.6   X11 server

XFree86

A central component of every Linux distribution is the X server from the XFree86 team. XFree86 is a nonprofit organization that is primarily involved in the further development of the X server on Intel-based UNIX systems. XFree86 gives special attention to

XFree86 server

the support of up-to-date PC graphic boards. For this reason, the XFree86 server also demonstrates performance that sometimes even exceeds what can be expected from RISC workstations. The SVGA server (XF86_SVGA) supports all common VGA graphic boards in all possible resolutions and vertical sweep frequencies. With special servers that exploit the possibilities of modern accelerator boards (Mach, S3), significantly better results can be achieved. However, if the performance of the XFree86 server still does not suffice, or if

Accelerated X

24-bit support is required, the commercial server Accelerated X by X Inside can be employed.

8.7   Linux as X terminal

PC as X server

A PC running under Linux and XFree86 is superbly suited as an X terminal. This proves especially interesting when expensive software packages are available on a workstation and are intended to be utilized decentrally.

Numerous X servers are available that run under MS-Windows. However, their performance is usually significantly below that of XFree86 servers because they translate the X protocol commands into slower MS-Windows calls.

performance

To give the reader a more precise picture of the possibilities afforded by using Linux as an X terminal, we present an example of such an application in a heterogeneous network. On a network (see Figure 9.3) we have a powerful graphics program available on a Sun workstation (sun) that is to be used by a Linux workstation (zeus). First, external access must be permitted to the local X server with the command xhost. The permissions can be defined separately for each machine. In general, however, the following input suffices:

xhost

```
zeus:/home/strobel> xhost +
access control disabled, clients can connect from any host
zeus:/home/strobel>
```

Then the Linux user logs in with telnet or rlogin on the computer sun:

telnet

```
zeus:/home/strobel>
zeus:/home/strobel> telnet sun
Trying 141.7.1.20...
Connected to sun.
Escape character is '^]'.

SunOS UNIX (sun)
login: strobel
Password:
Last login: Mon Aug 30 09:59:51 from zeus
SunOS Release 4.1.2 (NEWKERN) #1: Wed Dec 23 11:02:57 MET 1992
sun:/home/strobel>
sun:/home/strobel> setenv DISPLAY zeus:0.0
```

Next the DISPLAY environment variable is set so that the X library redirects all graphical output to the Linux machine. In the C shell, as the above example shows, this is done with the command setenv, in a Bourne shell with the following:

DISPLAY

```
sun:/home/strobel> export DISPLAY=zeus:0.0
```

If an X client is started now on sun, then all windows will appear not on sun but on the display of the Linux computer (zeus). In this way multiple applications from different workstations can be output on one display and operated from one machine. Linux even spares the user from setting the DISPLAY variable, since this is handled automatically by telnetd.

rsh

Alternatively, an X application can be started on a remote computer with the rsh command. This requires a corresponding entry in the .rhosts file on the respective machine (more details are provided in section 10.7). The following statement starts the application xterm on sun and redirects its output to zeus. The option -display is supported by almost all X applications.

xterm

```
zeus:/home/strobel> rsh sun "xterm -display zeus:0.0"
```

pop-up menu

To simplify the redirection of output from a remote application, it makes sense to make an entry in one of the pop-up menus of the window manager. How this functions is shown under the configuration of fvwm in section 8.9.

8.8   X11 configuration

Installing the X Window System under Linux normally consists of simply unpacking the programs and files from the various tar archives. With most Linux packages this occurs during the installation of the operating system and so it poses no problem. The configuration task grows complicated when the X server must be adapted to the available video board and monitor. Then configuration requires modifying the central configuration file XF86Config, which resides in the directory /etc or /usr/lib/X11.

tar archive

XF86Config

The XF86Config file

This file is divided into sections. Here we list these sections and explain their most important aspects in detail.

Files

defines the paths required by the X server for the RGB color table and the font directories.

ServerFlags

sets the server's general flags, including whether the server can be terminated with [Ctrl] + [Alt] + [Backspace] and how the server should react to UNIX signals.

Keyboard

defines the connected keyboard and the function of special modifier keys.

Pointer

adapts the mouse driver by specification of its type and the interface used.

Monitor

determines the limit values and the timing data of the monitor(s).

Device

describes video boards.

Screen

assigns monitor, definitions, and video board to an X server.

The files section

Installation packages usually handle the settings for the RGB table and font paths correctly. Font paths can be entered in individual lines or in a single line delimited by commas. Font servers are specified as `transport/hostname:portnumber`, for example, `tcp/zeus:7100`. The following example shows a file section:

font server

```
Section "Files"

RgbPath      "/usr/X11R6/lib/X11/rgb"
# Examples of font server entries:
#    FontPath    "tcp/127.0.0.1:7100"
#    FontPath    "tcp/font.server.de:7100"
     FontPath    "/usr/lib/X11/fonts/misc/"
     FontPath    "/usr/lib/X11/fonts/Type1/"
     FontPath    "/usr/lib/X11/fonts/Speedo/"
     FontPath    "/usr/lib/X11/fonts/75dpi/"
     FontPath    "/usr/lib/X11/fonts/100dpi/"

EndSection
```

185

The server flags section

Two options apply in this section. NoTrapSignal is only interesting debugging for debugging purposes, and DontZap prevents terminating the server with ⎡Ctrl⎤ + ⎡Alt⎤ + ⎡Backspace⎤:

```
Section "ServerFlags"

# If the following option is activated, the X server dumps
# a core file when it receives a signal.  Here the option is
# disabled as a comment.
#     NoTrapSignals

# Activating the following option disables the key combination
# <Crtl-Alt-BS> to terminate the servers.
DontZap

EndSection
```

The keyboard section

The keyboard driver is adapted here. Standard protocol should always be used. In addition, on non-English keyboards, note that the right ⎡Alt⎤ key (⎡AltGr⎤) must be redefined as ModeShift to allow the use special characters of special characters such as @ and ¦. Many example files employ the American keyboard and use the right ⎡Alt⎤ key as Compose.

```
Section "Keyboard"
Protocol     "Standard"
# Delay and repeat rate for autorepeat
AutoRepeat   500 5
# Numlock to be handled by the server
serverNumLock
# Which LEDs can the user influence (e.g., with xset)
#    Xleds        1 2 3
# Function of modifier keys
     LeftAlt     Meta
     RightAlt    ModeShift
     RightCtl    Compose
#    ScrollLock  ModeLock
# Switching consoles with SysReq (normally not used in Linux)
#    VTSysReq
# Command to be executed on opening of the virtuellen terminal
#    VTInit "command"
EndSection
```

The pointer section

mouse For the mouse driver, it normally suffices to specify the type of mouse and the interface used. Usually, installation creates a link for this interface as /dev/mouse, which can be used here.

```
Section "Pointer"

# One of the following mouse protocols must be selected.
# This need not correspond to the name of the mouse.
# Most generic mice and many Logitech mice
# use Microsoft protocol:
#     Protocol    "Microsoft"
# All normal bus mice:
#     Protocol    "BusMouse"
# Many new serial Logitech mice use the following
# (also see ChordMiddle):
#     Protocol    "Mouseman"
# Older Logitech mice:
#     Protocol    "Logitech"
# Other mice:
#     Protocol    "MouseSystems"
#     Protocol    "MMSeries"
#     Protocol    "PS/2"
#     Protocol    "MMHitTab"
# The following should not be used under Linux:
#     Protocol    "Xqueue"
#     Protocol    "OSMouse"
Protocol    "Microsoft"

# Mouse interface:
Device      "/dev/mouse"

# BaudRate and SampleRate (only for some Logitech mice)
#     BaudRate   9600
#     SampleRate 150

# Emulation of a 3-button mouse, where 3rd mouse key is
# is simulated by simultaneously pressing left and right
# mouse key.
#     Emulate3Buttons

# ChordMiddle is an option for some 3-button Logitech
# and Mouseman mice.
#     ChordMiddle

# The following resets the DTR line of serial mouse port to 0.
# This option is needed for some MouseSystems mice.
#     ClearDTR
# Some mice also require ClearRTS option, which sets RTS to 0.
#     ClearRTS

EndSection
```

The monitor section

This section has several purposes. It sets the limit values and the timing data of a monitor, and there can be multiple occurrences of the section. Thereby each monitor is assigned an identifier with which it can later be referenced. The limit values are the maximum horizontal synchronization, the vertical refresh rate, and the bandwidth.

bandwidth

These data can be found in the technical documentation of the monitor. If nothing else is specified, the bandwidth is assumed in MHz, the horizontal synchronization in KHz, and the vertical refresh rate in Hz. Specifying these values in the configuration serves to protect the monitor. On startup, the server tests whether a specified

protection

video mode exceeds the monitor's range and discards the mode if it does.

video modes   After the technical data of a monitor, the section lists various video modes that are adapted to the respective monitor. The definition of video modes is discussed in detail below.

```
Section "Monitor"
Identifier  "VESA Generic Monitor"
VendorName  "Unknown"
    ModelName    "Unknown"
    BandWidth   300
    HorizSync   23-38
VertRefresh 50-60
# 640x480@60Hz Non-Interlaced mode
# Horizontal Sync = 31.5kHz
ModeLine "640x480" 25 640 664 760 800 480 491 493 525
# 640x480@64Hz Non-Interlaced mode
# Horizontal Sync = 33.7kHz
#ModeLine "640x480" 28 640 664 704 832 480 489 492 525
# VESA 640x480@72Hz Non-Interlaced mode
# Horizontal Sync = 37.9kHz
#ModeLine "640x480" 31.5 640 664 704 832 480 489 492 520
# VESA 800x600@56Hz Non-Interlaced mode
# Horizontal Sync = 35.1kHz
ModeLine "800x600" 36 800 824 896 1024 600 601 603 625
# VESA 800x600@60Hz Non-Interlaced mode
# Horizontal Sync = 37.9kHz
ModeLine "800x600" 40 800 840 968 1056 600 601 605 628
# VESA 800x600@72Hz Non-Interlaced mode
# Horizontal Sync = 48kHz
#ModeLine "800x600" 50 800 856 976 1040 600 637 643 666
# VESA 1024x768@60Hz Non-Interlaced mode
# Horizontal Sync = 48.4kHz
#ModeLine "1024x768" 65 1024 1032 1176 1344 768 771 777 806
# 1024x768@42.6Hz, Interlaced mode
# Horizontal Sync = 34.8kHz
ModeLine "1024x768" 44 1024 1040 1216 1264 768 777 785 817 Interlace
# 1024x768@43.5Hz, Interlaced mode (8514/A standard)
# Horizontal Sync = 35.5kHz
ModeLine "1024x768" 45 1024 1040 1216 1264 768 777 785 817 Interlace
# VESA 1024x768@70Hz Non-Interlaced mode
# Horizontal Sync=56.5kHz
#ModeLine "1024x768" 75 1024 1048 1184 1328 768 771 777 806
# 1024x768@76Hz Non-Interlaced mode
# Horizontal Sync=62.5kHz
#ModeLine "1024x768" 85 1024 1032 1152 1360 768 784 787 823
# 1152x900@60.14Hz, Non-Interlaced mode
# Horizontal Sync=57.4kHz
##ModeLine "1152x900" 85 1152 1192 1384 1480 900 905 923 955
# 1152x900@48.5Hz, Interlaced mode
# Horizontal Sync=45.6kHz
##ModeLine "1152x900" 62 1152 1184 1288 1360 900 898 929 939 Interlace
# 1152x900@48.5Hz, Non-Interlaced mode
# Horizontal Sync=76.1kHz
#ModeLine "1152x900" 110 1152 1284 1416 1536 900 902 905 941
# 1280x1024@44Hz, Interlaced mode
# Horizontal Sync=51kHz
##ModeLine "1280x1024" 80 1280 1296 1512 1568 1024 1025 1037 1165 Interlace
# 1280x1024@61Hz, Non-Interlaced mode
# Horizontal Sync=64.25kHz
##ModeLine "1280x1024" 110 1280 1328 1512 1712 1024 1025 1028 1054
# 1280x1024@70Hz, Non-Interlaced mode
# Horizontal Sync=74.4kHz
#ModeLine "1280x1024" 125 1280 1296 1552 1680 1024 1024 1032 1062
# 1280x1024@74Hz, Non-Interlaced mode
# Horizontal Sync=78.85kHz
#ModeLine "1280x1024" 135 1280 1312 1456 1712 1024 1027 1030 1064
```

```
EndSection

Section "Monitor"
Identifier "EIZO FlexScan T660"
VendorName "EIZO"
ModelName "FlexScan T660i-T/TCO"
    BandWidth    135.0
    HorizSync    30.0-82.0
VertRefresh 55.0-90.0
ModeLine "1024x768" 80 1024 1088 1152 1280 768 770 772 778
ModeLine "1280x1024" 135 1280 1328 1408 1688 1024 1025 1026 1060
ModeLine "1536x1152" 168 1536 1616 1760 2048 1152 1154 1158 1188
EndSection
```

The device section

This section specifies the available video boards. Like Monitor, it can   video board
occur repeatedly. For many boards, neither the chipset nor the dot
clocks need to be specified, since the server can collect these data
automatic ally on startup. For more complicated boards, however,
specification becomes necessary.

```
Section "Device"
Identifier  "Generic VGA 16 Color"
#server     "XF86_VGA16"
VendorName  "GENERIC"
BoardName   "GENERIC"
EndSection

Section "Device"
Identifier  "Generic SVGA"
#server     "XF86_SVGA"
VendorName  "GENERIC"
    BoardName    "GENERIC"
    VideoRam     1024
EndSection

Section "Device"
Identifier  "Generic SVGA, VideoRam limited to 1MB"
#server     "XF86_SVGA"
VendorName  "GENERIC"
    BoardName    "GENERIC"
    VideoRam     1024
EndSection

Section "Device"
Identifier "Sigma Legend ET-4000"
#server     "XF86_SVGA"
VendorName "Sigma"
BoardName "Sigma Legend ET-4000"
Option "legend"
EndSection

#From: koenig@tat.physik.uni-tuebingen.de (Harald Koenig)
#Date: Sun, 25 Sep 1994 18:55:42 +0100 (MET)

Section "Device"
Identifier "Miro 10SD GENDAC"
#server     "XF86_S3"
VendorName "MIRO"
BoardName "10SD GENDAC"
#    Clocks 25.255 28.311 31.500  0     40.025 64.982 74.844
#    Clocks 25.255 28.311 31.500 36.093 40.025 64.982 74.844
```

```
      ClockChip "s3gendac"
      RamDac    "s3gendac"
EndSection
```

clocks

Even if the server can determine the clock frequencies automatically, sometimes it still makes sense to specify them manually because the detected values are used as an identifier. The definitions of video modes refer to this identifier in the mode lines of the monitor definition. If there should be fluctuations during the detection of the clock frequency and a clock were identified at 49.5 Hz instead of 50, then the X server might not identify the frequency used by a video mode and would thus terminate with an error message.

In addition, the server's automatic detection of clock rates can cause problems with some hardware. Specification of the clock frequencies in a board's definition suppresses automatic detection.

computing clocks

To establish the available clock frequencies, remove the `clocks` line from the `Xconfig` file and restart the X server with the option `-probeonly`. The X server then displays the detected clock frequencies and other driver information in text mode and then quits.

The screen section

Each special server (SuperVGA server, monochrome server, S3 server, etc.) can be assigned in this section to a monitor and a video

screen

board. When the server starts, it selects the appropriate screen and thus has the data of the video board and the monitor. In addition, this section lists possible video modes that refer to mode lines from the corresponding Monitor section. At run time the user can switch between these modes with the key combinations [Ctrl][Alt][+] and [Ctrl][Alt][-] on the numeric keyboard.

```
Section "Screen"
Driver "vga256"
Device "Generic SVGA"
Monitor "IDEK VisionMaster 17 (1)"
Subsection "Display"
Moof the "1280x1024" "1024x768" "800x600" "640x480"
EndSubsection
EndSection

Section "Screen"
Driver "accel"
Device "Miro 20SD"
Monitor "IDEK VisionMaster 17 (1)"
Subsection "Display"
```

```
Moof the "1024x768" "800x600" "640x480"
EndSubsection
EndSection
```

Setting the video modes

The most difficult and dangerous part of configuration is setting video modes, since this directly defines the synchronization frequencies (timings) of the monitor, and a low-priced monitor, without protective circuitry against exceeding its frequency limits, can be damaged by incorrect values. To prevent damage, the frequency limits of the monitor should be entered in the configuration file from the start.

synchronization

The advantage of this kind of configuration of the video mode is that the available monitor can be used to full advantage. For example, a 14" monitor whose maximum horizontal synchronization frequency (HSF) is too low to display 800×600 pixels flicker-free could be operated at a resolution of 800×550 with 72 Hz screen refresh rate (RR).

optimization

no flicker

For each mode, the configuration file specifies the clock to be used as well as four values each for horizontal and vertical synchronization. The specification can be in a single line (as ModeLine) or distributed across several lines. The two definitions in the following example are identical:

vertical timing

```
#          Mode    Clock  horizontal            vertical
ModeLine "800x600"  45   800  840 1030 1184   600  600  606  624

# The same mode in a different notation:
Mode "800x600"
    DotClock        45
    HTimings        800 840 1030 1184
    VTimings        600 600 606 624
EndMode
```

As an option, flags can be specified at the end of a mode definition, including interlace, +hsync, +vsync, and csync. These flags influence the interlace mode and the type of synchronization.

interlace mode

```
Mode "1024x768i"
    DotClock        45
    HTimings        1024 1048 1208 1264
```

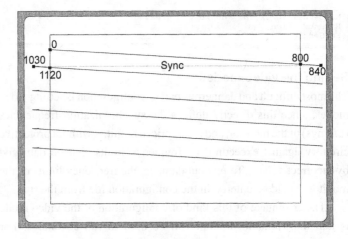

Figure 8.4. Schematic representation of the composition of a screen

```
        VTimings        768 776 784 817
        Flags           "Interlace"
EndMode
```

The values for horizontal timing, in order, are the respective meanings of the values in each group of four numbers:

- the maximum number of pixels after which the picture ceases to be displayed;
- the number of dot-clock ticks to the start of the horizontal synchronization pulse (sync), whereby the values are counted ongoing;
- the number of dot-clock ticks until the horizontal synchronization pulse ends and the second guard time of the electron beam begins;
- the total number of dot-clock ticks to the end of a cycle (frame).

```
ModeLine "800x5"   45   800 840 1030 1120     540 540 546 558
```

This example defines a mode with a resolution of 800x540 pixels, which is assigned the name "800x5."

The horizontal resolution is 800 pixels, and after the end of a visible line a guard time begins for the electron beam to rest. The guard time lasts until 840 pixels; then the synchronization pulse begins. It lasts 190 dot-clock ticks until 1030. Then there is a guard time until 1120. Thereupon the next horizontal cycle begins. After 540 horizontal cycles (that is, scan lines), the vertical synchronization intervenes, lasting six horizontal cycles. Then there is another guard time until the 558th cycle. After the guard time, the next screen starts.

sync pulse

The files `video.tutorial` and `VideoModes.doc` in the directory `/usr/lib/X11/doc` describe in depth the rules for determining the exact values for such a video mode.

determination of values

However, it is often simpler to find a corresponding entry in one of the many example files and to modify it. There is also a table for the simple spreadsheet program `sc`, which simplifies the computation of the values. This can be found on the FTP server `sunsite.unc.edu` and its mirror servers in the directory `/pub/Linux/X11/install` with the file name `modegen.taz`.

spreadsheet

The limiting factor for simple monitors is usually the maximum horizontal synchronization frequency. This is the frequency with which the electron beam moves from left to right and from scan line to scan line. This frequency is computed by dividing the driving clock rate, specified in MHz, by the largest (right) number of the block for horizontal timing:

horizontal timing

computation

$$f_{horizontal} = \frac{f_{pixel}}{N_{pixel}}$$

In the above example, the required horizontal sweep frequency would be 45 MHz/1120, or approximately 40 KHz. This is the upper limit for the monitor in our example.

Refresh rate

To compute the vertical synchronization frequency (vertical timing or screen refresh rate), divide the horizontal synchronization frequency by the number of scan lines (i.e., horizontal cycles) necessary for a complete screen. This is the rightmost number in the block for vertical timing.

computation

$$f_{vertical} = \frac{f_{horizontal}}{N_{scan\ lines}}$$

193

In our example we have 40 KHz/558, or 72 Hz. If 600 lines rather than 540 are to be displayed, then the vertical synchronization frequency falls significantly below 72 Hz, which the user notices as *flicker* light flicker ing of the monitor.

With a better monitor whose maximum horizontal synchronization frequency is, for example, 60 KHz, and a newer video board that *better performance* offers a faster clock, the driving clock frequency could be raised to achieve a higher refresh rate.

copying a mode To modify an existing video mode, we recommend copying and modifying the mode repeatedly and entering each modified mode in a mode line of the Screen section with a different name. Then start the X server and compare the effects of the modifications by switching modes with [Ctrl]+[Alt] and the [+] or [-] key on the numerical keypad. If the monitor no longer synchronizes with a new mode, i.e., it fails to show a stable picture, quickly change modes or end the X server *avoid damage* with [Ctrl] + [Alt] + [Backspace] to avoid damage to the monitor.

vgaset The program vgaset provides a valuable aid in adjusting the picture. Started in an xterm, it permits interactive manipulation of the picture position. At the touch of a key the borders can be increased or decreased, and the duration of the synchronization signal can be changed. The eight values to be entered for the current settings in the file Xconfig are constantly displayed.

Keyboard layout configuration

The X Window System manages the keyboard independently of the kernel. An American keyboard is initialized as the default. *xmodmap* Country-specific keyboard tables can be loaded with the utility xmodmap. When the X server is launched in a normal configuration, xmodmap is invoked with the file .Xmodmap. The utility seeks this file first in the user's home directory and then in the directory /usr/lib/X11/xinit.

If a given keyboard layout is to be modified systemwide, it must be adapted in the directory /usr/lib/X11/xinit. Ready .Xmodmap files are included in some distributions, or they can be drawn from FTP servers such as sunsite.unc.edu in the directory /pub/Linux/X11/misc.

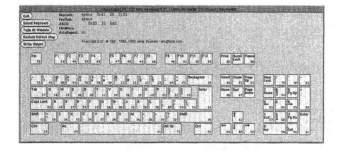

Figure 8.5. xkeycaps

Since xmodmap is normally invoked in an xinitrc script, the   xinitrc
invocation might need to be modified to seek the file .Xmodmap in
another directory or under another name. In case of doubt, examine
the script that starts the X server, usually startx.

Using the xkeycaps utility certainly proves to be a more   xkeycaps
comfortable alternative. It is included in many Linux distributions
and can be found on the usual FTP servers. This program offers an
X11 user interface (Figure 8.5). The user can display the current
keyboard layout and interactively change it with the mouse.

American Linux distributions frequently lack other country-
specific keyboard layouts. Hence we give an example of a German
.Xmodmap as an example of country-specific keyboard adaptation.
Note the keyboard symbol number 12, which is often erroneously
configured with the symbol paragraph instead of section.   paragraph

```
keycode    8 =
keycode    9 = Escape
keycode   10 = 1 exclam
keycode   11 = 2 quotedbl twosuperior
keycode   12 = 3 section threesuperior
keycode   13 = 4 dollar
keycode   14 = 5 percent
keycode   15 = 6 ampersand
keycode   16 = 7 slash braceleft
keycode   17 = 8 parenleft bracketleft
keycode   18 = 9 parenright bracketright
keycode   19 = 0 equal braceright
keycode   20 = ssharp question backslash
keycode   21 = apostrophe grave
keycode   22 = BackSpace
keycode   23 = Tab
keycode   24 = q Q at
keycode   25 = W
keycode   26 = E
keycode   27 = R
keycode   28 = T
```

195

```
keycode  29 = Z
keycode  30 = U
keycode  32 = O
keycode  33 = P
keycode  34 = Udiaeresis
keycode  35 = plus asterisk asciitilde
keycode  36 = Return
keycode  37 = Control_L
keycode  38 = A
keycode  39 = S
keycode  40 = D
keycode  41 = F
keycode  42 = G
keycode  43 = H
keycode  44 = J
keycode  45 = k K Arabic_kaf
keycode  46 = l L Arabic_lam Greek_lambda
keycode  47 = Odiaeresis
keycode  48 = Adiaeresis
keycode  49 = asciicircum degree
keycode  50 = Shift_L
keycode  51 = numbersign apostrophe
keycode  52 = Y
keycode  53 = X
keycode  54 = C
keycode  55 = V
keycode  56 = B
keycode  57 = N
keycode  58 = m M mu
keycode  59 = comma semicolon
keycode  60 = period colon
keycode  61 = minus underscore
keycode  62 = Shift_R
keycode  63 = KP_Multiply
keycode  64 = Alt_L
keycode  65 = space
keycode  66 = Caps_Lock
keycode  67 = F1
keycode  68 = F2
keycode  69 = F3
keycode  70 = F4
keycode  71 = F5
keycode  72 = F6
keycode  73 = F7
keycode  74 = F8
keycode  75 = F9
keycode  76 = F10
keycode  77 = Num_Lock
keycode  78 = Scroll_Lock
keycode  79 = Home KP_7 KP_7 Home
keycode  80 = Up KP_8 KP_8 Up
keycode  81 = Prior KP_9 KP_9 Prior
keycode  82 = KP_Subtract
keycode  83 = Left KP_4 KP_4 Left
keycode  84 = Begin KP_5 KP_5 Begin
keycode  85 = Right KP_6 KP_6 Right
keycode  86 = KP_Add
keycode  87 = End KP_1 KP_1 End
keycode  88 = Down KP_2 KP_2 Down
keycode  89 = Next KP_3 KP_3 Next
keycode  90 = Insert KP_0 KP_0 Insert
keycode  91 = Delete KP_Decimal KP_Decimal Delete
keycode  92 = 0x1007ff00
keycode  93 =
keycode  94 = less greater bar
keycode  95 = F11
keycode  96 = F12
keycode  97 = Home
keycode  98 = Up
keycode  99 = Prior
keycode 100 = Left
keycode 101 = Begin
keycode 102 = Right
```

```
keycode 103 = End
keycode 104 = Down
keycode 105 = Next
keycode 106 = Insert
keycode 107 = Delete
keycode 108 = KP_Enter
keycode 109 = Control_R
keycode 110 = Pause
keycode 111 = Print
keycode 112 = KP_Divide
keycode 113 = Mode_switch
keycode 114 = Break
```

Figure 8.6. German X11 keyboard layout adaptation

8.9   Configuration of X applications

Most X clients come with an *application defaults* file that is copied
into the X11 system region (`/usr/lib/X11/app-defaults`). This
file contains the important default settings for the application, such
as size, position, and color of graphical objects and error messages
in the respective country-specific language.

application defaults

Every application was assigned a class name by its programmer
that corresponds to the name of its resource file. Class names
always begin with a capital letter. Change the background color
of xterm (class name XTerm) in the file `/usr/lib/X11/app-
defaults/XTerm`.

class names

Various environment variables (XFILESEARCHPATH, XAP-
PLERESDIR) affect the search path for resource files. XFILE-
SEARCHPATH allows specification of multiple search paths delimited
by colons and handles several special characters as follows:

XFILESEARCHPATH

%C

value of customization resource (`*.customization`)

%L

language, local codeset

%l

language

%N

class name

%T

file type (`app-defaults`)

197

A useful definition of this variable could be as follows:

```
XFILESEARCHPATH=/usr/lib/X11/%T:/usr/local/%T/%N:$HOME/%T/%N
```

Resource files will now be searched for in three directories:

1. /usr/lib/X11/app-defaults/*class*
2. /usr/local/app-defaults/*class*
3. *home-directory*/app-defaults/*class*

xrdb   Another way to configure X11 applications is the command xrdb, which loads the passed resource file into one of the properties (RESOURCE_MANAGER or SCREEN_RESOURCES) of the X server.

property   A *property* is a global memory region in the X server that can be assigned a name. On launching of an X application, the resource manager evaluates the resource definitions contained in these properties. Configuring applications by means of resource properties particularly makes sense if applications are started on another computer and the local look and feel is to be affected. xrdb has a number of parameters:

-all
> Operation refers to both properties

-screen
> Operation refers only to the property SCREEN_RESOURCES

-global
> Operation refers only to the property RESOURCE_MANAGER

query
> Displays current contents of a property

merge *file*
> Merges contents of a file with a property

edit *file*
> Saves contents of a property to a file

remove
> Removes a complete property

load *file*
> Overwrites a property with contents of a file

In addition, users can create their own .Xdefaults files in their home directories and thus override the global default settings.

.Xdefaults

The following list gives an overview of the files and paths that are processed sequentially to determine the current widget attributes on starting an application. If a resource is assigned a value at more than one location, then only the last defined value applies.

widget attribute

- Within an application: Fallback resources
- Application-specific:
  1. /usr/lib/$LANG/app-defaults/*class*
  2. /usr/lib/X11/app-defaults/*class*
- New search path: $XFILESEARCHPATH
- User-specific:
  1. $XUSERFILESEARCHPATH
  2. $XAPPLRESDIR/$LANG/*class*
  3. $XAPPLRESDIR/*class*
  4. $HOME/$LANG/*class*
  5. $HOME/*class*
- Screen-specific: SCREEN_RESOURCES property (xrdb)
- Display-specific:
  1. RESOURCE_MANAGER property (xrdb)
  2. $HOME/.Xdefaults file
- Host-specific:
  1. $XENVIRONMENT variables
  2. $HOME/.Xdefaults-*hostname*
- Command line: Command-line options

Widget attributes

These resource values are represented in ASCII format. To distinguish them within a resource file, the programmer assigns each application a name (class), which seldom corresponds to the program file (instance). Likewise each widget and widget attribute that is externally configurable has a name and belongs to a class. To uniquely reference a widget, the name does not suffice. Instead, as with a file system, this requires a path that represents an excerpt from the widget hierarchy.

resource values

widget path

wildcards

     To allow manipulation of the attributes of multiple widgets simultaneously, wildcards (?, *) are permitted in the path. The following is the exact syntax of the resource specification:

```
object.subobject[.subobject...].attribute: value
```

The individual elements have the following meanings:

object
> class or name of program

subobject
> class or name of widget

attribute
> resource name

value
> value

.
> delimiter

*
> wildcard, any number of, or no, names

?
> wildcard, any individual name

attribute

     The first column of the resource file specifies the attribute to be manipulated. This usually corresponds to a widget resource. However, the programmer can define new, application-specific resources. The hierarchy and the names of the available resources can be taken from the respective Manual page. Example of a resource file:

```
Xterm*background:       gray90
XTerm*ScrollBar:        true
XTerm*Foreground:       white
XTerm*Background:       gray20
XTerm*IconName:         XTerm
XTerm*WaitForMap:       true
XTerm*MarginBell:       false
XTerm*JumpScroll:       true
```

Likewise, individual widget attributes can be collected into class es. Making use of class identifiers can make a resource file significantly shorter and more readable. The attributes `cursorColor` and `pointerColor` of `xterms` both belong to the class `Foreground`. Therefore the following:

```
XTerm*foreground:        green
XTerm*cursorColor:       green
XTerm*pointerColor:      green
```

can be abbreviated as:

```
xterm*Foreground:        green
```

Releases 5 and 6 of the X Window System contain an interactive resource manager (`editres`) that permits comfortable manipulation of all resource values of a running program and saves them on demand to an ASCII file. It is particularly noteworthy that this can be done at run time. Thus the user gets immediate feedback on the effects of changes. Unfortunately, the `editres` protocol is not yet supported by all widget sets, which naturally restricts the use of the tool. The generated ASCII files can easily be integrated into available resource files or appended to the `.Xdefaults` file.

editres

protocol

Configuration of the window manager

The user can configure not just the look of individual applications, but of most X window managers as well. Since many Linux users probably use `fvwm`, we go into detail only on this window manager. The parameters of this window manager are set in the file `system.fvwmrc` in the directory `/usr/lib/X11/fvwm`. Alternatively, each user can provide a file named `.fvwmrc` in the user's home directory.

fvwm

Using the M4 preprocessor provides additional flexibility. This allows linking additional configuration files or testing conditions, for example. The main file (`system.fvwmrc`) thus becomes relatively comprehensible (Figure 8.7)

M4 preprocessor

```
###############################################################
#
# system.fvwmrc - fvwm configuration
#
###############################################################
# Paths

ModulePath  /usr/lib/X11/fvwm/modules
PixmapPath  /usr/lib/X11/pixmaps:/usr/local/lib/pixmaps
IconPath    /usr/include/X11/bitmaps/

###############################################################
# External configuration files

include(/usr/lib/X11/fvwm/fvwm.options)

include(/usr/lib/X11/fvwm/fvwm.menus)

include(/usr/lib/X11/fvwm/fvwm.functions)

include(/usr/lib/X11/fvwm/fvwm.bindings)

include(/usr/lib/X11/fvwm/fvwm.styles)

include(/usr/lib/X11/fvwm/fvwm.goodstuff)

include(/usr/lib/X11/fvwm/fvwm.modules)

###############################################################
# Initialization and restart function

Function "InitFunction"
    Module  "I"    GoodStuff
    Module  "I"    FvwmPager 0 1
    Exec    "I"    exec xterm -sb -sl 400 -geometry +75+390 &
    Exec    "I"    xsetroot -solid LightSlateGray
EndFunction

Function "RestartFunction"
    Module  "I"    GoodStuff
    Exec    "I"    xsetroot -solid LightSlateGray
    Module  "I"    FvwmPager 0 1
EndFunction
```

Figure 8.7. `system.fvwmrc`

fvwm.options

In addition to color and font definitions, the file `fvwm.options` contains a number of other options that determine the look and feel.

```
###############################################################
#
# fvwm.options - general options
#

DeskTopSize 2x2
DeskTopScale 32

# Standard colors
StdForeColor        Black
StdBackColor        #d3d3d3

# Window colors
HiForeColor         Black
HiBackColor         #5f9ea0
StickyForeColor     Black
```

```
StickyBackColor         #60c0a0

# Menu colors
MenuForeColor           Black
MenuBackColor           grey
MenuStippleColor        SlateGrey

# Fonts
Font                    -adobe-helvetica-medium-r-*-*-12-*-*-*-*-*-*-*
WindowFont              -adobe-helvetica-bold-r-*-*-12-*-*-*-*-*-*-*
IconFont                fixed

# Rectangles in which icons are positioned
IconBox 5 -80 -140 -5
IconBox 5 -160 -140 -85
IconBox 5 -240 -140 -165
IconBox 5 -320 -140 -245

# Motif look and feel
MWMFunctionHints
MWMHintOverride
MWMDecorHints
MWMBorders
MWMButtons

# Moves all windows with contents
OpaqueMove 100

# Suppress automatic desktop change
EdgeScroll 0 0

# Delay in changing desktop section
EdgeResistance 250 50

NoPPosition

# Automatic positioning of new window
RandomPlacement

# Forces decoration in transient shell
DecorateTransients
```

Figure 8.8. `fvwm.options`

The user can create new menus and assign them to a user action.   fvwm.menus

```
###############################################################
#
# fvwm.menus - Menu configuration
#
Popup "Shells"
        Title    "Shells"
        Exec     "MXterm"           exec mxterm &
        Exec     "Color XTerm"      exec color_xterm &
        Exec     "Rxvt"             exec rxvt &
EndPopup

Popup "Editors"
        Title    "Editors"
        Exec     "GNU emacs"        exec emacs &
        Exec     "NEdit"            exec nedit &
        Exec     "Textedit"         exec textedit &
EndPopup

Popup "Graphics"
        Title    "Graphics / Viewer"
```

```
        Exec    "XPaint"          exec xpaint &
        Exec    "XV"              exec xv &
EndPopup

Popup "Modules"
        Title   "Modules"
        Module  "GoodStuff"       GoodStuff
        Module  "Identify"        FvwmIdent
        Module  "SaveDesktop"     FvwmSave
        Module  "Pager"           FvwmPager 0 1
        Module  "FvwmWinList"     FvwmWinList
        Module  "FvwmIconBox"     FvwmIconBox
EndPopup

Popup "Window Ops"
        Title   "Window Ops      "
        Move    "&Move   Alt+F7"
        Resize  "&Size   Alt+F8"
        Lower   "&Lower Alt+F3"
        Raise   "Raise   "
        Stick   "(Un)Stick       "
        Iconify "(Un)Mi&nimize  Alt+F9"
        Maximize "(Un)Ma&ximize Alt+F10"
        Maximize "(Un)Maximize Vertical "  0 100
        Nop     "  "
        Destroy "&Kill  Alt+F4"
        Delete  "Delete "
EndPopup

Popup "Window Ops2"
        Move    "&Move   Alt+F7"
        Resize  "&Size   Alt+F8"
        Iconify "(Un)Mi&nimize  Alt+F9"
        Maximize "(Un)Ma&ximize Alt+F10"
        Lower   "&Lower Alt+F3"
        Nop     "  "
        Destroy "&Kill  Alt+F4"
        Delete  "Delete "
        Nop     "  "
        Module          "ScrollBar"    FvwmScroll 2 2
EndPopup

#############################################################
# Mainmenu

Popup "Programs"
        Title   "Programs"
        Exec    "Xterm"           exec xterm -sb -sl 400 &
        Popup   "Shells"          Shells
        Popup   "Editors"         Editors
        Popup   "Graphics"        Graphics
        Popup   "Modules"         Modules
        Exec    "Screen Lock"     exec xlock &
        Nop     "  "
        Restart "Restart Fvwm"    fvwm
        Quit    "Exit"
EndPopup
```

Figure 8.9. fvwm.menus

Within the configuration file of fvwm, new functions can be defined that are usually assigned to a keyboard or mouse action.

```
#############################################################
#
# fvwm.functions - function definition
```

```
#
Function "Move-or-Raise"
        Move            "Motion"
        Raise           "Motion"
        Raise           "Click"
        RaiseLower      "DoubleClick"
EndFunction

Function "maximize_func"
        Maximize        "Motion" 0 100
        Maximize        "Click" 0 80
        Maximize        "DoubleClick" 100 100
EndFunction

Function "window_ops_func"
        PopUp   "Click"         Window Ops2
        PopUp   "Motion"        Window Ops2
EndFunction

Function "Move-or-Lower"
        Move            "Motion"
        Lower           "Motion"
        Lower           "Click"
        RaiseLower      "DoubleClick"
EndFunction

Function "Move-or-Iconify"
        Move            "Motion"
        Iconify         "DoubleClick"
EndFunction

Function "Resize-or-Raise"
        Resize          "Motion"
        Raise           "Motion"
        Raise           "Click"
        RaiseLower      "DoubleClick"
EndFunction
```

Figure 8.10. `fvwm.functions`

The file `fvwm.bindings` contains the mappings between mouse and keyboard actions and the associated actions.

`fvwm.bindings`

```
##############################################################
#
# fvwm.bindings - keyboard- and mouse configuration
#
# Structure of a configuration line:
#
#       <key>       <context> <modifier> <function>
#
#       <key>       (mouse) key
#       <context>   R - root window
#                   W - application window
#                   T - title bar
#                   S - window sides
#                   F - window frame
#                   I - icon
#                   A - everything but title bar
#                   0,1,2,... - window element
#       <modifier>  N - no modifier key
#                   A - alternate
#                   C - control
#                   M - meta
```

```
#                       S - shift
#                       mod1-mod5 - X11 modifiers
#           <function>  fvwm function
#

# mouse click on root window
Mouse 1  R       A      PopUp "Programs"
Mouse 2  R       A      PopUp "Window Ops"
Mouse 3  R       A      Module "FvwmWinList" FvwmWinList Transient

# window element
Mouse 0  1       A      Function "window_ops_func"
Mouse 0  2       A      Function "maximize_func"
Mouse 0  4       A      Iconify
Mouse 1  F       A      Function "Resize-or-Raise"
Mouse 1  TS      A      Function "Move-or-Raise"

# icon actions
Mouse 1  I       A      Function "Move-or-Iconify"
Mouse 2  I       A      Iconify

# window operations
Mouse 2  FST     A      Function "window_ops_func"
Mouse 3  TSIF    A      RaiseLower

# keyboard shortcut
Key F1   A       M      Popup "Window Ops"
Key F2   A       M      Popup "Programs"
Key F3   A       M      Lower
Key F4   A       M      Destroy
Key F5   A       M      CirculateUp
Key F6   A       M      CirculateDown
Key F7   A       M      Move
Key F8   A       M      Resize
Key F9   A       M      Iconify
Key F10  A       M      Maximize
```

Figure 8.11. fvwm.bindings

fvwm.styles The file fvwm.styles establishes the look and feel of individual applications.

```
##################################################################
#
# fvwm.styles - Style configuration
#
Style "*"           BorderWidth 7, HandleWidth 5
Style "FvwmPager"   Sticky, NoTitle
Style "FvwmBanner"  StaysOnTop
Style "GoodStuff"   Sticky, WindowListSkip, NoTitle
Style "xterm"       Icon terminal.xpm
Style "xcalc"       Icon rcalc.xpm
Style "xman"        Icon xman.xpm
Style "xvgr"        Icon graphs.xpm
Style "Mail"        Icon sndmail.xpm
Style "emacs*"      Icon editor2.xpm
```

Figure 8.12. fvwm.styles

fvwm.modules Each of the fvwm modules has its own configuration possibilities, which are summarized in the file fvwm.modules.

```
##############################################################
#
# fvwm.modules - Module configuration
#

#################### Window identifier ######################
*FvwmIdentBack MidnightBlue
*FvwmIdentFore Yellow
*FvwmIdentFont -adobe-helvetica-medium-r-*-*-12-*-*-*-*-*-*-*

#################### FvwmWinList ############################
*FvwmWinListBack #d3d3d3
*FvwmWinListFore Black
*FvwmWinListFont -adobe-helvetica-bold-r-*-*-10-*-*-*-*-*-*-*
*FvwmWinListAction Click1 Iconify -1,Focus
*FvwmWinListAction Click2 Iconify
*FvwmWinListAction Click3 Module "FvwmIdent" FvwmIdent
*FvwmWinListUseSkipList
*FvwmWinListGeometry +0-1

######################## FvwmIconBox #########################
*FvwmIconBoxIconBack    #cfcfcf
*FvwmIconBoxIconHiFore   black
*FvwmIconBoxIconHiBack   #5f9ea0
*FvwmIconBoxBack    #cfcfcf
*FvwmIconBoxFore    blue
*FvwmIconBoxGeometry    1x5+0+89
*FvwmIconBoxMaxIconSize 64x38
*FvwmIconBoxFont    -adobe-helvetica-medium-r-*-*-12-*-*-*-*-*-*-*
*FvwmIconBoxSortIcons
*FvwmIconBoxPadding    4
*FvwmIconBoxLines    10
*FvwmIconBoxPlacement        Top Left
#
# mouse bindings
#
*FvwmIconBoxMouse    1        Click        RaiseLower
*FvwmIconBoxMouse    1        DoubleClick  Iconify
*FvwmIconBoxMouse    2        Click        Iconify -1, Focus
*FvwmIconBoxMouse    3        Click        Module "FvwmIdent"
ndings
#
# Key bindings
#
*FvwmIconBoxKey      r        RaiseLower
*FvwmIconBoxKey      space    Iconify
*FvwmIconBoxKey      d        Close
#
# FvwmIconBox built-in functions
#
*FvwmIconBoxKey      n        Next
*FvwmIconBoxKey      p        Prev
*FvwmIconBoxKey      h        Left
*FvwmIconBoxKey      j        Down
*FvwmIconBoxKey      k        Up
*FvwmIconBoxKey      l        Right
#
# Icon file specifications
#
*FvwmIconBox    "*"            unknown1.xpm
*FvwmIconBox    "Mosaic"       www-shape.xpm
*FvwmIconBox    "xterm"        terminal.xpm
*FvwmIconBox    "GoodStuff"    toolbox.xpm
*FvwmIconBox    "*ircon*"      daffy.xpm
*FvwmIconBox    "*anual*"      xman.xpm

######################## Pager ############################
*FvwmPagerBack #908090
*FvwmPagerFore #484048
*FvwmPagerFont -adobe-helvetica-bold-r-*-*-10-*-*-*-*-*-*-*
```

```
*FvwmPagerHilight #cab3ca
*FvwmPagerGeometry 0+0
*FvwmPagerLabel 0 Strobel
*FvwmPagerLabel 1 Uhl
*FvwmPagerSmallFont 5x8
```

Figure 8.13. fvwm.modules

fvwm.goodstuff

The configuration of the GoodStuff module resides in its own file, named fvwm.goodstuff. GoodStuff enables including the most important applications in an icon bar. A click on an icon launches the corresponding program. The Swallow option enables depicting programs like xload and xclock in the icon bar.

```
##############################################################
#
# fvwm.goodstuff - Goodstuff . configuration

*GoodStuffBack gray60
*GoodStuffGeometry 65x715-1+0
*GoodStuffColumns 1
*GoodStuffFont -adobe-helvetica-medium-r-*-*-12-*-*-*-*-*-*-*

#        Name      Icon          Action  WindowTitle command

*GoodStuff " "      " "           Swallow "xclock"    xclock -bg gray60 &
*GoodStuff " "      " "           Swallow "xload"     xload -bg gray60 &
*GoodStuff " "      " "           Swallow "xbiff"     xbiff -bg gray60 &
*GoodStuff XTerm    terminal.xpm  Exec "xterm"        xterm -sb -sl 400 &
*GoodStuff NetScape www.xpm       Exec "Netscape"     netscape &
*GoodStuff Xman     xman.xpm      Exec "Manual Page"  xman -bothshow -notopbox &
*GoodStuff Mail     sndmail.xpm   Exec "Mail"         xterm -T Mail -e pine &
*GoodStuff Emacs    editor.xpm    Exec "emacs"        emacs &
*GoodStuff Exit     lbolt.xpm     Quit
```

Figure 8.14. fvwm.goodstuff

system.fvwmrc

The above classification of the fvwm configuration is not absolutely necessary. However, it does add some structure to the otherwise incomprehensible configuration file system.fvwmrc.

## Chapter 9

Networking

A significant aspect in the discussion of modern workstations and their operating systems centers around networking capability, that is, the possibility to integrate the system into an existing network.

The complete development of Linux would have been impossible without the Internet. Thus even very early versions of the kernel included TCP/IP and the necessary drivers for PC network boards.

Internet

This chapter presents the basics of networking and describes the configuration of lower network levels. Since discussing all the details of TCP/IP would lead far beyond the scope of this book, we have simplified some of the issues. For further information we refer to the RFCs (see Section 9.2) and the numerous books on TCP/IP and network administration dealing exclusively with this subject.

basics

RFC

9.1 Network hardware

Connecting to a network requires little in the way of hardware: two computers can be connected in an elementary local area network (LAN) with two simple Ethernet boards, a piece of thin Ethernet cable, two T-connectors, and two terminal resistors. This makes networking affordable even for private users. Linux supports various pocket adapters and Arcnet boards as well as drivers for nearly all the popular Ethernet boards. You can connect computers at even less cost using a parallel or serial cable and modems. Special protocols like SLIP, CSLIP, PPP, and PLIP support such networking.

LAN
Ethernet

SLIP; PPP

209

9.2   TCP/IP

TCP/IP   The de facto standard for networking UNIX computers is TCP/IP, a protocol that was developed for the Internet in the early 1970s and has since become available for almost all computer platforms. The history of TCP/IP is closely connected to that of the Internet, so these two subjects are usually treated together.

History

ARPA   TCP/IP evolved as a protocol for ARPA NET (later DARPANET and
Internet   then Internet), which at the time primarily interconnected American universities. The network was commissioned and financed by the Advanced Research Project Agency. This U.S. government agency was involved primarily in military projects; hence it is no surprise that TCP/IP was also declared as the standard of the U.S. Department of Defense. Meanwhile the Internet has grown to include many subnetworks worldwide.

RFCs

TCP/IP is not a standard like those of ANSI, ISO, and IEEE, but
information   a manufacturer-independent definition that is available to everyone in the form of a Request for Comment (RFC). An RFC is usually a description of a protocol or a proposal for a new protocol. Not every RFC is a standard, however. Many have a more informal
e-mail   character. RFCs are available via FTP or e-mail from an RFC archive or from many other FTP servers. In Germany, for instance, this is `ftp.uni-stuttgart.de`, where the RFCs are listed in the directory `/pub/doc/standards/rfc`. You can also retrieve RFCs via e-mail from the official RFC archive of the InterNIC (`ds.internic.net`). To do this, you send a message with the contents `help` to the address `mailserv@ds.internic.net`. The server usually responds within half an hour with a description and detailed instructions.

Structure

four levels   TCP/IP essentially consists of four *levels*, which, with some
ISO/OSI layers   deviations, correspond to today's standard ISO/OSI Reference Model

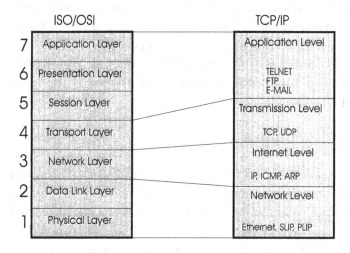

Figure 9.1. Correspondence of ISO/OSI layers and TCP/IP levels

(Figure 9.1). The lowest-level is termed the network level and corresponds to *layers* one and two of the ISO/OSI Reference Model. As a rule, Ethernet is used at this level.

network level

The second level is the Internet level with its Internet Protocol (IP). This level approximates the ISO/OSI layer three. This layer enables the transfer of data packets (datagrams) independently of the actual network that makes the connection. On this level, networking software identifies a computer by its unique IP address. The third level corresponds to ISO/OSI layer four and offers TCP and UDP protocols. TCP stands for Transmission Control Protocol and makes a virtual connection, while UDP means User Datagram Protocol and offers a simple packet service.

Internet level

protocol level

The fourth level of TCP/IP covers ISO/OSI layers five to seven and is termed the application level. While levels one to three are normally components of the operating system (in Linux they are part of the kernel), level four consists of normal programs. The simplest and most propagated services on this level are telnet for the virtual terminal, FTP for transferring files, and e-mail for transferring electronic correspondence. Telnet and FTP exist as programs of the

application level

telnet, FTP, and e-mail

same respective names that the user can launch directly. E-mail is supported from the TCP/IP end with only a simple transfer mechanism that is used by various other programs.

In the following we will describe primarily the lower levels of TCP/IP in greater detail. The next chapter is devoted to Internet and other applications.

9.3   IP

data packets

The Internet Protocol (IP) transports data packets between network interfaces, usually of different computers. Data that is sent by a higher protocol, such as TCP, goes to the IP level, where it is packed in IP

routing

packets. Based on its routing table, the IP level makes a decision about where to actually send the packets and passes them on to the appropriate network level accordingly. We will illustrate this with an example after the following explanation of the basic concepts.

Addresses

In a network connection with TCP/IP, each network interface of a computer receives an IP address that is unique worldwide. The address consists of four numbers between 0 and 255, separated by periods, for example, 141.7.1.40. This address consists of a network

network and
host address

component and a host address. It must be set when the computer is started up.

For small private networks that lack connections to other networks, the IP address is relatively insignificant; users can select

default values

them at will or assume the default values suggested by the installation program. Here it is only important to assure unambiguity within the local-area network.

Network classes

The IP addresses are important when setting up an Internet connection. The Network Information Center (NIC) assigns one or more network addresses for the new connection. These addresses

network classes

belong to one of the classes A, B, or C, (Figure 9.2) and consist of 1, 2, or 3 bytes, depending on the class. The first bits of an address indicate the class to which the address belongs. The network address

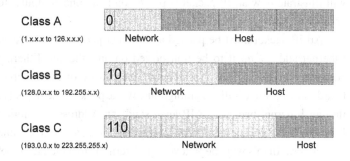

Figure 9.2. Network classes

constitutes the start of the IP address. The local network administrator can assign the remaining bits. In a class C network, the IP addresses consist of an officially determined network address with 3 bytes and a local component with 1 byte. Since addresses ending with 0 or 255 have a special meaning, a class C network can encompass up to 254 IP addresses. Aside from the classes A, B, and C, there are also class D and E addresses. These are reserved for multicasting and extensions.

0 and 255

The local component of the IP address can be either used directly for addressing the individual machine or divided into a subnetwork address and a host address by means of a network mask. However, we do not discuss the use of subnetworks further here. Details can be found in RFC 950.

subnetworks

network mask

Loopback device

Even for computers that do not actually possess a network interface there is a virtual interface named *loopback*. As its name suggests, everything that is output via this interface is input again directly. This allows TCP/IP connections for a machine to itself. Thus the TCP/IP programs can be used even without a network interface. The IP address of the loopback interface is usually 127.0.0.1.

virtual interface

loopback address

ARP

We briefly explain addressing at the network level in order to provide better understanding of the following section. An Ethernet example

Ethernet

213

will illustrate how an IP packet is passed on from one computer to another.

An IP packet must be packed as Ethernet packets and have an Ethernet address on it to be transported on an Ethernet. Ethernet addresses are determined directly in the hardware of the Ethernet boards and are universally unambiguous. While packing the IP packet into an Ethernet packet, the IP level sends an Address Resolution Protocol (ARP) packet as a broadcast to all computers in the same subnetwork. In this way the IP level can determine to which Ethernet address the packet should be sent. You could interpret the ARP broadcast as a question like this: "Please respond if you know the Ethernet address of the interface with the IP address a.b.c.d." If the desired address is in the same subnetwork, the appropriate computer will respond with an ARP reply communicating the Ethernet address. The first computer can then pack the IP packet in a correctly addressed Ethernet packet and send it.

Ethernet addresses

ARP

ARP broadcast

ARP reply

Routing

Not only the Internet, but even large companies and universities do not consist of only a single Ethernet to which all computers are directly connected. Rather, they consist of many heterogeneous partial segments connected via repeaters, bridges, and routers.

Since IP should be independent of the network levels used beneath it, packets can only be directly addressed from computer A to computer B, for instance, with an Ethernet address if A and B are in the same physical subnetwork. If two computers are separated by one or more routers, then communication must go via the routers. This means that packets on the network level must be addressed to the router. Every computer needs to know whether the target address is in the same subnetwork when addressing an IP packet. If the target address is in the same subnetwork, the computer can get the Ethernet address with an ARP request and send the packet directly. If the address is in a different subnetwork, then the computer must address the packet to the appropriate router's Ethernet address. In addition, one computer can have several network interfaces and thus be connected to several subnetworks simultaneously. The computer

repeater, bridge, and router

router

ARP request

therefore also needs to find out to which interface a particular packet should be sent.

This decision is called *routing*, and it is made by every computer and the designated routers. The IP level is equipped with a table of network or host addresses and an interface, or the address of the next router. A special entry, the *default route*, specifies to whom packets are to be forwarded when they do not fall under any of the other rules.

routing

A Linux computer as router

To employ a Linux computer as a router, compile the kernel with the option CONFIG_IP_FORWARD. Normal kernels drop IP packets that are addressed to outside IP addresses; router kernels forward these packets based on the routing table. A Linux router requires no further preparations.

Example

This example starts with a class B network, which is divided by a network mask into further subnetworks. The officially designated network address is 141.7.0.0, and the network mask used is 255.255.255.0. Three bytes are available for addressing the network and 1 byte for addressing the individual computer in the subnetwork. The configuration of the IP address on startup of the computer determines the network mask. A Linux PC working as a router contains two network boards and is connected to the subnetworks 141.7.1.0 and 141.7.11.0. It establishes the connection between these two subnetworks. The addresses of the respective network interfaces are 141.7.11.1 and 141.7.1.41. Figure 9.3 demonstrates this example.

network mask
network address

The Linux router's routing table contains the following entries:

target	gateway	interface
141.7.11.0	*	eth0
141.7.1.0	*	eth1
default	FH router	eth0

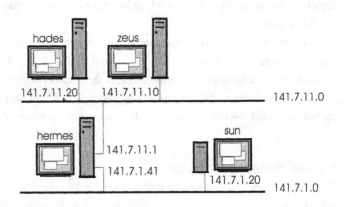

Figure 9.3. Network example

The router is directly connected to the two subnetworks 141.7.11.0 and 141.7.1.0. It cannot reach other IP addresses directly. The default route entry determines that packets for other addresses are passed on to the central FH Heilbronn router. The network mask for its two interfaces, eth0 and eth1, is 255.255.255.0.

default route

The routing table for the other computer in the 141.7.11.0 subnetwork contains the following entries:

routing table

target	gateway	interface
141.7.11.0	*	eth0
default	141.7.11.1	eth0

This table determines that the computer can send packets only to other computers in the same subnetwork. Other packets are sent to the Linux router at address 141.7.11.1.

same subnetwork

If a computer with address 141.7.11.10 sends a packet to the computer with the address 141.7.11.20, then the network masks and the routing entries determine to which address and via which interface the packet will actually be forwarded. The network mask 255.255.255.0 compares only the first three bytes of the IP address with the routing table entries. Thus 141.7.11.20 and 141.7.11.0 match.

The routing entry states that the target address can be reached directly via the interface eth0. If the Ethernet address for 141.7.11.20 is still unknown, then the computer sends out an ARP broadcast to all the other computers in its subnetwork and asks for the Ethernet address for 141.7.11.20. The target computer will respond with its own Ethernet address in an ARP reply. The computer with the address 141.7.11.10 can then pack its IP packet in an Ethernet packet and send it directly to the receiver.

target address

Ethernet packet

The process becomes more complicated when a packet is sent to a different subnetwork. The sending computer finds an entry in its routing table with a gateway address. Then it must attempt to find out the gateway's Ethernet address in order to send the packet there. The gateway, which is the Linux router in this example, receives the Ethernet packet and unpacks it. When the gateway determines that the IP packet it has received is actually directed to a different address, it attempts to send the packet on using its routing table.

gateway address

Configuration

We describe the configuration of a PC in the subnetwork 141.7.11.0 as in the previous example. First configure the network interfaces with the command ifconfig. Then determine the IP address, the network mask, and the broadcast address for each interface. Use the broadcast address to send packets to all the computers in the same subnetwork. In the simplest case and in our example, this is the network address ending with 255 instead of 0, i.e., 141.7.11.255. You will find details on the parameters and the invocation of ifconfig on the appropriate manual page.

ifconfig

The drivers list the names of the available network interfaces with the booting process. Some common names are, for example, eth0 for Ethernet, lo0 for loopback, or sl0 for the first serial interface for SLIP.

interface names

You should use numbers between 2 and 253 for the last byte of addresses for normal computers in a subnetwork. The numbers 1 and 254 are usually reserved for routers, and the numbers 0 and 255 are assigned to network or broadcast addresses.

routing table

Once you have configured the interfaces, you must make the entries in the internal routing table of the kernel which records which addresses can be reached via which interfaces. Do this with the command route.

rc.inet1

The example below shows the script /etc/rc.d/rc.inet1, which makes the necessary settings for a computer with the IP address 141.7.11.10.

```
HOSTNAME=stef1

# Activate loopback
/sbin/ifconfig lo 127.0.0.1
/sbin/route add net 127.0.0.0

# Parameters for this computer:
IPADDR="193.48.121.37"
NETMASK="255.255.255.0"
NETWORK="193.48.121.0"
BROADCAST="193.48.121.255"
GATEWAY="193.48.121.1"

# Activate Ethernet interface
/sbin/ifconfig eth0 ${IPADDR} broadcast ${BROADCAST} netmask ${NETMASK}

# Routing for the local network
/sbin/route add net ${NETWORK} netmask ${NETMASK}

# Routing for other addresses via the router
/sbin/route add default gw ${GATEWAY} metric 1
```

Testing connections

After the network interface has been configured with ifconfig and the necessary routing information has been entered, the connection test can be test ed. The help program ping is frequently used for this. It sends small data packets at regular intervals to the target machine, which then responds.

```
linux0:/home/tul> ping linux1
PING linux1.openconcepts.com (192.0.2.130): 56 data bytes
64 bytes from 192.0.2.130: icmp_seq=0 ttl=119 time=2 ms
64 bytes from 192.0.2.130: icmp_seq=1 ttl=120 time=1 ms
64 bytes from 192.0.2.130: icmp_seq=2 ttl=121 time=1 ms
64 bytes from 192.0.2.130: icmp_seq=3 ttl=122 time=1 ms
64 bytes from 192.0.2.130: icmp_seq=4 ttl=123 time=1 ms

--- linux1.openconcepts.com ping statistics ---
5 packets transmitted, 5 packets received, 0% packet loss
round-trip min/avg/max = 1/1/2 ms
linux0:/home/tul>
```

This also allows the assessment of the transmission speed. Network configuration should proceed only after the connection has been tested successfully with `ping`. If `ping` detects problems, the settings of the parameters can be tested and controlled with the commands `ifconfig` and `netstat`. If `ifconfig` is invoked without options, it outputs the status of all the network interfaces. Some Linux distributions use a `netstat` command that recognizes the option `-i`.

ping

```
zeus:/root# ifconfig
lo        IP ADDR 127.0.0.1 BCAST 127.255.255.255 NETMASK 255.0.0.0
          MTU 2000 METRIC 0 POINT-TO-POINT ADDR 0.0.0.0
          FLAGS: 0x004B ( UP BROADCAST LOOPBACK RUNNING )

eth0      IP ADDR 194.45.197.100 BCAST 194.45.197.255 NETMASK 255.255.255.0
          MTU 1500 METRIC 0 POINT-TO-POINT ADDR 0.0.0.0
          FLAGS: 0x0043 ( UP BROADCAST RUNNING )
```

You can display the routing table of the kernel by invoking the command `route` without options or the `netstat` command with the option `-r`.

```
zeus:/root# netstat -r
Kernel routing table
Destination net/address   Gateway address   Flags RefCnt    Use Iface
141.7.11.0                *                 UN        0   47854 eth0
127.0.0.0                 *                 UN        0       0 lo
default                   hermes            UGN       0    4070 eth0
```

Firewall features

A *firewall* is a set of measures, software packages, behaviors, chipcards, people, configurations, shell scripts, monitoring cameras, ideas, and paranoia that collectively serve to protect your own computer or your computer network from intruders (hackers) on the Internet. Hackers intrude into others' computer systems in part out of sporting ambition, but sometimes also to damage computer installations or to access classified data (an exciting and informative story can be found in Clifford Stoll's classic *Cuckoo's Egg* [29]). The basis of a firewall is a clearly defined *policy*, where the goal is not maximum security (which is achieved simply by decoupling from the network), but an optimal compromise between security, economy, and comfort. Thus the Linux kernel contains no firewall as such, but several tools that support the realization of firewalls. The construction and operation of a firewall requires professional

firewall

Hackers

policy

optimal compromise

219

expertise and complete familiarity with system administration and the operating system.

Packet filters One of the most important firewall tools is the IP packet filter. Every IP packet contains the number of the next highest protocol level (e.g., TCP or UDP) and a port number (which in combination with the protocol number specifies the receiver on the respective host). Many Internet services use fixed protocols and ports. The mail daemon, e.g., receives arriving mail on TCP port 25.

packet denial

Packet filters can be configured so that they deny certain IP packets based on protocol and port rather than forwarding them. If a router denies all IP packets addressed to TCP port 25 of a computer in a LAN, then no computer in the LAN can receive mail—even if someone has started a mail daemon in violation of security policy.

services = risks

Here you need to know that each Internet service (such as e-mail) that the LAN provides represents more or less of a security risk—the more powerful the service and the more extensive the underlying protocol, the greater the risk. For this reason, one could refuse to forward mail arriving from the Internet to certain computers, but collect it centrally on a particularly carefully maintained mail server that might communicate with the rest of the LAN only through a firewall.

The packet filter must be included in the kernel by selecting the option IP_FIREWALL. In this context we also recommend the option IP_ALWAYS_DEFRAG, with which the kernel reassembles

packet defragmentation

fragmented packet defragmentation before forwarding them (see Section 9.3). CONFIG_IP_FIREWALL_VERBOSE causes the packet filter to log information on delivered packets (per klogd).

configuration
lists of rules

The packet filter is configured with the help of the package ipfwadm.* Under Linux there are three lists of rules: Input (arriving IP packets for local processes), Output (outgoing IP packets), and Forward (packets between other hosts that need to be routed). A single rule includes the following specifications:

policy
    accept (forward) or deny (throw away)

---

*ftp://ftp.xos.nl/pub/linux/ipfwadm/

protocol

> TCP, UDP, ICMP, or all

source

> IP address of source and source port

destination

> IP address of destination and destination port

interface

> Network interface on which the packet arrived (e.g., eth0).
> Source IP addresses in packets can be manipulated; only   bogus IP address
> the distinction by arrival interface can decide with certainty
> whether the packet came from the LAN or the Internet.

The following is a configuration example for a router that connects a LAN (Class C subnet 141.7.11.*) with the outside world.

```
#!/bin/sh

lan=141.7.11.0/255.255.255.0
mailserver=141.7.11.2
all=0.0.0.0/0.0.0.0

# Our IP address on LAN
lan_ip=141.7.11.1

# Our IP address on Internet
inet_ip=141.7.1.42

# Incoming mail only to our mail server...
ipfwadm -F -a accept -P tcp -S $all          -D $mailserver 25 -V $inet_ip
ipfwadm -F -a accept -P tcp -S $mailserver 25 -D $all -V $inet_ip

# ...nowhere else
ipfwadm -F -a deny -P tcp -D $lan 25 -S $all -V $inet_ip -o

# Permit mail to outside
ipfwadm -F -a accept -P tcp -S $lan    -D $all 25 -V $lan_ip
ipfwadm -F -a accept -P tcp -S $all 25 -D $lan    -V $lan_ip    # DANGER

# Display result (-e displays interfaces as well)
ipfwadm -F -l
```

This produces the following output:

```
golem:~> ./setup_fw
IP firewall forward rules, default policy: accept
typ prot source              destination          ports
acc tcp  anywhere            141.7.11.2           any -> smtp
acc tcp  141.7.11.2          anywhere             smtp -> any
den tcp  anywhere            141.7.11.0/24        any -> smtp
acc tcp  141.7.11.0/24       anywhere             any -> smtp
acc tcp  anywhere            141.7.11.0/24        smtp -> any
```

The option -o causes the kernel to display log messages if a packet matches the defined rules. In addition to the use of ipfwadm, this example also demonstrates the tricks of the IP packet filter: the last rule is marked with DANGER. If a local host sends mail to an outside server, then this server responds to the various steps of the protocol with small status reports, which naturally also must pass the firewall. Which port the mail server occupies is not clear, however; the replies on outside port 25 could just as well be output from a hacker tool that makes the local mail program carry out unforeseeable actions. This danger can still be handled, but various other defense mechanisms cannot be realized with packet filters.

IP filter handicaps

ipfwadm also has other purposes: the configuration of the IP accounting (activated with CONFIG_IP_ACCT) and IP masquerading (CONFIG_IP_MASQUERADE).

IP accounting

A basic introduction to packet filters and firewalls would by far exceed the scope of this book; this section is only intended to introduce the Linux-specific details and to give some first impressions. More information on firewalls can be found in the book by Cheswick and Bellovin [3].

IP masquerading Let L be a host in the LAN and A another host somewhere on the Internet. The router R between them masks L so that A has the impression that it is exchanging packets with R; from A's viewpoint, L is invisible. However, R inserts its own IP address in packets from L to A and directs packets from A to itself on to L. However, this procedure cannot easily be applied to every protocol and often requires additional provisions (e.g., for FTP sessions).

Masquerading can have two purposes: First, the supply of 32-bit IP addresses of IP version 4 will soon be exhausted—it is becoming increasingly difficult and expensive to reserve large IP address spaces for a local network. Thus unofficially within some LANs IP addresses of outside address spaces are being assigned to local computers. Naturally packets with such addresses must not leave the LAN since they would otherwise be delivered to the rightful owners of the addresses. Thus the router must practice IP masquerading.

dangers

Second, masquerading is often used in the realm of packet filtering in firewalls. Cheswick and Bellovin [3] advise against masquerading—if packets with borrowed addresses reach the Internet, this can introduce confusion into routing tables and have other dangerous effects.

Transparent proxies A proxy is first of all a popular all-purpose term, and second a process on a computer between a client and a server that monitors, protocols, influences, or even censors their communication—usually as a security proxy in a firewall (but also as WWW proxy for central WWW caches). Traditional proxies often require troublesome reconfiguration or even reinstallation of communication software (e.g., for SOCKS).

classical proxies

Transparent proxies are the newest toys of security gurus: At the firewall such an invisible proxy autonomously switches itself into the connection to prevent testing of security-critical services or other suspicious actions. Packets arriving at a certain port are redirected to another port where this proxy resides. Redirections are created and deleted with special system calls. Actual transparent proxy software is not available yet, but is expected to appear soon.

transparent proxy

IP tunneling

IP tunneling is the encapsulation and transmission of IP packets via a different network protocol. This allows using the protocol *IPIP* to send IP packets as data encapsulated in IP packets via an IP network—a *tunnel*. The name tunnel comes form the firewall field, where tunnels are often used to circumvent packet filters (tunneling is used by both firewall administrators and hackers). If a router filters out packets with destination port 25, such packets can be encapsulated, sent through the firewall using another port number, and then unpacked and sent on normally. This requires the receiver to likewise use the protocol IPIP (e.g., between two Linux machines). Other encapsulations will appear, such as "IP in IPX"—TCP/IP communication via a pure IPX network without IP support. IP tunnels are also interesting for mobile computers.

IPIP

mobile computing

IP defragmentation

When an IP packet on its way through the Internet is transmitted through a link whose MTU (maximum transfer unit) is smaller than

reason for
fragmentation

the packet size, the packet is *fragmented*. Normally the fragments are sent on individually to the destination host and reassembled there. If the kernel option IP_ALWAYS_DEFRAG is activated, then the Linux kernel fully reassembles all IP packets before forwarding them. This

firewalls

behavior is interesting for packet filters in firewalls—only the first fragment of an IP packet contains the TCP or UDP port number by which the filter can decide whether the packet may be forwarded. Fragments beyond the first one are never filtered by the Linux packet filter. However, this is seldom dangerous. IP masquerading and transparent proxies require this option in any case.

9.4 IP aliasing

Linux 2.0 features *network interface aliasing*, the assignment of

several addresses
per interface

multiple addresses to a single network interface. Presently aliasing is only supported for IP addresses. Aliasing proves useful if one server assumes the tasks of another—the former simply inherits the other's IP address, which saves some reconfiguration. An interface with several addresses appears as multiple logical interfaces: e.g., dummy0 can become dummy0 (as was), dummy0 : 0, dummy0 : 1, dummy0 : 2, ...

Configuration example:

```
ifconfig eth0 141.7.11.12 broadcast 141.7.11.255 netmask 255.255.255.0
ifconfig eth0:0 141.7.11.10 broadcast 141.7.11.255 netmask 255.255.255.0
route add 141.7.11.12 dev eth0
route add 141.7.11.10 dev eth0:0
```

9.5 Serial connections

Information on the serial port and modem operation can also be found

Serial-HOWTO

in the Serial-HOWTO (see Section 11.4).

Hardware

external modems
internal modem card

To allow modem operation, the kernel must support the serial port. External modems are simply connected to one of the serial ports. Functionally, an internal modem card behaves like a serial port card with an attached external modem. However, since the computer generally already has one or two serial ports, some preparations need to be made. The serial ports generally occupy the following IO ports (in this order): 3F8h, 2F8h, 3E8h, 2E8h. If the internal modem is the third or fourth port, it additionally needs its own interrupt (IRQ 2 or IRQ 5). Under Linux this IRQ must be set with setserial, e.g., as follows (third serial port, IRQ 5):

IO ports

IRQ

setserial

```
> setserial /dev/cua2 irq 5
```

Setting the proper baudrate is also important. The default setting of 115200 baud is something of a joke in relation to telephone lines. For a 28800 baud connection:

baudrate

```
> setserial /dev/cua2 baud_base 28800
```

General information

In order to install a TCP/IP connection via a modem line, use SLIP (Serial Line Internet Protocol) or PPP (Point-to-Point Protocol). This kind of protocol-based system has an advantage over normal modem connections in that it can be used by several users simultaneously.

SLIP, PPP

Figure 9.4 shows our familiar example network with an additional serial modem connection. zeus has now taken over the task of the SLIP/ PPP server. It has two interfaces with the same IP address, which is easily possible with a point-to-point connection. Normally, serial interfaces are not configured at system startup, but only when they are actually needed. First you must check whether the kernel in use actually provides PPP or SLIP. The following command outputs a list of the available interfaces:

PPP server

serial interfaces

```
zeus:/home/uhl> cat /proc/net/dev
Inter-|   Receive                    |   Transmit
 face |packets errs drop fifo frame|packets errs drop fifo colls carrier
   lo:       0    0    0    0     0   18443    7    0    0     0    0
 ppp0:    1425    1    0    0     0    1406    0    0    0     4    0
 ppp1:       0    0    0    0     0       0    0    0    0     0    0
 ppp2:       0    0    0    0     0       0    0    0    0     0    0
 ppp3:       0    0    0    0     0       0    0    0    0     0    0
  sl0:       0    0    0    0     0       0    0    0    0     0    0
  sl1:       0    0    0    0     0       0    0    0    0     0    0
  sl2:       0    0    0    0     0       0    0    0    0     0    0
  sl3:       0    0    0    0     0       0    0    0    0     0    0
 eth0:  308413    0    0    0     0  287117    0    0    0    28    0
zeus:/home/uhl>
```

225

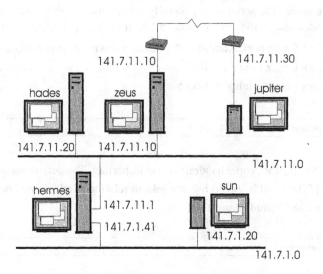

141.7.11.10   141.7.11.30

hades   zeus   jupiter

141.7.11.20   141.7.11.10

141.7.11.0

hermes   sun

141.7.11.1

141.7.1.41

141.7.1.20

141.7.1.0

Figure 9.4. TCP/IP compared to a modem

eth0, sl0, ppp0

In the example above, four SLIP devices (s10-s13) and four PPP devices (ppp0-ppp3) are available in addition to one Ethernet device (eth0).

SLIP

SLIP   With SLIP, individual IP packets are sent unchanged through the lines. Due to high overhead, this leads to relatively low transfer

CSLIP   speeds. For this reason, an improved protocol variant called CSLIP (Compressed Serial Internet Protocol) is used more often now. CSLIP compresses the IP header before transfer, which results in a noticeable improvement in transfer speed.

dip   The utility dip is for dialing the telephone number and making the connection to a SLIP router or server. It can be used interactively or controlled from a script. The following example is a simple script

dip script   for dialing a Linux SLIP server. It is invoked with dip *scriptname*.

```
# DIP - Login Script (for dip 3.3.7)
main:
  # determine IP addresses
```

```
  get $local opcon.franken.de
  get $remote wuff.mayn.sub.de

  # configure port
  port cua1
  speed 38400
  reset

  # initialize modem
  send ATQ0V1E1X4\r

  # wait for OK
  wait OK 2
  if $errlvl != 0 goto modem_trouble

  # dial telephone number
  dial 993322
  if $errlvl != 0 goto modem_trouble

  # wait for CONNECT
  wait CONNECT 60
  if $errlvl != 0 goto modem_trouble
login:
  sleep 2

  # wait for login message
  wait ogin: 20
  if $errlvl != 0 goto login_error

  # send login name (linux)
  send linux\n

  # wait for password prompt
  wait ord: 20
  if $errlvl != 0 goto password_error

  # send password (linus)
  send linus\n

loggedin:

  get $mtu 296
  default

done:
  print CONNECTED $locip ---> $rmtip
  mode .CSLIP
  goto exit

prompt_error:
  print TIME-OUT waiting for SLIPlogin to fire up...
  goto error

login_trouble:
  print Trouble waiting for the Login: prompt...
  goto error

password:error:
  print Trouble waiting for the Password: prompt...
  goto error

modem_trouble:
  print Trouble ocurred with the modem...
error:
  print CONNECT FAILED to $remote

exit:
```

Once the connection has been established, dip automatically configures the SLIP interface and defines a standard routing entry to pass all packets on to the Linux server.

9.6   PPP

PPP

The Point-to-Point Protocol (PPP) is another way to establish a TCP/IP connection via modem. Unlike SLIP, PPP has been standardized in several RFCs. In addition, PPP also enables the

IPX, Appletalk

transfer of other protocols such as Appletalk and Novell's IPX. PPP also has its own authentication protocol, which provides a measure of security with a dial-in connection. Another advantage

dynamic IP address

of PPP is the possibility of dynamic IP address assignment. This means that the server can assign an appropriate address to the client when establishing the connection. Like CSLIP, PPP supports the compression of IP headers, which results in a considerable increase in transfer speed.

Configuration

PPP client

The configuration of a PPP client under Linux is similar to that of a SLIP connection and is equally simple. It requires the PPP

PPP daemon

daemon pppd and a program called chat. The PPP packages for Linux contain both. The superuser authorization must be running when you install the daemon. The file owner must be root, and the SetUID bit must be set:

```
jupiter:/root> ls -l /sbin/pppd
-rwsr-xr-x   1   root     root        96301 Aug 29 20:02 /usr/sbin/pppd
jupiter:/root>
```

pppd completely takes over establishing the connection and directing the transfer of IP packets. Due to the number of options available, the command line may appear somewhat confusing. We

command line

therefore recommend creating a shell script.

```
#!/bin/sh
# pppcall: Establishing a PPP connection

# Telephone number
NR=0815
```

```
# Login
PROMPT1=login:
LOGIN=ppp

# Password
PROMPT2=password:
PASSWD=joshua

MODEM=/dev/cua0

DIAL=ATDT
PPPD=/usr/sbin/pppd

echo "Connecting to PPP server ($NR) ..."

$PPPD connect "chat -v ABORT BUSY ABORT 'NO CARRIER' ''\
        $DIAL$NR CONNECT '' $PROMPT1 $LOGIN $PROMPT2 $PASSWD"\
        $MODEM -detach crtscts modem defaultroute
```

Naturally you need to adapt the strings LOGIN and PASSWD for yourself.

Another alternative is to enter frequently used options in a file called /etc/ppp/options. This file must exist whether or not it is used. *(options)*

```
# /etc/ppp/options: Global options of pppd
#
lock # UUCP conform lock file
modem # modem connection
crtscts # hardware flow control
-detach # no fork
```

As the script shows, the chat command takes care of dialing the remote modem and logging in. The chat script can also send character strings to the modem or wait to receive a sequence, so it is similar to the chat script for establishing a UUCP connection. *(chat script)*

The chat program should also contain the interrupt strings BUSY and NO CARRIER, as in the script above. This will avoid having to wait long for an interruption when the connect ion is being structured. In this particular example, chat dials the number 0815, then waits for a CONNECT response and a log-in prompt. Before a PPP connection is established, ppp is given as the log-in name and joshua as the password. It may be necessary to make some changes in the script because log-in prompts coming from the server may differ from time to time. *(BUSY, NO CARRIER; CONNECT)*

The chat debug options are very helpful in looking for configuration errors. Using the -v option in chat results in a protocol *(debug option)* of all activities via the syslog daemon. With pppd, do this by transferring -debug.

pppd also accepts the desired baudrate as an option. Since it does not recognize all baudrates (e.g., not 28800 baud), this option should be omitted and the baudrate should be set with setserial (see above).

default route

The option noipdefault is used to accept a dynamically assigned address from the server (it should be used when dialing in to a terminal server). The option defaultroute should be transferred as well, so that the default route is automatically set to the PPP server. If you do not wish to assign a default route, the routing can also be explicitly defined.

ip-up

To do this, pppd invokes the shell script ip-up in the directory /etc/ppp after the connection has been successfully established. The name of the network interfaces, the path of the serial interfaces, the local address, and the remote station's IP address are passed on as parameters. Any routes can be set, depending on the transfer parameters, in a script like this:

```sh
#!/bin/sh
# IP UP Script for PPP connections
#
case $5 in                     # IP address of the affiliate
        192.7.11.1)
            /sbin/route add -net 192.7.11.0 gw 192.7.11.1 ;;
        195.9.12.1)
            /sbin/route add -net 195.9.12.0 gw 195.9.12.1 ;;
esac
```

ip-down

The shell script ip-down is analogous to ip-up and makes it possible to carry out any number of actions after ending a PPP connection.

To interrupt a PPP connection, it suffices to send a termination signal (TERM) to the pppd with the command kill or killall. The process ID of the running daemon is in /var/run/pppN.pid,

connection interrupt

whereby N is the number of the associated interface. The following command interrupts the connection:

```
zeus:/root# killall pppd
```

If several daemons are running in parallel, then only the correct pppd should be terminated. This can be achieved with the following command:

```
zeus:/root# kill `cat /var/run/ppp0.pid`
```

This ensures that only the pppd responsible for the interface ppp0 is terminated.

Troubleshooting

pppd and chat log messages and replies of the other end per syslog. Thus while the connection is being established you should watch the corresponding log files, e.g., with **tail -f /var/log/messages**.

Depending on the replies from the other end, PROMPT1 and PROMPT2 might have to be modified. If the modem dials successfully and the call is answered, but then there is no reply, you probably have an incorrect baudrate. Normally you can hear the dialing and initialization of the connection. If the modem does not dial, then IO ports or IRQs are wrong.

Authentication

It makes sense to install additional security measures for a dial-in connection in order to guard against intruders. PPP provides two different authentication protocols for this purpose. The Password Authentication Protocol (PAP) basically acts like a simple log-in mechanism. It checks a user name and an optional coded password at the start. The Challenge Handshake Authentication Protocol (CHAP), which is explained further below, provides considerably greater security. CHAP effects an exchange of special information at regular intervals, with which the communicating stations can check each other's identity.

security

authentication

PAP

CHAP

The keyword auth must be added to the file /etc/ppp/ options (or to the pppd command line) in order to enforce this kind of mutual authentication. For each connection, distinct secrets, which are matched to each host, can be defined. Depending on the protocol, these are in either /etc/ppp/pap-secrets or /etc/ppp/chap-secrets. A CHAP authentication is always attempted first, then a

secrets

PAP authentication. If neither of these two files can be found, the connection is terminated.

A file with CHAP secrets can take the following form:

```
#
# CHAP Secrets for zeus.heilbronn.de
#
# Client          Server           Secret                 address
#------------------------------------------------------------------------
zeus.demo.de      jupiter.demo.de  "catbox"               zeus.demo.de
jupiter.demo.de   zeus.demo.de     "Eat brown rice, Baby" jupiter.demo.de
*                 zeus.demo.de     "00Schneider"          141.7.11.50
```

remote station

The first column contains the name of the respective remote station. The server column contains the name of the machine where the authentication takes place. The third column contains the agreed secret. The final column may optionally contain a host name or an IP address from which the client must log in. This is important for systems allowing any number of clients.

hostname

For trouble-free authentication, the client machine must be configured to respond with a fully qualified name (including the domain) when `hostname` is invoked. If `hostname` only responds with a simple name, then the domain can be determined through the `domain` option of the `pppd`.

PPP

Fortunately, the PPP daemon under Linux can also be used to create a PPP server. This requires entering a user in the file `/etc/password` that has `ppp`, for example, as a user name.

```
ppp:m3eNH3fgw:200:50:public PPP
account:/tmp:/etc/ppp/ppplogin
```

ppplogin

A script called `ppplogin` is used as a log-in shell and may look like this:

```
#!/bin/sh
#
# ppplogin - Log-in shell for PPP log-in
#
# prevents terminal output via write (1)
mesg n
# turns echo off
```

```
stty -echo
# starts pppd in server mode
exec /usr/sbin/pppd -detach silent modem proxyarp crtscts
```

The option `silent` causes the daemon to wait for incoming silent
packets before attempting to establish a connection. `proxyarp`
ensures that the server reacts to ARP requests (see Section 9.3)
concerning the remote station in a point-to-point connection. In this
way, a computer connected to a modem can be addressed like a
machine in the local Ethernet.

9.7   Parallel connection

The parallel port and a protocol called PLIP (Parallel Line Internet PLIP
Protocol) provide an economical TCP/IP connection. Two computers
are connected with a null printer cable via free parallel ports. null printer cable
This type of network proves particularly attractive for data transfer
between a notebook and a workstation.

In principle, the configuration of a PLIP interface works exactly configuration
like that of a serial network interface (SLIP, PPP). The name of the
first parallel interface is `plip0`. Be sure to choose the PLIP option for
the compilation of the kernel (see Section 6.2). To configure a point-
to-point connection, the option `pointtopoint` and the IP address
must be transferred to the remote station when `ifconfig` is invoked.

```
#!/bin/sh
# PLIPUP - init PLIP interface
#
IPADDR="141.7.11.30"        # IP address
NETMASK="255.255.255.0"     # network mask
BROADCAST="141.7.11.255"    # broadcast address
POINTOPOINT="141.7.11.10"   # point-to-point connection

echo "Setting up PLIP interface..."

/sbin/ifconfig plip0 ${IPADDR} \
              pointopoint ${POINTOPOINT} \
              netmask ${NETMASK} \
              broadcast ${BROADCAST}

/sbin/route add ${POINTOPOINT} dev plip0

/sbin/route add default hermes.demo.de

echo "PLIP is running."
```

233

9.8 ISDN

Especially for companies, ISDN has become a quasi-standard for Internet access as a compromise between slow analog connections and expensive dedicated lines. A standard ISDN interface (*basic rate interface*, *BRI*, *S0 interface*) provides two B-channels at 64 kbit/s for data transfer as well as a 16 kbit/s D-channel for control information. Both B-channels can be bundled for a transmission rate of 128 kbit/s.

ISDN support has been integrated into the kernel. It is activated with the option CONFIG_ISDN (and can also be compiled as a module). The corresponding device files need to be created under /dev. This is handled by the Makefile of the isdn4k-utils:

```
golem:/usr/local/src/isdn4k-utils-2.0> make devices
...
```

Linux 2.0 supports the following ISDN adapters:

- ICN 2B and 4B
- PCBIT-D
- Teles S0-16.0, S0-16.3, S0-8 and compatible, e.g., NICCY 1016PC and Creatix

configuration   ISDN interfaces are configured with the package isdn4k-utils.* This package contains tools for general ISDN configuration (isdnctrl) and for certain adapters (telesctrl, icnctrl, pcbitctrl).

Configuration for IP via ISDN:

```
#!/bin/sh

# ISDN Setup
# "rc.isdn start": Setup
# "rc.isdn stop":  Shutdown

# Euro-ISDN: Our MSN
# National ISDN: EAZ
EAZ=0049123423456

# Remote phone number to call for outgoing IP traffic
OUTPHONE=0049123456782
# Remote phones that may call us and deliver incoming IP packets
INPHONE="004912345678?"
```

*Source: ftp://www.franken.de/pub/isdn4linux/isdn4k-utils-2.0.tar.gz

```
# Our IP
IP=141.7.11.12
BROADCAST=141.7.11.255
NETMASK=255.255.255.0

# Our card
CARD=teles

if [ $1 = "start" ]; then
        # Load modules (usually requires kernel parameters)
        modprobe $CARD

        # The right place to load firmware (PCBit, ICN, ...)

        # Register new ISDN interface
        isdnctrl addif isdn0

        # Set EAZ/MSN
        isdnctrl eaz isdn0 $EAZ

        # Telephone number to dial for outgoing packets
        isdnctrl addphone isdn0 out $OUTPHONE

        # Select peers that may deliver incoming packets
        isdnctrl secure isdn0 on
        isdnctrl addphone isdn0 in $INPHONE

        # IP configuration
        ifconfig isdn0 $IP
        ifconfig isdn0 broadcast $BROADCAST
        ifconfig isdn0 netmask $NETMASK
else
        ifconfig isdn0 down
        isdnctrl delif isdn0
fi
```

For the PCBit and ICN adapters you also have to load some firmware (see comment in script).   firmware

This script configures the ISDN adapter only for raw IP connections. If the provider or peer does not support this protocol   raw IP connections
or if other network protocols such as IPX are to be used on the channel, PPP (see Section 9.6) must be used as IP basis. The   PPP
isdn4k-utils contain a corresponding PPP daemon ipppd that also supports bit-synchronous PPP (this requires kernel support: synchronous PPP
CONFIG_ISDN_PPP).

For further details see /usr/src/linux/Documentation/ isdn and the documentation for the utilities, especially the Manual pages isdnctrl(8), telesctrl(8), icnctrl(8), pcbitctrl(8), and ipppd(8).

9.9 TCP and UDP

Internet applications rarely use the IP level routines directly. Instead, they use the TCP or the UDP protocol, which provide more address possibilities and abstraction than IP.

virtual connection

TCP establishes a virtual connection. This means that a connection on the TCP level can be considered a secure data channel. Anything that is sent from one end of the channel can be read on the other end. TCP breaks down the files to be sent and uses IP to send them. Should a transfer error occur or IP packets be lost, the TCP level's task is to repeat the transfer.

packets

checksum

UDP can only send individual packets. It compares the contents of the packet with a checksum. If the receiver notices a transfer error, the packet is not sent again, but rather deleted. UDP is not as convenient to use as TCP; however, it is more efficient.

Ports

In addition to the network address, making a connection at this level

port number

also requires a port number, which usually corresponds to a particular network service. This permits multiple independent connections via a single network interface. Several of these port numbers are reserved for standard TCP/IP applications: for example, port 23 is for telnet, and ports 20 and 21 are for ftp. These *well-known ports* are designated in the file /etc/services.

Sockets

In order to provide a uniform interface for the programming of

BSD UNIX

Berkeley sockets

network applications, the developers of BSD UNIX introduced the Berkeley sockets in the early 1980s. These are a series of kernel routines that are needed to make a connection between two computers and for transferring data between them. Both TCP and UDP connections can be realized via sockets.

Note that it does not matter whether the data transfer takes place within a local-area network (LAN) or in a global wide-area network (WAN). The programming interface is always the same.

The Linux kernel also includes such a socket interface, which makes most well-known UNIX network applications available.

9.10 Host names

Most users do not consider the direct input of an IP address address to be a very comfortable solution. This provided the stimulus for introducing symbolic addresses. Such a symbolic address consists of a host name and a domain name.

symbolic name

The host name in conjunction with the domain name identifies the computer uniquely around the world. Instead of the IP address 141.7.1.40, for example, a user could enter the symbolic address linux1.rz.fh-heilbronn.de. In this case linux1 is the host name and rz.fh-heilbronn.de the name of the domain, which is a subdomain of fh-heilbronn.de.

host name

The correspondence of IP address and symbolic address can be specified locally in the file /etc/hosts. Here additional names, or alias es, can be defined for a host. Aliases serve to define shorter names and thus to make the entry of addresses more comfortable. The following is an excerpt from the file /etc/hosts:

/etc/hosts
alias

```
#IP address    symbolic address          alias

141.7.1.40     linux1.rz.fh-heilbronn.de  linux1

127.0.0.1      localhost

141.7.1.20     sun1.rz.fh-heilbronn.de    sun1
141.7.1.25     risc11.rz.fh-heilbronn.de  risc1   news   newsserver
```

DNS and name server

Since maintaining hundreds or thousands of entries in this file proves impossible, a hierarchical system of name servers was set up to manage these symbolic names and to automatically exchange addresses among themselves. For each domain, i.e., all machines with a certain domain name, there is a responsible name server. A detailed description of the concepts *domain name*, *subdomain*, and *name server* can be found in RFC 1034 and RFC 1035.

name server

The UNIX TCP/IP programs convert the host name to the corresponding IP address by invoking a C library routine. This routine, called resolver, reads the file /etc/hosts and makes a connection to the next name server if necessary (i.e., if the address

resolver

is outside its own domain). The order in which this is to occur can be specified in the file /etc/host.conf.

```
# /etc/host.conf
order hosts, bind
multi on
```

/etc/hosts   The entry order hosts, bind indicates that the file /etc/hosts is to be read first. If it contains no entry for the host name in question, then the name server is contacted. The address of the next name server is stored in the file /etc/resolv.conf. The line multi on means that the resolver should return all valid addresses to a host when multiple addresses in are entered in the file /etc/hosts. The On-Line Manual page for resolv+ describes these and other options in detail.

/etc/resolv.conf   The actual configuration of the resolver is stored in the file /etc/resolv.conf. This file also contains the address of the nearest name server, the name of the local domain, as well as possible host name extensions for querying name servers.

```
# /etc/resolv.conf
domain demo.de
nameserver 141.7.11.1
nameserver 141.7.1.25
search demo.de
search beispiel.de
```

search   The line with search indicates that for a name server query both demo.de and beispiel.de should be tried as extensions of the host name. The host name is thus sufficient without the domain name for a computer from either domain, assuming that the host name is unambiguous.

Name server

daemon   Many Linux installation packages include the name server daemon
NAG   namednamed. The configuration of this name server is no simple matter, however, and for smaller networks a name server usually proves superfluous. For detailed descriptions of how a name server functions and of TCP/IP configuration files, refer to the *Linux*

Network Administration Guide (NAG). *DNS and Bind*, published by O'Reilly, contains a very detailed description. This section merely provides a general overview of the files and programs used.

The first configuration file of the name server daemon named is /etc/named.boot. This file determines the (primary) domains for which the server is responsible, the (secondary) domains for which it should regularly manage the names and addresses, and the files in which the respective tables are stored (Figure 9.5).

configuration file

```
; boot file for primary nameserver
; Domain demo.de
;

directory        /etc/bind

; --- definition file for zone of authority
primary          demo.de                        db.demo
;
; reverse mappings for local (.11) subnet..
primary          11.7.141.in-addr.arpa          db.141.7.11
;
; --- file defining localhost
primary          0.0.127.in-addr.arpa           db.127.0.0
;
; --- file to hold cached IN addresses
cache            .                              db.cache
```

Figure 9.5. File /etc/named.boot

In this example, the individual tables are stored in the directory /etc/bind. This directory is also specified in /etc/named.boot. The tables can be separated into two types: One type provides addresses and further information on a host name; the other provides the host name of an address. Figures 9.6, 9.7, 9.8, and 9.9 show sections from each type of table.

tables

```
; Address to hostname mappings for net 127.0.0.1
@         IN SOA hermes.demo.de.  dns.demo.de. (
                                  1994120600 ; Serial
                                  21600      ; Refresh
                                  1800       ; Retry
                                  3600000    ; Expire
                                  86400 )    ; Minimum
          IN      NS     ns.demo.de.
          IN      PTR    localhost.
```

Figure 9.6. File db.127.0.0

239

```
; Address to host mappings for 141.7.11
; local subnet demo.de
@               .IN SOA   hermes.demo.de. dns.demo.de. (
                          1995010302   ; serial
                             43200     ; refresh : 12h
                              1800     ; retry   : 30 min
                           3600000     ; expire  : 41 Tage
                             86400 )   ; minimum : 24h
; nameservers
                IN    NS      ns.demo.de.

; Hosts
1               IN    PTR     hermes.demo.de.
10              IN    PTR     zeus.demo.de.
20              IN    PTR     hades.demo.de.
30              IN    PTR     jupiter.demo.de.
```

Figure 9.7. File db.141.7.11

```
;
;   demo.de
;   host to address mappings
;
@               IN SOA    hermes.demo.de. dns.demo.de. (
                          1994010402   ; serial
                             43200     ; refresh : 12h
                              1800     ; retry   : 30 min
                           3600000     ; expire  : 41 Tage
                             86400 )   ; minimum : 24h
; nameservers
                IN    NS      hermes.demo.de.
;
; mx record for demo.de
                IN    MX      10 hermes.demo.de.
;
;   Hosts
hermes          IN    A       141.7.11.1
                IN    HINFO   "i486" "Linux"
                IN    MX      10 hermes.demo.de.
news            IN    CNAME   hermes.demo.de.
ftp             IN    CNAME   hermes.demo.de.
www             IN    CNAME   hermes.demo.de.
ns              IN    CNAME   hermes.demo.de.
;
zeus            IN    A       141.7.11.10
                IN    HINFO   "i486" "Linux"
                IN    MX      10 hermes.demo.de.
;
hades           IN    A       141.7.11.20
                IN    HINFO   "i486" "Linux"
                IN    MX      10 hermes.demo.de.
;
jupiter         IN    A       141.7.11.30
                IN    HINFO   "i486" "Linux"
                IN    MX      10 hermes.demo.de.
;
```

Figure 9.8. File db.demo

db.cache   File db.cache has particular significance. It stores the addresses of the root name server. Its contents rarely change.

```
; Root Nameserver Cache
      .                 99999999 IN NS NS.INTERNIC.NET.
      .                 99999999 IN NS AOS.ARL.ARMY.MIL.
      .                 99999999 IN NS NS1.ISI.EDU.
      .                 99999999 IN NS C.PSI.NET.
      .                 99999999 IN NS TERP.UMD.EDU.
      .                 99999999 IN NS NS.NASA.GOV.
      .                 99999999 IN NS NIC.NORDU.NET.
      .                 99999999 IN NS NS.ISC.ORG.
NS.INTERNIC.NET.        99999999 IN A 198.41.0.4
AOS.ARL.ARMY.MIL.       99999999 IN A 128.63.4.82
AOS.ARL.ARMY.MIL.       99999999 IN A 192.5.25.82
NS1.ISI.EDU.            99999999 IN A 128.9.0.107
C.PSI.NET.              99999999 IN A 192.33.4.12
TERP.UMD.EDU.           99999999 IN A 128.8.10.90
NS.NASA.GOV.            99999999 IN A 192.52.195.10
NS.NASA.GOV.            99999999 IN A 128.102.16.10
NIC.NORDU.NET.          99999999 IN A 192.36.148.17
NS.ISC.ORG.             99999999 IN A 192.5.5.241
```

Figure 9.9. File db.cache

Finding errors

The program nslookup is frequently used to look for errors involving name servers. With this program, a name server can be queried interactively. The program can be invoked either with a name in the command line or without arguments. If no arguments are given, nslookup responds with a prompt, and the user can enter special commands and search names. The command help displays the most important commands.

nslookup

help

9.11 UUCP

UUCP stands for UNIX to UNIX Copy and probably represents the oldest possibility of connecting UNIX machines to one another via a network. Establishing the connection normally takes place between the individual machines using a serial cable and a modem. A UUCP network can transfer any amount of data and commands. In general, however, it provides the most economical mail and news link.

UNIX to UNIX copy

modem

UUCP works on the principle of *data forwarding*. This means that in one session it transfers first a data packet and then a command to process the transferred data on the remote machine. When mail is transferred, for instance, the command rmail is transferred along with the actual contents of the mail. Data are not usually transferred immediately as they occur, but rather only at certain times (batch system). This keeps telephone costs as low as possible by taking

data forwarding

rmail

241

advantage of low rate times. Data are copied into a special directory as they occur and then deleted after successful transfer.

UUCP not only allows the transfer of data between two directly connected computers, but, based on the principle of *store and forward*, the transfer can also be carried out over several stations. Here, however, the exact transfer route must be known. This possibility is no longer used as widely as it was in the early phases of UUCP use. Since the administration of routes with UUCP maps is quite complicated for larger networks, people usually prefer IP-based transfer now. UUCP is currently used primarily to transfer data from a server connected to the Internet through TCP/IP to a smaller system without an on-line connection.

UUCP assigns every job a *grade* according to its importance. Grades are defined with a character in the range 0-9, A-Z, and a-z, with 0 having the highest priority. Mail usually has a grade of B or C, news a grade N. The commands uux and uucp can define the desired priority with the option -g.

Data transfer can be carried out through various protocols. Not every UUCP package understands all variants. The g protocol is the oldest and most widespread. System V favors the g variants. Taylor UUCP also recognizes an extremely fast, bidirectional i protocol. This, however, can only be used between Taylor systems. The Taylor UUCP packet consists of a series of commands. The following briefly explains the tasks of these commands.

uucico

establishes a connection to another UUCP system, sends and receives the occurring data, and subsequently invokes the processing of the accompanying commands, such as rmail or rnews via uuxqt.

uuxqt

carries out the commands required via uux on a remote system.

uucp

enables copy ing data between any UUCP systems.

Margin notes:
store and forward
grade
protocols
Taylor UUCP
connection
commands
copy

`uux`

      enables execution of certain commands on a remote system.   commands
In addition to the command name, data that are to be used in
the target system may also be transferred.

`uustat`

      lists current UUCP jobs. Jobs that are not yet completed may   jobs
also be removed from the UUCP queue.

`uuname`

      outputs all known local UUCP systems.

`uulog`

      outputs the contents of the UUCP log file. The output can be   log files
limited to certain systems or users.

`cu`

      establishes an interactive connection to a remote UUCP   interactive
system.

Configuration

A series of various UUCP packages has developed over the years;
they differ primarily in their configuration. The most comfortable
UUCP variant is the Taylor UUCP, which is available for free. It   Taylor UUCP
supports not only the configuration modes of the antiquated V2   V2, HDB
and the HDB, but also its own particular variant, the Taylor mode,
which should be used. Old configuration files can be transformed
into this format with a converter. In the following we therefore
discuss only configuration in the Taylor mode. We assume that all the
configuration files may be found in the directory `/usr/lib/uucp`.
This path can be defined upon compilation. The following files are
found under this path:

    `config, sys, port, dialer`   configuration files

    The name of the local system is defined in the file `config`:   config

```
# Name of the local UUCP system
#
host name         kirk
```

    A neighboring UUCP system must be made known to the local
computer in order to establish a connection between the two. This

243

sys   is achieved with the `sys` f ile, which can contain a series of options in addition to the name of the system, its telephone number, log-in name, and password. Such a file looks like the following:

```
#
# Global settings for all systems
# -------------------------------------
#
#
# Systems may be contacted any time
#
time              any
#
# After a successful connection, wait 15 minutes (900 seconds)
# before establishing a new connection
#
success-wait      900
#
# ---------- gallien ----------
# 'gallien' is the name of the UUCP feed
#
system gallien
#
#
#
call-login asterix
call-password obelix
#
# Telephone number
#
phone 0713566354
#
# 'gallien' supports the bidirectional i-Protocol
#
protocol-parameter i packet size 1024
#
# serial port
#
port    zyxel
```

port   The parameters, such as the name and transfer speed of the port, are defined in a separate `port` file.

```
#
# ZyXEL modem
# -----------
#
# Name of the port
port zyxel
# Modem is connected to port 'ttyS1'
device /dev/ttyS1
# Transfer speed between modem and computer
speed      38400
# Dialer
dialer     zyx-fast
```

If the connection is established via a modem, this requires a dialer `dialer` file containing all the data relative to the modem.

```
#
# Zyxel Modem
#
# Name of the dialer from the port file
dialer zyx-fast
#
# chat string
#
# \T -> Send telephone number
# \r -> Send carriage return (CR)
# \c -> Suppress carriage return at end of string
# \d -> Delay of 1 second
# \s -> Send space
#
chat "" AT&K4&N17 OK ATDP\T\r\c CONNECT
#
# Error strings. Chat is terminated, as soon as one of the
strings is recognized. #
chat-fail        BUSY
chat-fail        NO\sDIALTONE
chat-fail        NO\sCARRIER
#
# after successful connection
#
complete         \d\d+++\d\dATH0Z\r\c
#
# after connection interrupt
#
abort            \d\d+++\d\dATH0Z\r\c
```

Log files

All the activities of the UUCP system are recorded in several log files. These are also very helpful for configuration. The file /var/spool/uucp/Log contains general protocol information; the file /var/spool/uucp/Stats contains statistics on the transfer speeds that have been achieved (also see uulog). If uucico is started with the command line option -x in debug mode, then a detailed debug protocol is created under /var/spool/uucp/Debug.

uulog

Automatic connections

The UUCP user should create a separate crontab (see Section 2.9) to automate establishing the connection. The cron daemon can also facilitate repeat dialing if a line is busy. It is useful in this case to have uucico not allow multiple execution within a set interval following a successfully established connection. For instance, to establish a connection to the system gallien daily between 7:00 p.m. and 7:15 p.m., the crontab below suffices.

crontab

```
# (root.crontab installed on Wed Sep 7 18:23:50 1994)
# (Cron version -- $Header: crontab.c,v 2.2 90/07/18 00:23:56 vixie Exp $)
SHELL=/bin/sh
#
```

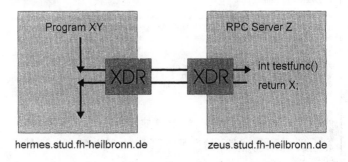

Figure 9.10. RPC invocation

```
# mail any output to 'uucp' no matter whose crontab this is
MAILTO=uucp
#
# daily call to system 'gallien' after 7:00 p.m.
0,3,6,9,12 19 * * *              /usr/lib/uucp/uucico -s gallien
#
# abbreviate the UUCP Log files by 20.00
#
00 20 * * *      /var/lib/smail/savelog -m 300 -c 2 -t /var/spool/uucp/Log
00 20 * * *      /var/lib/smail/savelog -m 300 -c 2 -t /var/spool/uucp/Stats
```

restart interval   The length of the restart interval in this case would have to be set at 15 minutes (`success-wait` 900). The other two `crontab` entries serve to shorten the constantly growing UUCP log files.

9.12   RPC

RPC   Some network services, including the Network File System (NFS), are based on the Remote Procedure Calls (RPC) from Sun. This refers to a mechanism allowing execution of individual routines on a remote computer in the network. There is an RPC server, which provides the subprograms, and clients, which use parameters to invoke these subprograms (Figure 9.10). RPC is thus a special type communication of communication between processes via a network. Unlike network programming through sockets, in this case one communication channel is abstracted.

The eXternal Data Representation (XDR), a machine-independent type of data representation, is usually used together with RPC to exchange data between computers with differing processor architectures. One frequently occurring difference between various processors, for example, is the representation of integral numbers. The XDR description allows the definition of an RPC routine's parameters, so that they can be converted through the appropriate subroutine between the machine-independent format and the internal format of an individual computer.

XDR

parameters

The program `rpcgen` allows automatic invocation of these routines and the internal RPC routines. It generates C source code for the RPC server and the client from a formal description of the RPC routines.

rpcgen

In order to establish a connection to an RPC server on a different machine, the `portmap` must be running on that machine. This daemon recognizes the available services, and it forwards the RPC invocation from the network to the appropriate RPC server. The information on registered programs that the `portmap` daemon has stored can be queried for diagnostic purposes with the `rpcinfo` program.

portmap

9.13 NIS

Since the consistent management of accounts and their passwords on a network can be quite arduous, Sun Microsystems developed the Network Information System (NIS). Instead of storing user information, available network services, and other system configuration information on each machine, a central NIS server manages these data. If the administrator creates a new user or if a user changes a password, NIS handles the necessary forwarding of this information to all affected machines.

configuration

The NIS client software is already included in many distributions or can be drawn from most FTP servers, for example, from the directory `/pub/linux/local/yp` on the server `ftp.uni-paderborn.de` (University of Paderborn, Germany).

Paderborn

9.14 NFS

Network File System

The Network File System (NFS) makes it possible to mount file systems that are released (exported) by other computers, as a part of the local machine's own file systems. This provides transparent access to the directories of the remote computers.

The example below shows access to files in the /home directory of a remote computer (stef1) on the network. Initially, the directory /stef1 on the machine dirk1 was empty. After the mount procedure, this directory contains (quasi) all files of the directory /home of computer stef1. The following is an example of an NFS mount procedure.

mounting

```
dirk1:/# ls
bin/           install/       lost+found/    stef1/         var@
dev/           lastlog@       mnt/           tmp/           vmlinux
etc/           lib/           proc/          user/
vmlinux.old
home/          linux@         root/          usr/
dirk1:/# ls stef1
dirk1:/# mount stef1:/home /stef1
dirk1:/# ls stef1
dirk/     fritz/    ftp/      peter/    root/    stefan/
dirk1:/#
```

NFS was developed by Sun Microsystems. Because Sun released the definitions of the protocol, many other manufacturers were able to integrate NFS into their operating systems. Thus NFS became a standard that asserted itself on almost all platforms even though it was not controlled by any higher authority. NFS is available for almost all UNIX variants, MS-DOS, and other operating systems.

stateless server

A significant feature of NFS is the *stateless server*. This means that the NFS server that exports directories does not store any state information on the clients, but only carries out simple read and write operations. For example, if an NFS server needs to be restarted for whatever reason while an NFS client is copying a file from a directory exported by the server, the client's copying procedure is not interrupted; instead, the client waits until the server responds again and then continues the copying procedure. This procedure becomes problematic when it comes to the synchronization of access by multiple clients who want to write to the same file.

parallel access

Another drawback of NFS is the security of its protocol in terms of privacy and unauthorized access. Newer distributed file systems such as the Andrew File System (AFS) or the Distributed File System (DFS) prove superior to NFS. DFS is part of the Distributed Computing Environment (DCE) of the Open Software Foundation (OSF). However, neither AFS nor DFS has attained the level of proliferation that NFS enjoys.

AFS

Linux also provides a network file system. However, the respective drivers must have been compiled into the kernel. Then at run time the `portmap` daemon as well as the `rpc.nfsd` and `rpc.mountd` daemons must be running to allow the use of NFS. The NFS daemon `rpc.nfsd` replies to read and write requests from NFS client computers. The daemon `rpc.mountd` is responsible for the mounting information itself. It manages directories and checks the client's authorization for a mount requests.

kernel

nfsd and mountd

This daemon's most important configuration file is `/etc/ exports`, which lists all directories that can be mounted by other machines via NFS, along with their respective permissions. To make modifications effective, you must terminate `rpc.nfsd` and `rpc.mountd` and restart them (here the signal HUP has no effect). In addition, the daemon `rpc.portmap` must be running. Here is an example of this file:

configuration file

```
#
# Exported directories
#
/                linux1(rw)
/home            141.7.1.49(rw)
/home/prog       risc1(rw)
```

First, specify the name of the exported directory, then the hosts that are granted access (IP or host name; wildcards are permitted). However, this access restriction is rather easy to circumvent. After each host name you can specify options in parentheses, such as `rw` for read and write permissions or `ro` for read only (also see `exports(5)`).

Normally a remote user is handled the same as a local user. **Here the UID remains the same, but not necessarily the username!** If possible, NFS client and server should share a common

/etc/passwd. Access by a remote user root can also be treated locally like access by the user nobody (nobody has no particular permissions). **In some versions this is standard behavior, contrary to the specification in the Manual page**; if root is to have root privileges on the NFS server, you need to specify the option no_root_squash for the respective file system in /etc/exports.

9.15 LAN manager

SMB

One of the most frequently used network protocols in the PC world is the SMB protocol of the LAN manager. Both IBM and Microsoft offer servers under OS/2 and Windows NT, respectively. The biggest drawback of these solutions is the high price of this software. To overcome this problem, a project was started on the Internet to

Samba

develop a UNIX-based LAN manager server called Samba. This freely available server can be used both as a file server and as a print server.

Since Samba runs as a normal process in user space, it does not require any manipulations of the kernel. Since a UNIX kernel normally only recognizes TCP/IP, Samba is also not able to support

SMB in IP

the actual SMB protocol. Instead it packs individual SMB packets into an IP packet. In principle, any number of network protocols can be sent via an IP network infrastructure this way. By using this trick, this LAN manager protocol, which is not capable of routing, can also be used for a WAN.

TCP/IP stack

A TCP/IP stack must be installed on the client end, however. Fortunately, Microsoft provides the appropriate software for DOS and Windows free of charge on an FTP server (ftp.microsoft.com). The TCP/IP stack is integrated into Windows 3.11 via the network setup (Figure 9.11).

Server installation

compilation

Once the Samba packet is ready as source code, the two daemons smbd (LAN manager server) and nmbd (name server) need to be compiled. First activate the respective locations for Linux in the makefile. Copy the programs created into the directory /usr/sbin, where most of the other network daemons are. Since both daemons

Figure 9.11. TCP/IP stack under WfW 3.11

can be started via the Internet daemon, make an entry in the file
/etc/inetd.conf accordingly: inetd

```
#
# Samba Lanmanager-Server
#
netbios-ssn stream tcp nowait root /usr/sbin/smbd smbd
netbios-ns dgram udp wait root /usr/sbin/nmbd nmbd -G WORKGROUP
```

Server configuration is carried out by a corresponding ASCII   configuration
file, as usual under UNIX. This file's search path is defined
on compilation. The example configuration that accompanies the
Samba packet should be used as the basis for custom settings.
A public account provided there enables access to the UNIX-end
home directory of the individual user as well as the use of UNIX
printer services. The following excerpt from the configuration file is
responsible for this form of server access:

```
;
; Example configuration of the SMB server
;
[global]
        print command = /usr/bin/lpr -r -P%p %s
        lpq command = /usr/bin/lpq -P
        printer name = lp
        printcap name = /etc/printcap
        guest account = nobody
        password level = 1

[homes]
        comment = Home Directories
        read only = no
        create mode = 0750
        print ok = yes

[printers]
        comment = All Printers
        path = /usr/spool/public
        printable = yes
```

```
public = yes
writable = no
create mode = 0700
```

sections A Samba configuration file is divided into several sections that each define a server service. The sections global, homes, and printers have special functions. The individual sections attributes consist of a series of attributes with assigned values that define the characteristics of a service. A series of global parameters or default values is defined in the global section.

If a home section exists, then a service is created, which allows all users known to the server to log in from a client and access the home directories home directories. This means that it is not necessary to declare an individual log-in service for each user. The server takes the password needed for logging in from the file /etc/passwd. The path variable is set to the corresponding home directory of the user.

printer The printer section is similar to the homes section, except that it refers to printer services rather than log-in services. This way, clients can access all printers (/etc/printcap) known to the PostScript system. A particularly interesting feature is that a PostScript printer queue is provided on the server machine. A corresponding lpr filter and Ghostscript make this possible.

In this way, the Linux system can be turned into an economic RIP Raster Image Processor (RIP), even if no PostScript printer is available. Before a file can be printed, it is copied to the server. You can find it in the /var/spool/public directory.

attributes The list below explains all the attributes that can be modified for a service. The list differentiates between global attributes (G) and service attributes (S). The appropriate default settings are given in parentheses.

allow hosts	GS	List of clients allowed to use a service; wildcards are permissible: *.fh-heilbronn.de, 192.0.2.*
available	S	Client may use service (yes)

copy	S	Copy of the definition of the previous service
create mask	GS	Mask when a new file is created
create mask	G	Standard mask when a new file is created
dead time	G	Time in minutes until an inactive connection is interrupted
debug level	GS	Debug level
default service	G	Standard service for requesting an unknown service
deny hosts	GS	List of machines prohibited from accessing server
dfree command	G	Script for determining free memory
dont descend	S	List of directories that should appear empty on the client end (none)
getwd cache	G	Cache of current directory (yes)
guest account	G	Standardized user name for guest services
guest ok	S	Guest access available to any users (no)
guest only	S	Exclusively for guest access (no)
keep alive	G	Send a keep alive packet every n minutes
lock directory	G	Path for lock files
locking	G	Control locking (yes)
lpq command	GS	Access path on `lpq`
mangled names	G	Replace UNIX file names (yes)
map hidden	S	Execute bit should be set for hidden files (no)
map system	S	Execute bit should be set for system files (no)
max connections	G	Maximum number of simultaneously active connections
max xmit	G	Maximum size for transferred packets
only user	GS	Controls whether only registered users have access

password level	G	Maximum number of capital characters in password.
path	GS	Path of respective services
print command	GS	Command for output of transferred printer files
print ok	S	Printer access allowed (no)
printcap name	G	Path of the `printcap` file
printer name	S	Name of the default printer
protocol	G	Protocol version used
read only	S	Service allows only readable access (yes)
read prediction	G	Enables prediction reading
read raw	G	Reads data in large packets
root directory	G	Server performs `chroot` on transferred directory
set directory	S	User may use `setdir` command to change directories (no)
username	S	Name of server user
wide links	G	Allows following any links
write raw	G	Writes in large packets

CD-ROM

With the Samba server, a PC client can also easily use other server resources, such as a CD-ROM drive or a central removable hard disk drive.

Client configuration

A PC client has access to a Samba LAN manager server via access paths in the following form:

```
\\server name>\service
```

access path

To access the directory /home/pcuser on the server, the access path must look like the following:

```
\\master\pcuser
```

Figure 9.12. WfW connection

You can reach the printer ps of the server phoenix like this:

```
\\phoenix\ps
```

Under Windows for Workgroups, the configuration of this kind   Windows for
of server connection is carried out in the file or printer manager, as   Workgroups
Figure 9.12 shows.

An appropriate password must be entered the first time the server   password
is accessed.

SMB file system

Using Linux as an SMB client requires kernel support for the SMB   kernel support
file system and the package utilities smbfs.* This package also   utilities
contains kernel patches for Linux 1.2. However, you only need the
two programs smbmount and smbumount in the subdirectory util/.
Installation proceeds as follows:

```
golem:/usr/local/src/smbfs> make
...
golem:/usr/local/src/smbfs> make install
...
```

*Sunsite: system/Filesystems/smbfs/smbfs-*version*.tgz

255

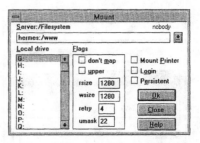

Figure 9.13. Mounting a directory via NFS

9.16 PC/NFS

Not only does NFS work well for connecting UNIX computers, it can also be used to integrate DOS PCs into a UNIX network. Aside from the numerous commercial products, you can also use a
xfs shareware package (xfs/xfs32). As with Samba, the TCP/IP stack from Microsoft is a prerequisite for xfs32. The PC/NFS daemon
pcnfsd (pcnfsd) must be running on the server end in addition to the NFS and mount daemons. The former is primarily needed for user authentication and printer administration. Most Linux distributions already contain these. They are usually activated at startup in one of the rc startup scripts (see Section 7.2). A spool directory for printer jobs is transferred as a parameter. Outstanding printer jobs are stored here.

```
/usr/sbin/rpc.pcnfsd /var/spool/xfs
```

printer With PC/NFS, you can access files and reach printer queues known to the server. A PC/NFS server is configured for access permission via the file /etc/exports (see Section 9.14), as usual for NFS. After installation on a PC client, an exported directory can
menu be mounted in the file manager under the new menu selection Xfs32.
printer queue Access to the Linux printer queue is carried out according to the same principle (Figure 9.13).
authentication The authentication can take place during the mounting or later through a special dialog in the file manager (Figure 9.14).

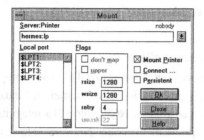

Figure 9.14. Access to the Linux printer queue

Without authentication, the user has access only to the public directories, because the user ID -2 is assigned to the user from the server side. The user assignment can be subsequently modified at any time.

public directories

9.17 ISODE

As explained in Section 3.2, a dedicated ISO standard covers the structure and implementation of networks. TCP/IP was already in existence when this standard was defined. Although TCP/IP can be mapped to the ISO/OSI model, it is not compatible with the standard. A developer who wants to create OSI-compatible applications under Linux can use the freeware ISO/OSI stack named ISODE (by Marshall T. Rose), which has been ported to Linux. This freeware can be found, for example, on the server sunsite.unc.edu in /pub/Linux/system/Network/isode.

ISO/OSI

Marshall T. Rose

Figure 9.15. Authentication

9.18   Novell Netware

Linux as Netware client

DOSemu

Linux 1.2 enabled contacting a Novell file server only from DOSemu or by patching `ncpfs` tools into the kernel. In Linux 2.0 the `ncpfs`

mounting Netware
volumes

file system (named after the NCP protocol) is integrated in the kernel. Now it is no problem to mount Netware volumes and to access

utilities

Netware printers. You need to install the package `ncpfs`* and also

IPX support

activate IPX support [†] and the NCP file system.[‡]

The following example mounts the volume SYS from server NW1 (as user LUTTI):

```
golem:~> ncpmount -S NWA -V SYS -U LUTTI /mnt
Logging into NWA as LUTTI
Password:
golem:~>
```

If you want to access Netware servers from DOSEmu and do not have access to Netware utilities for DOS, you can use the free

mars_dosutils

package `mars_dosutils`.*

Linux as Netware server

Meanwhile there are also two (free) Netware servers for Linux.

lwared

One is `lwared` [†]; because it requires a kernel patch that is not yet available for Linux 2.0, we introduce `mars_nwe`[‡] instead. `mars_nwe` offers everything that a commercial Netware server provides: The

file server, print
server, Bindery server

package contains file server, print server, Bindery server,[§] and an RIP/SAP daemon(for IPX routing). A small additional kernel patch

RIP/SAP daemon

(also available for Linux 2.0.*) accelerates `mars_nwe` by 30–50%; this puts the speed (according to measurements by the authors) in the

speed

range of Novell's Netware servers.

---

*Source: Sunsite, `system/Filesystems/ncpfs`

[†]Option `CONFIG_IPX`

[‡]`CONFIG_NCP_FS`

*Sunsite: `system/Filesystems/ncpfs`

[†]Sunsite: `system/Network/daemons/lwared`

[‡]`ftp://ftp.gwdg.de:/pub/linux/misc/ncpfs/mars_nwe`

[§]Bindery: small relational database for user management, etc.

After installation you still need to copy the file nw.ini to
/etc/nwserv.conf and modify it (network addresses, users,
volume directories, ...). If you enter the value 99 at option 15,
then all users are read from the /etc/passwd and entered in   users
the Netware Bindery. They initially receive a uniform password,
which can be changed (e.g., with nwpasswd from the ncpfs tools).
/etc/nwserv.conf contains detailed explanations. The following
is a simple example: Netware via the loopback interface (you can try
anything without introducing chaos into the network environment).

```
# Directories to be exported as volumes'
        1       SYS             /var/nwe/SYS/            k
# Server name
        2       MARS
# local host IP as internal server network address
        3       0x7f000001
# IPX devices (frame protocol is irrelevant here)
        4       0x10    lo      802.3   1
# Persistent IPX routing database?
        5       0
# Which server version is to be emulated?
        6       0
# Encrypt passwords for login and changing?
# 0 = yes for both
        7       0
# Two flags, normally uninteresting
        8       0x0
# Modes for newly created directories (first code) or files (second)
        9       0755    0664
# UID and GID of ''nobody''
        10      65534
        11      65534
# Supervisor login; third entry (= UNIX user) should never be root!
        12 SUPERVISOR   nw-adm    kar3/2Qi
# Normal user logins
        13      LUTTI   lutti   bukowski
# Section 15: automatic mapping of logins (decision required)
# 99: Users in /etc/passwd are automatically created in Bindery
# and receive the following password.
# 99 should be changed to 0 after the initial server startup!
        15      99      top-secret
# Several tests on server startup
16      1
# Printer queue(s)
        21      DJET            SYS:/PRINT/D    lpr
# Various debug levels
        100     0               # debug IPX KERNEL (0 ¦ 1)
        101     1               # debug NWSERV
        102     0               # debug NCPSERV
        103     0               # debug NWCONN
        104     0               # debug (start) NWCLIENT
        105     0               # debug NWBIND
        106     1               # debug NWROUTED
# Log configuration
200     1                   # 0 = no log file and don't daemonize nwserv/nwrouted
                            # 1 = daemonize nwserv/nwrouted and use log file
201     /var/log/nw.log     # file name of log file
202     0                   # 1=creat new log file, 0=append to log file
# Timing
210     1                   # 1 .. 600  (default 10) seconds after server
                            # really goes down after a down command
211     60                  # 10 .. 600 (default 60) broadcasts every x seconds
# Logging routing information
```

```
300    1
301    /tmp/nw.routes
302    0x1
# Watchdogs
310    7
# Station file for special handling of stations
400  /etc/nwserv.stations  # for syntax see file in the examples directory
# Handling of ''get nearest server request''
401    0       # 0 = ignore entry 400, get nearest response ever enabled
               # 1 = 400 are excludes, get nearest response normally enabled
               # 2 = 400 are includes, get nearest response normally disabled
# Handling of ''create connection call''
402    0
```

startup

automatic IPX

configuration

nwserv launches all services. With corresponding entries in
/etc/nwserv.conf, nwserv automatically configures the IPX
interfaces. You will find information on the status of the IPX system
in the files /proc/net/ipx*. The following is an example of the
above dummy configuration:

```
> cat /proc/net/ipx*
Local_Address  Remote_Address              Tx_Queue  Rx_Queue  State  Uid
7F000001:4000  Not_Connected               00000000  00000000  07     000
7F000001:0452  Not_Connected               00000000  00000000  07     000
7F000001:0453  Not_Connected               00000000  00000000  07     000
7F000001:4001  Not_Connected               00000000  00000000  07     000
7F000001:4002  Not_Connected               00000000  00000000  07     000
7F000001:4003  Not_Connected               00000000  00000000  07     000
7F000001:0451  Not_Connected               00000000  00000000  07     000
7F000001:4004  Not_Connected               00000000  00000000  07     000
Network     Node_Address    Primary   Device    Frame_Type
7F000001    000000000001    Yes       Internal  None
Network     Router_Net      Router_Node
7F000001    Directly        Connected
```

status messages

nwserv does not use syslog for status messages, but writes
them to the terminal from which it was started. It also uses the log file
/tmp/nw.log; in /etc/nwserv.conf, however, you can specify
another file.

## Chapter 10

Network applications

In the previous chapter we explained the theoretical basis of TCP/IP and the lower protocol levels. We will now discuss the programs and servers that use these lower levels.

10.1   Network daemons

As we have already mentioned, the operating system core does not contain most TCP/IP server services. These are realized with separate daemons. Among these are servers for telnet, FTP, and e-mail, in particular. The list below provides an overview of the most important network daemons available under Linux. Depending on the distribution, the names sometimes have the prefix `rpc.` or `in..` These prefixes were omitted in the list.

server
daemons
telnet, FTP, mail

bootpd
> needed for booting diskless workstations and X terminals.

fingerd
> enables the user to finger other users, who are active on a (different) system.

ftpd
> used for transferring data from one system to another with FTP.

gated
> implements routing protocol for dynamic routing.

httpd
> WWW server daemon.

identd

> User Identification Server, implements the protocol defined
> in RFC1413 for identifying a user to a connection.

imapd

> imap server. This is used for access to mailboxes with imap
> clients such as pine.

ipop2d

> and ipop3d Server for POP2 or POP3 Protocol for accessing
> mails.

lpd

> Printer daemon includes the possibility to access a printer
> from a remote computer.

mountd

> permits using a file system of another computer in the local
> system.

nfsd

> makes data available as NFS server.

nmbd

> Netbios name server; has nothing to do with the DNS name
> server.

nntpd

> delivers News from Usenet.

ntalkd

> server for a talk variant.

pcnfsd

> server for PC NFS allowing PCs to access a system's files
> and printer.

pppd

> daemon for the PPP protocol (see Section 9.6)

rlogind

> enables login from a remote system using an rlogin
> command.

routed

> also responsible for dynamic routing; can be used instead of
> gated.

rplayd

> server for the rplay command for playing sounds.

rshd

>   permits executing a command from a remote system.

rstatd

>   server for rstat; outputs the kernel's statistical data.

rusersd

>   server for the rusers command; provides information on
>   the users that are logged in.

rwalld

>   server for the rwall command; outputs announcements to
>   users.

rwhod

>   server for rwho; provides and collects data on users that are
>   logged in.

sendmail

>   sends and receives mail in the network; smail can be used
>   as an alternative.

smail

>   sends and receives mail in the network. However, it is also
>   important without a direct IP connection; for instance, in a
>   UUCP configuration.

smbd

>   the SMB/LAN manager server (see Section 9.15)

talkd

>   enables interactive communication with other users through
>   the command talk.

tcpd

>   TCP wrapper daemon. Actual servers can invoke it and check
>   the address and permissions of the clients.

telnetd

>   similar to rlogind; enables a user to log in from a remote
>   computer.

tftpd

>   used like bootpd for booting other machines in the network.

timed

>   time synchronizer daemon; synchronizes the local com-
>   puter's time with that of the other computers in the
>   network.

xntpd

> another time daemon; implements the NTP protocol as
> defined in RFC135.

10.2   Internet daemon (inetd)

daemons   Most TCP/IP daemons are activated only when there is actual demand
for such services from another computer. If they were always active
in the background like other daemons, they would unnecessarily
consume memory and computation time. Therefore, these daemons
are not automatically started with the booting of the system.

Internet daemon   A UNIX system normally provides an Internet daemon (Internet
superserver), which waits for messages from the network and is
always active, unlike other network daemons. Every service has a
port number   fixed port number. The file /etc/services contains a registry of
services and their respective port numbers (Figure 10.1). Another
inetd.conf   file (/etc/inetd.conf., Figure 10.2) lists the respective daemons
that offer the requested service. Only when an actual connection is
requested does inetd start the respective daemon that takes over the
connection. Upon termination of the connection, the daemon is also
ended, while inetd continues to run.

```
tcpmux       1/tcp       # TCP Port Service Multiplexer
rje          5/tcp       # remote job entry
echo         7/tcp
echo         7/udp
discard      9/tcp       sink null
discard      9/udp       sink null
systat       11/udp      users
systat       11/tcp      users
daytime      13/udp
daytime      13/tcp
daytime      13/udp
netstat      15/udp
netstat      15/tcp
qotd         17/udp      quote
quote        17/tcp      # quote of the day
chargen      19/tcp      ttytst source
chargen      19/udp      ttytst source
ftp-data     20/tcp
ftp          21/tcp
telnet       23/tcp
smtp         25/tcp      mail #Simple Mail Transfer
nsw-fe       27/tcp      # NSW User System FE [24, RHT]
```

Figure 10.1. Section of a file /etc/services

These files are normally not changed. They only need to be modified if new services are added or if new options become necessary with a daemon update.

```
telnet     stream  tcp  nowait   root  /etc/telnetd    telnetd
ntalk      dgram   udp  wait     root  /etc/ntalkd     ntalkd
ftp        stream  tcp  nowait   root  /etc/ftpd       ftpd -l
finger     stream  tcp  nowait   root  /etc/fingerd    finger
shell      stream  tcp  nowait   root  /etc/rshd       rshd
login      stream  tcp  nowait   root  /etc/rlogind    rlogind
tftp       dgram   udp  wait     root  /etc/tftpd      tftpd /home/ftp
# Internal to inetd
echo       stream  tcp  nowait   root  internal
echo       dgram   udp  wait     root  internal
discard    stream  tcp  nowait   root  internal
discard    dgram   udp  wait     root  internal
daytime    stream  tcp  nowait   root  internal
daytime    dgram   udp  wait     root  internal
chargen    stream  tcp  nowait   root  internal
chargen    dgram   udp  wait     root  internal
```

Figure 10.2. The file /etc/inetd.conf

10.3 Telnet

The telnet protocol is one of the oldest in the Internet. It enables a user to log in to other computers in the network. This means that all the client's keyboard entries are sent to the server and all screen output is sent from the server to the client. The client thus simulates a virtual terminal.

logging in

virtual terminal

Under Linux and most other UNIX variants, telnet is implemented by the server daemon telnetd and the client program telnet. Telnet client programs also exist for most other operating systems, including even DOS.

telnetd

To log in on a different computer, the user invokes the program with a computer name or an IP address. A TCP connection is then established with the telnet daemon of the computer named.

name or IP address

```
linux2:/home/stefan>telnet sun1
Trying 141.7.1.20...
Connected to sun1.
Escape character is '^]'.

SunOS UNIX (sun1)

login:
```

265

port number

SMTP

NNTP

help

escape code

breaking connection

terminal trouble

xboard

Internet services

FAQs

news.answers

The `telnet` program only uses the port number of the telnet daemon to reserve a connection. A port number can be specified optionally after the host name, when telnet is invoked. For example, with `telnet hostname 25`, the user can establish a connection to port 25 of the computer. This port is reserved for SMTP, which is the e-mail protocol. With the appropriate port number, the user can also establish a connection to the NNTP daemon of a newsgroup (port 119). This feature even allows the user to enter `help` to receive a description from the server daemon of its protocol commands. Such features are very useful for debugging.

With the escape code (on German keyboards [Ctrl][AltGr][9]) you can enter TELNET control mode. By entering `quit` you can break the connection.

Sometimes the (UNIX) host does not recognize the Linux terminal—this causes messages like `'linux': Unknown terminal type` and can be accompanied by curious colors, output errors, incorrectly converted characters, etc. In this case you should change the environment variable TERM in `vt102`.

In addition, on certain ports some servers offer games such as text adventures, multi-user dungeons (MUDs, see Section 12.11), or chess. The program `xboard`, which normally serves as the graphical front end for the GNU chess program, is able to establish such a telnet connection and in parallel to represent the positions graphically.

Lists of sources for such Internet services are stored on various FTP servers under the name `internet.services` or `internet.resources`. Along with FAQs (frequently asked questions), such lists are published regularly in the newsgroup `news.answers`. Particularly newcomers to the Internet should learn to use a news reader, since this eases access to other servers and information sources (see Section 10.9).

10.4 Secure shell

password snooping

The traditional `telnet` is quite insecure because the entire session is transmitted as plain text. In particular, hackers can read passwords. Thus an alternative is the secure shell `ssh` by Tatu Ylonen (`ylo@cs.hut.fi`). It encrypts all transmitted procedures with the

methods DES or IDEA and provides better authentication (public · encryption
key cryptography) than traditional UNIX passwords. If the host that · better authentication
is the source of the ssh connection has a private key and the server
knows the corresponding public key *and* trusts the client, then there
is no need for the user to enter a password. This allows executing
commands on the remote machine á la rsh (only more securely)
without a login procedure (even from shell scripts). However, · secure automatic login
ssh is a tool rather than a solution, and if it is used incorrectly,
can even cause additional security problems. Thus you should
read the documentation carefully and be familiar with elementary
cryptography concepts. Cryptography and ssh configuration are
described in Chapter 15 in more detail.

10.5   FTP

FTP is a protocol used to transfer data via the Internet. FTP stands
for File Transfer Protocol and is usually implemented under Linux · File Transfer Protocol
and other UNIX versions through the FTP server daemon ftpd · ftpd
and the client program ftp. Washington University's wu-ftpd · wu-ftpd
daemon is frequently used as an alternative to the simple ftpd. This
daemon offers enhancements particularly in the areas of security and
configurability.

Simply stated, the term FTP server usually refers to a computer
offering anonymous access via FTP, rather than the server daemon · anonymous FTP
ftpd. Large FTP servers are generally equipped with several
gigabytes of hard disk capacity and offer a large selection of freeware, · software
shareware, and public domain programs.

Using FTP

To establish a connection to the most important Linux FTP server · Linux FTP server
in Finland, enter ftp nic.funet.fi. This starts the FTP program
that attempts to establish a TCP connection to the other computer via
the fixed port number 21 of the FTP daemon. Once this connection · port 21
has been established, the guest is requested to enter a user ID. With
FTP servers that are freely accessible, guests can enter the user name · e-mail address
ftp or anonymous and should use their own e-mail address as a · as password

267

password. With the commands of the ftp program, such as cd, dir, get, or put, the user can then search for and transfer files.

protocol

These commands do not correspond to the commands used by the FTP protocol internally, but the FTP program recognizes them and translates them into the appropriate protocol commands like port or retr. Only these protocol commands are transferred. For data transfer, a second TCP connection is established to link the data.

help

You can find individual commands on the ftp Manual page or in the help files of the ftp program, which can be retrieved by entering help. The most important commands are summarized below.

The following example demonstrates an FTP session:

```
linux2:/home/stefan>ftp sun1
Connected to sun1.
220 sun1 FTP server (SunOS 4.1) ready.
Name (sun1:stefan): ftp
331 Guest login ok, send ident as password.
Password (sun1:ftp): strobel@demo.de
230 Guest login ok, access restrictions apply.
ftp> ls
200 PORT command successful.
150 ASCII data connection for /bin/ls (141.7.1.41,1157) (0 bytes).
total 6
drwxrwxrwx  2 0      150       512 Jul 16 16:14 Incoming
-rw-r--r--  1 0      1         139 Aug 22 12:33 README
drwxr-xr-x  2 0      150       512 May 10 09:51 bin
drwxr-xr-x  2 0      150       512 May 10 09:54 dev
drwxr-xr-x  5 0      150       512 Jun 20 15:36 pub
drwxr-xr-x  3 0      150       512 May 10 09:52 usr
226 ASCII Transfer complete.
ftp> get README
200 PORT command successful.
150 ASCII data connection for README (141.7.1.41,1158) (139 bytes).
226 ASCII Transfer complete.
142 bytes received in 0 seconds (0.14 Kbytes/s)
ftp> bye
221 Goodbye.
```

graphical front ends

ftp.x.org

You can also transfer files more comfortably with one of the graphical front ends for FTP rather than with the command-line–oriented ftp program. Many different variants of graphic front ends are available from the usual Linux FTP servers or the official server for X11 programs, ftp.x.org. The XView-based ftptool is also quite popular (Figure 10.3).

Important commands include the following:

get *file*	download a file from FTP server
mget *pattern*	download all files matching the *pattern*. For each file, ftp prompts the user for whether to download; the question can be toggled off with prompt
hash	on a download, for each transferred kilobyte an # is output
cd *directory*	change directory
ls	display directory contents
close	end session
bye	end session and quit ftp

Tips:

- On a login or change of directory, FTP servers often return long infotexts, which can be quite time consuming on a slow connection. On login, enter a dash (-) before the login name to disable server info.   *suppressing server info*
- Newer Netscape versions can also download files from FTP servers. Enter the URL as follows: ftp://*ftp-server/path*
- You can create a file .netrc in your home directory and store in it your login name and password for FTP login on various servers. ftp then attempts to use these values for an automatic login. This is an example of a .netrc file: *.netrc*

```
machine lemming.stud.fh-heilbronn.de
        login elling
        macdef init
                hash
                bin

default
        login anonymous i
        password elling@stud.fh-heilbronn.de
        macdef init
                hash
                bin
```

For automatic login, ftp employs the specifications for the respective FTP server (machine); if the server does not agree with any of the specifications, the default is used. If you have

269

Figure 10.3. ftptool

specified a password for a login other than anonymous, then
.netrc must not be readable for other users (in this case ftp
refuses to do an automatic login). The correct permissions are
set with **chmod 0600 .netrc**. However, you should still not
record any passwords in the file, especially not critical ones like
the root password. Along with the macdef init entries, several
commands are listed for execution after an automatic login.

Providing FTP services

The FTP server daemon wu-ftpd* is included in most Linux
distributions. It is invoked by inetd when a connection request
reaches the FTP port.

All operations executed in an FTP session are executed on the
FTP server as user ftp. This user is configured in four files that
in part already contain appropriate settings. Thus we discuss only
several options here.

ftpaccess

    upload

        specifies the directories in which the FTP user can
        store files (/pub/incoming).

*Sunsite: system/Network/file-transfer/

`email`

    mail address of FTP administrator.

`passwd-check`

    specifies how strict the authentication should be; for security reasons you should always specify `rfc822 warn` or `rfc822 enforce`.

`chmod, delete, overwrite, rename, umask`

    allows configuration of users with permissions for deleting or overwriting files, etc. It is unnecessary and risky to give FTP users such permissions; the FTP administrator should work locally or via `telnet` or `ssh`.

`message`

    If an FTP user changes to the specified directory, the specified file is displayed. You can employ placeholders that are replaced with the current time, etc. when displayed.

`class`

    defines a certain class of users; usually `local` (connections from the same host) and `remote` are already defined.

`limit`

    limits the number of users in a certain class.

`ftpusers`

    This lists the users who *cannot* log in to the FTP server. You should at least list the login names that have special privileges (in particular, you need to prevent a login by `root`).

For additional details, see `ftpd(8)`, `ftpaccess(5)`, `ftpconversions(5)`, and `ftpusers(5)`.

10.6   Archie

Given the vast number of FTP servers and the huge amount of free software available on them, it can be quite difficult to find the right software to cover a particular requirement. This is where Archie servers provide valuable help. An Archie server furnishes access

finding programs

271

software database — to a multiple-gigabyte database that contains an index of the most important FTP servers on the Internet. This database is updated automatically at regular intervals.

Archie servers are located at the following addresses:

- archie.th-darmstadt.de (Germany)
- archie.funet.fi (Finland)
- archie.ans.net (New York)
- archie.au (Australia)
- archie.doc.ic.ac.uk (Great Britain)
- archie.switch.ch (Switzerland)

telnet — To submit a query to an Archie server, log in to one of the respective hosts with `telnet` with the user name `archie`* and use a simple query language to search for programs.

xarchie — The graphical front end `archie`,† also available under Linux, provides this service with more comfort. The user needs only to enter the keyword and select the search mode, and `xarchie` establishes the connection to the already set-up server. Soon the files and their server browser — locations are displayed in a browser. Newer versions of `xarchie` can even start an FTP transfer directly to retrieve the desired files from their respective FTP servers.

whatis — In addition to searching for programs by name, an Archie server provides a `whatis` database in which the `whatis` command yields a description — concise description of a specific program. If the name of a program is not known at all or only in part, `whatis` can display a list of a relevant subset of all registered programs by name along with a description of each.

query per e-mail — In lieu of Internet access, an Archie server can be queried per e-mail. Here the appropriate command is sent to the user `archie` on such a server. As with FTP mail servers, sending the command `help` to the Archie server in the first line of the mail produces a more detailed description.

---

*Sunsite: `system/Network/info-systems`
†Sunsite: `X11/xapps/networked`

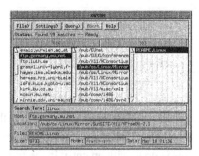

Figure 10.4. File search via xarchie

10.7 Berkeley r-utilities

The University of California at Berkeley's BSD UNIX exerted a great deal of influence on networking capability under UNIX. Through the successful integration of TCP/IP into the UNIX operating system, this implementation made a significant contribution to the further proliferation of TCP/IP.

The Berkeley r-utilities are a group of programs whose names begin with the letter r, the most important being rlogin, rsh, and rcp. The r stands for remote. The Berkeley r-utilities belong to the standard software of a networked UNIX workstation. Over time they have been enriched by a number of programs such as rwho and ruptime. As in many proprietary UNIX variants, utilities from the Berkeley Distribution were ported to Linux.

The basic idea of these utilities is to provide a user who has an account on multiple computers on a network, a simple way to log in to other computers on the network, to run programs, or to copy files, without having to enter a password each time. To do this without creating a security flaw, certain users from other computers can be defined as *trusted users*. Only such users can then log in to the computer and use its services without having to enter a password. This definition is systemwide in the file /etc/hosts.equiv or in .rhosts in the home directories of the respective users for their own accounts.

BSD UNIX

rlogin, rsh, rcp

porting

logging in

without password

trusted users

273

```
#
# Accepted hosts and users
#

zeus.demo.de
hermes.demo.de strobel
sun.demo.de arnold
```

hosts.equiv

.rhosts

different user IDs

Only the system administrator can modify the file /etc/
hosts.equiv. If an individual user wants to grant access permission
to another user, this is done with an entry in the file .rhosts in the
respective home directory. This type of file is particularly useful when
a user has different user IDs on different machines in the network.
Appropriately set .rhosts files make network-wide access to a
user's own directories considerably easier.

reserved port

superuser privileges

Reserved ports provide an additional security measure. Here
the server checks the TCP port number of the client: if it is not a
privileged port, the server denies the connection. Reserved ports on
UNIX machines are available only for users with superuser access
privileges. This prevents a normal user with another, self-written
program from feigning a false computer or user name in order to gain
access to another computer. However, this means that the r-utilities
have to run with the user ID *root* for this service.

Kerberos

Newer implementations of the Berkeley r-utilities also support
Kerberos, which achieves an additional increase in security. The
Kerberos system, which checks passwords and user IDs, was
developed at the Massachusetts Institute of Technology (MIT).

rlogin

telnet

For the user, the remote login program rlogin functions similarly to
the telnet program, except that with an appropriate configuration
it requires no user ID or password. rlogin does not permit the
specification of a deviating port number.

```
hermes:/home/strobel> rlogin zeus
zeus:/home/strobel>
```

In some Linux distributions the rlogind daemon in.rlogind
(in /usr/sbin) has a bug. This prevents automatic login

without a password. To work around this, copy the daemon to `in.rlogind.old` and create a shell script named `in.rlogind`:

```
#!/bin/sh
exec /usr/sbin/in.rlogind.old $@
```

Don't forget to set execute permissions!

rcp

`rcp` supports remote copying of files between computers. However, the exact access path must be specified. Therefore, in many cases   access path
users prefer the interactive `ftp` utility or access via a Network File
System (NFS). In contrast to normal FTP, `rcp` can also recursively   NFS
copy subtrees of file hierarchies.

```
zeus:/home/strobel> ls
Amster.txt  README       hn-net.tki  lainel/     maurer.txt
Buch/       emacst.txt   kernel.txt  mail/       mib.txt
zeus:/home/strobel> rcp -r strobel@sun1:/home/prog/xprogs
zeus:/home/strobel> ls
Amster.txt  README       hn-net.tki  lainel/     maurer.txt
Buch/       emacst.txt   kernel.txt  mail/       mib.txt
xprogs/
```

rsh

The remote shell `rsh` allows a user to execute programs on other   programs
computers. Beyond the command to be executed, the name of the
remote computer and, optionally, a user ID are specified. The output
of the executed command is then routed back to the local machine
via the network.

Beyond the remote execution of commands on other machines,
this program is also adept at fast data transfer between computers.   data transfer with rsh
Here the user exploits the `rsh` feature that allows combining the
local machine's own standard input and output with the program that
it executes on the target computer. For example, this enables making
a backup of files from a local hard disk onto a streamer on another   backup files
computer on the network.

275

```
stef1:/home/strobel> rsh lia "ls .em*"
.emacs
.emacs-bkmrks
.emacs-places
.emacs-places~
.emacs-skp
.emacs~
stef1:/home/strobel>
stef1:/home/strobel> rsh lia "tar cfz - .em*" | tar xvfz -
.emacs
.emacs-bkmrks
.emacs-places
.emacs-places~
.emacs-skp
.emacs~
stef1:/home/strobel>
```

10.8 Mail

daemon

The TCP/IP e-mail service usually consists of a daemon, which transfers messages to other computers with the SMTP protocol, and programs for reading and writing mails. These are also called mail

mail readers

readers.

sendmail and smail

Under Linux, both the popular sendmail program and the alternative smail are available for transferring mails. Aside from transport via a TCP/IP network, these also work well for UUCP. Most packets contain pine and elm as mail readers. In addition, there are also graphic programs such as mumail, which allows for easy mail administration under X11.

elm

older, but widely

elm is a somewhat older, but widely propagated program for reading

propagated

and writing e-mail (Figure 10.5). It exists for most UNIX platforms. When elm is first started up, two subdirectories are created in the user's home directory: a configuration directory and a directory for

list

storing received mails. A list displays new mail with the sender and the title of the message. The mail can be selected with the cursor keys, then read and stored as files.

external editor

To write mails, the user defines an external editor in the elm options. elm also handles mails in Multipurpose Internet Mail

MIME

Extension (MIME) format, which can contain graphics, sounds, or

metamail

programs. These MIME mails can be output with the metamail program and the respective presentation programs.

Figure 10.5. elm

Pine

`Pine`, which stands for "Pine Is No longer Elm" or Program for Internet News & E-mail, affords more comfort than `elm`. One of its major differences with respect to `elm` is `pine`'s feature allowing access to the Internet News (see Section 10.9). `Pine` contains an editor called `pico` that significantly eases the production of mail. Since `pine` uses the IMAP2 protocol, it can also manage mailboxes that are located on a remote machine. This proves particularly interesting for a user who often switches among several machines. IMAP2 assures consistent access to the mail of the home machine and now supports the MIME standard as well.

Internet News

IMAP

Use the file `.pinerc` in the user's home directory to configure Pine. Settings for all users can be stored in the file `pine.conf`, which is normally located in the directory `/usr/local/lib`. Below are some of the most interesting settings:

.pinerc

pine.conf

Figure 10.6. The mail front end Pine

```
user-domain=demo.de
```

This defines the domain name in outgoing mails. If someone

sender address with the user name `mueller`, for example, at the computer
`hermes.demo.de` sends a mail, then the sender address is entered
as `mueller@demo.de` according to the setting shown above.

```
inbox-path=mail/inbox
```

path for incoming   The setting `inbox-path` determines the path of the folder for
incoming mails. This folder is usually a file with the user's name

/var/spool/mail   in the directory `/var/spool/mail`. Inside Pine, the folder has the
name INBOX. If mail arrives in a different directory, or if a program
such as `deliver` automatically sorts the messages into different files,
the file path can be changed.

```
incoming-folders=Linux mail/linux,
        Projekt mail/project,
        Zeus {zeus.demo.de}
```

additional mailboxes   Additional mailboxes can be entered in the `incoming`
`folders` line. These folders may be other local files or mailboxes

title and path   on other computers. A title and a path are defined for every folder. If
a mailbox is on another computer, the name of the computer is given
in brackets before the path. The mailboxes are accessible in this case

IMAP   via the IMAP2 protocol.

feature-list   With the variable `feature-list` you can influence pine's
behavior. Possible settings are described in the commentaries of

old growth   the `.pinerc` file. Frequently used settings are `old-growth` and
`auto-move-read-msgs`. The latter automatically moves mail that
has been read into the folder called `read-messages` when pine is
closed.

```
feature-list=old-growth, auto-move-read-msgs
```

You can also define the program that pine invokes to view

graphics   graphics in MIME mails.

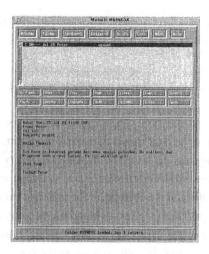

Figure 10.7. Mail front end MuMail

```
image-viewer=xv
```

MuMail

One program with a graphic interface is mumail (Figure 10.7). This
program uses X11 and can be comfortably used with the mouse. The
range of its functions is approximately the same as elm. MuMail can
also be used to create and view multimedia mail.

X11

deliver

There are several programs available for automatically sorting mail,
deliver and procmail being among the most widespread. We use
deliver as an example to show how this kind of program works
and how to configure it.

sorting mail

First of all, deliver must have control over incoming mail. A
user who wishes to have mails sorted can pass them on to deliver
with an entry in the file .forward. The contents of this file then
looks like this:

incoming mail

```
|/usr/bin/deliver benutzername
```

You can also use `.forward` to forward arriving mail to another host (if the user has moved):

```
user@host
```

As an alternative, you can integrate `deliver` directly into the configuration of the mail transport daemon transport.

Following this, `deliver` is invoked with every arriving mail, and the message is transferred to `deliver`'s standard entry. `deliver` writes the header and the contents of the mail in a temporary file and

.deliver

user

invokes a script called `.deliver` in the user's home directory. This script determines the mail's target. The individual user must create the script, and it must be able to analyze the contents of the mail. The analysis is usually based on keywords in the sender address or the subject line.

standard output

The script outputs to the standard output what should happen with the message. The syntax of the most important output possibilities is listed below.

`:Mailbox`

Appends the current mail to the file listed.

`Command`

Invokes the defined command and transfers the mail to the standard input.

The following example demonstrates such a script:

```
user="$1"
KENN='/usr/bin/header -f To -f CC -f SENDER -f Reply-To $HEADER'
SUBJECT='/usr/bin/header -f Subject $HEADER'

# Filter Mailinglisten
case "$KENN" in
*tkined@ibr.cs.tu-bs.de* )                       echo :Mail/IN/tkined;    exit ;;
*samba@* )                                       echo :Mail/IN/samba;     exit ;;
*-new-tty* )                                     echo :Mail/IN/linux;     exit ;;
*linux* | *Linux* )                              echo :Mail/IN/linux;     exit ;;
*Firewalls-Digest* | *firewalls-digest*)         echo :Mail/IN/firewall;  exit ;;
esac

case "$SUBJECT" in
*Daily Usenet report*)                           echo :Mail/IN/news;      exit ;;
*Quota usage on*)                                echo :Mail/IN/system;    exit ;;
esac
```

```
# Andere Mails
echo ":Mail/IN/default"
```

The system administrator can install deliver to invoke a central   central scripts
script before the .deliver scripts, so that mails are delivered to the
various users first. You will find more details on the Manual page for
deliver.

smail configuration

There are various programs available for simply transport ing mails.   transport
Some distributions use the program sendmail, but most use smail.   smail
In this section we describe the configuration of smail for a computer
with a direct Internet connection connection. The modifications for
a UUCP connection are explained subsequently.   UUCP
The files in the directory /var/lib/smail contain the   /var/lib/smail
configuration of the smail daemon. Some distributions combine
the configuration files with the help programs in the directory
/usr/lib/smail. smail can be customized on compilation or   compilation
later in the configuration files. In the latter case, the settings in the
file overwrite the values defined on compilation, which are normally
unusable.
The most important configuration files are

• config
• routers
• transports
• directors

The config file contains global settings such as the name of the   global settings
computer. The entries are normally in the form *attribute=value*.
The # character introduces a comment.

```
#
# smail configuration for hermes (our mail server)
#

hostname=hermes.demo.de
more_hostnames=demo.de
```

hostname defines the name of the local computer. It is used in the header of outgoing messages and also for recognizing incoming

more_hostnames

messages to the local computer. more_hostnames lists alternative names. In the example above, hermes is the mail server for the domain demo.de. The entry more_hostnames=demo.de effects that the actual computer name can be left out of mail addresses. Thus strobel@demo.de is sufficient, rather than the long address strobel@hermes.demo.de.

routers, transports,
and directors

The files routers, transports, and directors have more complicated tasks. They use the address to determine the path and the type of delivery. First the address is separated into a *target*

target address

address and a *remainder*. In the address strobel@demo.de, the target address is demo.de and strobel is the remainder. The target

local

address provides information about whether the mail is local or whether it needs to be forwarded to another computer. For local mail, the file directors helps to determine how the mail should be

route

delivered to the addressee. The file routers determines the route for remote addresses and defines the protocol to be used. The options of the various types of transport (SMTP via TCP/IP, UUCP, etc.) are defined in the transports file.

routers

The file routers contains a list of router entries. These routers have nothing to do with IP routers. They define an instance, which has

driver

a driver assigned to it, within the smail program. smail forwards the mail addresses one after the other to the defined routers, which then check whether they can process each address.

attributes

Generic and driver-specific attributes are defined for every router in the file routers. The generic attributes can be entered for each computer and they define the driver and the transport to be used. The

characteristics

specific attributes can influence the individual characteristics of the particular drivers.

The routers file in the following example contains definitions for a computer with both an Internet connection and UUCP connections. Since entries for MX records resolution are missing in many distributions, smail cannot be used for Internet without reconfiguration.

```
#
force_paths:
        driver=pathalias,
        transport=uux,                  # Use the uux transport
        always;                         #
        file=forcepaths,                # Name of the file
        proto=lsearch,                  # direct access (no dbm files)
        optional,                       # The file is optional
#
match-inet-addrs:
        driver=gethostbyaddr,           # processes IP addresses in []
        transport=smtp;                 # Transport is smtp
        fail_if_error,
        check_for_local
#
match_mx_hosts:
        driver=bind,                    # Resolution of MX records
        transport=smtp;                 # TCP/IP SMTP
        defnames,
        defer_no_connect,               # retry if name server is down
        local_mx_okay,
#
match-inet-hosts:
        driver=gethostbyname,           # resolve host names with resolver
        transport=smtp;
        domain =
#
smart_host:
        driver=smarthost,               # special-case driver
        transport=smtp;                 # by default deliver over SMTP
```

The first router entered here is only necessary if UUCP
connections are used in addition to an Internet connection. The router
enables the creation of a file called forcepaths, which contains the
domain names and target addresses for uucp. Mail to domains that
are entered in this file is sent to the target address entered in this file.

Internet and UUCP

The router match-inet-addrs makes it possible to use
IP addresses in a mail address. If it is not possible to resolve
a symbolic name for any reason, you could use the address
strobel@[141.7.41] instead of strobel@hermes.demo.de.

IP addresses

match_mx_hosts is the router normally used for mail on the
Internet. It resolves the MX entry for a symbolic address.

MX records

The match-inet-hosts entry can resolve addresses with
help from the resolver (see Section 9.10). This enables the use of
symbolic addresses in the form name@host. In this case, however,
MX records cannot be resolved. Thus a mail could be delivered
to strobel@hermes.demo.de, but not to strobel@demo.de,
because there is no computer with this name. There is only an MX
record that refers to hermes.

resolver

smarthost
gateway

The smarthost router forwards all mail to another computer. This router is used if there is a central mail gateway that is responsible for mail delivery, and the local computer is not intended or able to deliver mail directly. The address of the mail gateway to which the smarthost driver should forward mail is usually defined with the variables smart_path in the config file. The transport (see below) can also be entered with the variable smart_transport in the config file. These settings overwrite the attributes that may have been entered in the file routers.

smart_path
smart_transport

We discuss the use of the smarthost router further in conjunction with the uucp settings.

transports

The characteristics of the individual transport possibilities are defined in the file transports. This has the same structure as the file routers. Both generic and driver specific attributes can be entered for every transport.

```
local:  driver = appendfile,          # append message to a file
        return_path,                  # include a Return-Path: field
        local,                        # use local forms for delivery
        from,                         # supply a From_ envelope line
        unix_from_hack;               # insert > before From in body
        file = /usr/spool/mail/${lc:user},
        group = mail,                 # group to own file
        mode = 0660,                  # group can access
        suffix = "\n",                # append an extra newline
        append_as_user,
#
pipe:   driver = pipe,                # pipe message to another program
        return_path, local, from, unix_from_hack;
        cmd = "/bin/sh -c $user",     # send address to the Bourne Shell
        parent_env,                   # environment info from parent addr
        pipe_as_user,                 # use user-id associated with address
        umask = 0022,                 # umask for child process
        -log_output,                  # do not log stdout/stderr
        ignore_status,                # exit status may be bogus, ignore it
        ignore_write_errors,          # ignore broken pipes
#
file:   driver = appendfile,
        return_path, local, from, unix_from_hack;

        file = $user,                 # file is taken from address
        append_as_user,               # use user-id associated with address
        expand_user,                  # expand ~ and $ within address
        suffix = "\n",
        mode = 0644
#
uux:    driver = pipe,
        uucp,                         # use UUCP-style addressing forms
        from,                         # supply a From_ envelope line
        max_addrs = 5,                # at most 5 addresses per invocation
        max_chars = 200;              # at most 200 chars of addresses
        cmd = "/usr/bin/uux - -r -g$grade $host!rmail $((${strip:user})$)",
        umask = 0022,
        pipe_as_sender
```

```
#
smtp:    driver = smtp,
         -max_addrs,
         -max_chars
```

The transport `local` delivers mail to local users. It appends
the text to the mailbox file of the appropriate user in the directory
`/var/spool/mail`. The driver used for this is called `appendfile`.
Its specific attributes define the user, the group, and the access
permissions with which the mailbox file is to be written.

local mails
/var/spool/mail

attributes

The transport `pipe` is used when mail is to be forwarded to a
program with a pipe upon delivery to the local computer. This may
be the case if users have created a file `.forward` in their home
directory, which contains a pipe with a program name as an address,
for instance `|/usr/bin/deliver user`.

pipe

.forward

`smail` uses `file` implicitly if an address contains a path name.
As with `local`, it uses the `appendfile` driver.

file

The transport `uux` delivers mails via `uucp`. As with the transport
`pipe`, it uses the driver `pipe` to forward mail to a program's standard
output. Using the `-r` flag in the invocation of `uux` prevents immediate
delivery of mail. In this case, they are stored in the `uucp` spool
directory and forwarded at the next poll.

-r

The process of delivering local mail is defined in the file
`directors`. The entries in this file primarily direct internal
features, such as the expansion of addresses from the file
`/usr/lib/aliases.` or forwarding mail via the file `.forward.`
It has the same format as the files `routers` and `transports`.

directors

aliases

```
aliasinclude:
        driver = aliasinclude,
        nobody; copysecure,
        copyowners,

forwardinclude:
        driver = forwardinclude,        # use this special-case driver
        nobody;
        copysecure,                     # get perms from forwarding director
        copyowners,                     # get owners from forwarding director

aliases:
        driver = aliasfile,             # general-purpose aliasing director
        -nobody,
        owner = owner-$user;            # problems go to an owner address
        file = /usr/lib/aliases,
        modemask = 002,
        #proto = dbm,                    # use dbm(3X) library for access
```

```
            proto = lsearch,                    # use linear search through text file

    forward:
            driver = aliasfile,                 # general-purpose aliasing director
            -nobody,
            owner = real-$user;                 # problems go to an owner address
            file = /var/lib/smail/forward,
            modemask = 002,
            proto = lsearch,

    dotforward:
            driver = forwardfile,               # general-purpose forwarding director
            owner = Postmaster,                 # problems go to the site mail admin
            nobody,
            sender_okay;                        # sender never removed from expansion
            file = ~/.forward,                  # .forward file in home directories
            checkowner,                         # the user can own this file
            owners = root,                      # or root can own the file
            modemask = 002,                     # it should not be globally writable
            caution = daemon:root,              # don't run things as root or daemon
            unsecure = "~uucp:~nuucp:/tmp:/usr/tmp"

    user:   driver = user;                      # driver to match usernames
            transport = local                   # local transport goes to mailboxes

    lists:  driver = forwardfile,
            caution,                            # flag all addresses with caution
            nobody,                             # and then associate the nobody user
            owner = owner-$user;
            file = lists/${lc:user}             # lists is under $smail_lib_dir

    owners: driver = forwardfile,
            caution,                            # flag all addresses with caution
            nobody,                             # and then associate the nobody user
            owner = postmaster;
            prefix = "owner-,"
            file = lists/owner/${lc:user}       # lists is under $smail_lib_dir

    request: driver = forwardfile,
            caution,                            # flag all addresses with caution
            nobody,                             # and then associate the nobody user
            owner = postmaster;
            suffix = "-request,"
            file = lists/request/${lc:user}     # lists is under $smail_lib_dir
```

lists

mailing lists

address

The entries under lists, owners, and requests are especially interesting. They make it possible to create mailing lists very simply. Here it is sufficient to create a file in the directory /var/lib/smail, which uses the address of the list as a name. The addresses of all list recipients are entered in this file.

smail and deliver

deliver

If there are a number of users who want their mail sorted into different mailboxes by a program such as procmail or deliver, we recommend integrating the program directly into the transport (local). Using the example of deliver, we will demonstrate in this section how the necessary changes should be made.

The transport `local` uses the driver `pipe` instead of the driver `appendfile`. Use the complete path of `deliver` as the program. Normally this is `/usr/bin/deliver`.

pipe

```
local:  driver = pipe,
        return_path,                    # include a Return-Path: field
        local,                          # use local forms for delivery
        from,                           # supply a From_ envelope line
        unix_from_hack;                 # insert > before From in body
        cmd = "/usr/bin/deliver ${lc:user}",
        parent_env,                     # environment info from parent addr
        pipe_as_user,                   # use user-id associated with address
        umask = 0022,                   # umask for child process
        -ignore_status,
        -ignore_write_errors,
```

Users wishing to have their mail automatically sorted into various folders then only need to enter a script with the name `.deliver` into their home directories.

.deliver

smail and UUCP
If you do not have a direct Internet connection or want to transport mail only via UUCP for other reasons, then the simplest method is to use the `smarthost` router and forward all outgoing mails to a computer with a better connection. To do this, remove all entries except `smarthost` from the file `routers` and set the variable `smart_path` to the address of the mail gateway and the variable `smart_transport` to uux in the `config` file.

smarthost

smart_path
smart_transport

You will find more detailed information and the configuration details on the Manual page for `smail`.

10.9   News

The Internet News is one of the most important sources of information about new developments and many other subjects.

information

Structure and makeup
The principle is quite simple. News servers have been set up at many locations around the Internet, for example, at almost every university. A news server manages various news groups, which amount to bidirectional electronic bulletin boards, each on a certain subject

news server

many topics

287

area, for posting, reading, and replying. These subjects range from operating systems and programs to sports, computer games, and other recreational activities, to matters of social interest. Several thousand such newsgroups exist worldwide.

several thousand groups

All news servers are constantly exchanging postings with neighboring news servers, so that a message that is posted on a given news server in a certain group quickly propagates to all news servers. These postings remain on the news servers for a certain time, for example, two weeks, before they are deleted.

The entirety of all computers that exchange these postings in the form of news is called Usenet. Communication between these machines was originally based on modems and UUCP (UNIX to UNIX copy). This made it significantly slower than the current connections on the Internet, which meanwhile uses a special protocol called NNTP instead of UUCP.

Usenet
UUCP
NNTP

Newsgroups

newsgroup names

The newsgroups are structured hierarchically, as shown in Figure 10.8. Their full names, separated by periods, reflect their position in this hierarchy. comp.os.linux .announce, for example, means that this newsgroup resides under the heading comp, which deals with computers, software, and computer science in general. os indicates operating systems, and comp.os.linux is the leader for all names of groups under the comp hierarchy that have to do with Linux.

comp

Linux

In addition to comp there are many other important hierarchies such as sci for groups that discuss scientific subject matter and alt for a broad range of alternative subject areas.

sci

Moderated groups

Groups can be either open to any NetNews participant or moderated. In the latter case a moderator decides which proposed postings might be of interest to the readership of the newsgroup; these are posted, while the rest find their way into a black hole. For example, a moderated newsgroup for Linux is comp.os.linux.announce, which posts exclusively announcements of new programs or system extensions. This is especially necessary because the number of postings in the other Linux groups is so overwhelming that a

moderator

new programs

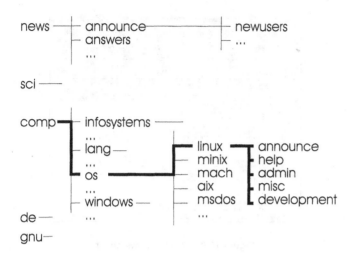

Figure 10.8. Excerpt from the newsgroup hierarchy

participant has to invest a great deal of time to read them and keep up to date.

Unmoderated groups are open, so that every participant can post statements, questions, and replies. *open groups*

Rules and netiquette

A new newsgroup is created if it is recommended by a Usenet participant and the suggestion is accepted in a network vote. Discussions about proposed new groups usually take place in the *discussions* group news.groups. *new groups*

When a participant wants to post a message to a newsgroup, certain rules should be observed, the *network etiquette*, or *netiquette*. *rules* Insulting comments or personal attacks are not tolerated. The *netiquette* newsgroup news.announce.newusers presents an overview of these rules of network behavior.

News reader

Reading the NetNews requires a news reader and a news server that is accessible via network or modem. At universities this is usually no problem since they generally operate their own news server.

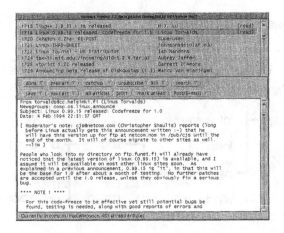

Figure 10.9. xvnews newsreader

available options   News readers have become available for almost all computer platforms and operating systems that support a network. Well-known

tin, xrn, xvnews   news readers include rn, trn, tin, xrn, and xvnews for the X Window System and trumpet for PCs. Almost all of these news readers exist under Linux. The only configuration required for most

NNTPSERVER   news readers is an environment variable named NNTPSERVER, which must contain the name of the news server.

xrn   Another workable option is xrn, which is available in an Athena widget version and a Motif variant (see Section 8.5).

News server

installation   Installing a news server is somewhat more complicated than installing a client. For a news reader, it suffices to copy the program to the computer and set an environment variable. A server, however,

several programs and   needs to have several programs and configuration files installed. In

configuration files   order to receive news, you need another news server that forwards the news to you.

INN   Internet usually uses the server INN in addition to the older

C news   server program C news. The configuration of INN is described in a text file in the tar file of the server source code.

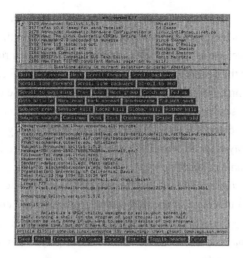

Figure 10.10. xrn under OSF/Motif

10.10   IRC

Internet Relay Chat (IRC) offers a means to converse directly with several participants on the Internet. Similar to NetNews, IRC represents a system of networked servers that exchange information among themselves. As with NetNews there is a hierarchical structure according to subjects, called *channels* under IRC (Figure 10.11).

What distinguishes IRC from NetNews is that the exchange of messages occurs without delay and the user can converse directly

Internet Relay Chat

channel

real-time conversations

Figure 10.11.   IRC

291

with the other participants. This proves particularly interesting when there is an acute problem that needs to be discussed with others.

irc client

/ commands

The user gains access with a special `irc` client program that establishes the connection to the next IRC server. The IRC client has certain commands that all begin with a slash (`/`). These commands enable the user, for example, to sign on to and sign off from a channel. Text that is entered without a command is immediately transferred and is displayed for all other IRC participants that are currently signed on to the same channel.

Linux channel

IRC also has a channel that is dedicated to Linux discussions. To take part in this discussion, start the IRC program and enter `/join #linux`. `/join` is the command to sign on to a channel. Then every message that is posted on the channel is displayed along with the name of the sender.

new channels

The number of channels changes constantly, since every user can open new channels. This is also done with the `/join` command. If the specified channel does not exist, it is created. Normally hundreds of channel are active simultaneously; all currently active channels can be displayed with the `/list` command.

/list

Besides its on-line discussion feature, IRC protocol also permits the exchange of smaller files. Furthermore, private messages can also be transmitted.

exchange of files

Participating in IRC is also possible and considerably more convenient with the graphical client `zircon` (Figure 10.12). Zircon is operated entirely with the mouse and displays every open channel in a separate window.

zircon

tcl/dp

`Zircon` is written with Tcl/Tk (see Section 14.6) and requires an enhanced Tcl interpreter named `tcl-dp` to access TCP/IP and sockets.

10.11   Gopher

Gopher is an Internet service that makes available many other services provided by universities and other institutions worldwide and combines them under a single user interface. Gopher presents itself to the user as a single, large, hierarchical menu. Within this structure the user can move from one server to another and employ

single user interface

Figure 10.12. The graphic IRC front end zircon

various network services. The offer includes literature databases, weather services, all kinds of documents (text, pictures, sound), cafeteria menus at various universities, telnet sessions, and gateways to other services such as WAIS. An increasing number of institutions are providing information via their Gopher service that previously was available only in printed form.

databases

menu structure

To be able to use Gopher, the user needs a Gopher client. Under Linux this could be the xgopher that runs under X11. When it is

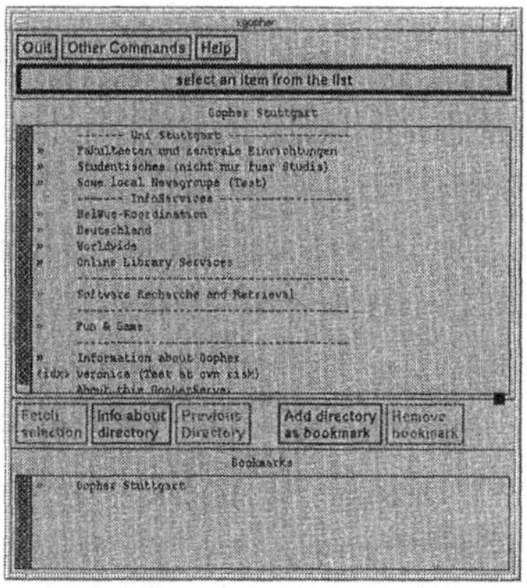

Figure 10.13. xgopher

started, `xgopher` establishes a connection to a Gopher server, and the user can move freely in the Internet (Figure 10.13).

decreasing significance

The significance of Gopher has greatly decreased in the past few years with the growing popularity of the World Wide Web. Almost all of the institutions that originally offered information via Gopher have now switched over to WWW.

10.12   World Wide Web

WWW

World Wide Web (also referred to as WWW or W3) is an Internet service that employs distributed multimedia hypertext documents that can contain not only formatted texts but also references to other documents, pictures, videos, or sound files. These documents are described in the HyperText Markup Language (HTML) in ASCII format. A special protocol called HyperText Transfer Protocol (HTTP) is used for data transfer.

documents, pictures,
videos, and sound
HTML
HTTP

References in HTML documents are specified with Uniform Resource Locators (URLs). The URL syntax is `proto-col://host[:port]/path`. Specification of the port number is optional; if no port is specified, the standard port for the specified protocol is used. Such URLs permit the expression of references to other HTML files as well as almost all kinds of addresses of services on the Internet. For example, the URL for the directory `/pub` on the FTP server `tsx-11.mit.edu` is `ftp://tsx-11.mit.edu/pub`.

URL
port number

all types of addresses

Using WWW

To retrieve information on the WWW, you need a WWW client. Currently the most widespread client, available for almost all platforms, is Netscape. Beyond simply displaying HTML pages, Netscape also features editing capabilities, interpretation of Java scripts, access to FTP servers, RSA encryption for secure data transfer and authentication, and mail and news reading. In addition, the browser features numerous unofficial HTML extensions such as frames. Netscape for Linux can be used without fees by educational institutions and their staff.

Netscape

Sometimes Netscape freezes without any comment. If you move another window over the Netscape window, window contents can be

Figure 10.14. The WWW client Netscape

deleted. This is usually when Netscape is trying to resolve a host name to an IP address. During this time, nothing works. Be patient. If Netscape fails to continue after ten seconds, something is wrong with the name resolution. Try to resolve the host name in the URL with the command `nslookup` and correct the problem on the basis of the error message. Also refer to Section 9.10.

Netscape troubles

Frequently, pictures in hypertext pages prove disturbing because they consume so much network capacity. If you want to do without the color pictures switch the option "Auto Load Images" off under "Options."

stripping images

Now and then newer versions of Netscape start with the message that apparently another Netscape browser is already running and so the session is read-only (the bookmarks directory cannot be stored, etc.). This seems to be a Netscape bug. It suffices to delete the file `.netscape/lock` to work around this problem.

A normal host is generally quite busy with a single Netscape browser; starting several in parallel is usually hardly possible.

Figure 10.15. The browser Amaya

However, this is not necessary at all: under "File" you can open a new browser window with "New Web Browser."

For the new HTML 3.2 standard, the W3 Consortium released the reference browser Amaya.* Amaya is not nearly so multifaceted as Netscape, but is markedly faster than its mammoth relative Netscape. In addition, Amaya is completely free and also supports editing Web pages.

Amaya

*Sunsite: `system/Network/info-systems/www/`

Recently an increasing number of editors are being equipped with WWW features; two such editors are xemacs (see Section 12.3) with its new WWW mode (start with **w3-fetch**) and the word processor in the office software package StarOffice (see Section 12.2).

There are also other older freeware browsers such as Mosaic and Arena. Via telnet login or on hosts without X-Windows, lynx* proves interesting; it runs on ordinary text consoles.

With the help of an HTTP server, a distributed information system can be constructed easily under Linux. Such a server, running in the background as a daemon, waits for a socket connection via a defined port; after a connection has been established by a WWW client (e.g., Mosaic), the server furnishes access to the files in certain directories. If direct Internet access is possible, the local documents can offer appropriate links to other HTTP servers. Interesting servers for Linux users can be found at the following URLs:

HTTP Server

daemon

links to other servers

http://www.linux.org/
> WWW server with an extensive list of FAQs, HOWTOs, manuals, and other WWW servers.

http://www-i2.informatik.rwth-aachen.de/Linux.html
> WWW server of the Linux archive at the RWTH Aachen (Germany). It contains information on Linux, access to other FTP servers, and other WWW servers.

http://www.linux.org.uk/
> This British server is managed by Alan Cox. It contains a list of commerical software for Linux.

WWW-Server under Linux

Under Linux you can choose from among three freeware WWW servers:

* httpd from CERN (Conseil European pour la Recherche Nucleaire)
* httpd from NCSA (National Center for Supercomputer Applications)

*Sunsite: system/Network/info-systems/www/

- The Apache server (a greatly modified NSCA server)

In the following we discuss the installation and configuration of Apache.* The Apache server (version 1.1.1) has several advantages:

- High speed
- Modular extensibility (e.g., by an interpreter for CGI scripts)
- SSL support (Secure Socket Layer, encrypted transmission of requests and Web pages, and authentication)

By default, Apache uses `/usr/local/etc/httpd` as installation directory. In the following, path names are relative to this directory. The example uses version 1.1.1.

- Create `/usr/local/etc/`, unpack `apache_1.1.1.tar.gz` there, and rename `apache_1.1.1` to `httpd`.
- Compile Apache:
  - Change to `httpd/src`
  - Copy `Configuration.tmpl` to `Configuration`
  - In `Configuration`, comment out `AUX_FLAGS` under "Linux" (remove hash)
  - Enter **make**
  - Copy `src/httpd` to `bin`
- Configuration: the configuration files reside under `conf`; the original files still have the suffix `-dist`, which must be removed.
- In `conf/httpd.conf`:
  `ServerAdmin`
     Enter the e-mail address of WWW administrator.
  `ServerName`
     Enter here the host name under which the server is to run. The name must actually exist; the option serves to select from among several aliases for one host (e.g., `ftp.stud.fh-`
     `heilbronn.de` and `www.stud.fh-heilbronn.de`).
- In `conf/srm.conf`:

*Sunsite: `system/Network/info-systems/www/servers`

DocumentRoot

> This is the directory in which the Web pages are stored (default `/usr/local/etc/httpd/htdocs`). A request for a document via URL `http://`*server*`/titel.html`, e.g., returns `/usr/local/etc/httpd/htdocs titel.html`.

UserDir

> The initial entry here is `public_html`. This allows users to store Web pages under `public_html` in their home directory.

Alias

> Here you can enter alias paths for HTML pages, etc. For example, in the following the path, `/icons/` in a URL is translated into `/usr/local/etc/httpd/cgi-bin/` in the Linux directory tree:

```
Alias /icons/ /usr/local/etc/httpd/icons/
```

ScriptAlias

> This is like `Alias`, but here directories are specified where CGI scripts are located. CGI scripts serve to realize dynamic Web pages that are created by a CGI script only on a request. A CGI script can insert the current time or current information from a database. CGI scripts must be executable files. For programming CGI scripts, see [14]. *CGI scripts*

The WWW server can now be launched with **/usr/local/ etc/httpd/bin/httpd**; this invocation should be entered in the boot scripts. As a test, you can request the page `http://local-host/`.

10.13 Network management

`tkined` is a particularly interesting tool for the area of network management (Figure 10.16). It allows supervision and administration of local TCP/IP networks and WANs. Its functions include automatic recognition of a network structure, appealing graphical *TCP/IP networks*

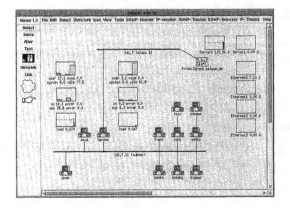

Figure 10.16. tkined

monitoring representation, monitoring connections and individual components, administration of SNMP-enabled elements, and many others. Since tkined was developed with Tcl/Tk, it is relatively easy to enhance it and make it suitable for particular needs. It uses an enhanced Tcl

scotty interpreter named scotty, which enables access to the protocols TCP, UDP, ICMP, DNS, and SNMP under Tcl (see Section 14.6).

## Chapter 11

Support and help

O ne argument that is frequently posed, especially in commercial settings, to reject free or public domain software is the lack of a licensing company that provides support and a hotline. In the USA some companies have recognized this market niche and offer commercial support for free software. A similar trend is developing in Europe as well.

hotline

free software

Apart from such support, there are many possible ways to receive information and help via the Internet or directly from the Linux system for concrete problems. This chapter offers an overview of these possibilities and of the available documentation for Linux.

Internet

11.1   man, xman

As with every UNIX system, a simple source of information is the on-line documentation. These are files that each describe one command, one C library routine, a device, or the contents of a configuration file. The command for displaying these On-Line Manual pages is man. For this reason, these files are usually called Manual pages, or simply man pages.

on-line documentation

The On-Line Manual pages are divided into sections according to contents. These sections are labeled with the numbers 1 to 9 and the letters n and l as follows:

1 Commands for the user
2 System calls
3 Routines of the C library
4 Device-files in /dev
5 File formats (usually configuration files)

301

6 Games

7 Miscellany

8 System administration

9 Kernel routines

n Other categories (at present, particularly Tcl Manual pages)

1 Local Manual pages

directories

/usr/man

You can find the Manual pages in various directories, where the individual files of a section are stored in subdirectories. Usually the directories /usr/man and /usr/local/man are used. The example below shows the subdirectories for the sections in the directory /usr/man.

```
hermes:/usr/man# ls
cat1/    cat6/    de/       lpman    man4/    man8/    mann/
cat2/    cat7/    doman*    man1/    man5/    man9/    nl/
cat4/    cat8/    fix.so*   man2/    man6/    manX/    whatis
cat5/    catX/    german/   man3/    man7/    manl/
hermes:/usr/man#
```

Other directories or subdirectories can be used as well, depending on the version and the configuration of the man command.

administrator

whatis

The system administrator can use the command makewhatis to create an index file of the Manual pages from the brief descriptions contained in them. The index file contains only the name of the commands and a one-line description. This file already exists in most of the common Linux distributions. The user can use the commands whatis and apropos to search for key words.

```
hermes:/usr/man# whatis gcc
gcc (1)              - GNU project C and C++ Compiler (v2.4)
hermes:/usr/man# whatis groff
groff (1)            - front end for the groff document formatting system
groff (1)            - formatiert Texte (z.B. Manualpages)
hermes:/usr/man# apropos gif
gif2tiff (1)         - create a file from a GIF87 format image file
giftopnm (1)         - convert a GIF file into a portable anymap
giftorle (1)         - Convert GIF images to RLE format
ppmtogif (1)         - convert a portable pixmap into a GIF file
rletogif (1)         - Convert RLE files to GIF format.
hermes:/usr/man#
```

The greatest problem for UNIX newbies is that they know exactly what they want to do, but do not know the corresponding command. Since typical Linux commands contain hundreds of commands, it is impossible to search all Manual pages. Therefore, this book presents a reference for the most important UNIX commands organized by subject (see Chapter 16).

Format of the On-Line Reference Manual pages

The On-Line Manual pages are sometimes available in two or three different formats. The original format is usually source code for nroff and is located in the directories man1 to man8. This format is unsuitable for direct screen output and so must be translated by the text-formatting program nroff or groff (see Section 12.5).

nroff

groff

For more complex On-Line Manual pages, this procedure takes some time; therefore, after the files have been translated once, they are stored in readable form in the directories cat1 to cat8. To do this, however, the user must have write permissions for these directories. If desired, the files can also be compress ed with compress, which only insignificantly increases the time required for displaying them but radically reduces disk storage consumption.

cat1 to catn

compress

If additional On-Line Manual pages have been installed in a directory other than /usr/man (e.g., /usr/local/man), the path for the On-Line Manual pages can be defined with the environment variable MANPATH. The following defines the path for the On-Line Manual pages in a Bourne shell:

MANPATH

```
export MANPATH=/usr/man:/usr/openwin/man:/usr/local/man
```

This example defines the path for the On-Line Manual pages in a C shell:

```
setenv MANPATH /usr/man:/usr/openwin/man:/usr/local/man
```

Naturally, this setting should be made in the appropriate startup file (.profile or .login).

xman

The X11 affords the somewhat more comfortable utility xman (Figure 11.1). Here the user first selects a section of the Manual. Then the

X11

303

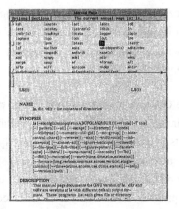

Figure 11.1. xman

utility provides an overview of all On-Line Manual pages in that section. With the mouse the user can select an On-Line Manual page from this overview for display.

When a problem arises with a command or with the configuration of a program, the first point of reference should always be the respective On-Line Manual page. Naturally the man command also has its corresponding On-Line Manual page, which the user invokes with man man.

11.2   Info

GNU

The documentation of many FSF programs is available in GNU Info format. GNU Emacs uses this format to provide hypertext-like navigation through these documents. Newer versions of the Emacs

Emacs 19   editor, such as Lucid Emacs and Emacs 19, permit controlling the navigation with the mouse under the X11. There are also programs

tkinfo   like xinfo and the TCL/Tk-based tkinfo that were conceived exclusively for displaying info files (Figure 11.2).

Emacs   Within the Emacs editor the user invokes the info mode (Strg +
H I) and selects from the menu of available info documents the needed text. In this text the user can navigate hierarchically from keyword to keyword.

Figure 11.2. tkinfo

Examples of Info documents include the documentation to the GNU C compiler and the GNU AWK utility.

11.3 Newsgroups

Since Linux continues to be developed on the Internet, the many communication services of the Internet are utilized to the fullest. Among these services, the newsgroups provide an information source of particular interest to Linux novices (see Section 10.9). Linux enjoys several newsgroups that provide a forum for discussion of questions about the system and its installation as well as other subjects. The most important newsgroups are the following:

Linux groups

- comp.os.linux.announce (c.o.l.a.)
- comp.os.linux.help comp.os.linux.misc
- comp.os.linux.admin
- comp.os.linux.development.apps
- comp.os.linux.development.system
- comp.os.linux.hardware
- comp.os.linux.networking
- comp.os.linux.setup
- comp.os.linux.x
- comp.os.linux.advocacy

comp.os.linux.announce is a moderated newsgroup for the announcement of new programs or ports to Linux. Messages intended for posting in a moderated group are not posted directly, but are

moderated

first filtered by a moderator who is responsible for maintaining the respective rules within the newsgroup. The other four groups have no restrictions. Any participant can post messages or questions here. However, users should be aware that every message that is posted to

propagated around the world

a newsgroup is propagated around the world and consumes storage on every news server.

Currently over 100 new postings appear in these newsgroups daily. This makes it difficult to keep up to date without perusing these postings more often than on a weekly basis. A newsgroup observer can often solve problems simply by reading the newsgroup postings

shared problems and solutions

and following the problems and solutions that other users share.

11.4   FAQs and HOWTOs

Another important information source that is closely linked to the

frequently asked questions

newsgroups is the FAQs (frequently asked questions). This is a list of questions that arise often in postings and, more important, the answers to these questions.

FAQs cover a broad range of subjects. They are usually compiled by active participants of the newsgroup, with the intention of avoiding the repeated posting of the same questions. A FAQ thus consists of

questions and answers

a series of such questions and the corresponding responses provided by various competent newsgroup participants.

HOWTO

Some of the original Linux FAQs have evolved into HOWTOs. These documents resemble FAQs but contain more detailed text.

text files

Both FAQs and HOWTOs are plain text files, so that they can be read and printed with any text editor, with the UNIX more command, or even with DOS. As a rule, Linux FAQs and HOWTOs do not

general UNIX questions

cover general UNIX questions. A dedicated newsgroup exists for this purpose (comp.unix.questions) with its own FAQs. Thus UNIX novices might also want to browse the UNIX FAQs.

Sources for FAQs

The best source of FAQs of all kinds is a special newsgroup entitled

news.answers

news.answers. Many groups regularly post their FAQs here. In addition to FAQs on Linux, UNIX, and programming languages, a

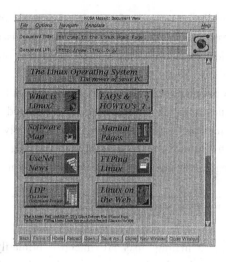

Figure 11.3. WWW site with references to Linux information

new explorer can find FAQs on other subjects of interest outside the realm of computer science.

The special Linux FAQs are posted regularly in the newsgroup `comp.os.linux.announce`. Naturally, current FAQs can also be found on the many FTP servers, usually in a subdirectory `doc` under `Linux`. For example, the FTP server `nic.funet.fi` stores them in `/pub/OS/Linux/doc/FAQ`.

subdirectory doc

The Linux HOWTOs are located at Sunsite under `docs/HOWTO/`. They are also included in most Linux distributions.

11.5 WWW

World Wide Web (WWW) is one of the most attractive and by now perhaps the most frequently used service on the Internet (see Section 10.12). There are many WWW servers for Linux as well, which offer FAQs, HOWTOs, manuals, and other information (Figure 11.3).

WWW server

11.6 Mailing lists

Various mailing lists have been created for kernel hackers and other active Linux system collaborators. These mailing lists primarily new developments   support the exchange of news of developments, problems, ideas, and patches. Messages sent to the address of the mailing list are collected and forwarded several times a day to all addressees on the mailing list.

channels   To join the mailing list for a certain subject, called a *channel*, the user sends a message containing the command `help` to the address `Majordomo@vger.rutgers.edu`; the reply will contain detailed instructions for using the mailing list. In the simplest case the following command suffices to request help for mailing lists:

```
echo help | mail Majordomo@vger.rutgers.edu
```

developers   Since these mailing lists are intended primarily for Linux developers, a novice should not pose questions through the normal channels.

11.7 Other documents

LDP   Manuals on Linux have been compiled by various authors from the Linux Documentation Project (LDP). Beyond the *Linux User's Guide* and the *Linux Installation Guide*, this documentation also includes

Network Administration Guide   more complex documents such as the *Network Administration Guide* (NAG), which covers almost all aspects of network installation under

Kernel Hacker's Guide   Linux. The *Kernel Hacker's Guide* (KHG) The *Kernel Hacker's Guide* deals with the structure of the kernel and the development of device drivers for Linux. It also provides an excellent glimpse into the inner workings of Linux.

These manuals can be procured via FTP and printed. Some book stores sell printed-out and bound copies of these manuals. The public

sunsite.unc.edu   domain files can be drawn from the FTP server `sunsite.unc.edu` in the directory `/pub/Linux/docs/LDP`.

11.8 Other sources

Besides the sources identified here, there are many other Internet services and organizations that provide information and document. This section identifies some of them.

WAIS

WAIS (Wide Area Information System) is an Internet service that
supports searching WAIS servers worldwide for documents of all
kinds by keywords. Through WAIS it is possible to obtain manuals
and FAQs. Clients, a list of WAIS servers, and a detailed description
of WAIS can be drawn per FTP from the host `think.com` or from
the comp.infosystems.wais news group.

documents

FAQs

README files

As with most larger programs, the Linux kernel documentation is
complemented by release notes and README files files containing
important instructions for its installation and operation. These files
normally reside in the same directory as the system or the source
code of the system.

release notes

source code

For example, the directory `/usr/src` contains many subdirectories with system components and utilities. Almost all of these
subdirectories contain their own README files. Hence in the directory `/etc/lilo` we usually find the Linux Loader (LILO) along
with a README file that describes both installation and configuration
in detail.

Applications

A n operating system without applications is only interesting for a very few. Linux has not been a system of that kind for a long time now. Aside from the vast number of free applications available from the Internet, there are also numerous commercial applications available. In addition, many applications for other PC UNIX versions can be run under Linux with the iBCS2 emulation. We can only present a small selection of all the available applications here.

Internet applications

iBCS2

12.1 Desktop environment

Today's computer systems usually offer the user a graphical environment for the administration of files and programs. The file managers that are available for Linux at no cost are usually inferior to the commercial versions. The *Freedom Desktop*, which can be run on all the common UNIX platforms, has also been ported to Linux (Figure 12.1). It should satisfy even sophisticated requirements. The program manager permits grouping individual files, programs, or shell scripts for a better overview. Files can be conveniently managed with the file manager. Both program manager and file manager support drag and drop. The Freedom package also includes several other additional utilities, such as a graphical front end for the `find` command and a print manager.

Freedom Desktop

drag and drop

12.2 StarOffice

One old and resilient edge of Microsoft's Windows family over Linux has been the availability of WYSIWYG (what you see is what you get) word processing, spreadsheets, and other office applications,

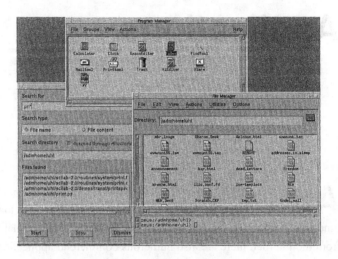

Figure 12.1. Freedom Desktop for Linux

especially those of the Microsoft Office suite. Since July 1996 Linux has nullified the lead in this area; Microsoft's new rival, Star Division of Hamburg, has ported StarOffice to Linux. What is particularly interesting is that the Linux versions can be used free of license fees by private users.

free for private users

StarOffice contains the word processor StarWriter with the formula editor StarMath, the spreadsheet StarCalc with the diagram tool StarChart, and the presentation program with the graphic tool StarImage. Of particular interest is its Internet integration: StarWriter enables you to edit HTML pages, you can embed URLs in normal StarOffice texts as hypertext references, and on opening a new file you can specify a URL for downloading instead of a file name. If the WWW server supports corresponding operations, edited HTML pages can be stored directly on the server (Figure 12.2).

word processor
formula editor
spreadsheet
diagram tool
presentation program
graphic tool

Much in StarOffice has been modeled after big brother Microsoft Office, especially the location of menus and user interface elements. However, the package does require some getting used to.

close to MS Office

StarDraw corresponds quite exactly to Microsoft PowerPoint. The slides can be decorated with text and graphics, and some style sheets are provided. As in PowerPoint there is a layer view, so that you can make notes on each slide, and you can change the

Figure 12.2. Springer home page in StarWriter—ready to edit

slide sequence in the slide overview. StarDraw even provides special effects when changing slides. You can integrate any objects from the other StarOffice components, including tables, diagrams, and graphic files. StarGallery includes a number of graphics for decoration.

Likewise StarCalc provides functionality comparable to Microsoft Excel. The formula editor StarMath uses a rather cryptical language and does not completely fulfill the WYSIWYG concept. The quality of the results does not compare to what can be achieved under Linux with TEX in terms of conjuring up filigree formulas, and in fact it is not quite up to par with the formula editor in Microsoft Word. StarImage enables embedding graphic files in documents, but also features a number of operations such as mirroring, various filters, and palette modifications—the scope corresponds approximately to that of xv.

StarOffice also makes rich use of shared libraries, comprising some 60% of the overall code. StarOffice is written almost completely in C++ and was compiled (for Linux) with gcc. The majority of the source code is platform independent and is based on the class library

StarView (which Star Division also offers separately for developers). StarOffice uses OLE to blend graphics, tables, and text.

StarOffice for Linux requires Motif 2.0 for the graphical user
requirements   interface. An average installation demands over 100 MB of hard disk capacity, while the minimum version (not recommended) takes more than 50 MB—but then we are all aware that office packages do not fit on a boot disk. To work rather swiftly with StarOffice, you need 32 MB of RAM.

source   StarOffice for Linux is available (currently as beta version) on Sunsite under `apps/staroffice`. You need all `disk-*` files and `setup.starOffice`. The `disk-*` files are compressed with `zip`, so further compression with `gzip` is fruitless. After you have collected all files locally in a directory, you can invoke `setup.starOffice`. The installation already uses the Motif user interface. By default StarOffice is installed under `/usr/local/StarOffice3.1`. To be able to work with the programs, you have to insert the installation directory in the file `sd.sh` for `sd_inst` and `SVHOME` and insert the following line in `/etc/profile`:

```
. /usr/local/StarOffice3.1/sd.sh
```

C shell users must modify `sd.csh` and invoke it in `/etc/csh.log-in`):

```
source /usr/local/StarOffice3.1/sd.csh
```

12.3   Editors

text   Text editing programs are one of the most important components of a computer system. Nearly a dozen such editors are available under Linux. Several of them are available on every UNIX system, while others have to be purchased separately with proprietary systems.

vi

The standard editor of every UNIX system is certainly vi.* Since this is a rather aged program, it is no wonder that its user comfort level leaves room for improvement in several points. vi's distinction between command and input mode irritates most users. Without a doubt, this approach has its advantages, but it also requires some adjustment. For example, it is possible to repeat the last command string and to replace the next three words in a step with a new word.

command mode

Since the source code of the vi editor is not available, a vi clone tends to be used under Linux. Even here there are two alternatives, elvis and vim, both of which emulate (almost) all commands of the original and provide several extensions as well.

elvis, vim

In some situations (such as editing configuration files during installation or repairing a Linux system or working with telnet) vi is better suited than emacs. Thus we briefly introduce the basics of using vi:

vi (in essence) has two modes: command mode and insert mode. From insert mode you return to command mode with ⟨ESC⟩.

:q	quit vi
:q!	quit even if changes were not saved
:w	save editor contents
:wq	save and quit (ZZ is equivalent)
h	character left
l	character right
j	line up
k	line down
G	end of file
nnnG	jump to line nnn
dd	delete entire line
D	delete to end of line
x	delete character under cursor
p	paste last deleted text after character under cursor
P	paste last deleted text before character under cursor
i	insert before text under cursor (insert mode)

*Sunsite: apps/editors/vi

o   insert a new line after the current line and insert text (insert mode)

o   insert a new line before the current line and input text (insert mode)

sed

stream editor   Not an editor in the usual sense, sed is rather used as a stream editor to modify a data stream by means of commands in a control file. sed's

vi commands   commands are largely compatible with those of vi, but the user does not input them interactively; instead, they are read from a file or from

shell scripts   the command line. sed often comes to play in UNIX shell scripts or for processing extremely large files that normal editors cannot load.

joe

joe is short for "Joe's own Editor." This editor finds appreciation

changeover   among converts from DOS because its extended keys rely strongly

Wordstar   on that of the well-known PC word processing program Wordstar

blocks   and the Turbo Pascal editor. The command and editing modes are not separate. Marked text blocks are displayed inversely, which is not always a given under UNIX. joe can divide the screen into multiple windows, format paragraphs, and use hyphenation mode.

People looking for a more powerful editor, who nevertheless prefer not to give up the Wordstar-compatible extended keys, should

Emacs   take a closer look at the Wordstar mode of the GNU Emacs editor.

xedit

X11   xedit is part of the X Window System package. Contrary to the above editors, xedit is not confined to an ASCII environment. Although xedit runs under a graphical user interface, it does not

less comfort   offer the level of comfort that would be expected; its available

Athena widgets   commands are essentially limited to the possibilities given by the Athena text widgets. While this editor is not likely ever to enjoy broad propagation, it does suffice for simple tasks.

axe

axe is another editor that runs only under the X Window System.

Athena widgets   It also uses the Athena text widgets but provides much more

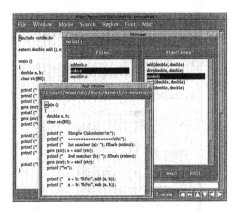

Figure 12.3. xcoral

functionality than `xedit`. The user can open an arbitrary number of text files in different windows, open and save files interactively via a file selection dialog, seek or replace text, and format paragraphs. Simple on-line help gives quick information on available commands. `axe` proves to be a multifaceted and user-friendly editor under Linux for the X Window System.

several windows

seek/replace

xcoral

`xcoral` also requires the X Window System environment (Figure 12.3). Although `xcoral` uses no standard toolkit, it has a pleasing look with a menu bar and a scroll bar. `xcoral` particularly interests C and C++ programmers because of its integrated function and class browsers. When `xcoral` is started, it scans all C/C++ files and displays all the identifiers contained therein in an alphabetical list. From the browser the user can then branch to the respective location in the source code. In particular, this facilitates a programmer's familiarization with already-existing source code. For writing new programs, the programmer can select an optional mode that handles uniform formatting and can create function and class templates. Keyboard commands in `xcoral` bear a strong resemblance to the Emacs editor.

menu bar

C++

browser

317

Figure 12.4. xemacs as Web browser

asedit

Motif   asedit uses the Motif widget set, which is reflected particularly in its consistent interface. Although this editor offers the most important commands, such as loading and saving texts and search-and-replace, few functions   it is quite Spartan otherwise. Its hypertext help deserves special mention.

Emacs and variants

The most popular editor for UNIX is certainly Emacs in all its variants. A major reason for its popularity is that it runs both on ASCII and X11   pure ASCII terminals and in a graphical X11 environment.

xemacs   xemacs* is a popular Emacs variant emanating from lemacs of the Lucid company, which was developed on the basis of an early Emacs 19 version (Figure 12.4). xemacs provides a much improved X-Windows interface compared to Emacs.

GNU Emacs   We will describe GNU Emacs in more detail in the next chapter.

*Sunsite: apps/editors/xemacs

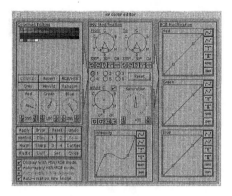

Figure 12.5. xv

12.4   Graphic programs

Many graphic programs are available for the X Window System. Their function extends from vector-oriented drawing programs to picture processing, and conversion. Only a few of these programs exist in a special Linux version. Usually they can be directly translated under Linux. Linux distributions already contain the most important of these programs.

drawing, painting
processing,
and converting

XV

J. Bradley's xv*, a very powerful program for the display and manipulation of graphics of all kinds, enjoys wide dissemination in the UNIX world. It is available from the usual FTP servers; however, it is not free, but rather shareware. It has a very mature interface and is easy to use despite its many powerful features. xv loads and saves all common graphic formats such as GIF, TIFF, PostScript, JPEG, and PBM (Figure 12.5).

shareware

graphic formats

A graphic to be loaded is selected from a file selection menu or (since version 3.00) via an integrated file manager that can display selected files as mini-pictures ("Visual Schnauzer"). The size of a loaded graphic can be changed freely. A graphic-processing menu permits the modification of numerous parameters such as brightness, contrast, and tone by means of numerous buttons and slide switches

file manager
scale

colors

*Sunsite: X11/apps/graphics/viewers

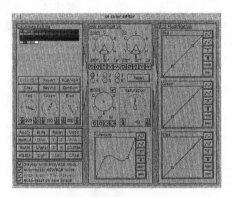

Figure 12.6. xv color editor

as well as mouse-modifiable curves (Figure 12.6). xv also contains a grab utility that supports snapshots of any other X-Windows window as well as processing and saving these.

modifications   A graphic loaded into xv can be modified in various ways, such as by using an algorithm like "Oil Painting" or "Emboss."

background   Furthermore, it can be displayed in various forms as a background graphic and is retained even after quitting the program.

xfig

vector graphics   xfig*, a program for creating vector graphics under Linux, offers all the usual drawing tools as well as the possibility of embedding text in various fonts (Figure 12.7). One of its interesting features is

formats   the export of graphics in various formats. Besides its own fig format,

PostScript, HPGL, TEX   xfig supports standards like PostScript, HPGL, and TEX in variants. This makes it quite suitable for creating graphics for TEX documents.

idraw

InterViews   Stanford University's InterViews package contains a quite powerful, vector-oriented drawing program named idraw (Figure 12.8). Besides the usual graphical elements such as lines, rectangles, circles,

Bézier curves   and Bézier curves, it also supports the free rotation of texts in various fonts.

*Sunsite: X11/xapps/graphics/draw

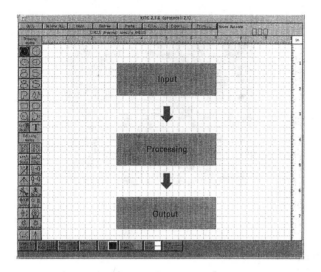

Figure 12.7. The drawing program xfig

The only file format that this program supports is PostScript. Unfortunately, the program places high demands on the hardware, which makes the program uninteresting for 386 computers.

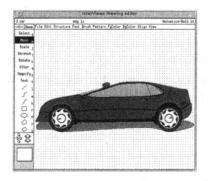

Figure 12.8. idraw

321

Figure 12.9. xpaint

xpaint

MacDraw

graphic elements

xpaint* is a program for the creation and manipulation of graphics that borrows from the Apple Macintosh MacDraw program. xpaint can process multiple graphics in different windows. Various tools support the drawing of any kind of figures: not only simple elements such as lines and circles, but also freehand curves as well (Figure 12.9).

A fill-pattern editor permits the creation of additional patterns. The adjustable zoom function proves quite practical; it displays an excerpt from the graphic in a separate window. It is noteworthy that all drawing functions are supported in the zoom window as well. The xpaint font browser offers a clear selection of fonts, including scalable fonts as available under X11 R5 and R6.

fonts

GIMP

cutting operations

The graphic tool gimp (General Image Manipulation Program)* is much more powerful than xpaint. It features very powerful cutting operations: rectangles, ellipses freehand forms, and contiguous regions around a selected color can be mirrored, rotated, cut out, moved, and copied. In addition to the obligatory spray cans and paint buckets, the gimp toolbox contains features for color transition between two points. You can choose paint brushes with sharp or

*X11/xapps/graphics/draw
*Sunsite: X11/xapps/graph/gimp

fuzzy borders. Color bleeding can be scaled so that background parts of a graphic can show through. You can create colors in the palette from the three RGB values or by selecting from a spectrum and regulating brightness and saturation—the dialog elements of the respective other method automatically adjust. Multiple undo is supported, with the maximum number of levels being selectable. Some elementary filters such as soft drawing and edge detection are provided. GIMP provides real-time zooming and parallel processing of multiple images (with the same toolbox and the capability to copy areas from one image into another).

GIMP does not support quite as many graphic formats as xv and is still inferior to xv in its palette manipulation, but it does handle reading and writing the most important formats: GIF, JPEG, PNG, TIFF, TGA, and XPM. It is notable that all of GIMP's graphic functions are realized with plug-ins—GIMP can be extended at will with new modules. An interesting feature for graphics on Web pages is the capability to mark a certain color as transparent in GIF graphics (although `giftool` also offers this feature. GIMP principally requires Motif, but there is a statically linked Linux version that gets by without the Motif libraries.

modular architecture

POV-Ray

POV-Ray (Persistence Of Vision RAYtracer) is a popular and powerful ray-tracing program that evolved from the former DKB Raytracer. From a scene (objects, light sources, observer, size of picture) that is defined in a `.pov` file, POV-Ray generates a TARGA graphic file. Optionally, under X-Windows you can observe the picture being constructed. A set of demos and many surface textures are included. The extensive HTML documentation explains the structure of scenery files. In addition to ray-tracing features, POV-Ray provides fractals as patterns for object surfaces and several flexible objects beyond the usual polyhedrons. The inside of an object can be filled with particles that can also emit light, so that fog effects or fire can be simulated ("halo").

scenery files

POV-Ray is available at Sunsite under `apps/graphics/rays`. The file `povray-version.ELF.tar.gz` contains the precompiled version. In addition, there is PostScript documentation. The archive with the precompiled version of POV-Ray can be unpacked with `tar` to an appropriate location, e.g., `/usr/local`:

```
golem:~> tar xzvf povray-version.ELF.tgz -C /usr/local
```

In `/usr/local/etc/` you should create the configuration file `pov.ini`:

```
Library_Path = /usr/local/povray3/include
+D
```

The Manual page `povray.1` can also be copied to `/usr/local/man/man1` to complete the installation. Under `pov3demo/` you will find a number of finished scenery files.

To use POV-Ray on X-Windows, enter

```
golem:/usr/local/src/povray/pov3demo/showoff> x-povray -Idiffract.pov
...
```

this command visualizes one of the demo scenes supplied with POV-Ray.

If everything went well, POV-Ray should open an X11 window while it is computing to allow you to follow the construction of the picture.

Like so many UNIX programs, POV-Ray has no graphical user interface. However, there are several X11 front ends such as mnm.*
programming scenes   On the other hand, the definition of scenes in a dedicated language is precisely the advantage of POV-Ray: Descriptions of complex scenes can be generated with programs in more powerful languages like Tcl or Perl.

xfractint

In addition to POV-Ray, the fractal generator `xfractint` is another must. `xfractint`[†] supports over 100 types of fractals, naturally

---

*Sunsite: `apps/graphics/rays/pov/`
[†]Sunsite: `X11/toys/`

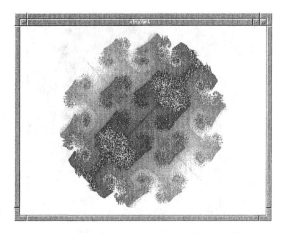

Figure 12.10. A Popcorn Julia fractal

including Mandelbrot and Julia (Figure 12.10) sets, Barnsley's IFS fractals, and the Lorenz Attractor. Also interesting are the L-systems (Koch Curve und others) and "Plasma." On a fractal (or other GIF picture) you can create a 3D relief map—low color values indicate valleys and high values are mountains. View a very psychedelic screen saver with $\boxed{\mathsf{C}}$ $\boxed{\mathsf{Space}}$ on the plasma fractal—xfractint supports palette rotation!

Ghostscript/Ghostview

An important component of the Linux system is the PostScript interpreter Ghostscript* (gs). Together with its graphical front end Ghostview, it permits the comfortable display of PostScript files (Figure 12.11). But Ghostscript implements more than just the screen output; it also transforms an ordinary dot matrix or ink jet printer into a full PostScript printer.

PostScript

Ghostscript

When color graphics are printed on a monochrome device, Ghostscript uses dithering to achieve reasonable quality. Ghostscript in the current version even supports PostScript Level 2.

dithering

To be able to handle text that uses any of the copyrighted Adobe fonts, Ghostscript includes a package of similar fonts, but their

Adobe

---

*Sunsite: apps/graphics/viewers

Figure 12.11. Ghostview with PS graphic

quality is noticeably poor. Fortunately, Ghostscript also allows the installation and use of the original fonts.

MPEG video player

Any of the many MPEG videos from the Internet can be viewed under Linux using the MPEG Player from the University of California at no special hardware Berkeley* (Figure 12.12). Note that this requires no special hardware and that the output can be redirected to other screens. Unfortunately, the performance of the computer and its graphic board strongly influences the speed of the player.

Some videos from the Internet come in the Apple Quicktime format. The program xanim is needed to play these.

Figure 12.12. MPEG video player

*Sunsite: apps/graphics/viewers

giftool

giftool[†] is a small shareware utility for processing GIF files. It provides the following functionality:

- Set interlace mode (the rows and columns of a picture are stored not in the normal sequence, but so that a picture with increasingly fine details results—this makes sense for Web pages, where pictures should already be visible during loading.
- Display or set GIF file comments.
- Select a certain color as transparent—also important for Web pages: instead of transparent pixels, the browser's background color is used.
- Output other information on the file: picture dimensions, color depth and all entries in the color palette.

PNM Tools

While picture formats such as GIF, TIFF, and JPEG were developed for compression of a picture, PNM graphics are particularly easy to process with computer programs. PNM is not a format itself; it is a collective term for the three formats PBM (bitmaps), PGM (greyscale image), and PPM (color image). PNM files store the pixels in a matrix; for bitmaps each pixel is represented by a bit, for greyscale pictures by an integer, and for color pictures by three integers for red, green, and blue. Large surfaces in a single color are not compressed, but stored as they are. This simplifies manipulating PNM graphics with small, self-penned programs or UNIX commands. PNM Tools is nothing more than a collection of 176 such UNIX programs. The vast majority of them (111) are programs for conversion between other graphic formats and PBM/PGM/PPM. For example, to convert a GIF graphic to a TIFF graphic, you can convert the GIF graphic to a PNM graphic and then the PNM graphic to a TIFF graphic. This makes the PNM Tools an incomparably powerful conversion library—we doubt that any graphic program reads more formats, much less saves them. Because the PNM formats have no compression, they avoid any losses.

simple format

PNM Tools as converter

[†]Sunsite: apps/graphics/giftool

Even if you only want to manipulate images in a conventional graphic program, it is worth installing PNM Tools. They are used by several other programs, e.g., xemacs. Each PNM Tool also has a Manual page. In addition to the conversion tools there

image manipulation

are some quite universal image manipulation tools: concatenation (pnmcat), rotation (pnmrotate), and mirroring (pnmflip), as well as cutting out parts of images (pnmcut), but also smoothing filters (pnmsmooth), contrast amplifier (pnmhisteq), and powerful universal filters like pnmconvol (links two images in an operation known in image processing as convolution, and with which many interesting filters such as smoothing or edge and line detection can be realized). pnmindex creates an overview image from a large number of PNM images; each image is included as a 100×100 stamp (practical for FTP or WWW servers that provide image archives).

No graphic program does everything. The PNM formats are well

PNM programming

suited for your own image processing programs; therefore, the PNM package* also contains a C library with include files in addition to the utilities. If you want to program a special filter, take a look at these include files; in line with the simplicity of the PNM formats, they contain only few primitives, so that programming should be no problem. We present a simple example as a demonstration. It decomposes a bitmap into two parts by superimposing a random pattern. Applying a favorite trick from cryptography, the individual parts now contain no information (assuming an ideal random pattern) about the original image; if you print them on two slides and overlay them exactly, the original image becomes visible again (with some noise; recombination in the computer produces the exact image).
vernam.c:

```
#include <pbm.h>

main()
{
  bit **inn,**out1,**out2;
  int xb,yb;
  int x,y;

  inn = pbm_readpbm (stdin, &xb, &yb); /* Read pbm from stdin; size in xb/yb */
  srand(time());                       /* initialize random number generator */
  out1 = pbm_allocarray (xb, yb); /* Allocate space for new images */
  out2 = pbm_allocarray (xb, yb);
```

Sunsite: apps/graphics/convert/netpbm

```
    for (y = 0; y < yb; y++)              /* Iterate over pbm array */
      for (x = 0; x < xb; x++) {
        out1[y][x] = (rand() & 1);       /* WEAK random numbers! */
        out2[y][x] = inn[y][x] ^ out1[y][x];
      }
    pbm_writepbm (stdout, out1, xb, yb, 0); /* Write first pbm to stdout */
    pbm_writepbm (stderr, out2, xb, yb, 0); /* Write second pbm to stderr */
}
```

Compile as follows:

```
golem:~/vernam> gcc -o vernam vernam.c -lpbm
golem:~/vernam> ./vernam < test.pbm > pic1.pbm 2> pic2.pbm
```

12.5   Word processing

Most text-processing systems under Linux are not word processors.
Generally, control sequences are inserted appropriately into ASCII
text in order to influence the formatting of the text. This approach
might seem quite inconvenient at first, but it does have its advantages,
particularly for large documents.

groff

The classical way to create formatted documents under a UNIX
system is to process an ASCII text with the command nroff. This is   ASCII text
a package for formatting texts, tables, formulas, and simple graphics.
The user enters text in ASCII format and influences the layout with
corresponding format commands. Output can be on a text-oriented
or a graphical device.

All UNIX On-Line Manual pages were created in this way.
Normally the primary use of this utility is to display Manual pages.   Manual pages
nroff's functionality can be extended with external macros, and
macro packages are available for various tasks. There is a dedicated   macro packages
macro file (an) for formatting a Manual page. The command looks
like this:

```
zeus:/home/uhl> nroff -man /usr/man/man1/ls.1 ¦ more
```

Linux provides an enhancement rather than the original nroff.   nroff
The command nroff is only a script that invokes groff with the

groff · correct parameters for ASCII output. If `groff` is invoked directly without these parameters, then PostScript text is output. This proves practical for printing Manual pages on a PostScript-compatible printer, since the text is properly formatted and output with various fonts.

```
linux2:/> groff -man /usr/local/man/scotty.1 >scotty.ps
```

TEX

D. E. Knuth · The typesetting system TEX (pronounced "teck") by Donald E. Knuth represents a world of its own. On first contact, the user of a modern WYSIWYG word processing system may feel projected back to the stone age of computers. Nevertheless, TEX affords some features that make it superior to normal word processing in several ways.

free availability · One advantage of the system is its free availability for almost all computer platforms and thus the portability of the generated texts.

TEX processes files that contain special formatting commands in ASCII format. The powerful program proves especially suitable for typesetting mathematical material, but the quality of normal texts also exceeds that of word processing programs. TEX translates an

DVI format · ASCII input file to a DVI (device-independent) file, which can be displayed on the screen or printed. The format of the DVI file is identical on all computer systems, which makes transferring a TEX file problem-free. The file can also be output to a linotronic machine.

Numerous macro packages and auxiliary programs exist for TEX that are also available under Linux. These include a graphical

Previewer · previewer (`xdvi`), a utility for sorting an index file, and a program to automatically generate missing fonts. There are also many drivers that convert DVI files to PostScript (`dvips`) or output them on non-PostScript printers (dot matrix, ink jet, laser). Graphics can be embedded with LATEX commands or with externally created PostScript files.

LATEX · LATEX   One of the best-known macro packages is LATEX, by Leslie Lamport, which appreciably eases working with TEX. Naturally, there are also versions for non-English texts. LATEX supports the automatic generation of a table of contents and an index. LATEX also eases the formatting of tables and lists. The following example shows a LaTeX input file followed by its output:

```
\documentstyle{article}
\topmargin -15mm \headsep 0mm \textwidth 16cm
\textheight 26cm \oddsidemargin 0cm \parindent 0mm

\begin{document}
\thispagestyle{empty}

\centerline{{\Huge Typesetting with \TeX}}
\vspace{1cm}

\TeX\footnote{pronounced ''teck'', or, better, with a Greek chi}
and the macro package \LaTeX\/ enable the production of
manuscripts in typeset quality. It proves especially suitable for
articles, books, letters, mathematical material, and documentation.
Particularly \LaTeX\/ provides numerous features for formatting
formulas, tables, and lists. Tables of contents and scientific
numbering of chapters can be generated automatically. Even the
management of footnotes proves to be no problem. Various fonts and
styles are available for emphasizing text:

\begin{center}
{\rm Roman}, {\bf Bold Face}, {\tt Typewriter}, {\it
Italic}, {\sl Slanted}, {\sc Small Caps}, {\sf Sans Serif}
\end{center}

The size of the text can also be varied:

\begin{center}
{\tiny tiny}, {\scriptsize very small}, {\footnotesize
smaller},
{\small small}, {\normalsize normal}, {\large large},
{\Large larger}\\
{\LARGE even larger}, {\huge huge}, {\Huge gigantic}
\end{center}

Mathematical formulas could look like this:
\begin{displaymath}
        \int_0^\infty f(x)\,dx \approx \sum_{i=1}^n w_i
e^{x_i} g(x_i)
\end{displaymath}

\begin{displaymath}
        \sqrt[n]{\frac{x^n - y^n}{1 + u^{2n}}}
\end{displaymath}

Here is an example of a list:

\begin{itemize}
\item Hardware
\begin{itemize}
\item Computer \item Keyboard \item Monitor
\end{itemize}
\item Software
\begin{itemize}
\item Operating system \item User interface \item Application
program
\end{itemize} \end{itemize}

Tables are especially easy to typeset under \LaTeX\/:

\begin{center} \begin{tabular}{|r|l||c|rrr|c|c|} \hline
Rank & Team          & Sp. & S & U & N & Goals & Points\\
\hline\hline
1.   & Bavaria Munich & 33  & 19 & 13 & 1  & 66:31 & 51:15\\
\hline
```

```
2.   & Hamburg          & 33  & 18 & 9  & 6  & 65:37 & 45:21\\
\hline
3.   & Bor. M'Gladbach & 33  & 17 & 7  & 9  & 70:44 & 41:25\\
\hline
4.   & Bor. Dortmund    & 33  & 14 & 10 & 9  & 66:50 & 38:28\\
\hline
5.   & Werder Bremen    & 33  & 16 & 6  & 11 & 63:53 & 38:28\\
\hline
6.   & Kaiserslautern   & 33  & 15 & 7  & 11 & 64:47 & 37:29\\
\hline
\end{tabular} \end{center}

\newcommand{\absatz}{
\begin{minipage}[b]{7.5cm}
A text can also be wrapped in a text box. By the way, \TeX\/
naturally
features automatic hyphenation. Furthermore, individual letters are
moved to certain positions under one another. This process is
called
{\em kerning}.
\end{minipage}}

\absatz \hfill \absatz

\begin{center}
{\Huge W\/orld V\/at V\/A W\/orld}
\end{center}
\begin{center}
{\Huge World Vat VA World}
\end{center}

\end{document}
```

After compilation, the result can be displayed with the command xdvi, with the result shown in Figure 12.13.

An important FTP server for TEX is ftp.dante.de.

Letters in LATEX2e To write a business letter quickly, you can use the style brief (Dutch for letter) in LATEX2e (Figure 12.14). The style allows you to choose from among various country-specific styles. The following would be an American letter:

```
\documentclass[american,streepjes,twoside]{brief}
\begin{document}

\voetitem{Telefon}{0241/4093826}
\voetitem{EMail}{elling@stud.fh-heilbronn.de}

\begin{brief}{Mr R.R. Recipient\\
220 Arrival Drive\\
Receiver Valley, CA 12345}

\signature{Volker Elling}

\uwbriefvan{October 21, 1996}

\uwkenmerk{MX-1254}

\onskenmerk{cg8829}

\address{Volker Elling\\
Karlsgraben 65\\
```

Typesetting with TeX

TeX[1] and the macro package LaTeX enable the production of manuscripts with typeset quality. It proves especially suitable for articles, books, letters, mathematical material, and documentation. Particularly LaTeX provides numerous features for formatting formulas, tables and lists. Tables of contents and scientific numbering of chapters can be generated automatically. Even the management of footnotes proves to be no problem.

Various fonts and styles are available for emphasizing text:

Roman, **Bold Face**, `Typewriter`, *Italic*, *Slanted*, SMALL CAPS, Sans Serif

The size of the text can also be varied:

tiny, very small, smaller, small, normal, large, larger
even larger, huge, gigantic

Mathematical formulas could look like this:

$$\int_0^\infty f(x)\,dx \approx \sum_{i=1}^n w_i e^{x_i} g(x_i)$$

$$\sqrt[n]{\frac{x^n - y^n}{1 + u^{2n}}}$$

Here is an example of a list:

- Hardware
  - Computer
  - Keyboard
  - Monitor
- Software
  - Operating system
  - User interface
  - Application program

Tables are especially easy to typeset under LaTeX:

Rank	Team	Sp.	S	U	N	Goals	Points
1.	Bavaria Munich	33	19	13	1	66:31	51:15
2.	Hamburg	33	18	9	6	65:37	45:21
3.	Bor. M'Gladbach	33	17	7	9	70:44	41:25
4.	Bor. Dortmund	33	14	10	9	66:50	38:28
5.	Werder Bremen	33	16	6	11	63:53	38:28
6.	Kaiserslautern	33	15	7	11	64:47	37:29

Text can also be wrapped in a text box. By the way, TeX naturally features automatic hyphenation. Furthermore, individual letters are moved to certain positions near one another. This process is called *kerning*.

Text can also be wrapped in a text box. By the way, TeX naturally features automatic hyphenation. Furthermore, individual letters are moved to certain positions near one another. This process is called *kerning*.

World Vat VA World
World Vat VA World

---

[1] pronounced 'teck'

Figure 12.13. Example of TeX output

```
D-52064 Aachen\\
Germany}

\signature{Volker Elling}

\opening{Dear Mr Recipient,}

Three of the most important services provided by cryptosystems
are secrecy, authenticity, and integrity. Secrecy refers to denial
of access to information by unauthorized individuals. Authenticity
refers to validating the source of a message; i.e., that it was
transmitted by a properly identified sender and is not a replay of
a previously transmitted message. Integrity refers to assurance
that a message was not modified accidentally or deliberately in
transit, by replacement, insertion, or deletion. A fourth service
which may be provided is nonrepudiation of origin, i.e., protection
against a sender of a message later denying transmission.

\closing{Yours sincerely,}

\bijlagen{detailed report}

\end{brief}
\end{document}
```

LyX

One of the major criticisms of TEX is that it completely violates the WYSIWYG principle. The author of a text can see the formatted text only after compilation and invocation of xdvi. LaTeX ameliorates the problem somewhat because the text to be formatted is already entered in a structured way and style files handle formatting on the basis of this structuring. Usually the result is ready for print without major corrections. LyX* (originally by Matthias Ettrich) is

graphical LaTeX front end   a comfortable graphical front end for TEX and LaTeX (Figure 12.15). The TEX code is graphically prepared already on input and displayed nearly in its final form. LyX is still under development. Version 0.10.7 beta (October 1996) already supports division into chapters, sections, and paragraphs, WYSIWYG input of mathematical formulas and tables, as well as the choice of format templates with the creation of the document. TEX commands are highlighted in red to distinguish them from the rest of the text, which makes reading TEX code quite comfortable. If you have the GNU spelling checker ispell installed, you can turn it loose on the contents of the LyX editor.

---

*Sunsite: apps/editors

Volker Elling
Karlsgraben 65
D-52064 Aachen
Germany

Mr R.R. Recipient
220 Arrival Drive
Receiver Valley, CA 12345

Your letter of	Your reference	Our reference	Date
October 21, 1996	MX-1254	cg8829	December 15, 1996

Dear Mr Recipient,

Three of the most important services provided by cryptosystems are secrecy,
authenticity, and integrity. Secrecy refers to denial of access to information by
unauthorized individuals. Authenticity refers to validating the source of a message:
i.e., that it was transmitted by a properly identified sender and is not a replay of a
previously transmitted message. Integrity refers to assurance that a message was not
modified accidentally or deliberately in transit, by replacement, insertion or deletion.
A fourth service which may be provided is nonrepudiation of origin, i.e., protection
against a sender of a message later denying transmission.

Yours sincerely,

Volker Elling

Enclosures: detailed report

Telefon	EMail
0241/4093826	elling@stud.fh-heilbronn.de

Figure 12.14. LaTeX2e letter style

12.6 Multimedia environment Andrew

Developers at Carnegie-Mellon University have been working
together with IBM for several years on the formation of an extensive,
distributed multimedia user environment called AUIS (Andrew User
Interface System). This refers to a series of individual applications
that enable the processing of multimedia document (Figure 12.16).

AUIS

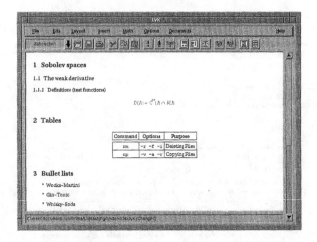

Figure 12.15. LyX—graphical TeX front end

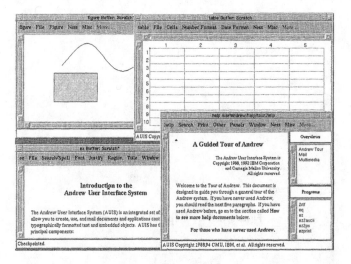

Figure 12.16. Andrew package

The applications include a simple text processor (ez), a spreadsheet (table), a drawing program (figure), and a painting program (image). A hypertext on-line help (help Andrew) documents the individual components.

A mail program capable of multimedia makes it possible to send the created documents. It is also possible to combine the individual components (text, graphics, tables, animations) in a document as needed. This process is often referred to as object embedding. Under AUIS the individual objects are called *insets*.

12.7 Databases

The following list of databases that run under Linux is only a small selection from a constantly growing group. Even systems for SCO UNIX, such as Foxpro for UNIX (Microsoft) and a commercial Ingres version, run under Linux with the help of the iBCS2 emulator. Of course, there is also a whole series of products that have been ported specifically for Linux. The Clipper-compatible database Flagship may be interesting for anyone wishing to port software from the PC area to Linux.

MSQL

MSQL* (mini SQL) was developed by David J. Hughes from the Bond University in Australia. It is a minimum database core for implementing a subset of the ANSI SQL standard. The available data types are currently restricted to character strings and whole or floating-point numbers. Unfortunately, MSQL does not yet recognize any Views. However, the system is probably sufficient for developing simple applications. Its performance is considerably better than that of other free database systems. In addition, the MSQL server can be addressed via a TCP/IP connection, which enables real client/server architectures. There is also a Tcl/Tk connection.

OBST

The object-oriented database OBST was developed within the framework of the STONE project (A Structured and Open

*Sunsite: apps/databases

Environment) at the Forschungszentrum Informatik (FZI) in Karlsruhe, Germany. Although this system was originally designed to be language-independent, the database description language is strongly oriented to C++. The program development, however, can be done in C, C++, and also in Tcl.

In addition to the rudimentary administration tools, a simple graphical database scheme editor is also available to the user.

commercial version A software company in Karlsruhe is currently developing a commercial OBST variant.

Ingres and Postgres

The database system Ingres* and its successor Postgres[†] from the University of California at Berkeley have been ported to Linux. However, do not confuse this version of Ingres with the commercial *SQL* SQL database system. The Linux version is significantly older and has a somewhat different query language instead of SQL.

object oriented Postgres is an object-oriented database, but unlike many of the proprietary systems, it is not based on C++ and persistent objects. It is rather an enhancement of the classical, relational approach. Both systems are quite interesting for educational purposes, but their usefulness is limited for developing applications.

YARD

SQL Anyone needing a complete SQL database under Linux should look at the products from Yard Software in Cologne, Germany. YARD-SQL is a robust database system that corresponds to ANSI standard. Aside *ESQL* from an ESQL-C port, it provides secure transactions, referential integrity, and the data type BLOB (Binary Large Object).

The graphical scheme editor can be used for database design. An *ODBC* ODBC port enables the connection of PC clients under MS-Windows.

Just Logic SQL

low-cost SQL The Just Logic Technologies company has developed a client/server SQL database in the low-cost range. The server can run on all the

*Sunsite: `apps/databases`
[†]Sunsite: `apps/databases/postgres`

common PC UNIX platforms. There are clients for DOS, Windows, and OS/2. An ODBC port and an Apple client are under development.

POET

Another commercial database system for Linux is POET. This database system is C++- based and object-oriented; it has been ported   C++ to all the common operating system platforms (UNIX, OS/2, MS-Windows) and is useful for implementing client/server solutions.   client/server Since POET is directed exclusively at C++ programmers, it only has a very rudimentary user interface.

12.8   Java

The Blackdown Project has ported the Java Developers Kit JDK to Linux. Sun Microsystems permits its use without license fees. JDK is located on `java.blackdown.org`. Linux requires `jdk.common.tar.gz` and `jdk-linux-shared.tar.gz`. If you have not installed Motif, instead of the latter you should download `jdk-linux-static.tar.gz`. To be able to use JDK, you must upgrade `libc`—preferably to Version 5.4.*. An introduction (in German) to Java with extensive references can be found in [15].

12.9   Mathematical applications

MuPAD

A particularly interesting program package for students is MuPAD*   MuPAD (Figure 12.17). This computer algebra system was developed at the   algebra University of Paderborn (Germany) and is furnished free of charge to noncommercial institutions. MuPAD supports the user in solving various types of mathematical problems. An integrated programming language enables the implementation of the user's own algorithms. MuPAD was especially designed to handle parallel problems.

MuPAD provides its own debugger with a graphical front end.   debugger MuPAD itself has a simple command-line–oriented user interface. However, an OpenLook- or Motif-based front end makes the program   OpenLook/Motif

*Sunsite: `apps/math/MuPAD/mu1`

339

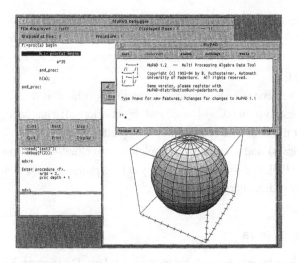

Figure 12.17. Computer algebra system MuPAD

appreciably easier to use. MuPAD's graphical output features, e.g., for depicting three-dimensional functions, are quite advanced.

on-line help   A hypertext on-line help function makes it possible to access all relevant information and function descriptions. A detailed manual for MuPAD was published by Birkhäuser.

Maple V

Waterloo Software   Waterloo Software has ported Version 3 of the well-known Maple V package to Linux (Figure 12.18). This system may well satisfy some users' exacting demands, but it is expensive.

12.10   Simulations

Neural network simulation

SNNS   The Simulator for Neural Networks (SNNS) developed by computer engineers at the University of Stuttgart (Germany) is one of the best for this sector (Figure 12.19). The graphical front end makes the development and analysis of more complex networks considerably easier. SNNS is extremely useful not only for demonstrating the

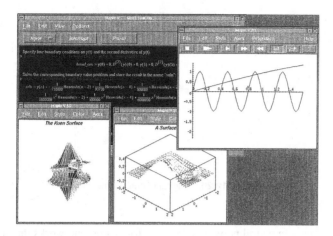

Figure 12.18. Maple V under Linux

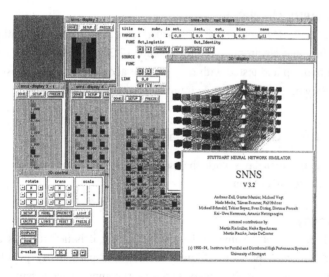

Figure 12.19. Simulation of neural networks with SNNS

341

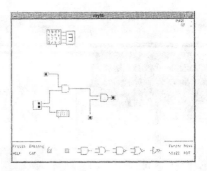

Figure 12.20. Digital circuitry simulation

processes in neural networks, but also for training networks that are actually usable.

Circuitry simulation

diglog

The Caltech Electronic CAD Distribution is useful for simulating digital and electronic circuitry (Figure 12.20). Digital circuits can be built up and tested with diglog.* In addition, a comprehensive library of components and circuit elements is available.

12.11   Games and recreation

To relax after a day's work, the user can enjoy one of the many games available under Linux.

Xteddy

XTeddy

XTeddy is not a game in the real sense, but it is nevertheless an indispensable program (Figure 12.21). It is particularly popular among family members who are not (yet) computer-dependent.

Tetris

playing pieces

Tetris is an extremely popular game that is also available under Linux in an attractive form. The player must try to place falling blocks in such a way that they do not pile up too high. This would happen quickly, of course, if completed rows did not disappear.

*Sunsite: apps/circuits

Figure 12.21. Electronic teddy bear

GNU Chess

For more challenging entertainment, have a look at xboard and GNU Chess. The chess skill of this program is astonishing. At chess competitions, GNU Chess has defeated commercial chess programs.

GNU Chess itself is not particularly user-friendly, so it requires the graphical front end xboard to make playing practical. xboard can also start GNU Chess twice and let the games play against each other. Another option allows chess parties on the Internet, making it possible to find an adequate partner somewhere in the world at any time, day or night (see Section 10.3).

MUDs and Crossfire

Games that can be played on a network by multiple participants prove especially interesting. One widespread form of such network games is MUDs (Multi-User Dungeons) (Figure 12.22). Each player logs in to a common server via telnet and can use commands like say, get,   telnet
or go, and can move. MUDs are normally limited to textual input and output.

Some addresses of MUDs that can be reached by telnet are (see Section 10.3):

- morgen.cs.tu-berlin.de, Port 7680
- padermud.uni-paderborn.de, Port 3000
- pascal.uni-muenster.de, Port 4711
- unitopia.uni-stuttgart.de, Port 3333
- mud.uni-munester.de, Port 4711

Further information is available in the many newsgroups on   newsgroups
MUDs and in the MUD FAQ (see Section 11.4).

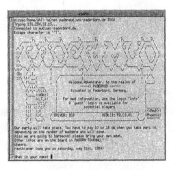

Figure 12.22. MUDs

A leap ahead of the text-oriented MUDs, the multi-user role-play
Crossfire requires special client software that graphically depicts
the virtual world in which the player moves (see Figure 12.23).
The source code of the game can be copied from the FTP server
`ftp.ifi.uio.no` in the directory `/pub/crossfire`.

fortune

`fortune`* is a small program that on login displays some deep
saying, a Dave Barry pearl, a quote from a StarTrek episode, or
(apparently) senseless babble from Zippy the Pinhead. The scope

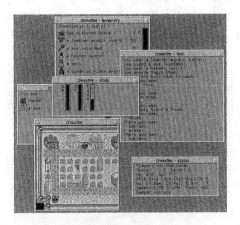

Figure 12.23. Crossfire

*Sunsite: `games/`

of the fortune database under /usr/games/fortunes suffices to prevent boredom even for dedicated UNIX hackers. It is strictly forbidden to invoke fortune manually or even to read through the fortune files! Fortunes are small jewels that should only be enjoyed in small doses. The origin of the name is naturally Chinese fortune cookies, which contain a small saying or fortune. This is a sample:

```
golem:~> fortune
Conscience is what hurts when everything else feels so good.
```

## Chapter 13

GNU Emacs

If you ask several experienced UNIX users which editor they use, most of them will answer either vi or Emacs. Most vi users will base their choice on having used this editor for 20 years and will point out that it is available on all UNIX platforms. The Emacs users, on the other hand, will point out that their editor is extremely flexible and functional.

This chapter introduces the application of Emacs and describes its concepts and features in more detail. A section on programming with Emacs Lisp explains the configuration by means of examples. The last section may be difficult to understand for readers who do not already have some knowledge of other programming languages. A more in-depth presentation, however, would by far exceed the scope of this book. The last part of this chapter therefore addresses readers who already have a basic knowledge of programming.

13.1 Overview

Richard Stallman, the founder of FSF, developed Emacs, which is available on nearly all UNIX platforms, DOS, and VMS. Emacs can be used not only in text mode on simple ASCII terminals, but also under the X Window System. This system provides pulldown menus, buttons, and scrollbars, and various colors and fonts. With the mouse the user can select, copy, and insert text as usual under X11.

Emacs provides a tutorial for novices as well as help for all the commands, key combinations, and internal variables. The complete documentation can be called up on-line in a form similar to hypertext.

With Emacs the user can work on different texts simultaneously in separate or divided windows. A backup copy of the texts is

vi or Emacs

application

configuration

FSF

X11

tutorial

automatic backup copy

automatically stored at regular intervals. The almost unlimited undo function is particularly remarkable. With the touch of a key, the user can undo any number of changes up to a definable limit.

Unlike vi and many other well-known editors, Emacs is much more than just an editor. It contains an interpreter for its own Lisp-based language, which is also available to the user. Almost all the functions that go beyond primitive editing functions are written in this Emacs Lisp, or Elisp for short. There are Emacs Lisp programs, for instance, which can create a mail front end, a newsreader, or a complete developing environment from Emacs.

Emacs Lisp

Due to its capabilities, the Emacs package is relatively extensive. The basic installation requires about20 MB of memory on the hard disk. The basic installation contains not only many Emacs Lisp programs, but also the complete documentation.

20 MB on the hard disk

With Emacs' numerous available major modes, the user can optimize the editor for specific tasks. The major modes support the programmer or author, for example, in formatting (source) texts. Directions in C and Lisp mode are automatically indented according to their box level. When the user enters a closing parenthesis, the appropriate opening parenthesis is automatically highlighted. Keywords, commentaries, or other language elements can be displayed in a different font or color if the user so wishes. These kinds of modes exist for all propagated programming languages and file types and are easy to customize.

modes

C

parentheses

13.2 Basic terms

Emacs uses some terms in the documentation and for names of functions, which other editors either do not have or use somewhat differently. We briefly explain those terms here in order to avoid confusion later.

The location between the user's current position in the text (the cursor) and the character before that is called the *point*. Aside from this, there is another important position, which the user can set explicitly; this is called the *mark*. The *region* is the area between the point and the mark. The region corresponds to a marked block in other editors. It can be deleted, cut out, or copied. Unlike in other

point

mark

region

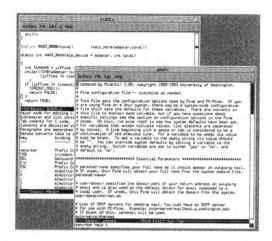

Figure 13.1. Emacs with multiple frames and windows

editors, in Emacs the region is always linked to the current cursor position (point).

A keyboard configuration is called *key binding* in Emacs, because it defines the connection between a key sequence and a specific function. Multiple bindings are stored together in a *keymap*. When a user works on a file in Emacs, work takes place in a *buffer*. A buffer usually contains the contents of a file, but it can also contain something completely different. Some examples of this are the input and output of the GNU debugger gbd when it is invoked under Emacs, or the contents of a directory if the user is in dired mode, explained below.

If a buffer is visible, it is displayed in a window. In Emacs jargon, however, a window does not correspond to a window under X11, but rather refers to a separate portion of the current window in which a buffer is displayed. A separate window under X11 is called a *frame* in this case, and it can contain several windows (Figure 13.1).

key binding

keymap

buffer

window

frame

13.3 Operation

As with any other editor, the user can invoke Emacs with a file name as parameter or without specifications. To work on the file .cshrc in the home directory, for example, invoke Emacs as follows:

invocation

349

```
golem:~> emacs ~/.cshrc
```

X11

text mode

Under X11, Emacs opens a new window on startup with a graphical menu bar. If Emacs is not invoked under X11, but rather in text mode, there is no menu bar and Emacs uses the entire screen of the terminal.

The user can operate Emacs with the cursor keys and function keys and also with special `Ctrl` or `meta` key combinations. We explain the configuration of the function keys in Section 13.8.

`meta`

`Esc`

There is a `meta` key on the keyboards of some workstations, but not on the MF2 keyboards common to PCs and not on simple ASCII terminals. The `Esc` key can be used instead of `meta`. For `meta` + `X`, press the `Esc` key, then press `X` on keyboards without `meta`. The `Alt` key is often redefined as `meta` under X11 (see Section 8.8), which makes the `Esc` route unnecessary.

The most important bindings of the standard keymap (without the function keys) are as follows:

- Cursor movements:

`Ctrl` + `F`	character forward
`Ctrl` + `B`	character backward
`Ctrl` + `N`	next line
`Ctrl` + `P`	previous line
`Ctrl` + `A`	beginning of line
`Ctrl` + `E`	end of line
`Ctrl` + `V`	scroll page forward
`Meta` + `V`	scroll page backward

- Delete:

`Del`	Delete character before the cursor (backspace)
`Ctrl` + `D`	Delete character under the cursor
`Ctrl` + `K`	Delete to end of line or blank line; this stores the deleted text in the *kill ring*, and it can be inserted again

- Mark, delete, and insert:

Ctrl + **Space**	Set the mark at the current position of the point
Meta + **w**	Copy the region (text between marking and point) to the kill ring
Ctrl + **w**	Copy the contents of the region to the kill ring and delete it from the text
Ctrl + **Y**	Insert the contents of the kill ring at the current cursor position

- Search:

Ctrl + **S**	search (by increments, see below)
Ctrl + **R**	search backwards (by increments)
Ctrl + **G**	interrupt search or the last command

- Miscellaneous:

Ctrl + **X** **F**	load file (find)
Ctrl + **X** **Ctrl** + **C**	end Emacs
Ctrl + **X** **O**	go to next window (other)
Ctrl + **X** **B**	go to a different buffer

Ctrl + **G** is a relatively important key. A beginner often feels somewhat lost in Emacs' combinations of multiple keys. If the user accidentally presses **Ctrl** + **X**, for example, Emacs expects a second entry, which in conjunction with **Ctrl** + **X** could result in a command. This can be aborted by pressing **Ctrl** + **G**.   *interrupt*

The user can find a clear and relatively complete list of all the Emacs key bindings in the Emacs reference card, which is   *reference card* stored in the Emacs `etc` directory. If Emacs is installed under `/usr/lib/emacs/19.28`, for example, then the `etc` directory is `/usr/lib/emacs/19.28/etc`. The reference card is named `refcard.ps` or `refcard.tex` as a TₑX file.

In addition, in Emacs the user can output a list of all key   *keyboard configuration* configurations at any time with **Ctrl** + **H** **B** ("B" for binding) or the meaning of a special key combination with $\boxed{\text{Ctrl}} + \boxed{\text{H}}\,\boxed{\text{k}}$

relevant key combination ("K" for key).

search   The incremental search within Emacs is a feature unknown to many other editors. It means that Emacs does not wait until the user has the entire text for the search; as soon as the first key is pressed, Emacs begins searching for the next occurrence of that character and positions the cursor at the appropriate place. If the user enters another character, Emacs looks for the next occurrence of these two characters together. This way, the user approaches the relevant text incrementally and may find it with far fewer keys than by having to enter the entire search term.

menus   Pulldown menus are available under X11 for the most important functions. In addition, all the (interactive) functions intended for the user can be invoked directly, regardless of whether they have been

$\boxed{\text{Meta}} + \boxed{\text{x}}$ assigned to a certain key. Press $\boxed{\text{Meta}} + \boxed{\text{X}}$ for this. Emacs then prompts the user to enter the name of the function to be invoked with a prompt in the minibuffer. An automatic name extension is

$\boxed{\text{Tab}}$ provided with $\boxed{\text{Tab}}$, as is almost always the case in Emacs. If more information is required for the function to be invoked, a query is made in the minibuffer. It is often practical to invoke less frequently used functions directly with $\boxed{\text{Meta}} + \boxed{\text{X}}$, especially if the user is not sure whether there is a binding for them at all.

13.4   Documentation and help

tutorial   The Emacs tutorial provides a quick introduction to the operation of Emacs. The tutorial is a text that is automatically loaded when the user enters $\boxed{\text{Ctrl}} + \boxed{\text{H}}\,\boxed{\text{T}}$. It contains directions that interactively present all the important editing commands step by step. The actual

functions   on-line help consists of a number of partial functions. The user can display the description of a function with $\boxed{\text{Ctrl}} + \boxed{\text{H}}\,\boxed{\text{F}}$; $\boxed{\text{Ctrl}} + \boxed{\text{H}}$ $\boxed{\text{A}}$ ("A" for *apropos*) searches a list of all the names of functions for a partial string (Figure 13.2). For example, if the user is looking for a function in order to go directly to a particular line, then $\boxed{\text{Ctrl}} + \boxed{\text{H}}$ $\boxed{\text{A}}$ *line* produces a list of all the functions containing *line* in their names, together with all the bindings that may be present. This list

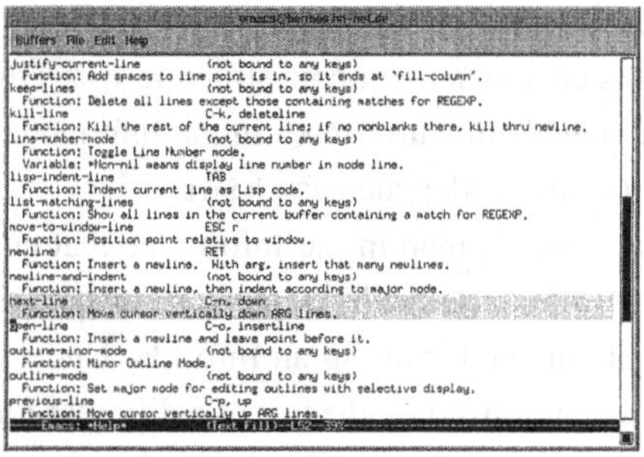

Figure 13.2. The apropos function

would contain such functions as `previous-line` and `next-line`, as well as the relevant function `goto-line`.

With Ctrl + H B the user can display a list of all current key bindings, and Ctrl + H M produces a description of the activated modes (see below). All of these help functions are also available in the help pulldown menu under X11.

key bindings

Ctrl + H A	apropos – list of all the functions whose names contain a particular text
Ctrl + H C	brief description of a key combination
Ctrl + H K	longer description of a key combination
Ctrl + H Ctrl + K	go into the info mode to the page where the command is described that is linked to the key combination
Ctrl + H I	go into the info mode
Ctrl + H M	mode – description of the activated modes
Ctrl + H F	description of an Emacs Lisp function
Ctrl + H V	description of an Emacs Lisp variable
Ctrl + H H	brief overview of all Ctrl-h commands

As with all FSF programs, the comprehensive documentation of the Emacs editor is originally in `texinfo` format. Info files are automatically created from this format on installation. Not only Info files, but also TEX files can be created from a `texinfo` file. This means that the documentation can also be printed out (see Section 12.5). Info files contain a hierarchic structure with cross references.

Info mode   The user can view them with Emacs in the Info mode (Figure 13.3) or with another Info reader such as tkinfo.

There is a new keymap in the Info mode that enables the user

cross references   to follow cross references with simple keys or with the mouse and thus to navigate hierarchically in an Info file. Under X11 the cross references are emphasized by the use of a different font or color.

The information on Emacs that is displayed in the Info mode

manual   corresponds to the printed Emacs manual, which can be obtained from FSF. The most important keys in the Info mode are as follows:

middle mouse button	Follow the clicked cross reference.
d	Go to the table of contents with the overview of all Info files (directory).
Return	Follow the cross-reference under the cursor.
l	Go back to the last page viewed (last).
n	Go to the next Info page (next).
p	Go to the previous Info page (previous).
u	Go to the Info page that is above the current page in the hierarchy (up).
s	Search for text (search).

Emacs Lisp   In addition to the normal Emacs manual, there is also a documentation for Emacs Lisp, which is also available in texinfo format. This manual has many hundreds of pages when printed, and it comprehensively describes all the internal details of the editor and its programming. The user can obtain this manual via FTP, for example, from any larger FTP server. The file is normally stored together with the Emacs source code and the other GNU utilities in a directory named gnu.

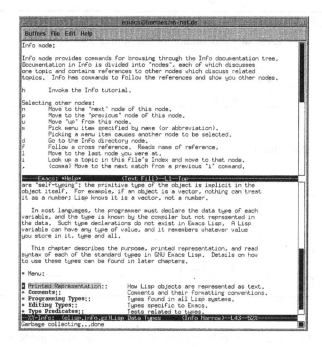

Figure 13.3. The Info mode in Emacs

13.5 Modes

One major mode and possibly one or more minor modes are assigned to every buffer. A major mode generally defines a new keymap and often provides new functions that set Emacs for a specific special function. Thus there are major modes for almost all common programming languages, but also for editing configuration files and normal text. Some modes are not intended for editing files, but rather use Emacs for other functions. Some examples of this are the `gnus`, `rmail`, and `dired` modes.

A minor mode provides certain features that can be activated in addition to the selected major mode. One example is the font-lock mode, which highlights commentaries and keywords of programming languages with different fonts and colors.

The table below lists examples of some major and minor modes along with a brief description of their most important functions.

Major modes:

major mode and minor mode

modes

c, c++	automatic indentation of the source text
lisp	automatic indentation of the source text, online help, evaluation of expressions
tcl	automatic indentation of the source text, evaluation of regions under Tcl

Minor modes:

font-lock	presents commentaries, keywords, strings, or other text areas in different fonts or colors
outline	inserts or removes text on different hierarchical levels
auto-fill	automatic word separation

loading

file extensions

Emacs automatically selects an appropriate major mode when files are loaded. The name of the major mode is displayed in the mode line of the corresponding window. The recognition characteristics for the mode selection are file names or file endings such as `.c`, `.cc`, or `.tcl`. These are assigned to their corresponding mode in a table. In addition, Emacs can determine the mode by the contents of the first line. In this case, it recognizes special commentaries such as `#!//usr/bin/wish`, `# -*-Tcl-*-`, or `# -*-Mode: Tcl;-*-`. The user can also activate a mode manually. To do so, press `meta` + `X` followed by the name of the mode, for example, `meta` + `x` **tcl-mode**.

13.6   Packages and enhancements

Lisp

Aside from the modes, there are also Emacs Lisp programs that provide general additional functions. They can also use the Lisp interpreter only to execute relatively independent applications. We will explain some of these enhancements in the following subsections.

Figure 13.4. The dired mode in Emacs

saveplace

`saveplace` saves the position of the cursor when a working file is closed. The next time this file is loaded, Emacs automatically places the cursor in the same position it was in when the file was closed. The user can activate this function generally for all files or only for certain files. The corresponding entry in the Emacs configuration file is

position of the cursor

```
(load "saveplace")
(define-key ctl-x-map "p" 'toggle-save-place)
```

dired

Although `dired` is actually a mode, it does not have much in common with a normal major mode for processing a file. As the name suggests, dired enables the user to work on directories. Files can be copied, renamed, or deleted (Figure 13.4).

files and directories

The key [F] (follow) permits branching into a subdirectory or loading a file into a different buffer. `dired` is automatically invoked when a directory is "loaded" instead of a file. The user can also activate it directly with [Meta] + [X] **dired**.

follow

357

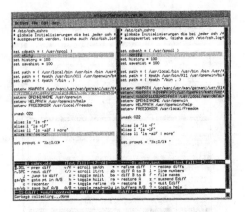

Figure 13.5. ediff in Emacs

ediff

versions   ediff is a valuable aid in combining different versions of a text. This
Emacs Lisp program opens two files and displays them either next
differences   to one another horizontally or vertically as selected. The differences
between the two files are highlighted with different fonts or colors
and can be accepted by either file from the other with a key entry
(Figure 13.5). ediff can be selected from the menu or invoked with
[Meta] + [X] ediff.

finder and lispdir

It is not easy for users to find their way around among all the Lisp
programs   programs and Emacs modes. The Emacs Finder program can be
helpful here. It groups the Lisp programs of the Emacs distribution
selection   under keywords and displays them in a selection list. If the user
selects a keyword with [space], then all the packages that correspond
to the keyword are displayed with a brief description (Figure 13.6).
load library   To start the Finder, load it first with [Meta] + [X] load-library.
Then start the program with [Meta] + [X] finder-by-keyword.

The Finder knows only the Lisp programs that the Emacs
package already contains. The user can use the GNU Emacs Lisp
Code Directory to get an overview of other Emacs programs. This
is a list with over 800 different Emacs Lisp packages, which can be
searched with a special program. The current version of this list can

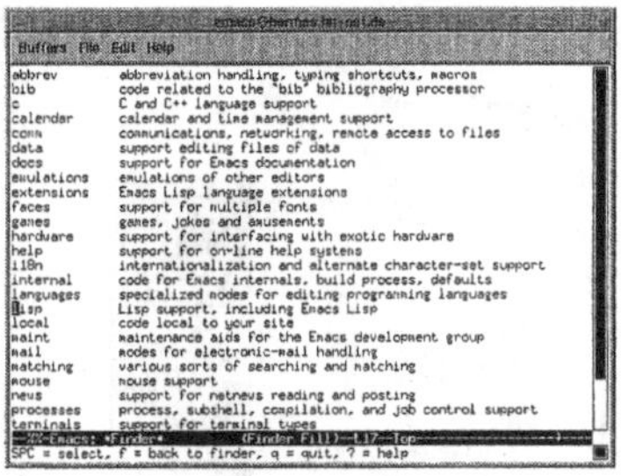

Figure 13.6. The Finder

be obtained from the server `archive.cis.ohio-state.edu` from the directory `/pub/gnu/emacs/elisp-archive`. The program for searching the archive is in the same directory as `lispdir.el.z` (Figure 13.7).

func-menu

The `func-menu` program is very practical for programming in C. It analyzes the C source code in the active buffer at a mouse click and displays a pop-up menu with all the defined function names (Figure 13.8). If the user selects one of these function names from the pop-up menu, Emacs jumps to the buffer location where the function is defined.

Figure 13.7. Result of a lispdir-query on `"tex"`

Figure 13.8. func-menu in a C source code

Tags

Although the management of tags is less convenient, it is functionally superior. The command `etags` creates a file in which all the function names are listed along with the file and the line where the function is defined. The user can then use Emacs Lisp functions such as `tags-search` and `tags-apropos` to search this list.

etags

search

13.7   Emacs Lisp

The Emacs editor contains it own Lisp interpreter, and most Emacs functions are written not in C, but in Emacs Lisp. Operating Emacs or adapting the keyboard does not require familiarity with Lisp. However, for writing functions or creating a more mature configuration, a basic knowledge of Emacs Lisp is unavoidable.

Naturally, a complete description of Emacs Lisp or a complete introduction to Lisp programming would exceed the scope of this chapter. The Emacs Lisp Manual of the Free Software Foundation (FSF) is hundreds of pages long, and Lisp textbooks on the average contain more than 500 pages. Instead, this chapter presents the most important elements of Lisp by way of several examples, in order to help the reader understand simple Emacs Lisp programs and to write smaller functions.

introduction

examples

If you want to enjoy the material in its full scope, we suggest the original manual of the FSF and the Emacs Lisp Info files as well as the many Lisp textbooks.

General information on Emacs Lisp

The name "Lisp" is actually short for LISt Processor. Some critics insist that the acronym harbors Lots of Irritating Single Parentheses. In fact, the most important fundamental structure of a Lisp program is a list delimited by parentheses. This means that expressions frequently consist of five or more nested levels of parentheses.

lists

However, do not let this be a deterrent. You quickly adjust to the look, and with the support of Emacs Lisp mode, which automatically indents expressions correctly and displays the pairing of opening and closing parentheses, there is never any temptation to count parentheses.

modes

Symbols

Symbols play a particular role in Lisp. A symbol represents a unique name that is used for access to data, functions, and property lists. (We do not handle property lists in detail here.) Imagine a symbol as a small container with several compartments: one each for the name, the value, the function definition, and the property list.

shelves

symbol
name
value
function
property list

The value of a symbol has a certain type, which need not be declared in advance as in many procedural languages (e.g., Pascal) but is implicitly contained in the value. Emacs Lisp knows the type of each value. This means that the use of a wrong type can be detected only at run time.

type

The most important primitive data types in Emacs Lisp are

primitive types

361

- Integer
- Floating point
- Character
- Array
- Strings (one-dimensional array)
- Symbol
- Function
- Macro
- Primitive function (written in C)
- Byte-code function (compiled function)

special types

Beyond these data types, which also exist in other Lisp dialects, there are special data types in Emacs Lisp that are used for editor functions. The most important of these are

- buffer
- window
- frame
- process
- stream
- keymap

specialization

The data types in Emacs Lisp partially overlap; a value can simultaneously belong to multiple types (Figure 13.9). This is because some types are a specialization of other types. The data type string, for example, represents a specialization of the type array, which in turn is a specialization of the type sequence.

true and false

t and nil

The values true and false as results of comparison or Boolean expressions are represented in Lisp with the special symbols t and nil. nil is a synonym for the empty list () and is thus also *atomic* (see below) and a list.

The interpreter

read-eval-print

The Lisp interpreter executes a read–evaluate–print cycle. This means that it reads an input, tries to evaluate it, and then prints the result. The expressions that the interpreter can evaluate are called *forms*, or *s-expressions*. The latter is a collective term for elements

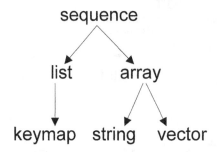

Figure 13.9. Excerpt from the type hierarchy in Emacs Lisp

such as numbers, strings, and symbols that are designated as *atoms*, and *lists*.

If the interpreter encounters a value such as a string or a number, then the result of the evaluation is the value itself. If the interpreter encounters a symbol, it outputs the contents of the compartment with the value of the symbol. The following example shows several inputs and the respective output of the Lisp interpreter.

numbers

symbols

```
1
1
"test"
"test"
fill-column
78
```

If the interpreter encounters a list, then interpretation depends on the first symbol in the list. The symbol is not evaluated, but it determines the kind of s-expression. If it is the name of a function, then the list is a function call. The interpreter then attempts to evaluate the remaining elements (all except the first) and to invoke the function with the results of the evaluation (Figure 13.10).

lists

function

In addition to lists that are interpreted as function calls, there are macros and special forms. In these cases the remaining list elements are not evaluated first. Special forms, for example, are conditions like if or cond. (Figure 13.10).

macros and special forms

A function call takes the following form:

function call

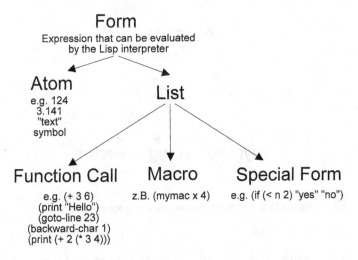

Form

Expression that can be evaluated
by the Lisp interpreter

Atom

e.g. 124
3.141
"text"
symbol

List

Function Call

e.g. (+ 3 6)
(print "Hello")
(goto-line 23)
(backward-char 1)
(print (+ 2 (* 3 4)))

Macro

z.B. (mymac x 4)

Special Form

e.g. (if (< n 2) "yes" "no")

Figure 13.10. Expressions in Emacs Lisp

```
function argument argument ...
```

prefix notation

This is a prefix notation as we know it from mathematics. The following example shows several function calls and the output of the interpreter.

```
(+ 1 4)
5
(substring "abcdefg" 2 3)
"c"
(* (+ 2 3) 3)
15
```

arguments

The individual arguments of the function calls can be symbols or lists, which again are interpreted as function calls. The evaluation of such a list is thus recursive.

special forms

Before we explain existing Lisp functions in more detail, we need to examine several of the special forms. Among other things, they help in realizing conditions and loops and in defining new functions.

Special forms

(defun *fname* (*P1* ... *Pn*) *comment form1* ... *formn*)

> Defines function *fname* with parameters *P1* to *Pn* and function definition *form1* to *formn*.

(defvar *symbol value comment*)

> Assigns to the symbol *symbol* a value if it has none; this is usually used in the definition of global variables.

(if *exp true false1* ... *falsen*)

> Evaluates the form *exp*. If its result is not nil, the form evaluates to *true* and this result is returned. Otherwise the forms *false1* to *falsen* are evaluated. The result is then the result of form *falsen*.

(cond (*exp1 forms1*) (*exp2 forms2*) ... (*expn formsn*))

> Similar to a case statement in Pascal, the expressions *exp1* to *expn* are sequentially evaluated until one is not nil. In this case the associated forms are evaluated; for *exp2* this would be the forms *forms2*. The result of the last associated form is returned as the result.

(while *cond forms*)

> Loop: The forms *forms* are evaluated sequentially until the condition *cond* produces a value other than nil.

(quote *list*)

> Returns *list* as a list without attempting to evaluate it. Abbreviation: '*list*.

(progn *forms*)

> The forms *forms* are evaluated sequentially and the last result is returned as the result of the special form.

(setq *sname nvalue*)

> Assigns the new value *nvalue* to the value compartment of symbol *sname*.

(let (*var1* ... *varn*) *forms*)

> Creates new links for variables *var1* to *Varn*, which can then be used within the forms as local variables. *var1* to *varn* can be either symbols, in which case they receive the value nil, or lists of type *var form*, in which case the symbol *var* is linked to the result of *form*.

```
(save-excursion forms)
```

The forms *forms* are evaluated sequentially as with `progn`, but the current state of the editor, i.e., the current buffer, the cursor position, and the position of the marker are saved and restored after evaluation of *forms*.

Additional special forms are explained when they are used in an example. An overview of all special forms in Emacs Lisp is in the Info document for Emacs Lisp.

Examples of special forms

```
(defvar TestVariable 123
  "This variable is only for test purposes.")

(setq TestVariable (+ TestVariable 2))
```

global variables   Here the symbol `TestVariable` is used as a global variable. First the variable is assigned the value 123. Then the `setq` form increments the value by 2. The result of this form is the new value of `TestVariable`, or 125.

testing   It is quite simple to test these small examples in Emacs. Start Emacs without a file name. Emacs displays the usual version number and the help commands. This message disappears when any key is pressed, presenting a buffer named `*scratch*`. The current mode is
Lisp interaction   "Lisp interaction," which indicates that the Lisp interpreter is ready. The mode contains key bindings for working with Emacs Lisp:

Tab	correct indentation of current line depending on nesting depth.
Meta + Tab	completion of the current symbol. Function names, variables, and special forms are automatically extended.
Meta + Ctrl + X	evaluates the `defun` special form to the left of the cursor.
Meta + Return	evaluates the form to the left of the cursor and feed key or outputs the result.

Unfortunately, PCs lack a special line-feed key. However, the function can be assigned to another key with the invocation of [Meta]+[X] local-set-key. Emacs then prompts with "Set key locally: -" for the key combination to be assigned. Here, for example, we might press [Meta-Return].

line feed

local-set-key

Emacs then asks for the function to be bound to the entered key combination. Here we specify eval-print-last-sexp. This assigns to the key combination [Meta] + [Return] the Emacs Lisp function eval-print-last-sexp, which evaluates the form to the left of the cursor and outputs the result. After entering a form, we can now simply enter [Meta] + [Return] instead of [Return], and the Emacs Lisp interpreter evaluates the form. The result for the above example looks like this:

function

meta return

```
(defvar TestVariable 123
  "This variable is only for test purposes.")   Meta + Return
TestVariable
(setq TestVariable (+ TestVariable 2))          Meta + Return
125
```

In the following example a simple function is defined that multiplies the sum of two numbers by 2. Then the new function is used in an invocation of print:

```
(defun doublesum (a b)
  "simple test function"
  (* 2 (+ a b)))
doublesum
(print (doublesum 2 3))
10
10
```

The Lisp interpreter outputs the result twice: once due to the function print, and again as the result of the overall form in which print was invoked.

double output

The preceding examples each specify a string as comment. This comment, also called a *doc string*, is saved along with the definition. These comments can later be read using the predefined functions describe-function and describe-variable, which are bound to [Ctrl]+[H][Ctrl]+[F] and [Ctrl]+[H][Ctrl]+[V], respectively. This

doc string

describe function

means that the same help function can be used for custom functions as was employed for predefined functions.

local variable   During programing, some intermediate result is needed in several subsequent steps, and thus it is stored in a local variable. In Lisp this works with the special form let, as the following example shows.

```
(defvar square 0
   "global value of square")
square
(defun f (n)
   "example function using let"
   (let ((square (* n n)))
      (print square)
      (print (- square 2)))))
f
(f 3)
9
7
7
square
0
```

let   The let form creates a new binding for the symbol square. This covers the global value of the symbol. The new binding only applies locally within the let form. On leaving the let form, the global value of square, which has not changed, applies again.

dynamic binding   Contrary to the late binding employed in Common Lisp, Emacs Lisp uses dynamic binding. This means that the values of new let variables are accessible from within functions that are invoked within let. The following example clarifies this:

```
(defvar a 100)
a
(defvar b 200)
b
(defvar c 300)
c
a
100
(defun fct1 ()
   "Test function using let"
   (print "in fct1")
   (print (format "a=%s, b=%s, c=%s" a b c))
   (let ((a 1) (b (+ 2 3)) c)
      (print "in fct1 in let")
      (print (format "a=%s, b=%s, c=%s" a b c))
      (fct2))
   (print "in fct1 again outside of let")
   (print (format "a=%s, b=%s, c=%s" a b c)))
fct1
(defun fct2 ()
   "Test function, invoked by fct1 and accessing variables
   from fct1"
```

```
  (print "in fct2")
  (print (format "a=%s, b=%s, c=%s" a b c)))
fct2
(fct1)

"in fct1"

"a=100, b=200, c=300"

"in fct1 in let"

"a=1, b=5, c=nil"

"in fct2"

"a=1, b=5, c=nil"

"in fct1 again outside of let"

"a=100, b=200, c=300"
"a=100, b=200, c=300"
```

Type-check functions

Predefined functions are a significant component of Emacs Lisp. Due   functions
to their sheer number, we can present only a small fraction of them.
However, the help functions in Emacs and the Info files for Emacs
Lisp provide a very practical reference of the available functions.

The fact that in Lisp the type of a symbol or a function   type
return value can often be determined only at run time necessitates
functions for type checking. The following table lists examples of
such functions, which test whether the passed expression is of a
certain type and then return t or nil. Their names usually derive   t or nil
from the name of the type with the extension p for predicate. Lisp
frequently uses this extension for functions that execute a test and
return t or nil.

arrayp
      tests whether the passed value is an array
bufferp
      tests whether the value for a buffer has been set
consp
      tests whether the value is a cons cell (in Lisp, the building
      blocks of lists)
listp
      tests whether the value is a list
numberp
      tests whether the value is numeric

Example:

```
(setq a "this is a string")
"this is a string"
(arrayp a)
t
(stringp a)
t
(numberp a)
nil
```

List functions

Lisp has numerous functions for processing lists. To understand these functions, it is important to understand the representation of lists in Lisp. Lists are formed by linking *cons cells*, which are cells consisting of two pointers. The first pointer, called car, references a value, and the second pointer, cdr, references the next cons cell of the next list element. The last cons cell of a list has a cdr value of nil. Figure 13.11 depicts the representation of the list (This is a list) with cons cells.

cons cells

If car of one element points to additional cons cells, this produces a nested list. The following table introduces the most important list functions.

nested lists

car

returns the first element of a list (the car of its first cons cell)

cdr

returns the rest of a list without its first element (the cdr of the first cons cell)

cons

creates a new cons cell

nth

returns an element of a list

list

creates a new list

append

merges two lists lists by appending

reverse

inverts a list

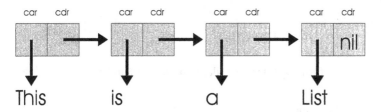

Figure 13.11. Internal structure of a list

`sort`

       sorts a list

In addition to the normal Emacs Lisp functions, after loading a special extension, Common Lisp functions can be used as well. Two macros for list processing are `push` and `pop`, which add an element to the front of a list and remove one from there, respectively.

push and pop

      Example:

```
(setq l1 '(This is a list))
(This is a list)
(car l1)
The
(cdr l1)
(is a list)
(cons 'This (cdr l1))
(This is a list)
(append '(and this too) (cdr l1))
(and this too is a list)
(nth 2 l1)
a
```

String functions

The type string in Lisp is a specialization of the type array. This means that all functions that process arrays also work with strings. The following table presents the most important functions.

array

`make-string`

      creates a string

`substring`

      returns a substring

`concat`

      concatenates strings

`string=`

> compares two strings

`format`

> formats a string similarly to `sprintf` in C

Example:

```
(setq a "this is a string")
"this is a string"
(stringp a)
t
(substring a 4 10)
" is a "
(make-string 10 32)
"          "
```

Cursor movement and text processing

The most important functions in Emacs Lisp are naturally those that process a text in a buffer, move the cursor, and insert or delete text. They allow automation of editor functions. The following table shows examples of such functions.

inserting and deleting

`point`

> returns the current cursor position

`goto-char`

> places the cursor at an absolute position

`forward-char`

> moves the cursor one character to the right

`forward-word`

> moves the cursor one word to the right

`search-forward`

> searches for a string in the buffer

`insert`

> inserts a string at the current cursor position in the buffer

`delete-region`

> deletes the current region in the buffer

Interactive functions

To permit the user to invoke a function with a key binding or with [Meta] + [X], this function must contain the function call interactive. This call is analogous to a declaration that specifies which arguments are to be passed to the function on invocation. The simplest case is a function without arguments, in which case it suffices to invoke interactive at the start of the function. The following example shows such a simple function that could be bound to the key combination [Shift] + [CursorRight], which would then simultaneously move the cursor one character to the right and mark the text.

arguments

```
(defun mark-move-right ()
  "move right and set the mark if it is not already active"
  (interactive)
  (if (not mark-active)
      (push-mark nil nil t))
  (forward-char))
```

It is possible to define a function that obtains its parameters via the user's minibuffer; this can also be done with the function interactive. As parameter a string containing a code character followed by a prompt is passed to interactive. The following example defines an interactive function that inserts a line composed of "-" characters into the text, whereby the length of the line is obtained first.

code characters

```
(defun line (len)
  "draw a -- line with length len"
  (interactive "nLength")
  (insert (make-string len 45)))
```

The code character used here is "n," meaning numeric input. If multiple parameters are passed, this is done in the same string but delimited by "\n." The following example shows a small extension of the above example that also allows specification of the character. The code character for inputting an individual character is "c."

inputting a number

```
(defun line (len lchar)
  "draw a line of lchar characters with length len"
  (interactive "nLength \ncChar")
  (insert (make-string len lchar)))
```

help

The complete description of all code characters can be obtained from the on-line help by typing `Ctrl`+`H` `F` `interactive` or from the Emacs Lisp Info files.

Notes on style

functional language

Lisp is a functional language, meaning that the most important structural element is the function. Pure procedures such as in Pascal, subroutines that do not return a value, do not exist in Lisp. Functional

variable assignments

programming means whenever possible variable assignments should be avoided in favor of working directly with the return value of a function or the value of an expression.

13.8   Configuration

configuration file
.emacs

To customize the keyboard layout within Emacs or to load additional functions and packages, the file `.emacs` in the user's home directory is generally adapted. Emacs loads this file on starting, and the Emacs Lisp interpreter evaluates it. Thus, it is also called the *initialization file*.

Alternatively, such settings can be made globally for all users in the files `site-start.el` and `default.el`. They must reside in a directory that Emacs automatically searches for Lisp files,

site-lisp

such as the directory `site-lisp`, which is usually located at `/usr/lib/emacs/site-lisp` under Linux. Other UNIX systems usually install Emacs under `/usr/local`. In this case the `site-lisp` directory would be at `/usr/local/lib/emacs/site-lisp`.

If the file `site-start.el` exists, then it is evaluated by a user-specific initialization file. The file `default.el` is also optional and serves as the default initialization file. It is loaded after the user-specific initialization file unless the user's initialization file sets the

inhibit-default-init

variable `inhibit-default-init` to a value other than `nil`. This makes three configuration files, all of which are optional, which are invoked in the following order:

`site-start.el`

for global settings made independently of the user-specific initialization file;

`~/.emacs`

for user-specific settings;

`default.el`

for global settings to be applied when the user does not disable them with the variable `inhibit-default-init`.

Configuration is carried out in these files with Emacs Lisp. The entries are Emacs Lisp function calls. As detailed in Section 13.7, these are parenthetical expressions in which the first list element represents the function name and the remaining elements are the parameters. If the parameters are symbols, they are evaluated unless they are quoted with an apostrophe (').   *Emacs Lisp*

Some of the paths of the configuration files contain the version number of Emacs. This number changes correspondingly with newer versions. In this section we describe version 19.28.   *path*

Beyond adapting the keyboard layout, the configuration files frequently modify global configuration variables and activate additional programs. A more advanced Emacs configuration file generally contains the following sections:

- Modification of global variables that toggle or change certain functions
- Settings for fonts and colors for Emacs under X11
- Loading of additional functions and packages
- Definition of commands whose invocation automatically loads the corresponding package or Lisp file
- Definition of hooks to be executed when a mode or a program starts
- Keyboard layouts

We now provide examples to explain these sections sequentially.

Global variables and settings

The following section of an `.emacs` file first loads the Common Lisp language extension (`cl`), which simplifies configuration. In addition,   *Common Lisp*

a small Lisp macro is defined as shorthand for the special form
condition-case for ignoring errors. We do not discuss this macro
further here. For detailed information on Lisp macros, refer to Lisp
textbooks or the Info files for Emacs Lisp.

ignoring errors

```
;; Load the Common Lisp language extension
(require 'cl)

;; macro to abbreviate condition-case
;; if all errors are to be ignored
(defmacro ignore-errors (&rest forms)
  "short form for a condition case"
  (list 'condition-case 'nil
        (cons 'progn forms)
        '(error nil)))

;; Path specification for Lisp programs
(push "/usr/lib/emacs/site-lisp/auctex" load-path)
(push "/usr/lib/emacs/site-lisp/swi" load-path)

;; Default mode for unknown file types
(setq default-major-mode 'text-mode)

;; Text width
(setq default-fill-column 78)

;; Make region visible
(setq transient-mark-mode t)

;; Permit eval with <Meta-Esc>
(put 'eval-expression 'disabled nil)
```

load-path

The variable load-path contains a list of path specifications
as strings. These paths are searched when an Emacs Lisp file
is loaded. In a normal Linux installation where no modifications
were made to Emacs, on startup this list at first contains an
entry for /usr/lib/emacs/19.28/lisp of the official Emacs
Lisp files and an entry for the Emacs site-lisp directory
/usr/lib/emacs/site-lisp.

site-lisp

If additional Lisp program packages, such as the AUCTEX
package, are installed in other directories, then this variable must
be extended. Since the data structure is a list, the Common Lisp
function push can be used to append an element to the front of the
list.

default-major-mode

The variable default-major-mode contains the name of the
major mode that is to be used if no other mode can be found
automatically for a file. The default is fundamental-mode. Since
normal text files, in contrast to program files, usually cannot be

distinguished by their name or extension, text-mode provides a reasonable alternative.

The variable default-fill-column permits specification of the column where word hyphenation can begin in a buffer with automatic hyphenation activated. Another such variable is default-tab-width, which enables setting the width of a tab mark in text.

default fill column

default-tab-width

The variable transient-mark-mode is a switch. If the variable contains a value other than nil, this deactivates the current selection of text, and thus the region, as soon as the buffer is modified. One side effect is that the current region cannot be highlighted when transient-mark-mode is set to nil. Thus the variable should always be set to t.

transient-mark-mode

The last line in the preceding section of code deviates somewhat from the other lines. It does not change a global variable, but reads the property list of a symbol. The key combination [Meta] + [Esc] or [Esc][Esc] actually represents the function eval-expression, which permits evaluating a Lisp expression directly in the minibuffer. Novices and former vi users who frequently need to terminate an accidental mode by pressing the [Esc] key would be too confused by this function. Therefore, this feature is originally deactivated, and [Meta] + [Esc] produces a corresponding message. Users who are more familiar with Emacs and who know that the Escape key is not [Esc] but [Ctrl] + [G] would tend to be irritated by this message. By setting the property disabled to nil, the normal function of [Meta] + [Esc] is restored. The simplest way to obtain a description of a variable is by entering [Ctrl] + [H] [V]. After this entry, the minibuffer prompts for the name of the variable, and Emacs displays its description in a new window.

other global variables and options

The function edit-options provides a very good overview of all global variables used as options in Emacs. In a new window it displays a list of all option variables along with their current values and their descriptions. The values can be modified directly in this window with simple keys, as Figure 13.12 shows.

Figure 13.12. The function edit-options

Fonts and colors

version 19 Since the release of version 19, GNU Emacs under X11 can open its own window with pull-down menus, is mouse-driven, and displays various fonts and colors in a buffer. This section explains the configuration of fonts and colors, while mouse operation and pull-down menus are explained later together with keyboard layout.

GNU Emacs manages various fonts and colors by means of faces *faces* (from "type faces"). A face is a specification of the font, the foreground color, the background color, and whether the font is underlined. Faces defined in this way can then be assigned in the text area.

If the `transient-mark-mode` is active, then Emacs employs the face `region` to display the current region. Various major modes Info mode also use faces to display text. In Info mode, for example, references

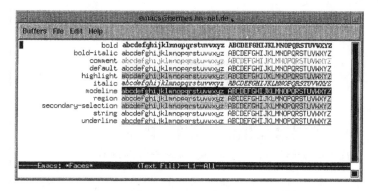

Figure 13.13. The output of list-faces-display

to other pages and options in menus are represented in special faces. For editing program files, the font-lock minor mode can be activated to display keywords, function names, comments, and strings with different faces.

Faces in Emacs Lisp are usually created with the functions `make-face` or `copy-face` and then modified with the functions `set-face-font`, `set-face-foreground`, `set-face-background`, and `set-face-underline-p`. The function `list-faces-display`, whose output is shown in Figure 13.13, provides an overview of the appearance of all defined faces.

The following excerpt redefines several faces.

make-face

overview

```
;;
;; fonts and faces
;; ===============

;; Set fonts in Emacs
(when window-system
  (ignore-errors
    (set-face-font 'bold
      "-adobe-courier-bold-r-normal-*")
    (set-face-font 'italic
      "-adobe-courier-medium-o-normal-*")
    (set-face-font 'comment
      "-adobe-courier-medium-o-normal-*")
    (set-face-font 'bold-italic
      "-adobe-courier-bold-o-normal-*")))

;; Set faces for font-lock mode
(when window-system
  (setq font-lock-function-name-face 'bold)
  (setq font-lock-comment-face       'italic)
  (setq font-lock-string-face        'default)
  (setq font-lock-doc-string-face    'default))
```

```
;; Set attribute for faces
(when window-system
   (ignore-errors

      ;; Region
      (set-face-foreground   'region "black")
      (set-face-background   'region "grey90")
      (if (not (x-display-color-p))
            (set-face-underline-p 'region t))

      ;; bold face
      (set-face-foreground   'bold   "black")
      (set-face-background   'bold   "white")
      (set-face-underline-p 'bold   nil)))

;; Additional faces make sense for color monitor
(when (and window-system (x-display-color-p))
   (ignore-errors
      (copy-face 'default   'comment)
      (set-face-foreground 'comment "grey60")
      (set-face-background 'comment "white")
      (setq font-lock-comment-face 'comment)

      (copy-face 'default   'string)
      (set-face-foreground   'string "gray10")
      (set-face-background   'string "white")
      (setq font-lock-string-face 'string)))
```

Loading/activating extensions

load   Extensions are load ed with the Lisp function `load`. However, this function reports an error if the file to be loaded does not exist.

ignore-errors   Therefore, we use the macro `ignore-errors`, which continues processing after an error. The package `func-menu` under X11 and in C mode can display a menu with all the functions defined in the current file. Selecting a function from this menu causes the cursor to jump to the definition of the function. This amounts to a simple but practical source code browser.

```
;; func-menu
(when window-system
   (ignore-errors
      (load "func-menu")
      (define-key global-map [S-down-mouse-3] 'function-menu)))
```

hooks   Hooks are used to change options that affect individual modes. Hooks are variables provided by every mode, in which Lisp expressions can be stored. These expressions are executed at certain times, depending on the type of hook; normally this is the

initialization   initialization of the mode for a new buffer. This means that certain functions can be executed each time a buffer is opened in a certain mode.

The following section of an Emacs initialization file uses this mechanism to activate the minor modes line-numbers and font-lock for buffers in C mode and in Emacs Lisp mode.

line numbers

```
;; line-numbers and font-lock for c
(add-hook 'c-mode-hook
          '(lambda ()
             (line-number-mode 1)
             (if window-system
                 (font-lock-mode t))))
;; line-numbers and font-lock for emacs-lisp
(add-hook 'emacs-lisp-mode-hook
          '(lambda ()
             (line-number-mode 1)
             (if window-system
                 (font-lock-mode 1))))
;; line-numbers and font-lock for tcl
(add-hook 'tcl-mode-hook
          '(lambda ()
             (line-number-mode 1)
             (if window-system
                 (font-lock-mode t))))
;; Auto fill in text mode
(add-hook 'text-mode-hook
          '(lambda () (turn-on-auto-fill)))
```

Emacs has numerous modes that are never activated without targeted configuration. To be used, they must be loaded using the autoload mechanism in Emacs, which allows loading specific Lisp files only when they are actually needed. The function autoload allows definition of such specifications. As parameters autoload receives a function name and the name of a file. When the function parameter is invoked, Emacs knows that the specified file must be loaded first.

To activate a new mode automatically when a file with a certain extension is edited, an entry must be made in the auto-mode-alist, a list containing pairwise entries of a pattern and a function. This specifies that the corresponding function is invoked when a file is loaded that matches the pattern. The following section establishes this correspondence for Ada files. With these settings, if a file is loaded whose name ends in .ada, then the function ada-mode is invoked. This function begins loading the file ada.el.

auto-mode-alist

Ada

```
;; Ada mode
(autoload 'ada-mode "ada"
  "Ada major mode." t)
(pushnew '("\\.ada$" .  ada-mode)
         auto-mode-alist)

;; Smalltalk mode
(autoload 'smalltalk-mode "st.el" "" t)
(pushnew '("\\.st$" .  smalltalk-mode)
         auto-mode-alist)

;; Modula-3 mode
(autoload 'modula-3-mode "modula3.el" "" t)
(pushnew '("\\.m3$" .  modula-3-mode)
         auto-mode-alist)
(pushnew '("\\.i3$" .  modula-3-mode)
         auto-mode-alist)

;; lispdir -- Search for/retrieve additional
;; packages in the Emacs Lisp Archive dir
(autoload 'lisp-dir-apropos "lispdir" nil t)
```

pushnew

lisp-dir-apropos

function of a key

The function pushnew is a Common Lisp macro that appends an element to the front of a list if the element is not already contained in the list. The autoload mechanism is also used in the above section for the function lisp-dir-apropos, which searches in the Lisp Code Repository (see Section 13.6).

Next we define three small Lisp functions to which we will later bind keys. The function mark-and-do is used together with the shift key. **Shift** + **ArrowRight** moves the cursor to the right and simultaneously extends the marking, or sets it if it is not active. The function generally tries to detect the function of the pressed key without the shift key and to invoke this function after processing the mark. Here it uses the function this-command-keys, which returns key combinations that triggered the function.

```
(defun S-Key (keysym)
  "return the keysym without S-"
  (let ((name (symbol-name keysym)))
    (vector
     (make-symbol
      (substring name 2 (length name))))))

(defun mark-and-do ()
  "set the mark if not active and
  do command without shift"
  (interactive)
  (if (not mark-active)
      (push-mark nil nil t))
  (let ((key (aref (this-command-keys) 0)))
    (call interactively
     (key-binding (S-Key key)))))

(defun mouse-describe-function (event)
  "describe function under the mouse-cursor"
  (interactive "e")
```

```
(save-excursion
  (mouse-set-point event)
  (let ((fn (function-called-at-point)))
    (describe-function fn)
    nil)))
```

The definition of key binding itself is relatively simple. The key and the function to be invoked are passed to the functions define-key and global-set-key. define-key is invoked again with the keymap where the binding is to be entered. The keymap named function-key-map plays a particular role here. It replaces key sequences with other keys or symbols, before they can be processed by the other keymaps. Entries in the function-key-map are generally made to adapt terminals that send function keys as ASCII sequences. The codes for simple cursor keys are usually already in the termcap or terminfo database of the system and thus also known to Emacs.

key bindings

function key-map

function keys

```
;; Special cursor Keys on Linux Console
(define-key function-key-map "\e[1~" [home])
(define-key function-key-map "\e[4~" [end])
(define-key function-key-map "\e[2~" [insert])

;; Control-cursor
(global-set-key [C-right] 'forward-word)
(global-set-key [C-left]  'backward-word)
(global-set-key [C-prior] 'beginning-of-buffer)
(global-set-key [C-next]  'end-of-buffer)

;; Shift-cursor
(global-set-key [S-right] 'mark-and-do)
(global-set-key [S-left]  'mark-and-do)
(global-set-key [S-up]    'mark-and-do)
(global-set-key [S-down]  'mark-and-do)
(global-set-key [S-end]   'mark-and-do)
(global-set-key [S-prior] 'mark-and-do)
(global-set-key [S-next]  'mark-and-do)

;; Function Keys
(global-set-key [f1]    'info)
(global-set-key [f2]    'save-buffer)
(global-set-key [f3]    'find-file)

(global-set-key [f5]    'goto-line)
(global-set-key [S-f5]  'what-line)
(global-set-key [f6]    'tags-search)
(global-set-key [S-f6]  'visit-tags-table)

(global-set-key [f9]    'compile)
(global-set-key [M-f8]  'next-error)
(global-set-key [f10]   'next-error)
(global-set-key [f12]   'advertised-undo)

;; Redefine home and end
(global-set-key [home] 'beginning-of-line)
(global-set-key [end]  'end-of-line)

;; Redefine backspace and delete
```

```
(define-key function-key-map [delete] [deletechar])
(define-key function-key-map [backspace] [DEL])
(global-set-key [DEL] 'delete-backward-char)

;; divers
(define-key ctl-x-map "p" 'toggle-save-place)
(define-key lisp interaction-mode-map [M-return]
       'eval-print-last-sexp)

(define-key emacs-lisp-mode-map [S-mouse-1]
 'mouse-describe-function)
(define-key lisp interaction-mode-map [S-mouse-1]
 'mouse-describe-function)
```

menus   A new menu is defined like a key binding and stored along with the normal key bindings. The following example defines a local menu for Emacs Lisp mode.

```
(when window system
 ;; New menu in elisp mode
 (define-key emacs-lisp-mode-map [menu-bar elisp]
   (cons "Elisp" (make-sparse-keymap "elisp")))
 (define-key emacs-lisp-mode-map [menu-bar elisp debonenoff]
   '("Cancel Debug on Entry" .  cancel-debug-on-entry))
 (define-key emacs-lisp-mode-map [menu-bar elisp debonen]
   '("Debug on Entry" .  debug-on-entry))
 (define-key emacs-lisp-mode-map [menu-bar elisp debdefun]
   '("Debug Defun" .  edebug-defun))
 (define-key emacs-lisp-mode-map [menu-bar elisp evalbuff]
   '("Eval buffer" .  eval-buffer))
 (define-key emacs-lisp-mode-map [menu-bar elisp evalreg]
   '("Eval Region" .  eval-region))
 (define-key emacs-lisp-mode-map [menu-bar elisp evaldef]
   '("Eval Defun" .  eval-defun)))
```

define-key

text and action

The first parameter of define-key contains the keymap, the second the position in the menu hierarchy. [menu-bar elisp] defines a new pull-down menu. The third parameter defines the text and the associated action. In the first invocation of define-key, the last parameter does not define any actual action, but a keymap for the new pull-down menu. The other invocations each contain a cons cell whose first element specifies the text for the menu and the second element the name of the function to be invoked.

## Chapter 14

Languages and tools

O ne particular feature of Linux is the large number of freeware programming languages in binary format available from Linux FTP servers and contained in the various Linux distributions. These freeware tools seldom take a back seat to proprietary systems. This chapter introduces the various compilers, interpreters, and software development tools that are available under Linux and identifies their most important features.

FTP servers

14.1   Languages

Undisputedly, C holds the position of the most important programming language for UNIX systems. Today's UNIX itself and all its utilities were developed largely in C. So it is not surprising that a C compiler serves as a central element of a UNIX development environment.

C and UNIX

As a rule, proprietary UNIX systems of the past have included a C compiler in their packages. However, this has changed recently. Newer PC UNIX implementations are now being marketed in user versions without a C compiler and without network support. The full version including these components costs significantly more. Programming languages supported under Linux range from C, C++, and Objective C to Lisp and Prolog and on to Smalltalk and Forth (Figure 14.1). Classical languages like Fortran and APL are also available under Linux. Even Basic programs can be developed with either of two interpreters.

C compiler

C++, Objective
C, Lisp, Prolog,
Smalltalk, Forth,
Fortran, APL, Basic

Compilers are available for Modula-2 and Modula-3 as well as for Oberon (Figure 14.2). Some of these compilers are commercial systems that are also available for other UNIX systems. In addition,

Modula

Oberon

385

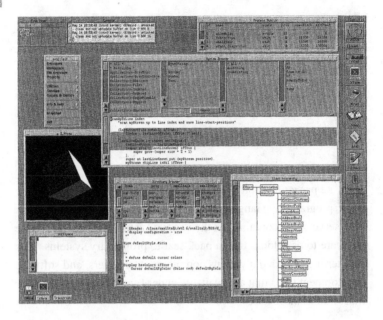

Figure 14.1. Smalltalk/X under Linux

there is the freeware ADA compiler GNAT, which supports the new standard Ada95 (see Section 14.5).

In view of recent developments, in the near future we can anticipate that almost every language will be available under Linux.

14.2 C compilers

gcc   The C compiler used under Linux is the GNU C Compiler (gcc) of the Free Software Foundation, which can generate optimized code. gcc's

porting   availability for numerous UNIX platforms facilitates the porting of software. The GNU C Compiler supports ANSI and K&R standards for C as well as C++ and Objective C. This compiler's detailed error

error messages   messages on syntax errors deserve special note.

Almost all program packages for Linux were written in C. Since every now and then there are problems in compiling the source code, the system administrator, and a programmer even more so, should also be familiar with the C compiler.

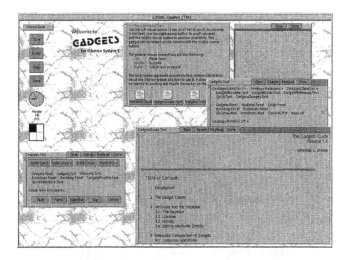

Figure 14.2. Oberon System 3 under Linux

Architecture of gcc

Before compilation, C or C++ programs first pass through a C preprocessor, which replaces #include statements with the contents of the associated header files and evaluates #define and #ifdef constructs.

The architecture of gcc is designed to handle many programming languages and to generate code for many architectures (Figure 14.3). Therefore, compilation is divided into two parts. First, from the source code, code is generated in an interlingua called RTL (Register Transfer Language). The Ada compiler gnat also (indirectly) generates RTL code; the rest of compilation is the same in the two languages. With the help of target specifications, the compiler then generates assembler code for a given processor from the RTL code. For the programmer, however, these two steps are transparent.

After compilation the assembler for the respective architecture translates the assembler code to an object file (.o). Multiple object files are often combined in a single archive file (.a). In the final step you can link multiple object files either to an executable program or to a shared library.

387

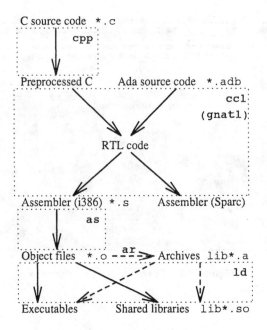

Figure 14.3. The architecture of gcc

Using gcc

The simple statement **gcc example.c** generates an executable file directly from a C program. Often it makes sense to interrupt gcc after a certain step. We have the following options:

-E Only preprocessing, no compilation
-s Compilation to assembler code: from example.c we get example.s.
-c Compilation and assembly: from example.c: we get the object file example.o.

The following is an example in which several C source code files are first compiled and then linked to a program.

```
golem:~/db> ls
main.c  files.c  db.c
golem:~/db> gcc -c main.c
golem:~/db> gcc -c files.c
golem:~/db> gcc -c database.c
golem:~/db> ls
```

```
main.c  files.c db.c    main.o  files.o db.o
golem:~/db> gcc -o db main.o files.o db.o
golem:~/db> ls
main.c  files.c db.c    main.o  files.o db.o    db*
```

The option **-o** *file* redirects the compiler's output to *file*.

Libraries   Several object files can be comfortably linked to a library with the command ar.

```
golem:~/db> ar -rc libstuff.a files.o db.o tools.o output.o
golem:~/db> ar -t libstuff.a
files.o
db.o
tools.o
output.o
```

When linking a C program, you can link the library as well with the option -l*libname*, where *libname* derives from removing the prefix lib and the suffix .a from the file name.

```
golem:~/db> gcc -o db main.o -L. -lstuff
```

Linking object files to a library saves you from specifying all the individual object files in the command. The option -L directs gcc to look for libraries in the working directory as well. **ranlib** *library* produces an index of all symbols in the various object files, which accelerates linking, especially with large libraries.

gcc searches several standard directories for libraries. Additional directories can be specified in the environment variable LIBRARY_PATH or with the option -L.

Generating debugging information

To allow debugging of a C program, it must have been compiled and linked with the option -g. This option causes the transfer of information from the source code to the executable file (position of variables and functions, etc.). This *symbol information* can radically inflate the size of the executable file, but it does not affect the speed of execution.

Optimizing

gcc features quite a number of optimizing strategies. The option -O*level* turns on code optimization. -O2 is a healthy level; above that gcc begins to increase memory requirements to promote performance.

14.3   Pascal, Fortran, Simula, and Modula-2

The GNU C compiler also provides the basis for the Pascal-, Simula-, and Fortran-to-C converters. These converters read existing Pascal, Simula, or Fortran source code and generate a C program, which is then compiled with the C compiler. Skillful integration in the make system can leave the intermediate stage in C completely unnoticed by the programmer.

converters

Beyond standard Pascal, the Pascal-to-C converter can even translate dialects of several Pascal variants, such as Turbo Pascal up to Version 5 and Macintosh Pascal. The Simula-to-C converter works according to the same principle. The German Association for Mathematics and Data Processing (Gesellschaft für Mathematik und Datenverarbeitung, GMD) has ported its Modula-2 development environment MOCKA to Linux. It is interesting that the compiler itself was implemented in Modula-2; its source code is included in the package. In contrast to the above tools, MOCKA generates object code directly. MOCKA also supports linking C routines as *foreign modules*.

Pascal

Simula

Modula-2

14.4   Lisp and Prolog

Since the programming languages used in the area of knowledge-based systems and artificial intelligence play an important role at universities, several implementations have become available. Here Lisp is of particular importance because it achieved relatively broad propagation as the programming language of the GNU Emacs.

AI

Emacs Lisp

One Common Lisp implementation with an object-oriented extension (a subset of CLOS) named clisp is included in most Linux distributions. The extensive GNU Common Lisp is based on

clisp

the previous akcl and orients itself to the new ANSI standard for
Common Lisp.

The FTP server swi.psy.uva.nl contains the extensive Prolog   Prolog
implementation of the University of Amsterdam, which is easy to
compile under Linux. It is based on the Warren Abstract Machine
(WAM) and provides practical on-line help. An interesting aspect is
the connection to XPCE, an object-oriented system that also comes   XPCE
from Amsterdam. This system provides a graphical programming
environment for Prolog.

14.5   Ada

For a long time the language Ada suffered the drawback that its
sheer complexity scared off potential compiler designers. The GNAT
project developed the Ada95 compiler gnat,* which uses gcc for
code generation. gnat is available for Linux, Solaris, and other UNIX
platforms as well as for DOS. It has been successfully validated
under Solaris. gnat employs a hand-coded parser and generates
quite informative error messages, making it quite suitable for Ada
novices. The Linux version also supports tasks. gnat can be found
at or . For Linux you should absolutely use the precompiled version.
Meanwhile a gdb patch has become available[†] that adds special
support for debugging Ada programs.

Ada source code files must bear the suffix .adb (package bodies
and procedures) or .ads (package specifications). They can be
compiled simply with **gnatmake** *unit-name* or **gnatmake** *file*.
There is also extensive documentation (as GNU Info hypertext).

14.6   Tcl

Whether editor, database, or modem program, good software needs
an extension language with which the user can write scripts or   extension language
macros. These can be used for automation of sequences or for simple

---

*ftp://cs.nyu.edu/pub/gnat or ftp://ftp.informatik.rwth-aachen.de/mirror/cs.nyu.edu/pub/gnat

[†]ftp://cs.nyu.edu/pub/gnat/gdb or ftp.//ftp.informatik.rwth-aaachen.de/mirror/cs.nyu.edu/pub/gnat/gdb

extension of the system. Well-known examples of such languages

Emacs Lisp, elk include Emacs Lisp, elk, and Microsoft Visual Basic for Applications (VBA).

At the end of the 1980s, John Ousterhout conceived Tcl (Tool Command Language) as such a language. Tcl has an uncomplicated syntax and contains a single simple data type, the character string.

strings Depending on requirements and context, these strings can be interpreted as numbers, lists, or other data types. The power of

high-level functions the language stems mainly from its many high-level functions and the fact that, similar to Lisp, it does not distinguish between data and program. Tcl code itself is stored and interpreted as strings. This makes it easy to realize an extension of language constructs or customized code.

C library The language was implemented as a C library and can be combined with existing programs by linking and executing a few functions. For independent programs there are directly executable

interpreter interpreters that read a single input, pass it to the Tcl interpreter of the Tcl library, and then output the result. Here we use small examples to introduce some of the most important language elements of Tcl. A Tcl interpreter can be started by entering `tcl` or `tclsh`.

The language

lists In Tcl a list is a string whose elements are separated by blanks,

statements tabs, or line breaks. A Tcl statement is a list, i.e., likewise a string, whereby the first element is the name of a function to be invoked. The remaining elements are passed as arguments to the function.

```
hermes:/home/strobel> tclsh
% set a 5
5
% puts $a
5
% puts "The value of a is $a"
The value of a is 5
```

In the above example the Tcl interpreter first evaluates the line

variable `set a 5`. The function `set` assigns a value to a variable, here a. A variable in Tcl need not be declared; it exists as soon as a value is assigned to it. The next line outputs the current value of a. Before the

Tcl interpreter evaluates a line of Tcl code, substitutions are made
that are induced by special characters. The $ character, e.g., causes
the subsequent name to be handled as a variable and replaces it with
its value. If there is no variable with the specified name, there is an
error.

This variable evaluation mechanism works anywhere in a
program line unless it is prevented by special quoting. The following
example shows that even the function name is no exception.

evaluation

```
% set fkt puts
puts
% set arg "The function $fkt was invoked here"
The function $fkt was invoked here
% $fkt $arg
The function $fkt was invoked here
%
```

In the last line the function puts is invoked. Its argument is the
string "The function $fkt was invoked here."

puts

Another type of evaluation is invoked by the square brackets
[]. The text between the brackets is evaluated as a Tcl function
invocation and then replaced by the returned function value. The
following example uses the function lindex, which interprets a
string as a list and returns a certain element. The numbering of list
elements in Tcl begins with the ordinal number 0.

function call

```
% set l "This is a list"
This is a list
% puts "The 2nd element is: [lindex $l 1]"
The 2nd element is: is
%
```

Another interesting aspect of Tcl is arrays, whose indices are not
restricted to numeric values. Arbitrary strings are permitted. These
are called associative arrays. The next example uses grade as an
array and the names of fictional students as indices.

associative arrays

```
% set grade(sam) 2.3
2.3
% set grade(fred) 1
1
% set grade(peter) 4
4
% puts $grade(fred)
1
```

```
% set name sam
hugo
% puts "The grade average for $name is $grade($name)"
The grade average for sam is 2.3
%
```

control constructs

Tcl provides the usual control constructs of procedural languages. In addition to if, switch, for, and while, there is a foreach that executes a block for each element of a list. This permits iteration over the elements of an associative array, as the following example shows:

```
% set students [array names grade]
peter fritz hugo
% foreach name $students {
    puts "The grade average for $name is $grade($name)"
}
The grade average for peter is 4
The grade average for fred is 1
The grade average for sam is 2.3
%
```

The function array returns information about existing arrays. With the argument names all indices are returned for which the array contains a value.

regular expressions

Tcl also provides functions for working with regular expressions (see Section 2.8). The function regexp compares a regular expression with a string and returns 1 if the expression was found. Optionally, substrings that match the specified expression or its subexpressions can be assigned to variables.

```
% set s "123abchello6677pplist7zz"
123abchello6677pplist7zz
% set pattern {hallo.*7([a-z]+)7}
hallo.*7([a-z]+)7
% regexp $pattern $s all sub1
1
% puts $all
hallo6677pplist7
% puts $sub1
pplist
%
```

curly braces

The curly braces { } have a function similar to that of the double quotation marks. However, they prevent further internal substitution. The regular expression in the above example had to be written in curly braces because otherwise the substring [a-z] would have been interpreted as a function call.

Custom functions can be defined in Tcl by invoking the function proc. The arguments of the new function can be defined as individual variables or as list variables. In the former case the number of parameters is fixed, while it is dynamic in the latter case.

```
% proc myFunction {arg1 arg2} {
    puts "The arguments are $arg1 and $arg2"
    return 1
}
% myFunction a b
The arguments are a and b
1
% proc funct2 args {
    puts "The arguments are $args"
    return "bye"
}
% funct2 a b c d e
The arguments are a b c d e
bye
```

Variables in a Tcl function are normally local. To allow access to global variables, they must first be specified in a global line:

```
% set name Sam
Sam
% proc Test {name} {
    puts "name is $name"
}
% Test
can't read "name": no such variable

% proc Test {} {
    global name
    puts "name is $name"
}
% Test
name is Sam
%
```

To enable using Tcl scripts as executable files, the Tcl interpreter is specified like a shell in the first line after #!. If users have execution permissions to the script file, then they can launch the script by entering its name. The following example shows the start of such a script file:

```
#!/usr/bin/tcl
puts "Hello world!"
...
```

Applications and extensions

script language

There are two basic approaches to writing applications with Tcl. First, an application written in C can be extended by a script language with the Tcl interpreter. Linking the script language to the application occurs via the definition of additional Tcl commands. This approach makes sense primarily with existing programs. For a new development, even the main application could be developed in Tcl. Functions that are not available can be realized as Tcl extensions in C and accessed via Tcl.

Tcl extensions

argc, argv

Extending Tcl is very simple. You define a C function, which, just as a main function in C, receives its parameters via argc and argv. Then in the initialization mode of the Tcl interpreter you invoke the function Tcl_CreateCommand, which registers the new function and assigns it a name within Tcl.

SQL

Many Tcl language extensions are available in the public domain. These extensions enable access to SQL databases or UNIX system invocations. For example, *tcl-dp* provides functions for network programming (sockets and RPC) and *itcl* extends Tcl by classes and methods for object-oriented programming. A debugger and a class browser are also available.

sockets

OOP

DNS and SNMP

In addition to TCP/IP sockets and Sun RPCs, the extension *scotty* also provides functions for accessing DNS and for communication via SNMP. The following example shows a simple server that was written with scotty. It opens a TCP socket and waits for connections. The telnet program is one option for a client. When a client connects to the server, the server sends the current date and time to the client and waits for a reply from the client.

TCP socket

```
#!/usr/local/bin/scotty -f

set port 1371

proc handleConnection {lsock} {
        set socket [tcp accept $lsock]
        # send date and time to client
        puts $socket [exec date]
        # wait for reply from client
        puts "Msg from Client : [gets $socket]"
        # end connection
        close $socket
}
```

```
set lsocket [tcp listen $port]
addinput -read $lsocket "handleConnection %F"
puts "waiting for connections on port $port ..."
```

The client's output could look like this:

```
hermes:/home/strobel> telnet hermes 1371
Trying 194.45.197.100...
Connected to hermes.stud.fh-heilbronn.de.
Escape character is '^]'.
Fri Jan  6 16:16:16 MET 1995
hallo
Connection closed by foreign host.
hermes:/home/strobel>
```

Tk

Tk is a widget set that has interfaces to both C and Tcl (Figure 14.4).   widget set
Thus it proves especially suitable for providing Tcl programs with a
graphical user interface. Due to the underlying interpreter language,
simple and rapid prototypes as well as complete applications can be   prototypes
developed.

Prominent examples of Tcl/Tk applications include Zircon,
tkined, Picasso, and many other systems that employ Tcl as their
extension language.

Tk Extensions

Two important Tk extensions are the packages Tix and blt (Figure
14.5). Both feature many additional widgets such as NoteBooks,
ComboBoxes, balloon help, file selection, directory trees, hypertext
edits, and LabelFrames.

XF

The interface builder XF for Tcl/Tk enables graphical and interactive   interface builder
design of a Tk user interface (Figure 14.6). This not only makes
implementing Tk interfaces simple, but allows subsequent loading
of existing Tcl/Tk programs and modifying or extending them.
Since XF itself was developed in Tcl/Tk, the user interface can be
tested in the course of development, and the representation during
development corresponds exactly to the finished program.

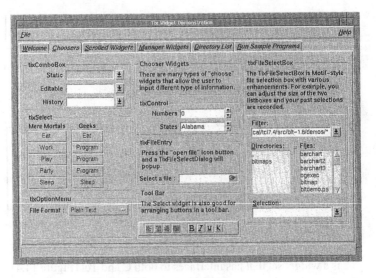

Figure 14.4. The Tix demo widget

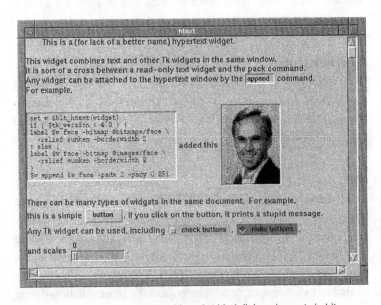

Figure 14.5. Hypertext with embedded dialog elements in blt

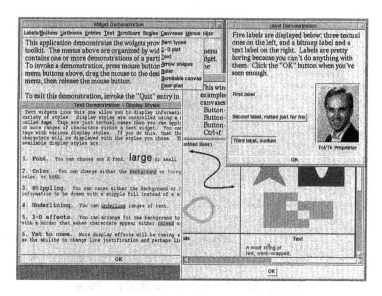

Figure 14.6. The Tcl/Tk interface builder XF

Tcl/Motif

To couple the advantages of Tcl with the Motif widget set, try
Tcl/Motif. This package uses normal Motif widgets to generate
graphical user interfaces. Thus Motif user interfaces can be designed
simply in an interpreter environment. The programmer can employ
almost all of the accustomed widget resources. Tcl/Motif even
supports the drag and drop mechanism of Motif 1.2.

Tcl/Tk and various extensions can be found on the Sunsite
under `devel/apps`. The following WWW home page provides an
overview of Tcl extensions, documents and programs:

`http://web.cs.ualberta.ca/~wade/Auto/Tcl.html`

Tcl/Motif

resources

WWW

14.7   Interface builders

The most comfortable way to produce X11-based applications is with
special software for the interactive design of graphical user interfaces.
These interface builders can usually generate C source code, which
the programmer can extend as needed. ParcPlace markets such an
interface builder, called ObjectBuilder (Figure 14.7). It permits direct

interactive design

ObjectBuilder

399

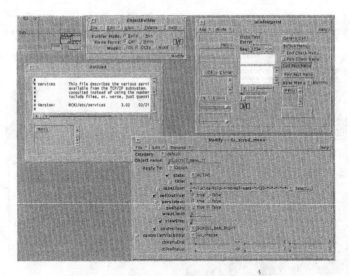

Figure 14.7. The interface builder by ParcPlace

ObjectLibrary

manipulation of graphic objects with the mouse and generates C++ source code. Together with the ObjectLibrary, user interfaces can be generated with the OpenLook or Motif convention. Command-line options determine the look and feel. Both products are available for all common UNIX Platforms, with a purchase price of over $1,000 U.S. dollars. Only the Linux version is available free and may be copied freely. For serious use, however, the user manuals, available directly from ParcPlace, should be at hand.

VXP

OSF/Motif

Although the free VXP interface builder by Young Chen is still under development, it easily suffices for creating simple OSF/Motif-based user interfaces (Figure 14.8). Contrary to the interface builder by ParcPlace, VXP generates pure Motif source code. All graphic objects can be positioned and manipulated by mouse. VXP then

makefiles

generates the corresponding C source code and an appropriate makefile. The functionality of the application has been implemented, as usual under Motif, within callback routines in C. VXP also manages the source code that the programmer adds. In addition, the C compiler can be started with a click of the mouse without leaving

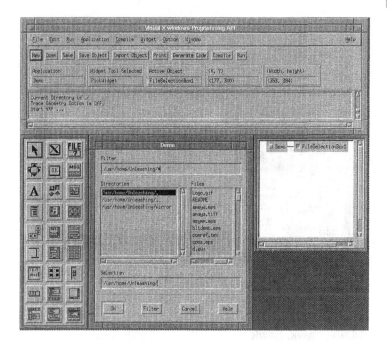

Figure 14.8. VXP Motif interface builder

the development environment. The source code generated by VXP needs no library routines other than the Motif library, making it easily portable to other UNIX platforms.

14.8   Metacard

Metacard is a system for developing Hypercard applications, e.g., as we know them from the Apple Macintosh. Fortunately, Metacard is able to load and process Apple Hypercard stacks. The integrated programming language permits easily developing smaller applications or prototypes for graphical user interfaces. Metacard is available on all common UNIX platforms, but it is commercial software (Figure 14.9).

Hypercard

Apple

401

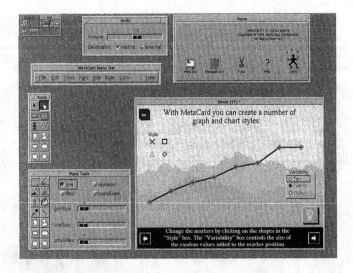

Figure 14.9. Metacard under Linux

14.9   awk, gawk

processing text files

awk is a traditional UNIX tool for the production of smaller scripts for processing strings and text files. The name of the program derives from the initials of its authors: Aho, Weinberger, and Kernighan. The strong resemblance of awk's interpreter language to C makes it relatively easy to learn.

awk does not distinguish between numeric and string variables and requires no variable declarations. For smaller projects, awk can prototyping serve as a prototyping tool. However, the size of an awk program should not exceed circa 200 lines of code.

The following script totals the sizes of all files in the current directory and displays the sum:

```
linux1:/> ls -l | awk '{sum += $5} END {print "Summe : " sum}'
```

The original utility is not available under Linux, but the GNU implementation of the Free Software Foundation called GNU awk (gawk) is. In addition to awk, commercial UNIX systems often contain the extended version called nawk.

14.10   Perl

Perl is also an interpreter language. It combines the most important features of sed, awk, and the usual UNIX shells and proves especially suitable for processing text files. One advantage over classical tools is the possibility of opening multiple files simultaneously.

    sed, awk

Perl permits the use of lists and associative arrays, with the size of the data structures limited only by available memory, which allows the processing of relatively large amounts of data. Naturally, Perl also has loops and other control structures, subroutines, recursion, and regular expressions. Various format statements for data output enable the creation of clear reports and tables. An integrated debugger allows the setting of breakpoints and stepwise execution of a program.

    lists and arrays

    loops

    debugger

Perl proves suitable for system administration because it allows the production of scripts that run with root permission. It is also noteworthy that almost all routines of the standard C library and the UNIX kernels can be used directly under Perl, including functions for network programming via sockets. The new version 5 of Perl offers object-oriented extensions.

    system administration

14.11   Editors

A compiler alone does not constitute a full-scale development environment. At least a befitting editor and a symbolic debugger are required as well. The GNU Emacs editor integrates these components (Figure 14.10). It can invoke numerous utilities like grep and RCS as well as the C compiler and the GNU debugger, so that the complete development cycle can run within the editor. Emacs is described in detail in Chapter 13.

    Emacs

Besides the GNU Emacs, Linux distributions furnish numerous other editors, which are introduced in Section 12.3.

14.12   GNU Debugger (GDB)

Description

The GNU Debugger (GDB) is a powerful symbolic debugger that supports C, C++, and Modula-2. In addition, patches were recently

    multiple languages

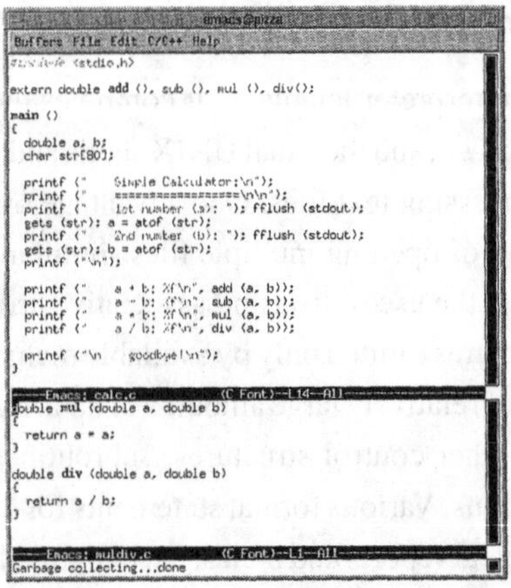

Figure 14.10. Software development with Emacs

released for Ada extensions. GDB provides all functionality that developers expect from such a tool. Programs can be executed stepwise. Breakpoints allow the interruption of the execution at defined points, and watchpoints interrupt the program when specified values are modified. An option allows the continuous display of the values of selected variables or objects.

Newer versions of GDB also permit remote debugging, which means that the debugger can run on a different machine from the program to be debugged. The connection between the machines can be either a serial interface or a network. Under Linux, even the operating system can be analyzed with GDB, and running processes can be debugged (see Chapter 16).

The GNU Debugger provides only a simple command-line–oriented user interface. However, there are graphical front ends that enable comfortable mouse-driven operation of the debugger. These front ends start GDB as a second process and redirect its input and output. Thus they simulate user input and redirect debugger output to various windows. One example of such a graphical front end is xxgdb (Figure 14.11).

The top pane displays the current position in the source code. The central area contains a number of command buttons that invoke basic debugger functions. The second pane from the bottom allows

breakpoints
watchpoints

remote debugging

graphical front ends

xxgdb

panes

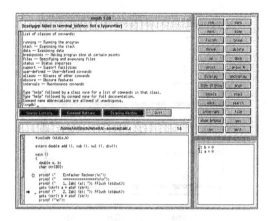

Figure 14.11. The GDB front end xxgdb

the user to enter textual commands when keyboard input seems more practical.

xxgdb permits the continuous display of variable values in the bottom pane. An expression that occurs in the C source code can be evaluated easily: select the expression in the source code pane with the mouse; then click on the print button, and the result is displayed in the bottom pane.

You can define a breakpoint similarly by positioning the text cursor at the respective position in the source code pane and pressing the corresponding button. Breakpoints are displayed with the symbol of a flat hand; a blue arrow marks the current position in the source code.

Another way to make the use of the GNU Debugger more comfortable is by integrating it with the Emacs editor. A special mode in Emacs permits debugging programs within a normal editor window, which is divided into two panes. The upper pane displays the source code and marks the current position with an arrow. The lower pane controls the debugger and allows input of commands.

Using GDB within Emacs (Figure 14.12) has some advantages for Emacs specialists, but it is certainly not as comfortable as using an X-based front end.

variable values

breakpoints

Emacs

for experts

Figure 14.12. GDB in Emacs

Invocation

Debugging programs For debugging, invoke gdb with the name of the executable file:

```
golem:~> gdb executable
```

Debugging core files core files are generated if a process terminates unexpectedly—due to a special signal (e.g., SIGQUIT) or due to a memory security violation during execution (segmentation fault). **Here you must set the corresponding resource limit value: ulimit -c** *max-core-size*; by default it is 0 ("generate no cores"). Various information can be extracted from the core file, such as the values of global variables and the position of the program termination:

```
golem:~> gdb executable core
```

Debugging running processes gdb can attach itself to running processes and detach itself again. As with normal debugging, you can set breakpoints and watchpoints and read variables.

```
golem:~> gdb executable PID
```

Debugging the kernel Kernel hackers recompile the kernel after they have complemented the assignments to CFLAGS and LD with -g in /usr/src/linux/arch/*arch*/Makefile and they debug (after installation and reboot) with

```
golem:~> gdb /usr/src/linux/vmlinux /proc/kcore
```

However, you can only read variables; any influence is naturally impossible.

The most important GDB commands

break	Sets a breakpoint in a certain source code line.
watch	Monitors an expression; whenever it changes, the program halts in the respective source code line.
delete	Deletes a breakpoint or watchpoint.
load	Loads another source code file into GDB.
list	Displays a certain line in a certain file. If no arguments are given, list shows the environment of the line of code that is currently being executed.
run	Begins execution of a program. After run you can also enter command line parameters.
continue	Continues program execution.
where	Displays current invocation stack.
frame	Selects a certain stack frame to read its local variables.
print	Evaluates a C expression, which can contain variables, but no function invocations.
display	Displays the value of an expression after each executed command.
quit	Quit GDB

Example

As an example, we compile and debug a C program:

```
int a;

sub()
{
        int i;

        i = a;
        a = 15;
}

main()
{
        a = 10000;
        sub();
        a = 500;
}
```

```
golem:/tmp# gcc -g -o main main.c
golem:/tmp# gdb main
GDB is free software and you are welcome to distribute copies of it
under certain conditions; type "show copying" to see the conditions.
There is absolutely no warranty for GDB; type "show warranty" for details.
GDB 4.15.1 (i486-linux), Copyright 1995 Free Software Foundation, Inc...
(gdb) list
6       {
7               int i;
8
9               i = a;
10              a = 15;
11      }
12
13      main()
14      {
15              a = 10000;
(gdb) Enter
16              printf ("%d\n", a);
17              sub();
18              a = 500;
19              printf ("%d\n", a);
20      }
(gdb) break 15
Breakpoint 1 at 0x8048163: file main.c, line 15.
```

Breakpoints are numbered sequentially; they can also be deleted by number: **delete 1**.

```
(gdb) run
Starting program: /tmp/main

Breakpoint 1, main () at main.c:15
15              a = 10000;
(gdb) list
10              a = 15;
11      }
12
13      main()
14      {
15              a = 10000;
16              printf ("%d\n", a);
```

```
17              sub();
18              a = 500;
19              printf ("%d\n", a);
```

`list` outputs the lines of code surrounding the position in the program. With the graphical front end xxgdb this is not necessary.

```
(gdb) watch a
Hardware watchpoint 2: a
(gdb) continue
Continuing.
10000
Hardware watchpoint 2: a

Old value = 0
New value = 15
sub () at main.c:11
11        }
```

The programmer has set a hardware watchpoint on the global variable a. In the function sub() it is assigned a new value, so gdb stops here. The watchpoints are numbered sequentially along with the breakpoints and can also be deleted with delete.

```
(gdb) list
6         {
7                 int i;
8
9                 i = a;
10                a = 15;
11        }
12
13        main()
14        {
15                a = 10000;
(gdb) where
#0  sub () at main.c:11
#1  0x8048185 in main () at main.c:17
#2  0x80480eb in ___crt_dummy__ ()
```

The command where displays the invocation stack—here the invocation of sub() is at the top, then that of main(). At the bottom are several internal invocations of the C library that we can ignore. Before the invocations where displays a number. frame allows you to select the associated stack frame and display the values of local variables:

```
(gdb) frame 0
#0  sub () at main.c:11
11          }
(gdb) print i
$1 = 10000
(gdb) frame 1
#1  0x8048185 in main () at main.c:17
17                 sub();
(gdb) print i
No symbol "i" in current context.
```

Only the local variables of the respective stack frame are
accessible—this makes it possible, by selecting the correct frame,
to evaluate variables that are actually not directly visible.

```
(gdb) quit
The program is running.  Quit anyway (and kill it)? (y or n) y
golem:/tmp#
```

14.13   Make utility

Another important component of the C development environment
is the make utility. This command significantly simplifies the
compilation of a project that consists of multiple modules. For
this purpose, the programmer stores the dependencies between the
makefile   individual program parts in a makefile. If the programmer modifies
the source code of one of these modules, then only the modified parts
and the modules dependent on them are recompiled.

GNU make   The GNU variant of make used under Linux has several options
that go beyond the normal make utility. For example, it supports
RCS   the Revision Control System (RCS), a collection of commands for
version management of source code. If a file cannot be found in the
current directory, GNU make seeks a subdirectory named RCS from
which it reads the newest version of a module automatically. This
even applies to the makefile.

implicit rules   GNU make also recognizes more implicit rules than other
versions of make. A makefile for a small C program consisting of
three files, for example, could take the following form:

```
CFLAGS = -g
LDLIBS = -lm

test: test.o sub1.o sub2.o
```

GNU `make` contains rules to create `.o` files from the corresponding `.c` files and to link the program `test` from all object files and with the specified libraries. The documentation for GNU `make`, which is contained in the Info system, provides an overview of all rules and variables.

linking

14.14 Imake

The differences between various UNIX variants often seriously encumber platform-independent software development. Hence it might become necessary to produce different versions of makefiles, each tailored to a respective system. Here the Imake utility known from the X Windows System provides support by generating a platform-specific `makefile` from a platform-independent `Imakefile`.

platform independence

Imake is normally invoked in the script `xmkmf`. For perfect functioning, this command requires *template files* that contain the system-specific data. These files are installed in the directory `/usr/lib/X11/config`.

xmkmf

14.15 RCS

The development of larger projects—consisting of a multitude of different modules and having new versions thereof evolving steadily—makes a version-management system indispensable. Such a system gains in importance when multiple programmers are working on a project simultaneously.

version management

Since all versions of a program in its development cycle are archived, if the need arises, a programmer can return to the source code of a long-since-outdated version. In addition to the Source Code Control System (SCCS) known from UNIX System V, Linux offers the more powerful Revision Control System (RCS). Normally the archive data are stored in a separate directory named `RCS` or `SCCS`.

all versions

SCCS

RCS

RCS provides numerous commands, the most important of which we outline here.

check in   `ci`   (check in) transfers the specified file into the RCS directory and thus freezes the current version. The complete version is not stored with each check-in; only the difference with respect to the predecessor version, as determined with the `diff` command, is stored. The version number of the module is automatically incremented.

check out   `co`   (check out) creates a nonmodifiable copy of the current version or of any predecessor of a module. If a module is to be modified, this must be indicated with the option `-l` ("lock"). This protects the file from simultaneous modification by another programmer, for it can be checked out only once by only one user.

status   `rlog` displays various information such as the status of an archive and the versions of the modules it contains.

Other commands permit, for example, merging two versions.

Emacs   To allow the version management and the rest of the development environment to work together smoothly, newer versions of the Emacs editor have a special mode for operating RCS.

14.16   xwpe

Borland   `xwpe` poses an interesting alternative to Emacs as a development environment. Users who are familiar with Borland products for DOS (Turbo C, Turbo Pascal, etc.) will soon feel at home, for `xwpe` greatly resembles them (Figure 14.13). Although `xwpe` is a text-oriented application, comfortable mouse operation is possible. `xwpe`'s author also developed a terminal emulation program with color support for the X Window System. However, `xwpe` also runs on a normal terminal, although its look suffers considerably.

mouse   The integrated editor permits processing multiple texts in different windows. Both the compiler (`gcc`) and the debugger (`gdb`) can be started with either the keyboard or the mouse. Error messages are displayed in a separate window, and breakpoints can be defined directly in the editor.

gcc, gdb

`xwpe` can be drawn from the FTP server `ftp.rrzn.uni-hannover.de` in the directory `/pub/systems/unix/xwpe`.

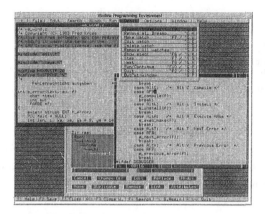

Figure 14.13. xwpe as a development environment

14.17 Example

To give the reader a better impression of working with the previous development environments, we introduce a small C program. The program consists of multiple modules to add, subtract, multiply, and divide two numbers that are input. The main program contains only the two input prompts and the output of the results. The computations take place in separate modules. (Naturally, this simple example could have been combined in a single file.)

C program

computations

To input the first file, invoke the Emacs editor with the file main.c as argument. Since the file does not exist, Emacs starts with an empty buffer, which is already in C mode, however. After the following source text has been input, it is saved with the key combination $\boxed{\text{Ctrl}} + \boxed{\text{X}} \boxed{\text{Ctrl}} + \boxed{\text{S}}$. This function could have been invoked from the menu instead.

Emacs

```c
#include <stdio.h>

extern double add (), sub (), mul (), div();

main ()
{
  double a, b;
  char str[80];

  printf ("     Simple Calculator:\n");
  printf ("     ==================\n\n");
  printf ("     1.  Zahl (a): "); fflush (stdout);
  gets (str); a = atof (str);
  printf ("     2.  Zahl (b): "); fflush (stdout);
```

413

```
    gets (str); b = atof (str);
    printf ("\n");

    printf ("    a + b: %f\n," add (a, b));
    printf ("    a - b: %f\n," sub (a, b));
    printf ("    a * b: %f\n," mul (a, b));
    printf ("    a / b: %f\n," div (a, b));

    printf ("\n    Goodbye!\n");
}
```

Figure 14.14. The file calc.c

Now the other modules can be entered. The key combination

new files   opens a new file.

```
double add (double a, double b)
{
  return a + b;
}

double sub (double a, double b)
{
  return a - b;
}
```

Figure 14.15. The file addsub.c

```
double mul (double a, double b)
{
  return a * a;
}

double div (double a, double b)
{
  return a / b
}
```

Figure 14.16. The file muldiv.c

Now the project consists of three files. This also has an effect on the makefile.

```
CFLAGS = -g
OBJS = calc.o addsub.o muldiv.o

calc: $(OBJS)
        $(CC) -o $@ $(OBJS)
```

Figure 14.17. The makefile

CFLAGS   First the environment variable CFLAGS is set with the option -g, so that the compiler generates debug code. The newly defined variable OBJS contains the names of all object files after their declaration. This declaration serves only to increase the readability and is not absolutely necessary. The target is defined as the compiled and linked program calc (Figure 14.14). Generating the target requires three object files. The following command links these object files after their compilation:

OBJS

target

```
$(CC) -o $@ $(OBJS)
```

No separate rule needs to be specified for the translation of a *.c file to a *.o file. This is implicit in the make mechanism. On entry of the makefile, note that a [Tab] must precede the link command. After the makefile has been saved, the complete project can be compiled and linked from within the editor using the command [Meta] + [X] **compile**. The editor window splits. The lower window pane logs the commands that are executed and displays any error messages that arise. In our case we deliberately omitted a semicolon in the function div of the module muldiv.c (Figure 14.16). The compiler will detect this syntax error when it compiles the source code.

rules

compile

The command **next-error** [Meta] + [X] allows the processing of the error in the editor and places the cursor at the position in the source code where the error occurred. After corrections, entering the command [Meta] + [X] **compile** starts the compiler again. Naturally, the programmer should assign each of the above commands to a keystroke combination (shortcut) to keep from having to enter the complete command each time. Such definitions are best placed in the file .emacs in the home directory (also see Chapter 13).

next error

If logical errors have found their way into the program, the GNU Debugger provides useful support in detecting them. Since the program was compiled with the compiler option -g, the debugger can be started immediately.

debugger

```
linux2:home/tul> xxgdb calc
```

First the required breakpoints need to be set. This can be done with the mouse or by entering the appropriate command. The cursor

breakpoints

415

is placed in the respective line in the text window where a breakpoint is to be set. A click on the break button of the debugger then sets the breakpoint. Sometimes it is easier to set a breakpoint via the command line, especially if the breakpoint is to be at the very start of a function.

```
gdb> break main
```

The preceding command stops the program as soon as it reaches main.

run   After all breakpoints have been defined, the program can be started with the run command. When execution stops at a breakpoint, it can be continued stepwise and the values of variables can be displayed.

```
gdb> print a
```

The above command displays the value of the variable a if it is within the current scope. The command display initiates the continuous display of variable values.

```
gdb> display b
```

The preceding command displays the value of variable b after each successive gdb command.

shell   The debugged program can be started directly from Emacs. However, first a shell must be opened with the command Meta + X shell. Then all UNIX commands can be used within the editor. The advantages of a shell that is executed within Emacs are the possibility to easily edit commands that have been executed and the ability to apply all editor commands, such as copying blocks, to the shell output.

## Chapter 15

Linux and security

In recent years the problem of computer security has increasingly awakened public agencies and various organizations, and sensitive data of all kinds traverse it: personal letters, credit card numbers, etc. The Internet has developed from a university playground to a communication network for private persons, companies, government agencies, and various organizations, and sensitive data of all kinds traverse it: personal letters, credit card numbers and bank account PINs, medical histories and examination results, management data, military secrets, and development plans of high-tech firms. Since ever more computers are networked, increasingly many computers are the targets of hackers. There are sporting hackers who want to demonstrate their intelligence by intruding into others' computer systems as well as professional hackers who target systems for destruction or to copy and sell classified information.

private data

hackers

The original development of the Internet as a network between universities and research facilities (alongside the military component) markedly shaped its technical basis. Since there was no fundamental mistrust among network participants, security was often a subordinate aspect in the development of new network protocols and concepts, as with computers and their operating systems. Electronic mail and passwords were and still are transferred unencoded across the network. When a hacker intercepts communication between two hosts, this often opens the door to intrusion into one or both of them.

early Internet

no security provisions

With regard to security, UNIX in its various flavors is ahead of various other operating systems. UNIX provides users and user groups with different permissions, login with password, and mutual isolation of processes. There are access permissions to files and

417

system invocations that only the superuser can invoke. Nevertheless, UNIX systems like Linux have many security problems.

15.1 Cryptology

There is no shortage of tools to attack these problems. Of primary importance for secure communication is cryptology, the science of secrecy. Even in early times military messages were often sent in encrypted form—although sometimes with quite simple methods that were easy to crack. Caesar, e.g., encoded messages by replacing each letter with its third successor in the alphabet. Meanwhile cryptology has evolved to an interdisciplinary science between mathematics and computer science. Powerful encryption algorithms have been developed whose security might be disputed, yet which could not be cracked after years or decades of analysis.

the science of secrets

Terminology

The cast of characters in cryptology are sender, recipient, and attacker (or *cryptanalyst*). The sender attempts to send messages to the recipient without allowing the attacker to read parts thereof. Here we assume that *physical* wiretapping of the communication channel cannot be precluded, so the message is sent in encrypted form as *ciphertext*, so that on wiretapping the attacker receives only an indecipherable mess of letters and numbers.

cryptanalyst

sender, recipient, attacker

ciphertext

The sender and recipient agree on an encryption method or *cryptosystem*, which contains algorithms for encoding and decoding as well as a key. The key is a code that is combined with the plain text for encoding or ciphertext for decoding. The attacker can attempt to guess the key, so the number of possible keys should be as high as possible. This is achieved by long keys. The key length is given in bits; for example, there are 2^{56} keys of length 56 bits. The fundamental principle of cryptography is that the cryptosystem itself must be so secure that its details can be published without danger. This is described by the motto "security instead of obscurity." *The total security of the protected communication rests in the secret key.* Over and again, new methods are introduced whose function is unknown (e.g., the Clipper chip of the US government). Such

security instead of obscurity

methods generally encounter rejection from the field of cryptology—a cryptosystem is recognized as adequately secure only if it resists the analysis attempts of scientists over a longer period of time. Even cryptosystems published by respected researchers are cracked, often within only a few weeks—and some even at the very conference at which they are introduced.

cryptosystem evaluation

Private-key cryptosystems

In *private-key cryptosystems* (or *symmetric cryptosystems*) the sender and recipient agree on a common key for their communication. With this key, both are encoded before transmission and then decoded after sending. Such methods have the drawback that the key is applicable to only one sender/recipient pair. If the recipient wants to receive messages from another sender, the recipient can use the same key for this connection as well; however, this risks that the first sender can eavesdrop on the communication. Otherwise a new key can be agreed upon; however, with a large number of communication participants, it is almost impossible to assign a key for each pair in advance. In a net with 1,000,000 hosts that exchange data, this would make 10^{12} keys. Well-known private-key cryptosystems include DES and IDEA.

private-key cryptosystems

drawbacks

DES
IDEA

Public-key cryptosystems

In *public-key cryptosystems* (also called *asymmetric* cryptosystems) there is not one common key, but two different ones. The sender has the *public key*, which is used to encode messages intended for the recipient. The recipient decodes the message with his/her *secret key*, often called *private key* (Figure 15.1). What is important is that only the *secret key* can be used for *decoding*. The *public key* is completely useless (ideally) for decoding. If the sender forgets the plain text that was encoded, then not even he/she can reconstruct it. As the names indicate, the *public key* is no secret—on the contrary, it should be known to as many communication participants as possible so that they can all send encoded messages to the recipient.

public key
secret key

The advantage of a public-key cryptosystem is that the sender need not be trustworthy. While a private-key cryptosystem has one key per sender/recipient pair, here there are only two keys per recipient. However, the drawback is the complexity of the known

sender need not be trustworthy
drawbacks

419

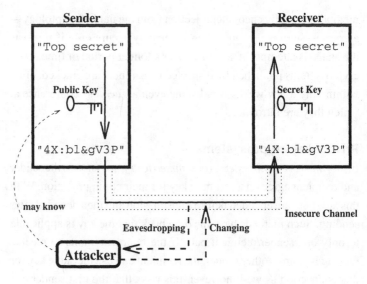

Figure 15.1. Asymmetric cryptosystem

public-key cryptosystems. They are orders of magnitude slower than the usual private-key cryptosystems, so they are seldom used (for encoding). The best-known public-key cryptosystem is RSA.

Digital signatures

As mentioned, private-key cryptosystems are often preferred for encoding larger data streams. A certain class of public-key cryptosystems, including RSA, can be used for digital signatures. In
decoding plain text these special methods, it does not matter whether encoding precedes decoding or vice versa; this method is *commutative*. The reverse order sounds ridiculous. Note, however, that encoding and decoding are simply two steps in a method with digital data, whereby anyone can encode, but only the owner of the secret key can decode (Figures 15.2 and 15.3). From now on, we will use "decoding" and "encoding" to designate these methods; the original meanings are no longer valid!
signing text If the sender "decodes" an authored text with his/her secret key, this creates a *digital signature*. The sender sends the message and the signature to a recipient; the recipient can "encode" the signature with
signature verification the public key. If everything is in order, then the result is identical to

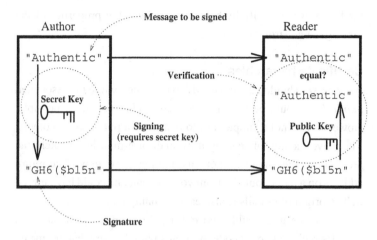

Figure 15.2. Digital signatures with public-key cryptosystems

the original message; the signature has been verified. The deciding factor is that only the owner of the secret key is able to generate the signature. The recipient thereby enjoys the security that the received message comes from the owner of the secret key rather than being a counterfeit.

Usually not the message itself is signed, but a short hash value that is generated from the message by a *secure hash function* such as MD5* or SHA. This accelerates the generation of the signature

secure hash function
MD5, SHA

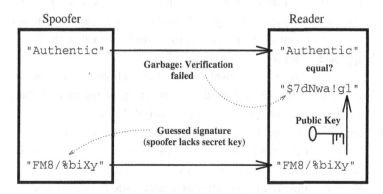

Figure 15.3. Failed attempt to fake a digital signature

*No longer seen as secure.

(and improves security by balancing unfavorable properties of the message, e.g., strong redundancy).

Certificate hierarchies

A *secret key* should be known only to its owner, while the associated *public key* should be known to as many other people as possible.

distributing public keys However, it is not a simple task to distribute a public key to others. The naive method of sending it by mail or e-mail has a catch: the recipient of the e-mail cannot trust the key it contains. The return address on a letter could be from you, or someone could have forged it. The origin of e-mails is also easy to manipulate.

Someone else could send out a public key in your name. A careless recipient could code messages with this key that are meant *dangers* for you, but actually can be decoded by the attacker. So that the sender does not become suspicious because you never respond to messages, the attacker could forward the decoded message to you—this time coded with the correct public key (a *"man in the middle"* attack). What is even more dangerous is when someone with the wrong public key attempts to verify your signature: the attacker can sign any messages in the name of the owner.

This means that anyone trusting digital signatures must be *information* informed about this danger. Actually, there are only two ways to deal with cryptosystems: either you are fully informed about their principles and flaws, or you do not depend on them. In a time when we carry a half dozen chip cards or magnetic cards in our pockets and have to remember various PIN codes for credit cards and home banking as well as the passwords for several computers, the latter approach is not so easy to sustain.

Furthermore, the original problem has not been solved: how do we get the public key to potential readers of signed messages so that we can be *certain* to whom the key belongs? The author could pass *physical key transfer* the public key for signature verification to the reader at a physical meeting; if the two persons do not know one another, they could require personal identification to assure the authenticity of the key. Naturally, this solution is completely unrealistic in communication networks—sender and recipient might be thousands of miles apart and only "know" each other for a matter of minutes.

Here is where the above digital signatures provide a solution. One approach is to have a third participant sign the sender's public key, creating a *key certificate*. Such a certificate would look like this:

key certificates

```
This key belongs to "sender" (sender@transmit.org):
XB581!fk;LX
Signatory: "third person" (third@hitchcock.com).
Digital signature:  sD1f93ka"rAF
```

This third person must be certain that this public key belongs to the sender. Likewise the recipient must trust the third person. This transfer method thus remains somewhat unrealistic—even via a third person, the field of acquaintances is not that large.

Naturally we could construct complete certificate chains— recipient trusts A, A trusts B, B trusts C, C certifies the public key of the sender. Such chains are more powerful, but they have another problem: the longer the chain becomes, the more likely it is that one of its members brings forged public keys into circulation. Certainly they would not deceive one of their friends, but the friend of a friend might not be so protected. Furthermore, a friend of a friend might be rather careless and certify the key of an unknown person without verification.

certificate chains

transitive trust

Certificate hierarchies provide a workable solution. The recipient might be an employee in a company or in a government office or a student at a university. The superordinate institution certifies the recipient's public key. Every institution in turn has another superordinate institution that certifies its public key—for the university it is the state, for the state the USA. At the highest level (e.g., between nations) public keys are exchanged at physical meetings. Higher instances tend to be unfriendly and mistrustful and thus well suited at least for the purpose of key distribution.

certificate hierarchies

With an existing certificate hierarchy the sender—assume a student at an American university—provides the recipient with his/her public key that has been certified by the university, then the certified public key of the university, of the state as certified by the US government and of the US government as certified by (say) the Federal Republic of Germany. The recipient only needs to possess the public key of Germany; this allows verification of the public key

solution

of the US government, which helps to verify the state, which in turn helps to verify the university and finally the student's key.

As with public keys for digital signatures, naturally keys for protected communication must be exchanged. This also occurs as described above, with the help of key hierarchies. At this point the private-key method returns to use: here it is possible, when creating a new connection, to generate a private key and to exchange it with *certification*. This avoids the drawbacks of the private-key method and allows making use of the speed advantage of private key cryptosystems. In practice, there is no longer a forced selection between private and public key cryptography; instead the two paradigms are mixed as described above: private key for privacy, public key for signatures.

Reality

However, all these theoretically well-functioning mechanisms are only partially implemented in practice. In particular, there are still no functioning worldwide key hierarchies. Some organizations, such as the various national CERT organizations, have built internal certificate hierarchies that might find use in the academic sector. In most Internet protocols, cryptosystems and security measures in general have yet to be installed; as far as this has already occurred, the new features are not yet very widespread.

Likewise, just how secure RSA, DES, and other established methods are, remains an open question. The only evidence of their security is that thus far no one has succeeded in cracking them, long-range security although they have been known for decades. However, there is no actual proof of their security. Furthermore, encoding and signatures, depending on their application, might have to remain secure for years to come. Since cryptoanalysis makes constant progress and ever more powerful computers become available for cracking keys, this can hardly be guaranteed.

Finally, cryptosystems and their software encounter political obstacles—many governments find it suspicious that criminals or foreign intelligence services can communicate without the least chance of decoding their messages. The USA, e.g., treats export restrictions cryptographic software like weapons—their export is strictly controlled. Selling or distributing encoding software overseas requires a permit that is hard to get. When the permit is issued, it generally bears the restriction that the key length must not exceed some set size. Software with DES encoding, e.g., can only be used with a key of at most 56 bits. Experts consider this key length inadequate and recommend variants, such as Triple DES, whose export is forbidden.

Bruce Schneier's book *Applied Cryptography* [25] is a standard in the field. But if you have an adversity to thick books, you will find an introduction with many software tips in newer editions of [3].

PGP

History   PGP ("Pretty Good Privacy") was written at the start of this decade by an American programmer named Phil Zimmermann, who made it available as freeware. PGP enables users of most common platforms to encode data with cryptographic methods and to employ and verify digital signatures. PGP uses DES or IDEA for encoding files and RSA for digital signatures and key certificates. PGP soon also appeared on European FTP servers. This led the state of California to initiate an investigation concerning violation of export restrictions for cryptographic software. Although Zimmermann was already known for PGP, this investigation made him a real folk hero. Extending over years, when the investigation was finally dropped in February 1996, the event was celebrated euphorically in many Usenet newsgroups. There were also problems with various patents that protect RSA and public-key cryptosystems in the USA, but these were attributed to an earlier version. If you want to use PGP in a commercial setting, you might have to procure a license (see the documentation).

Installation and use   PGP can be found on many FTP servers, e.g., at CERT. When downloading, you should observe the export restrictions mentioned above. There is an international PGP version* that is managed and updated outside the USA. It uses Phil Zimmermann's own RSA routines. Within the USA you should use

*ftp://ftp.ifi.uio.no/pub/pgp/

PGP

DES
IDEA
RSA

PGP investigation

international
PGP version

US version

the US version,[†] which the RSAREF library (MIT) uses, to avoid patent conflicts. You should not attempt to download other than the corresponding version—US citizens will face patent problems and non-US citizens will at least create problems for the operators of the American FTP server. Most American FTP servers check the host name of the FTP client and prevent foreigners from downloading PGP.

➡ To be able to use PGP, you absolutely must store the two files `pgpdoc1.txt` and `pgpdoc2.txt` in `/usr/local/lib/pgp`. **This section is not an exhaustive coverage of PGP. If you really want secure communication, also read (at least) the two files cited above and become familiar with the concepts of cryptography.**

key pair

First you should create a key pair. Here you can choose the key length. 512-bit length is no longer seen as secure; some time ago a worldwide combination of computers managed to crack a slightly smaller key. Also, it takes a certain effort to transfer the public key of the key pair to your communication partner (and to do so securely). Possibly signatures and encoding should remain secure over the years. Therefore, you should accept any possible reduction of speed and use a key of at least 1024-bit length.

pass phrase

To protect the secret key, the key itself is encoded with a password, the *pass phrase*. However, the pass phrase is only intended to cover the case where a hacker or burglar intrudes into the machine where your key is stored. The pass phrase is not suited for protecting the key in a multi-user system or for protecting a networked host: To encode and sign messages, the user must enter the pass phrase; if the host has been infiltrated by hackers, they can easily read along with the pass phrase. To achieve real security, you should use PGP

stand-alone machine

only on a stand-alone machine. Perhaps many persons use PGP only for reasons of prestige, but the consequences they risk if a hacker employs their signature with a stolen key are unclear.

random numbers

To achieve keys that are as random and thus secure as possible, PGP needs a source for random numbers (also called *entropy source*). Since here the key is generated interactively, the user can be prompted

---

[†]`ftp://bitsy.mit.edu/pub/pgp`

to make several hundred random keystrokes. PGP uses the time
between keystrokes to create the key.

```
golem:~> pgp -kg
Pretty Good Privacy(tm) 2.6.2i - Public-key encryption for the masses.
(c) 1990-1995 Philip Zimmermann, Phil's Pretty Good Software. 7 May 95
International version - not for use in the USA. Does not use RSAREF.
Current time: 1996/11/27 10:33 GMT
Pick your RSA key size:
    1)    512 bits- Low commercial grade, fast but less secure
    2)    768 bits- High commercial grade, medium speed, good security
    3)   1024 bits- "Military" grade, slow, highest security
Choose 1, 2, or 3, or enter desired number of bits: 3
Generating an RSA key with a 1024-bit modulus.

You need a user ID for your public key.  The desired form for this
user ID is your name, followed by your E-mail address enclosed in
<angle brackets>, if you have an e-mail address.
For example:  John Q. Smith <12345.6789@compuserve.com>
Enter a user ID for your public key:
Hans Dampf <dampf@nowhere.edu>

You need a pass phrase to protect your RSA secret key.
Your pass phrase can be any sentence or phrase and may have many
words, spaces, punctuation, or any other printable characters.

Enter pass phrase:
Enter same pass phrase again:
Note that key generation is a lengthy process.

We need to generate 728 random bits.  This is done by measuring the
time intervals between your keystrokes.  Please enter some random text
on your keyboard until you hear the beep:
    0 * -Enough, thank you.
..........................................................****
...****
Key generation completed.
```

PGP manages two *keyring* files: one contains all secret
keys (`~/.pgp/secring.pgp`); the other contains public keys
(`~/.pgp/pubring.pgp`) for the user and other communication
partners. The contents of both key rings can be viewed with **pgp
-kv**:

keyring

```
golem:~> pgp -kv
Pretty Good Privacy(tm) 2.6.2i - Public-key encryption for the masses.
(c) 1990-1995 Philip Zimmermann, Phil's Pretty Good Software. 7 May 95
International version - not for use in the USA. Does not use RSAREF.
Current time: 1996/11/27 11:14 GMT

Key ring: '/home/.pgp/pubring.pgp'
Type bits/keyID    Date       User ID
pub  1024/EADAF26D 1996/11/27 Hans Dampf <dampf@nowhere.edu>
1 matching key found.
```

```
golem:~> pgp -kv ~/.pgp/secring.pgp
Pretty Good Privacy(tm) 2.6.2i - Public-key encryption for the masses.
(c) 1990-1995 Philip Zimmermann, Phil's Pretty Good Software. 7 May 95
International version - not for use in the USA. Does not use RSAREF.
```

```
Current time: 1996/11/27 11:17 GMT

Key ring: '/home/lutti/.pgp/pubring.pgp'
Type bits/keyID    Date        User ID
pub 1024/4E650019 1996/11/27 lutti
1 matching key found.
golem:~> pgp -kv ~/.pgp/secring.pgp
Pretty Good Privacy(tm) 2.6.2i - Public-key encryption for the masses.
(c) 1990-1995 Philip Zimmermann, Phil's Pretty Good Software. 7 May 95
International version - not for use in the USA. Does not use RSAREF.
Current time: 1996/11/27 11:18 GMT

Key ring: '/home/lutti/.pgp/secring.pgp'
Type bits/keyID    Date        User ID
sec 1024/4E650019 1996/11/27 lutti
1 matching key found.
```

To be able to transfer the public key, copy it from the keyring to a file:

```
golem:~> pgp -kx
Pretty Good Privacy(tm) 2.6.2i - Public-key encryption for the masses.
(c) 1990-1995 Philip Zimmermann, Phil's Pretty Good Software. 7 May 95
International version - not for use in the USA. Does not use RSAREF.
Current time: 1996/11/27 11:19 GMT

A user ID is required to select the key you want to extract.
Enter the key's user ID: Hans Dampf <dampf@nowhere.edu>

Extracting from key ring: '/home/.pgp/pubring.pgp', userid "Hans Dampf
<dampf@nowhere.edu>".

Key for user ID: Hans Dampf <dampf@nowhere.edu>
1024-bit key, Key ID EADAF26D, created 1996/11/27

Extract the above key into which file? hd

Key extracted to file 'hd.pgp'.
```

By specifying -kxa you can extract the public key in ASCII format. However, observe that you should not send public keys via e-mail and you should not trust keys received by mail. You can only be sure about the origin of the key if the key was signed (certified) by someone else whose public key you already know and whom you trust.

If you are sure of the authenticity of the key even without a certificate (physical meeting), you can include it in the keyring for public keys as follows:

```
golem:~> pgp -ka lutti.pgp
Pretty Good Privacy(tm) 2.6.2i - Public-key encryption for the masses.
(c) 1990-1995 Philip Zimmermann, Phil's Pretty Good Software. 7 May 95
International version - not for use in the USA. Does not use RSAREF.
Current time: 1996/11/27 11:25 GMT
```

```
Looking for new keys...
pub  1024/4E650019 1996/11/27  lutti

Checking signatures...


Key file contains:
  1 new key(s)

One or more of the new keys are not fully certified.
Do you want to certify any of these keys yourself (y/N)? n
golem:~# pgp -kv
Pretty Good Privacy(tm) 2.6.2i - Public-key encryption for the masses.
(c) 1990-1995 Philip Zimmermann, Phil's Pretty Good Software. 7 May 95
International version - not for use in the USA. Does not use RSAREF.
Current time: 1996/11/27 11:25 GMT

Key ring: '/home/.pgp/pubring.pgp'
Type bits/keyID    Date       User ID
pub  1024/4E650019 1996/11/27 lutti
pub  1024/EADAF26D 1996/11/27 Hans Dampf <dampf@nowhere.edu>
2 matching keys found.
```

If you answer the certification question with $\boxed{y}$, then you can certify the public key. The key's owner can then distribute it per e-mail to others who trust your signature. In addition, you can specify with levels whether you trust the certificates of this partner. **pgp -kvv** lists the keys in a keyring as well as the certificates (`sig`). If you extract a key from the public keyring, certificates are automatically extracted with it.

certifying keys

For certification, you should be very clear about the ownership of the key, even more than for simple use of the key. Encoding with a non-authentic public key only means that a message can be read by the wrong person. But if the key was certified by you, you contribute to its proliferation and likewise make **encoded messages from persons who trust your certificates readable for the attacker**.

Encoding files:

```
golem:~> ls
test.txt
golem:~> pgp -ea test.txt
Pretty Good Privacy(tm) 2.6.2i - Public-key encryption for the masses.
(c) 1990-1995 Philip Zimmermann, Phil's Pretty Good Software. 7 May 95
International version - not for use in the USA. Does not use RSAREF.
Current time: 1996/11/27 10:53 GMT


Recipients' public key(s) will be used to encrypt.
A user ID is required to select the recipient's public key.
Enter the recipient's user ID: Hans Dampf <dampf@nowhere.edu>

Key for user ID: Hans Dampf <dampf@nowhere.edu>
1024-bit key, Key ID EADAF26D, created 1996/11/27
.
```

```
Transport armor file: test.txt.asc
> ls
test.txt test.txt.asc
```

The switch -a stores the encoded file in ASCII format to make it easy to send by e-mail. For e-mail signatures, use the options -sta:

```
> pgp -sta test.txt
Pretty Good Privacy(tm) 2.6.2i - Public-key encryption for the masses.
(c) 1990-1995 Philip Zimmermann, Phil's Pretty Good Software. 7 May 95
International version - not for use in the USA. Does not use RSAREF.
Current time: 1996/11/27 11:06 GMT

A secret key is required to make a signature.
You specified no user ID to select your secret key,
so the default user ID and key will be the most recently
added key on your secret keyring.

You need a pass phrase to unlock your RSA secret key.
Key for user ID "Hans Dampf <dampf@nowhere.edu>"

Enter pass phrase: Pass phrase is good.
Key for user ID: Hans Dampf <dampf@nowhere.edu>
1024-bit key, Key ID EADAF26D, created 1996/11/27
Just a moment....
Clear signature file: test.txt.asc
>
```

The following are the contents of test.txt.asc:

```
-----BEGIN PGP SIGNED MESSAGE-----

message

-----BEGIN PGP SIGNATURE-----
Version: 2.6.2i

iQCVAwUBMpwg8hkHxrrq2vJtAQEAoQP/YrT24UsFrNYyAmPoxTrVYoC1E4zegMlX
QLkcrRJ4D87/+Y0YCM3oljmLYhgi/jMY88gbLVbl+rXmG75zQB51QsXPOX8Iv/nS
EYGdKcaVtaAgfe7Tq7pIx3UQj0lUXtjYe8vWidjM0QrnorR5E3suxiOGDxW7VjbN
cVuDsGT1jR8=
=jIlF
-----END PGP SIGNATURE-----
```

Secure Shell

The Secure Shell ssh by Tatu Ylonen replaces the Internet service telnet. Telnet suffers the drawback that its complete communication is transferred unencoded—especially the passwords for logging in on the remote computer system. The Secure Shell provides both encoded communication and stricter authentication mechanisms than traditional UNIX passwords.

encoded
communication
stricter authentication
mechanisms

The Secure Shell is distributed as source code,* but thanks to its `configure` script, it is quite easy to install (also see Section 7.11). The package contains, among other things, the client `ssh` and the server `sshd`.

Configuration of sshd First use `ssh-keygen` to generate a host key pair for the current host. This host key pair serves to authenticate the host for others and is needed for encoding the Secure Shell protocol:

host key pair

```
golem:~> ssh-keygen
Initializing random number generator...
Generating p:  ............++ (distance 224)
Generating q:  ............++ (distance 152)
Computing the keys...
Testing the keys...
Key generation complete.
Enter file in which to save the key ($HOME/.ssh/identity): /etc/ssh_host_key
Enter passphrase (empty for no passphrase):
Enter same passphrase again:
Your identification has been saved in /etc/ssh_host_key.
Your public key is:
1024 33
10771084722788123928596733618960306348725397632070952834695351674769521160 96
64131805602382377315478003834411497460101787500643407877759684243551765595 77
49199858675758236889340182986875656881704286997649732388529543410897301905 92
42657077253703466459711545370094388482155911032166804296662307955788430661 16
84737 root@golem
Your public key has been saved in /etc/ssh_host_key.pub
```

The public key in `/etc/ssh_host_key.pub` can be transferred to multiple hosts and stored there in `/etc/ssh_known_hosts` or `~/.ssh/known_hosts`. In the former file it applies system-wide as certified public key of the other host; in the latter file it applies only for logins of the respective user. The key can be appended to either of these files with `cat`.

If the administrator allows only RSA authentication (see below), then every user employing the Secure Shell must generate an individual key pair. Like the host key, the public key `~/.ssh/identity.pub` can be transferred to another host and appended to the file `~ /.ssh/authorized_keys` there with `cat`.

```
golem:~> cat remote_host_key >> ~/.ssh/known_hosts
```

*ftp://ftp.dfn.de/pub/security/ssh

sshd is configured in /etc/sshd_config; the file was already installed with **make install**, but it needs to be modified. Check the following settings in any case:

PermitRootLogin

Determines whether root can log in via Secure Shell.

RhostsAuthentication

If yes is specified here, users can log in via ssh as with rlogin, with corresponding entries in ~/.rhosts even without a password. In this form the Secure Shell provides no security improvement over r-Tools.

RhostsRSAAuthentication

Here, too, the user can specify in ~/.rhosts from which hosts he/she can log in without a password. However, the other host must authenticate itself with its host key (ssh requires a SetUID flag to be able to read the private key in /etc/sshd_host_key). This provides additional security compared to the weak authentication via the address of incoming packets.

RSAAuthentication

This requires authentication of the user with the individual key. The public key of the key pair must have been stored locally on the remote host in ~/.ssh/authorized_keys (see above).

PasswordAuthentication

The user can log in with the normal UNIX password. This does not directly improve access control, but strengthens communication security.

AllowHosts

If this option is specified, logins are possible only from the specified hosts.

DenyHosts

If this option is specified, logins from the specified hosts are denied, but are possible from all other hosts.

The various authentication methods are alternatives: e.g., if the user has no RSA key, he/she can log in via UNIX password, assuming that yes was specified in PasswordAuthentication. The AllowHosts restriction applies only to the IP address (not to host authentication and key IDs).

You should also set defaults for users in /etc/ssh_config (users can configure these with individual values in ~/.ssh/config). The file is created already on installation, however, and contains sensible values.

15.2   UNIX system security

Passwords

Traditional UNIX passwords consist of eight characters—letters, numbers, or special characters. These passwords are easy to transform for use as 56-bit DES keys. In addition to the fact that a 56-bit key is not seen as adequate, the 2^{56} possible keys are not fully exhausted. Many users use their login name, their birthday, the name of a partner or child, their brand of car, or another password that is easy to guess. Plain text passwords are generally unsuitable: large dictionaries are circulating on the Internet, and hackers simply try out their complete contents.

no plain-text password

To enjoy the full security of UNIX passwords, you should mix letters with numbers and special characters in the password. One good method is using the acronym for a phrase that is easy to remember—a not too common saying or a passage from a book.

numbers and special characters

SetUID programs

Reports on new security flaws in a UNIX system frequently mention the *SetUID* programs. Executable programs can be provided with a *SetUID flag*. When you start such a process, it is executed not with the permissions of the user, but with the permissions of the file owner. An example is the program su. A user can invoke su to execute commands with root permissions after entering the root password. su can give the user such permissions only if it receives root permissions itself through the SetUID flag of the program file and its owner is root. Without the SetUID flag su would run

SetUID flag

433

only with the permissions of the user and could not grant other permissions.

The user receives `root` permissions only on input of the `root` password. `su` must prompt for the password, check the input, and refuse the user `root` permissions if the password is incorrect. Like any computer program, `su` can have errors that diminish its security. It might not react properly to certain passwords and open a `root` shell without controls.

Therefore, do not permit more SetUID programs than necessary and remove or defuse extraneous SetUID programs installed by a Linux distribution. Beyond that, the decision of whether a program needs a SetUID flag is difficult because the purpose of the flag might not be obvious.

15.3   Information sources

There are numerous useful computer newsgroups and mailing lists on security and cryptography, of which some are listed here:

- news://comp.os.unix.security
- news://sci.crypt
- news://alt.security.pgp
- `linux-security@redhat.com` (mailing list)
- `http://www.cert.org` CERT home page
- `http://www.ifi.uio.no/pgp/` home page of international PGP version
- `http://www.eff.org/` home page of Electronic Frontier Foundation

Much information and software resides on the CERT FTP servers `ftp.cert.org` and `cert.concert.dfn.de` and their mirrors.

## Chapter 16

Linux command reference

This command reference presents the most important Linux commands. Any Linux command comes with a variety of command line options. We only present the most important options; any others can be looked up in the corresponding Manual pages. Consequently, there may be more options than the command syntax—as presented in this reference—contains.

16.1   X-Windows

```
startx
```

Launches the X-server. With multiple users, you should configure and use xdm, because it includes (in addition to other features) a login prompt.

```
xhost {-¦+}[host]
```

xhost switches the X-display access control for the specified host or for all hosts off (+) or on (-). With activated access control, a user who wants to control a program on a remote host from the local X-Windows display needs the xdm cookie on the remote host (also see xauth).

```
xauth [-f xauth-file] extract file displayname
xauth [-f xauth-file] merge file
```

Normally only a user has the right to execute window and graphic operations under X-Windows. The user is authenticated with an access code in ~/.Xauthority. This code can be transferred to another user or to the user's account on the remote host. xauth serves to extract and add codes to ~/.Xauthority.

```
local> xauth extract x.key :0
local> telnet remote
...
remote> ftp local
...
ftp> get x.key
...
ftp> bye
...
remote> xauth merge x.key
remote> export DISPLAY=local:0
```

X-Windows via network   On a remote host, this sequence allows you to execute X-Windows programs that use the X-Windows server on the local host (i.e., especially local keyboard, mouse, and X-terminal). The variable DISPLAY tells X-Windows programs which display they should use. Normally this is :0 (i.e., the first X-Windows display of the local host). In the example we specify local:0, i.e., the programs on remote are controlled by the user from the X-Windows display on local.

```
xdm
```

The X Display Manager: In addition to many other features, its most important task is to operate X-Windows for multiple users. Its configuration file /usr/lib/X11/xdm/xdm-config contains links to other configuration files. The following is an overview of the life cycle of xdm.

Xsetup   xdm executes the file Xsetup and then opens a login window. Xsetup launches the X server and can handle several other small tasks (setting up a nice image background, etc.).

`Xstartup`   A user has logged in successfully. `xdm` first executes the file `Xstartup`—still with `root` permissions. In `Xstartup` those login operations should be executed that require `root` permissions, such as entries in login protocol files.

`Xsession`   `xdm` now executes the script `Xsession` with the permissions of the logged-in user. At the end of `Xsession` a window manager such as `fvwm` should be started; it handles the frames around the windows and provides some other comfortable features like pop-up menus, toolbars, and virtual screens.

`Xreset`   The user logs out again. `xdm` executes `Xreset` with `root` permissions. This might include a protocol entry like "User logged out at *time* in a log file." The life cycle continues with `Xstartup`.

```
editres
```

This is a small tool for editing the *resource files* of X-Windows   resource files
applications. Resource files are configuration files that affect primarily the user interface, but also the behavior of the programs. These files are located system-wide at `/usr/lib/X11/app-defaults/`. In multiple-user systems, however, there should be a separate directory `app-defaults` in each home directory with the paths stored in the environment variable `XUSERFILESEARCHPATH`.

```
fvwm
```

This is a popular window manager. Window managers decorate windows under X-Windows with buttons for expanding/shrinking/moving, title bars, etc. In addition, `fvwm` provides pop-up menus and a toolbar for starting X-Windows programs. A very powerful feature lacking under MS-Windows is virtual screens, which allow you to switch between multiple X-Windows screens. In addition, there is a small window, the Pager, in which the user can click to select a virtual screen or (with the middle mouse button) move windows between virtual screens. Virtual screens prove useful if you have numerous windows open and you have difficulty maintaining an overview.

```
openwin
```

Shell script to start the X11 environment and the olvwm window manager.

```
xfontsel
```

This command allows you to select a font for other X-Windows programs. If you click the Select button, you can paste the font name in another window, e.g., a configuration file currently being edited.

16.2   System and processes

```
depmod -a
```

This command determines the mutual dependencies of various kernel modules. The result is used by modprobe, among others. You should invoke **depmod -a** on installing a new kernel.

```
dmesg
```

In a circular buffer the Linux kernel stores its latest messages. **dmesg** displays these. Independently thereof, an active klogd regularly reads the buffer and directs the messages to the syslog system (see syslogd).

```
domainname [domain]
```

If domain is specified, then the (Internet) domain of the host (stored within the kernel) is set to this value. Otherwise the current domain name is read and displayed. Normally, on booting, the Linux host reads the domain name from a configuration file, so that the user need not do anything.

```
free
```

free displays the current degree of utilization of main memory (in KB). The values in the first line include I/O buffers (buffers for hard disk and floppy disk access as well as interprocess and network communication); the values in the second line (+/- buffers) do not.

```
fuser file
```

fuser allows you to determine which processes are currently accessing a *file*.

```
halt
```

Halts the system. The user should employ **shutdown -h** instead; otherwise in an error situation the system could halt without shutting down the file system.

```
hostname [-F file] [name]
```

Parameterless invocation displays the *name* of the host; otherwise the specified *name* is set. The host name is usually set on system startup and requires superuser permissions.

```
insmod [-f] [-m] [-s] module [symbol=value]
```

insmod loads a new *module* into the kernel.

-f   Loads a module even if the version number of the kernel and the module do not agree, in which case at least a warning is issued.

-m   Display error messages

-s   Protocol error messages with `syslog`

`symbol=value`   On loading, the module variable associated with `symbol` is assigned a `value`, which is specified in the usual C notation and corresponds to the type of the variable. Only arrays of element type `int` or `char[]` can be initialized (this incudes the types `int` and `char[]` as well, for they are treated as single-element arrays).

```
kerneld
```

`kerneld` is activated by the kernel when the kernel needs a module for and operation; `kerneld` loads the module. Likewise, from time to time `kerneld` removes unused modules. `kerneld` thereby makes modularization transparent and so spares the user and system administrator. However, some modules still need to be loaded manually (e.g., file system modules such as `msdos`).

```
kill [options] [-signal] PID
kill -l
```

This command is usually built into a shell. It sends a signal to one or more processes. Without further options, a TERM signal is sent, which orders a process to terminate. Only the system administrator can send signals to processes that she/he does not own. The processes are specified with their process number (`PID`). The signals can be specified numerically or symbolically.

-l   lists all signal names

-signal   sends a certain `signal` to the specified processes. The following signals are useful in this context:

No.	Name	Explanation
1	SIGHUP	Generated on interruption of a terminal connection; for many daemons it serves to read the configuration files anew
2	SIGINT	Equivalent to entering Ctrl C
3	SIGQUIT	Terminates a process and triggers a core dump
9	SIGKILL	Terminates a process; this signal cannot be intercepted
15	SIGTERM	Terminates a process (default).
10	SIGUSR1	User-specific signal whose meaning is different in each application
12	SIGUSR2	See SIGUSR1

```
killall [-signal] name
```

Like kill, except that not the PID, but the name of the program associated with the process is specified. If multiple processes are using the program, they all receive the signal.

```
golem:~> killall make gcc sh
```

This serves to terminate a compilation process. Several Makefiles compile files not sequentially but in a number of split-off processes in parallel.

```
klogd
```

klogd regularly reads kernel messages in the background and forwards them to syslogd.

```
ksyms [-a] [-h] [-m]
```

Lists the symbols currently exported by the kernel. Only functions and variables that are exported can be used by dynamically loaded kernel modules.

441

-m   Lists only symbols exported by kernel modules. In addition, the address, storage space, and name of the module is displayed.

-a   *Both* symbols exported by kernel modules and those exported by the kernel itself are listed. If the option -m was specified, address, storage space, and name of the module are listed.

```
ldconfig [-l] [-p] [-v] [-D] [-N] [-X] [file]
```
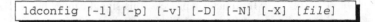

Re-creates links and cache files that are necessary for linking shared libraries. ldconfig should always be executed when a shared library is deleted, added, or replaced, e.g., on installation of certain program packages. This command must be executed by the superuser. Optionally you can pass a directory or the name of a library whose entries are to be updated. A list of all directories with shared librariess is maintained in /etc/ld.so.conf. If a program needs a shared library that could not be found, then the program invocation fails with the (misleading) message command not found. **ldd** *file* allows you to determine which shared libraries a program requires.

-l   Enables manual creation of links to a certain library.

-p   Displays all directories and libraries entered in cache.

-v   Displays the directory, name, and version number of the library that is currently being examined.

-D   Debug mode.

-N   Simply creates new links without regenerating the cache.

-X   Only regenerates the cache without changing links.

```
lilo [-R directory] [-q]
```

LILO, the LInux LOader, is introduced in detail in Section 5.5.

```
logger [-P level] message
```

Sends a protocol message from the syslog system. -P specifies the priority (default is user.notice.)

```
lsmod
```

Lists all loaded kernel modules, their storage space, and the number
of module locks on them. To be able to remove a module, the number
of locks must be 0; if it is not 0, the parts of the kernel are specified
that are using the module and thus have set a lock. (autoclean)
means that the module was loaded by kerneld and will also be
removed autonomously.

```
mkfifo Name
```

Creates a new FIFO queue. FIFO queues are used for simple data
exchange between two processes. The FIFO queue corresponds
approximately to a pipeline, but has a file name and can be accessed
in the directory tree. One process writes data in the queue, while
another reads from it.

```
mknod file {b|c|u} major minor
```

Creates a device file. Usually all important devices are already
created under /dev on installation of the Linux system. However, on
upgrading to a new kernel version, it might be necessary to modify
existing entries or to add new ones. You will find a list of all devices
and their numbers (major and minor) in the kernel sources under
linux/Documentation/devices.txt. A major device number
designates a driver that is responsible for the device; the minor device
number is the individual device (there are generally multiple devices
per driver; a printer driver might manage several parallel ports called
lp1, lp2, ...). /dev also often contains the script MAKEDEV, which
supports comfortable update of entries after installation of a new
kernel.

The name of a new device file must be followed by its type
specification:

b   Block device (hard disk, floppy drive, ramdisk, ...)
c   Character device (printer, serial port, terminals, ...)

u   Equivalent to c

```
golem:~> ls -l /dev/
```

Outputs device numbers of all device files.

```
golem:~> mknod /dev/sda2 b 8 2
```

Creates a new device file for the second partition of the first SCSI hard disk.

```
modprobe module
```

modprobe checks whether the specified kernel module is loaded or, if not, loads it. Any modules that this module requires, directly or indirectly, are also loaded.

```
golem:~> modprobe msdos
```

Assures that the driver for the MS-DOS file systems is loaded. File system drivers are not loaded on demand by kerneld!

```
nice [{-,+}adjustment] [-n adjustment] command
    args...
```

nice   Executes commands with a higher nice-level, i.e., a lower priority. nice is usually integrated in the shell. The maximum nice-level is 19. The system administrator can also specify negative values to -20. A default nice-level of 10 is used in lieu of a specification.

```
ps [-a] [-h] [-j] [-l] [-m] [-r] [-s] [-t
    terminal] [-u] [-w] [-x]
```

ps   Outputs a list of currently active processes.

-a   displays the processes of all users

-h   suppresses the header line

-j   outputs the process's group ID and session ID

-l   verbose output format

-m   provides an overview of storage allocation

-r   lists only currently running processes

-s   provides information on signal status

-t *terminal*   displays processes and their controlling *terminal*

-u   outputs the name of the process owner and the start time

-w   suppresses the truncation of command lines for wide output

-x   also displays processes without a controlling terminal (especially daemons)

The flags under STAT have the following meanings:

R   runable (is executing or ready for execution)

S   sleeping: the process is waiting for an event, e.g., new data from a file or a network connection or user input.

D   uninterruptable sleep: this process cannot even be terminated with the signal KILL. This is typical of processes that are currently carrying out disk operations.

T   stopped or traced: either the process was halted with the signal STOP or the key combination [Ctrl][S], or it is presently being analyzed by strace or gdb.

W   A process that "occupies no main memory" (Manual page for ps). Either it is a process in the kernel (since it uses kernel memory, it does not occupy any of the main memory pages available for user processes) or a process whose pages were completely swapped onto the hard disk (usually ones that have been inactive for a long time).

N   This process has a positive nice value: it has reduced priority, and other processes are favored over it.

<   This process has a negative nice value: it runs with increased priority and it is favored over other processes. Only the superuser can assign process negative nice values.

445

```
pstree [-a]
```

pstree lists all processes in a tree according to parent/child.

-a   The command line that launched the process is displayed also.

```
reboot
```

Reboots the system (system shutdown with subsequent reboot). **shutdown -r** is more secure.

```
renice
```

Like nice, only here the priority of a running process is changed afterwards.

```
rmmod [-r] module
```

rmmod removes a module from the kernel. This is only possible if the module is not being used by other modules, by a system invocation or to support a mounted file system (see lsmod).

-r   Also removes, if possible, all modules used by this module.

```
shutdown [-c] [-h] [-k] [-r] [-t sec] time
        [message]
```

shutdown   Changes the run level of the system or terminates the system. A time and a warning message can be passed as arguments. For an immediate shutdown, the time now is specified.

-c   interrupts a shutdown in progress
-h   halts the system with the termination of all processes and unmounts the file systems
-k   does not execute a shutdown, but only displays the warning

-r   reboots the system

-t *sec*   delay in seconds between the display of the warning
        message and sending the `kill` signals

```
swapoff {-a¦device}
```

Switches off the specified swap device; if -a is specified, all swap
devices listed in /etc/fstab are deactivated. This command is
automatically invoked on shutdown.

```
swapon {-a¦device}
```

Activates the swap device specified by *device*. -a activates all swap
devices specified in /etc/fstab. This command is automatically
invoked on booting.

```
sync
```

sync triggers the writing of all file system I/O buffers to the
respective block device. Most disk operations under Linux do not
write directly to the hard disk, but to a buffer that is written to disk
every 30 seconds or on unmounting of the file system. This is why
Linux (contrary to MS-DOS) write to disk impressively quickly, but
then requires extra time for unmounting.

```
syslogd
```

In the background, syslogd collects status and error messages of
various parts of the system, archives them in protocol files (see
var/log or /var/adm), or forwards them to a central log server
on the LAN. syslogd is configured in /etc/syslog.conf. If
klogd is active, then messages from the kernel are also processed
by syslogd.

447

```
top
```

top displays running processes and refreshes the list every five seconds. top is terminated with (q); however, there are a number of other keys (to change output parameter or to send a signal to a process).

```
ulimit [-S] [-H] [-a] [-c] [-d] [-f] [-s] [-t]
     [-v] [limit]
```

(only in bash!) Sets various resource restrictions for the shell and all processes started therefrom, or displays their current value.

-a   Outputs all limits
-c   Maximum core file size (0 = generate no cores)
-d   Maximum size of data segments
-f   Maximum size of generated files
-s   Maximum stack size
-t   CPU time that a process can take before it receives the signal SIGXCPU (which generally terminates the process)
-v   Maximum amount of virtual memory used (code, data, and stack including swapped memory pages)

See **man bash**, searching for **/ulimit**.

```
umount [device|directory]
```

umount *unmounts* the specified file system, removing it from the directory tree, and completely flushes the I/O buffers to disk.

```
uname [-a] [-m] [-n] [-r] [-s] [-v]
```

Outputs the name and version number of the current system.

-a   outputs all available information

-m   outputs hardware (processor) type

-n   outputs the host name

-r   outputs the version number of the operating system

-s   outputs the name of the operating system

-v   outputs the date and time of compilation of the kernel

```
golem:~> uname -sr
Linux 2.0.18
```

```
uptime
```

Outputs the current time, the time since the last reboot, the number of logged users, and the momentary system load.

```
golem:~> uptime
11:06pm  up  5:59,   3 users,   load average: 0.04, 0.05, 0.00
```

16.3   User and group management

```
chfn
chfn2
```

Changes the user description that is returned on a finger query (name, organization, telephone number, ...).

```
chsh
```

Changes the shell in which the user lands after logging in. Only certain shells are permissible. The shell's name (with its absolute path) is specified in /etc/shells.   /etc/shells

449

```
groups [user]
```

Outputs the groups to which the specified *user* belongs. A parameterless invocation lists all the current user's own groups, and with a parameter the groups of the specified *user*. The command evaluates the files /etc/passwd and /etc/groups.

```
id [-g] [-G] [-n] [-r] [-u]
```

Displays the real and effective user ID (UID) and all groups (GID) of the current user.

-g   displays only GID
-G   displays only the additional groups to which a user belongs
-n   displays GID or UID as name (only in combination with options
     -g, -u, -G)
-r   displays the real instead of the effective GID (only in combination with options -g, -u, -G)
-u   displays only UID

```
last [-f file] [-h host] [-t tty] [-N]
     [attribute]
```

Provides information from the login statistics (/etc/wtmp). Without additional arguments, it outputs a list of all login, logout, shutdown, and reboot activities. This list contains the name of the user or the event, the login terminal, the login host, and the time. A selection can be limited to certain entries by specifying search attributes (name, login terminal).

-N limits output to a certain number of lines
-f *file*   uses the specified *file* instead of /etc/wtmp as the database
-t *terminal*   lists only logins entered from a particular *terminal*
-h *host*   lists only logins entered from a certain *host*

```
hermes:/root# last uhl
uhl     ttyp4     mobby        Sun Jan 29 17:24    still logged in
uhl     ttyp2     tonne        Sun Jan 29 16:32 - 16:47 (00:15)

wtmp begins Sun Jan 29 15:18
hermes:/root#
```

```
passwd [username]
```

Changes the user's own password. The system administrator can also
change the passwords of other users.

```
su [-c command] [-] [user] [arguments]
```

Starts a new shell as a different user. This program is used to log
in on a terminal that is already being used by another user. Omitting
the user opens a root shell. The new shell is terminated by entering
exit or Ctrl + d. If - is specified as option, then su tries to mimic
a login as far as possible (environment variables like HOME are set
to other values, etc.). In addition, the option -c allows execution of
commands under a different user ID.

```
w [-h] [-s] [-f] [users]
```

Displays all currently logged users and their activities. Without
parameters, all users are output; with a name, only the specified
users.

-h   suppresses a title line
-f   determines whether the login terminal should also be output
-s   concise output format

```
who [-i] [-q] [-w] [-H] [file] [am i]
```

Outputs a list of users currently logged in, their terminals, the login
time, and the name of the host on which they logged in. If a file name
is specified in addition, then this file is used for evaluation instead
of /etc/utmp.

am i   outputs the user's own data

-i   outputs how long the user was inactive

-H   outputs column headings

-q   outputs only the login name and the number of users

-w   displays whether the user accepts (+) messages generated with
       write or not (-)

```
whoami
```

Displays the user name under which the user is currently logged in.

16.4   File and directory management

```
cat [-b] [-e] [-n] [-s] [-t] [-u] [-v] [files]
```

Reads multiple *files* and outputs them to the standard output
device. If no *files* are specified, the standard input device is read.
Entry is then terminated with **Ctrl** + **D**. For this command, output
is frequently redirected with >.

-b   sequentially numbers all nonempty lines

-e   can be specified along with -v and outputs $ for end of line
       (EOL)

-n   sequentially numbers all lines

-s   replaces a group of blank lines with a single one

-u   unbuffered output

-v   also outputs control characters and other nonprintable charac-
       ters

-t   can be specified along with -v and outputs ^I instead of tabs
       and ^L instead of page feeds

```
zeus:/home/uhl> cat >file.txt
This is the contents of the file!Ctrl + D
zeus:/home/uhl> cat file.txt
This is the contents of the file!
zeus:/home/uhl>
```

```
cd [directory]
```

Changes the current *directory*. This command is usually included in the shell. If no *directory* is specified, the current user's home directory is assumed by default. Specifying - returns to the previous directory.

```
chgrp [-c] [-f] [-v] [-R] group [files]
```

Changes the group membership of *files*. This command can be used by the system administrator or by the owner of the specified *files*. The *group* can be specified in the form of a numeric group ID or as the name of a group.

-c   displays the names of the *files* whose *group* membership actually changed

-f   suppresses error messages

-R   changes the *group* membership of *files* in subdirectories (recursively)

-v   describes each change in a verbose manner

```
chmod [-c] [-f] [-v] [-R] mode files
```

Changes the *permissions* of the specified *files*. This command can be used by the system administrator or the owner of the specified *files*. The *permissions* can be specified numerically (octal format) or with a command string. The command string can consist of: the designation for owner (u), group (g), or other (o); the command to add (+), remove (-), or set (=); the permissions to read (r), write (w), or execute (x); and the commands to set or reset the special flags *set user ID* (s) and *sticky* (t).

-c   displays the names of files whose permissions actually changed

-f   suppresses error messages

-R   also changes the permissions of files in subdirectories (recursively)

-v   describes each change in a verbose manner

Examples

```
golem:~> chmod u+x file
```

adds execution permission for the owner of the file

```
golem:~> chmod go-wx files
```

removes read and execution permissions for the specified files for
the group and other users

```
golem:~> chmod g+s file
```

sets the *set group ID* flag of the specified file

```
golem:~> chmod =r file
```

sets the file's permissions to read-only for everyone

```
golem:~> chmod 644 file
```

allows read and write permissions for the owner and read permissions
for all others

```
chown [-c] [-f] [-v] [-R] [user][{.|,|:}group]
      files
```

Changes the owner and optionally the group as well for the specified
files. The owner and the group can be specified as numeric IDs
or as names.

-c   displays the names of the files whose owner has actually
      changed

-f   suppresses error messages

-R   also recursively changes owners of files in subdirectories

-v   describes each change in a verbose manner

```
golem:~> chown -R newsadm.news /var/spool/news
```

Sets the user newsadm and group news as owners of the News files (useful if you happened to start the News spooler with root permissions, so that all News files belong to newsadm).

```
cp [-a] [-b] [-d] [-f] [-i] [-l] [-P] [-p] [-r]
    [-R] [-s] [-S] [-u] [-v] [-x] [-V] file(s)
    {file2|directory}
```

Copies file to file2 or the specified file(s) into the directory. If the target file (file2) already exists, it is overwritten (although option -i requires confirmation).

-a   combination of -d, -p, and -r

-b   creates a backup of files before overwriting them

-d   maintains symbolic and hard links during copying

-f   forces a copy and overwrites existing files

-i   asks for confirmation before overwriting an existing file

-l   creates a hard link rather than a copy of a file

-P   copies files into a target directory hierarchy (which is created if necessary)

-p   also copies the permissions and modification times of the files

-r   recursively copies subdirectories and their contents

-R   see -r

-s   creates a symbolic link rather than a copy of a file

-S suffix   changes the extension for backup files to suffix

-u   prevents the overwriting of a file that has the same name and a newer date

-v   displays the name of each file on copying

-x   ignores directories on any file system different from the source file

-V {numbered|existing|simple}   determines the kind of version control:

numbered   always creates a numbered backup

existing   creates a numbered backup only for files for which such a backup already exists, and in all other cases creates a simple backup

simple   always creates a simple backup

```
golem:~> cp -av /home /backup/home
```

copies the entire /home directory tree to /backup/home. All permissions and user/group ownerships of files are maintained, as is the structure of the tree. The names of all copied directories and files are displayed linewise.

```
dd bs=n cbs=n conv=flags count=n if=file
   of=file ibs=n obs=n skip=n
```

dd   copies from the standard input device or a specified file to the standard output device or another specifiEd file. The most frequent options are if to specify the input file and of to specify the output file. dd, for example, can be used to write a kernel image file directly onto a diskette or to make a boot diskette from a disk image.

bs=n   sets the block size for input and output to n bytes. Optionally, n can be specified with units, e.g., 8k for 8 kilobytes

cbs=n   determines the size of a field in converting to bytes

conv=flags   converts the input according to the following arguments:

ascii   EBCDIC to ASCII conversion

ebcdic   ASCII to EBCDIC conversion

ibm   ASCII to IBM EBCDIC conversion

block   converts variable-length fields to fields of length cbs and fills the spaces with blanks

 unblock   converts fixed-length fields (*cbs*) to variable-
    length fields

 lcase   converts uppercase to lowercase letters

 ucase   converts lowercase to uppercase letters

 swap   swaps every two bytes of the input file

 noerror   ignores errors during reading

 notrunc   does not truncate the output file

 sync   fills spaces in the input blocks of size *ibs* with zeros

count=*n*   copies only *n* blocks

if=*file*   specifies the input *file*

of=*file*   specifies the output *file*

ibs=*n*   sets the size of the input buffer

obs=*n*   sets the size of the output buffer

skip=*n*   skips *n* blocks of input

```
golem:~> dd if=/tmp/zImage of=/dev/fd0
```

copies a Linux kernel to start of diskette.

```
file [-c] [-f] [-m] [-l] [-Z] files
```

Outputs the types of specified *files*. The file type is recognized on the basis of an extensible rule file (/etc/magic).

-c   for checking the rule file

-f *file*   examines the files listed in *file*

-m *file*   uses the specified rule *file* instead of /etc/magic

-L   also follows symbolic links

-z   enables the processing of compressed files

```
find pathname constraints
```

This command recursively searches in directories for files that meet all the specified constraints. The list of constraints is evaluated from left to right. Individual constraints can be negated by a preceding exclamation mark (!). An OR conjunction between two expression is defined with -o. find is particularly useful in combination with other commands (e.g., cpio).

Numeric specifications:

+n   value larger than n

n   value equal to n

-n   value smaller than n

Available options (always true):

-depth   files contained in a directory are processed before the directory itself

-follow   also branches to directories indicated by symbolic links (follows symbolic links)

Possible constraints:

-amin n files accessed in the last n minutes

-anewer *file*   files accessed more recently than the specified *file*

-atime n files that were last accessed n days ago

-ctime n files that were last modified (either the file itself, the permissions, or the owner) n days ago

-fstype *type*   files in a certain *type* of file system (e.g., ext2, msdos, proc)

-group *group*   files belonging to a certain *group* (name or ID)

-inum n files with i-node number n

-links n files that possess n links

-local   files physically stored on the local system

-mtime n files that were last modified (only the file itself) n days ago

-name *pattern*   the names of the files match the specified wildcard *pattern*

-newer *file*   the last modification of the files must be more recent than the specified *file* (see also mtime)

-nogroup   files whose group does not exist in /etc/groups

`-nouser`   files whose owner does not exist in `/etc/passwd`

`-perm` *nnn*   the permissions of the files must match the octal representation *nnn*

`-size` *n*`[b|c|k|w]`   files of size *n* blocks, *n* bytes, or *n* kilobytes

    `-type` *c*   files of type *c*, where *c* must derive from the following list:

    b   block special file

    c   character special file

    d   directory

    p   FIFO or named pipe

    l   symbolic link

    f   normal file

`-user` *user*   files belonging to a certain *user* (name or ID)

Possible actions:

`-exec` *command* `{} \;`   executes the *command* for each file and tests whether the return code is 0. During execution, `{}` is replaced by the name of the current file

`-ok` *command* `{} \;`   like `-exec`, but the user must confirm the *commands* with **y**

`-print`   outputs files or directories found

`-printf` *format*   like `-print`, but the format of the output can be influenced by a *format* string

Examples:

```
golem:~> find . -type f -print
```

outputs all normal files in the current directory and its subdirectories

```
golem:~> find /usr/include -type f -exec grep "read" {} \;
-print
```

searches all normal files in `/usr/include` for the character string read

```
golem:~> find . -name '*.[chSs]' -print | grep session
```

searches for a C or Assembler source file whose name contains
"session." A simple **find | grep session** would also search
object files (.o) and others, which is usually not desirable.

```
ln [-s] [-f] [file1] [file2]
```

Creates a link. Without options, it creates a hard link to a file. With
the option -s a symbolic link is created that could also point to a
directory. If *file2* already exists and is a file, then an error message
is output. Only with the option -f is this file overwritten. If *file2*
is a directory, then the links are created in this directory.

-f   any existing files are overwritten without confirmation
-s   symbolic links are created

```
golem:~> ln -s
/usr/src/linux/Documentation/filesystems/ncpfs.txt ncpfs.txt
```

If the file is read frequently, this symbolic link spares the
time-consuming specification of the complete name.

```
locate string
```

Searches in the locate database for file paths that contain *string*.
locate searches in a tree and is therefore faster than a sequential
search with find. The corresponding database can be constructed
or updated with updatedb; it makes sense to run this as a cron job
at regular intervals.

```
ls [-a] [-A] [-B] [-b] [-c] [-C] [-d] [-f] [-F]
   [-G] [-i] [-k] [-l] [-L] [-m] [-n] [-r]
   [-R] [-s] [-S] [-t] [-u] [-x] [files]
```

Displays the contents of directories or lists specific *files*. If no *files* are specified, the contents of the current directory are listed. If *files* are specified, then only such files are listed that match the file name (with wildcards).

-a   displays all *files*, including those beginning with a period

-A   like option -a, but suppresses the entries . and . .

-B   ignores backup *files* that end in tilde (~)

-b   displays nonprintable characters as octal numbers

-c   sorts *files* by time of last status change

-C   displays only file names, but in multiple columns (default)

-d   on specification of a directory name, lists only the directory itself, not its contents

-f   unsorted output

-F   appends a special character to each file name to indicate the file's type (normal file, directory, executable file, link, ...)

-G   suppresses the output of group in long format

-i   displays the associated node for each *file*

-k   displays file size in kilobytes

-l   long format displays every *file* in a line along with its permissions, owner, group, size, etc.

-L   for symbolic links, shows the file or directory to which the link points rather than the link itself

-m   lists file names linewise, separated by commas

-n   lists UID and GID numerically

-r   lists *files* sorted backward

-R   recursively lists subdirectories and their contents

-s   lists file size in kilobytes before the file name

-S   sorts list by file size

-t   sorts list by date of last modification, with newer files coming first

-u   sorts list by time of last access

-x   lists *files* in horizontally sorted columns

-x   lists *files* sorted by file extension

```
golem:~> ls -l /dev
```

displays all files under /dev; since the long format is selected, permissions and in particular the minor and major device numbers are also displayed.

```
mkdir [-m perms] [-p] dirs
```

Creates directories.

-m *perms*   creates a new directory with the specified *perm*issions

-p   if a directory path is specified where individual subdirectories do not exist, then these are created also

```
mtools
```

This is a group of commands that permit simple access to MS-DOS file systems. Normally these are used to handle diskettes. Note that access to a DOS partition of a hard disk is simpler if it is mounted (see mount). The individual commands largely correspond to the DOS commands. This means that floppy disk drives can be accessed with DOS's usual letter designations (A:, B:) if the drives were correctly configured in the file /etc/mtools. If the specification of a file named in DOS file system contains wildcards (e.g., *.*), then the entire name must be put in quotes (e.g., ''*.txt''). Files in Linux file systems can be addressed in the usual way. Directory paths in DOS-file systems can be written either with the DOS (\) or in the UNIX way (with slashes /); however, the former again requires quotation marks because the backslash has a special meaning in the UNIX shell.

mattrib   modifies file attributes

mcd   changes the current directory

mcopy   copies files

mdel   deletes files

mdir   displays a directory listing

mformat   formats a low-level formatted diskette with a DOS file
   system

mlabel   changes the volume label

mmd   creates a subdirectory

mrd   removes a subdirectory

mren   renames a file

mtype   displays the contents of a file

```
mv [-b] [-f] [-i] [-u] [-S] [-V] path target
```

Moves files and directories or renames them. If the target already exists and it is a file, it is overwritten; if it is a directory, the specified files and directories are moved into the existing directory. If the `target` does not exist, then only a file or a directory can be specified as the source, and it is renamed to the `target` name.

-b   creates a backup of a file before overwriting it

-f   does not ask for confirmation before overwriting files

-i   asks for confirmation before overwriting files

-u   moves a file only if it is newer than a target file of the same
     name

-S   see cp command

-V   see cp command

```
rm [-f] [-i] [-r] [-v] files
```

Removes one or more `files`. Removing a `file` requires write permission in the containing directory. If the `file` is write protected, confirmation is required. Directories are removed with rmdir.

-f   removes `files`, even if write protected, without confirmation

-i   asks for confirmation for each `file`

-r   recursively removes subdirectories and their contents

-v   displays each file name on removal

```
golem:~> rm -r /home/undergrads/bukowski/
```

Bukowski was expelled because of some minor offenses against the campus rules.

```
rmdir [-r] directories
```

Removes subdirectories. A directory must be empty to be removed. Alternatively, rm can be used with option -r, which removes subdirectories and their contents.

```
split [-b bytes[bkm]] file
```

Decomposes a large file into several smaller ones (e.g., for transport on floppy disks). The target files are named xaa, xab, xac, etc.

```
golem:~> split -b 1250k linux-2.0.25.tar.gz
```

After transport, the files are reassembled with cat:

```
golem:~> cat xaa xab... > linux-2.0.25.tar.gz
```

```
updatedb
```

Creates or updates the database for locate queries.

```
zcat [files]
```

Decompresses the specified files and outputs their contents to the standard output device. The compressed files remain untouched.

16.5   Terminal

```
clear
```

Clears the screen.

```
dumpkeys
```

Outputs the current kernel keyboard layout, which determines the functions of each key; the functions range from simply inserting a character to rebooting (**Ctrl** + **Alt** + **Del**). Under X-Windows, however, the kernel keyboard layout table has only limited relevance.

```
kbdrate [-r rate] [-d delay]
```

kbdrate sets the speed of the keyboard.

-d *delay*   After *delay* milliseconds the kernel begins to repeat the action associated with the key pressed.

-r *rate*   *rate* sets the repetition rate.

```
loadkeys keytable
```

Loads a new keyboard layout table from `/usr/lib/kbd/keytables/` into the kernel.

```
script
```

Protocols all input/output of the current terminal in a file (until end of session). The default protocol file is `typescript`.

```
showkey
```

For any key pressed, outputs the key name in the kernel keyboard layout table. After ten seconds without a key pressed, the program terminates.

```
stty [-a] [--help] [modes]
```

Sets terminal IO *modes*. This includes all general settings of the terminal as well as speed and handshaking and the function of special characters. A list of all possible settings is displayed using the option --help.

-a   displays all current settings
--help   displays help text

```
tty
```

Outputs the name of the terminal on which tty was entered.

16.6   Viewers and editors

```
ed [file]
```

This is an antiquated standard editor which, apart from its use with the diff command, is no longer of any importance.

```
elvis
```

Although a somewhat spartan editor, on text-oriented consoles and via TELNET login elvis is more popular than Emacs. There is a tutorial package named vilearn that helps you learn the most important command shortcuts.

```
elvrec
```

. If an `elvis` session was interrupted by the crash of the TELNET
connection or otherwise, this utility allows you to save the file that
was in the editor just before the crash.

```
emacs [-nw]
```

GNU Emacs is certainly the best-known editor. In contrast to `elvis`,
Emacs has an enormous number of libraries and modes that support
writing C or other source code, including TEX files and much more.
Emacs can be configured with its built-in Emacs Lisp (also see the
Info files and the Lisp libraries). Normally Emacs detects whether it
was started under X-Windows and then opens its own window. To
suppress this, start Emacs with `-nw` in `xterm`. Chapter 13 is dedicated
to Emacs.

```
less [file]
```

This is a comfortable text viewer. Important commands include ⎡u⎤
and ⎡d⎤ for paging, ⎡/⎤, ⎡?⎤, and ⎡n⎤ for searching, and ⎡q⎤ to quit.
Additional help is available with ⎡h⎤. Its greatest advantage over
`more` is that it allows paging up. If `file` is not specified, text is read
from standard input and buffered; this makes `less` very suitable for
command pipelines.

```
more +N [-d] [-f] [-l] [-s] [-u] [files]
```

Displays `files` by (screen) page. ⎡Enter⎤ scrolls one line down and
the space bar advances to the next screen page. ⎡h⎤ displays help
with all commands and ⎡q⎤ quits the `more` command. If no `file` is
specified, then `more` reads from the standard input device.

+N begins with the specified line number
-d displays the message `Press space to continue, 'q'
    to quit` at the end of a screen page

-f   counts logical rather than screen lines for page breaks and counts broken lines only once

-1   ignores form-feed control character (^L)

-s   suppresses the output of multiple neighboring blanks

-u   suppresses underlining

```
vi [files]
```

Full-screen editor for processing ASCII *files*. It is largely based on ex and generally functions on all terminals.

```
zless [file]
```

Allows paging with less in compressed files (GNU Zip .gz or others).

```
zmore files
```

Corresponds to more, but allows pagewise display of files compressed with gzip or compress.

16.7   Archiving and compression

```
cksum [files]
```

Computes CRC checksums for the specified *files* and displays these along with their file size and file name.

```
compress [-b n] [-c] [-f] [-r] [-v] [-V]
    [files]
```

Compresses the specified *files* using the Lempel-Ziv method. The compression is indicated by appending .Z to the file name. All other file attributes are retained.

-b *n*   restricts to *n* the number of bits that may be used for coding
-c   outputs the results to the standard output device and does not
      change any files
-f   compresses without confirmation if the target file already exists
-r   also compresses files in subdirectories (recursively)
-v   provides a verbose status report
-V   displays the version number of the program

```
cpio [-0] [-a] [-A] [-b] [-B] [-c] [-C n] [-d]
    [-E file] [-f] [-F file] [-H format] [-i]
    [-I file] [-L] [-m] [-M msg] [-n] [-o] [-O
    file] [-p] [-r [user][;|.][group]] [-s]
    [-S] [-t list] [-u] [-v] [-V]
```

Copies files into an archive, displays the contents of an archive,
or extracts files from an archive. The archives can be on magnetic
tape, hard disk, or floppy disks. cpio has three modes of operation,
selected by the options -i (*copy in* = unpack), -o (*copy out* = pack),
and -p (*copy pass* = copy from directories). cpio was designed to
work with the find command.

-0   accepts file names terminated with null instead of newline (copy
      out and copy pass modes)
-a   resets the access times of files that are read so that the reading
      cannot be discerned from the file date
-A   adds files to an existing archive (with options -O or -F)
-b   during extraction (copy in), exchanges words and half-words
      (little/big endian)
-B   increases the input/output buffer from 512 to 5120 bytes
-c   uses the (old) portable ASCII format for the file headers
-C *n*   sets the input/output buffer to *n* bytes
-d   automatically creates the necessary subdirectories during
      extraction
-E *file*   extracts the files whose names are in *file* (copy in)
-f   copies only the files that do not match the specified search
      pattern

-F *file*   uses the specified *file* as an archive instead of the standard output device. *file* can also contain the name of a host in order to write the archive to a remote magnetic tape (-F zeus:/dev/tape)

    -H *format*   reads/writes header information in the specified *format*:

bin   old binary format

odc   old portable format (POSIX.1)

newc   new portable format (SVR4)

crc   new SVR4 format with CRC checksums

tar   old tar-compatible format

ustar   POSIX.1-compatible tar format

hpbin   old HP UNIX binary format

hpodc   portable HP UNIX format

-i   puts cpio in copy-in mode (extraction of an archive)

-I *file*   uses the specified file instead of the standard input device. A host name (zeus:/dev/tape) can be specified, for example, to access an archive on a remote magnetic tape drive

-L   de-references symbolic links, meaning that not the link but the file to which the link refers is copied

-m   the original modification date of a file is retained on creation of a new file

-M *msg*   enables multivolume archives. If a storage medium is full, the message msg is displayed on the screen. The variable %d can be used within the message to display the current number of the medium

-n   on display of the directory listing, the UID and GID are displayed as numeric values

-o   puts cpio in copy-out mode (creation of an archive)

-O *file*   uses the specified file instead of the standard output device. A machine name (zeus:/dev/tape) can be specified, for example, to access an archive on a remote magnetic tape drive

-p   puts cpio in copy-pass mode (copy directories locally)

-r [*user*][;¦.][*group*]   changes the file owner in copy-out and copy-pass modes and can only be used by the administrator

-s   exchange bytes in copy-in mode

-s   exchange halfwords in copy-in mode
-t *list*   displays a *list* of the contents of an archive
-u   permits overwriting of files with the same name and an older
     version
-v   displays a list of file names. A verbose version can be obtained
     by combining with the option -t.
-V   displays a period (".") for each processed file

Examples:

```
golem:~> find . -name '*.txt' -print | cpio -ocv > /dev/tape
```

backs up all files that end with .txt into an archive on magnetic tape

```
golem:~> cpio -icdv < /dev/tape
```

extracts all files from magnetic tape to the hard disk

```
golem:~> find . -print | cpio -pdv /tmp
```

copies all files from the current directory to /tmp

```
gzip [-a] [-c] [-d] [-f] [-l] [-q] [-r] [-S
    suffix] [-v] [files]
```

Compresses or decompresses *files* using the LZ77 method and
adds the extension .gz to the file name. If no file (or -) is specified,
then the standard input device is read and output goes to the
standard output device. gzip can also decompress files packed with
compress (ending in .Z).

-a   adapts the end of line in ASCII texts to the respective system
     (CRLF or LF)
-c   writes the results to the standard output device without
     overwriting the input file

-d   decompresses packed files

-f   forces an overwrite of existing files

-1   for a compressed file, displays its size in packed and unpacked
     form, the compression rate, and the name of the original file

-q   suppresses warnings

-r   recursively works through subdirectories

-S *suffix*   changes the file *suffix* for compressed files

-v   displays the name and the compression rate for each file

-N   sets the quality of compression from 1 (poor) to 9 (good), where
     default compression is 6

```
shar
```

For processing .shar archives.

```
tar [-c] [-r] [-t] [-u] [-x] [-b n] [-farchive]
    [-h] [-k] [-L] [-m] [-M] [-N date] [-o]
    [-O] [-v] [-z] [archive] [files]
```

Manages tar archives (originally on magnetic tape). This command
writes files to an *archive* or reads them from an archive. At least
one of the following operations must be passed as parameter.

Available operations:

-c   creates the archive

-r   appends files to an archive (not on tape)

-t   outputs the contents of an archive

-u   appends files to an archive if they are not already contained
     or if they have been modified (not on tape)

-x   extracts files from an archive

Additional options:

-b *n*   sets the blocking factor to *n*

-f *archive*   specifies the *archive*, which can be a normal file or a device file such as /dev/rmt0 for a tape drive or /dev/fd0 for a diskette

-h   archives referenced files instead of their symbolic links

-k   prevents overwriting of existing files

-L   follows symbolic links

-m   sets the modification time on extracting *files* to the current time

-M   creates or extracts from a multivolume *archive*, which can encompass multiple diskettes or tapes

-N *date*   archives only *files* that are newer than the specified *date*

-o   sets the owner on extracting *files* to the current user

-O   extracts *files* to the standard output device

-v   displays the file name on archiving or extracting

-z   compresses the *archive* on creation and decompresses on extraction

Examples:

```
golem:~> tar -cvf archive.tar *
```

saves all files and subdirectories of the current directory in an archive named archive.tar

```
golem:~> tar -cvf /dev/fd0 *.txt
```

saves all files in the current directory with the extension .txt from the diskette in the first floppy disk drive

```
golem:~> tar -xvfb20 /dev/rmt0
```

extracts all files from the first tape drive (block size 20)

```
golem:~> tar -tvf zarchive.tar.z
```

lists the contents of a compressed tar archive

```
uncompress [-c] [files]
```

uncompress   Restores an original file that was compressed with compress.

-c   outputs the file contents to the standard output device. Here
uncompress behaves like the command zcat.

```
unshar
```

Unpacks .shar archives.

```
unzip
```

Decompresses .zip archive and unpacks them.

```
zip
```

Creates or processes .zip archives.

```
zoo
```

For processing .zoo archives.

16.8   Disk management and file systems

```
df [-a] [-i] [-k] [-P] [-t type] [-x type]
   [paths]
```

Outputs the number of occupied and free blocks of file system. If no
path is specified, then a list of all current file systems is output. If
a path is specified, an overview is provided of the associated file

systems. Alternatively, the direct *path* of a device (/dev/hda1) on
which the file system is located can be specified. Normally only real
file systems with a storage volume greater than zero are output.

-a displays all current file systems, including those of size zero
-i instead of block information, displays i-node statistics
-k uses a block size of one kilobyte (default)
-P uses POSIX output format
-t *type*   restricts output to file systems of a certain type
-x *type*   ignores file systems of a certain type during output

```
du [-a] [-b] [-k] [-l] [-s] [-x] [files]
```

Outputs the sizes of the specified *files*.

-a outputs the sizes of all files, not just directories
-b outputs the file size in bytes
-k outputs the file size in kilobytes
-l outputs the sizes of (hard) linked files, even if this means
    handling them doubly
-s outputs the total size of all files and subdirectories
-x ignores directories in different file systems

```
e2fsck
```

Checks an Extended-2 file system for inconsistency and hardware
errors; also see fsck.

```
fdformat [-n] device
```

Executes low-level formatting of a diskette. The required parameter
is the path of the corresponding *device*. The first drive is addressed
as /dev/fd0XXX; the second, as /dev/fd1XXX. The -n option
suppresses subsequent verification of the diskette.

475

Device	Sectors	Tracks	Size	Capacity (KB)
/dev/fd0h1200	15	80	5¼	1200
/dev/fd0D720	9	80	3½	720
/dev/fd0H1440	18	80	3½	1440
/dev/fd0E2880	36	80	3½	2880

```
fdisk [device]
```

Partitioning hard disks. Caution: There are several fdisk variants; some are for interactive use, others rather for shell scripts.

```
fsck [device|-a]
```

Checks the integrity of one or more file systems. fsck is executed on booting for all file systems specified in /etc/fstab. A file system that has been unmounted without errors is not checked.

```
mkdosfs device
```

Creates an MS-DOS file system on device. The file system is fully compatible with DOS (and permits file names with a maximum of 8+3 characters).

```
mke2fs [-c] [-m percentage] [-i bytes] [-b
    bytes] file
```

mke2fs creates a new Extended-2 file system on a block device (hard disk, floppy disk, ramdisk, ...) or in a file; existing data are deleted. mke2fs can only be applied to file systems that are not mounted.

-c   Before creation of the file system the device is checked for errors by badblocks.

-m percentage   Determines how much disk space is reserved for root. When the hard disk is full, the administrator then has

one more reserve to regain some space. The default is 5%. For
diskettes or other portable media it can be set to 0.

-i *N*   Determines the number of bytes (*N*) per i-node. The default
is 4 KB per i-node. For bood disks this value should be reduced.

-b *N*   Determines block size; the default is 4 KB. A block can
only be filled with data from a single file, so the actual disk
space of a file is always a multiple of the block size. Large
blocks waste disk space, while small blocks encumber access
speed.

```
mkfs.minix [-c] [-i i-nodes] device blocks
```

Creates a MINIX file system an. -c triggers a preceding check with
badblocks. i specifies the number of *i-node* (not the byte/i-node
relationship as with mke2fs!). The number of 1 KB blocks must
always be specified; it is not set automatically.

```
mkswap device
```

Sets up a swap *device* (*swapping* = stores unused main memory
pages on hard disk).

```
mount [-a] [-f] [-n] [-o options] [-r] [-t
     type] [-v] [device] [mount_location]
```

Links new file systems into the directory tree. A file system is attached
to the UNIX file tree at a defined *mount location*. Unspecified
parameters are taken from the entries of the file /etc/fstab.

-a   automatically mounts all file systems specified in /etc/fstab
-f   suppresses the actual mount system invocation (practical with
option -v)
-n   suppresses entries in /etc/mtab
-o *opts*   additional *options* that depend on the respective file
system.

General options:

async   all input and output is asynchronous

auto   the file system can be mounted with the -a option

defaults   standard options: rw, suid, dev, exec, auto, nouser, async

dev   permits the use of character- and block-oriented devices

exec   permits execution of commands

noauto   can only be mounted explicitly, but not with the option -a

nodev   suppresses the use of character- and block-oriented devices

noexec   suppresses the execution of commands

nosuid   SUID and SGID bits have no effect

nouser   forbids a normal user to mount file systems

remount   permits remounting of a file systems, e.g., to change mount options

ro   mounts the file system as read-only; this option must be specified to mount CD-ROM file systems

rw   mounts the file system for reading and writing

suid   enables the execution of SUID and SGID commands

sync   all input and output operations are synchronous

user   permits a normal user to mount the file system

File-system-specific options:

case={lower|asis}   (hpfs) sets (upper/lower) case sensitivity

check=value   (ext2) enables the choice of consistency checks before mounting a file systems

none   no consistency checks

normal   check i-node and block bitmap (default)

strict   also checks consistency of free blocks

check=value   (msdos) determines the form for specifying file names

relaxed   case insensitive, long file names truncated

normal   special characters (*, ?, <, ...) not accepted (default)

strict   no long file names and no special characters

conv=*value*   determines whether end-of-line (EOL)
character is converted on access to file system
(msdos, hpfs, iso9660)

binary   no EOL conversion (default)

text   CRLF/LF conversion for all files

auto   no conversion on files with the following
extensions: exe, com, bin, app, sys, drv, ovl,
ovr, obj, lib, dll, pif, arc, zip, lha, zoo, tar,
z, arj, tz, taz, tzp, tpz, gif, bmp, tif, gl, jpg,
pcx, tfm, vf, gf, pk, pxl, dvi

block=*value*   specifies block size for iso9660 file systems

cruft   sets the cruft flag to overcome an error in certain
CD-ROM premastering programs (iso9660)

debug   creates debug messages (ext2, msdos)

errors=*value*   determines error handling (ext2)

continue   no special error handling (default)

remount ro   file system is remounted as read-only

panic   on error, force a kernel panic

fat=*value*   overwrites the automatically detected *value*
for the FAT type (available values being 12 and 16)
(msdos)

gid=*value*   establishes the GID for each file of the file
system (msdos, hpfs)

grpid   new files receive the same GID as the directory in
which they are created (ext2)

nocheck   equivalent to check=none (ext2)

nogrpid   new files receive the GID of the creating process,
as in System V (ext2, default)

norock   turns off Rockridge extensions, ending case
sensitivity and long file names (iso9660)

quiet   suppresses corresponding error messages on
attempts to execute the commands chmod and chown
(msdos)

sb=*value*   uses an alternative superblock at the specified
block position (normally at positions 1, 8193, 16385, ...)
(ext2)

sysvgroups   see nogrpid

uid=*value*   determines the GID for each file in the file
     system (msdos, hpfs)

umask=*value*   determines the umask for files (msdos, hpfs)

-r   file system is mounted as read-only

-t *type*   mounts a file system of a certain *type* (default: minix;
     possible values: minix, ext, etx2, xiafs, msdos, hpfs,
     proc, nfs, iso9660, sysv, xenix, coherent)

-v   outputs verbose messages

16.9   On-Line Manual

```
apropos terms
```

Searches the command descriptions in the Manual pages for the
terms passed as parameters and displays the descriptions of the
appropriate commands. This is equivalent to the command **man -k**.
(Also see whatis.)

```
info
```

Starts the GNU Info Browser. Info files are hypertext documentation
on GNU software packages.

```
man [-a] [-f] [-h] [-k] [-M path] [-w]
    [[section] name]
```

Displays On-Line Manual pages pagewise on the screen. These pages
are located in a subdirectory under /usr/man or in other directories
listed in the environment variable MANPATH. Under X-Windows there
is also the alternative xman.

-a   displays all Manual pages that match the specified name

-f   equivalent to the command whatis

-h   displays a help page

-k   equivalent to the command apropos

-M *path*   specifies a list of additional directories in which to
search for Manual pages (normally only the directories listed
in MANPATH are searched)

-w   displays not the contents but the access path of a Manual page

```
whatis [commands]
```

Outputs a short description of the specified commands from the
On-Line Manual.

```
whereis [-b|-m|-s] topic
```

Determines the path where the Manual page, the source code, or the
program file *command* reside.

-b   search only for program
-m   search only for Manual page
-s   search only for source code

```
xman
```

Like man, but with comfortable X-Windows interface. In addition,
you can search in the Manual tables of contents.

16.10   Development and installation

```
ar [-]{m|p|q|r|t|x}[a][b][c][d][i][o][s][u][v]
    [position_name] archive [files]
```

Processes an *archive* file, which is usually a C compiler library.
With this command you can combine any binary *files* to a library or
extract *files* from a library. Only one *operation* may be specified,
but multiple options are permitted.
    Available operations:

d   deletes the *files* from the *archive*

m   moves the *files* to the *archive* (with the position depending on additional arguments)

p   lists the *files* in the *archive*

q   appends the specified *files* to the end of the *archive*

r   replaces the specified *files* in the *archive* with the new files

t   lists the contents of an *archive* (with argument *v* providing a verbose list output)

x   extracts all files or only those specified from the *archive*

Available options:

a   places the *files* in the *archive* after *position name* (can be specified with *r* or *m*)

b   places the files in the *archive* before *position name* (can be specified with *r* or *m*)

c   creates the *archive*

i   see argument b

o   retains the original file date on extraction

s   creates the file table of the *archive* anew

u   replaces only files that have been modified (can be specified with *r*)

v   outputs detailed messages for every operation

```
as[options]
```

UNIX Assembler; under Linux GNU's i386-Assembler or Cross-Assembler. See GNU Info pages about as.

```
bison[-y]
```

GNU's Version of the UNIX parser generator yacc. -y activates full yacc compatibility. See GNU Info pages about bison.

```
cc
```

The traditional UNIX C compiler. Under Linux cc is only a link to gcc.

```
ci file
```

RCS check-in for a file: If the associated RCS file does not exist, it is created. If it does exist, the new version of the file is saved therein. If the previous version is locked, the file is stored anew under the next highest version number; otherwise the previous file is overwritten.

```
co [-l|-u]
```

RCS check-out: The newest version of a file is extracted. -l sets a lock on the current version to force incrementation of the version number on the next check-in. -u is the default and does not set a lock—the file is simply extracted for compilation or other use.

```
cpp
```

The C/C++ preprocessor.

```
ctags [-a] [-B] [-C] [-d] [-f file] [-F] [-H]
      [-i file] [-o file] [-S] [-t] [-T] [-u]
      [-v] [-V] [-w] [-x] files
```

Reads the specified C, Fortran, Pascal, LaTeX, or Lisp source *files*   ctags
and generates a list of functions and macros defined therein. This list
can be processed in the vi or emacs editor. A keyword list (tag file)
is generated with the name tags in the current directory.

-a   appends the names found to an existing list
-B   generates a search pattern for a backwards search in vi

483

-C   activates C++ mode, where `.c` and `.h` files are treated as C++ code

-d   generates entries for preprocessor definitions as well

-f *file*   writes the names it finds to *file*. If `-f` is not specified, then the file `tags` is used

-F   generates a search pattern for forward search in `vi` (default)

-H   displays a help text

-i *file*   continues the search for a tag in the specified *file*

-o *file*   changes the name of the output *file*

-s   ignores indents

-t   also generates a tag for type definitions

-T   also generates a tag for type definitions, structures, enumerations, and C++ member functions

-u   updates the tag list

-v   generates an index file in `vgrind` format and outputs it to the standard output device

-V   displays the version number

-w   suppresses warnings about duplicate entries

-x   generates a cross-reference list in `cxref` format and outputs it to the standard output device

```
flex
```

GNU's `lex` clone.

```
gcc
```

In addition to C, C++, and Objective C, the GNU C compiler supports back ends for other languages such as Ada and Pascal. A more detailed description of these features can be found in the GNU Info documents.

```
gprof
```

Profiler for programs that were compiled with the `gcc` option `-pg`. See GNU Info pages about `gprof`.

```
gdb [executable [core-dump | PID]]
```

The GNU Debugger allows debugging of programs that were compiled with the cc option -g. It is quite Spartan, but astonishingly powerful: it supports hardware watchpoints and breakpoints as well as debugging of running processes (with specification of *PID*) and the analysis of core files. A highlight is debugging of the running Linux kernel, although with restricted influence. See GNU Info pages about gdb.

```
g++
```

Compiler for C++ programs (can also be invoked via gcc).

```
ident file
```

Extracts the RCS identification (author/maintainer, version, version date, etc.) from a source code file.

```
indent file
```

Indents lines in source code according to the usual convention.

```
ld object_files
```

The linker links individual *object files* to an executable program. It is seldom invoked directly. Normally the C compiler or the make command automatically invokes the linker.

```
ldd [-d] [-r] [-v] [-V] [programs]
```

Lists the dynamic libraries that a *program* needs.

-d   carries out a relocation and lists missing functions (only ELF format)

-r   carries out a relocation for data and program code and lists
      missing objects (only ELF format)
-v   outputs the version number of the command
-V   outputs the version number of the dynamic linker

```
lex files
```

The scanner generator creates the output file lex.yy.c from a
scanner grammar as input file.

```
m4
```

This macro processor is used for various program files, in the GNU
Autoconf system, and for fvwm configuration files. The language is
described in the GNU Info system.

```
make [-C] [-d] [-e] [-f] [-I] [-k] [-n] [-p]
     [-r] [-s] [-t] [-w] [targets]
```

Reads a makefile and updates one or more targets. make is usually
used for compiling of source files. It is described in detail in the GNU
Info system.

-C directory   changes to the specified subdirectory before
                a makefile is read
-d   provides additional debugging information
-e   environment variables overwrite corresponding variables in the
      makefile
-f makefile   uses the specified makefile
-I directory   searches in the specified directory for
                imported makefiles
-k   on error, aborts only the current target, not the complete make
      process
-n   only outputs commands without executing them
-p   outputs internal macro definitions

`-r` uses no default rules

`-s` suppresses screen output

`-t` provides *files* to be processed with the current date without executing the corresponding operation

`-w` displays the current working directory before and after executing an operation

```
nm files
```

Outputs the symbol table of object *files* or libraries.

```
objcopy
```

Copies the contents of one object file (`.o`) to another.

```
objdump
```

Outputs various information from the headers of an object file or disassembles it.

```
patch
```

From standard input, reads a patchfile created by `diff` and *patches* the specified files. The format of the patchfile is usually recognized automatically. `patch` serves to integrate bugfixes or program extensions.

```
ranlib file
```

Searches through the object files contained in a `.a` archive and creates a global symbol table for the entire archive. This expedites linking to the archive file.

```
rcs
```

rcs processes RCS files. RCS (*Revision Control System*) is a system for managing versions of files (source code or configuration files).

```
rlog file
```

Outputs the file versions and comments in an RCS file.

```
strace [-f] [-o file] command arguments...
```

Protocols all system invocations of a process, including parameters and return values. This is a very useful utility for programmers and system administrators in search of errors.

-f child processes fork() ed by the started process are also controlled. The output has the corresponding PID in square brackets before each system invocation.

-o The protocol is redirected to a file.

```
strip files
```

Strips symbol, debug, line numbers, and other information from object *files* and programs, thus reducing their size.

16.11 File processing

```
awk [-f file] [-F c] [-v var=value] [program]
    files
```

awk is a simple interpreter with the combined functionality of grep and sed. It contains its own C-like language. awk is particularly suitable for evaluating ASCII files and for creating scripts for system administration.

-f *file*   reads the program from the specified *file* instead of the command line

-F *c*   sets the delimiting character for fields to *c*

-v *var=value*   assigns the variable *var* the specified *value*

```
cmp [-c] [-l] [-s] file1 [file2]
```

Compares the contents of two files bytewise. If the files are identical, 0 is returned; otherwise, 1. If - is specified as the file name, then the command reads from the standard input device. The same applies if *file2* is not specified.

-c   displays the characters that are different

-l   displays the offset and octal values of deviating bytes

-s   suppresses all screen output

```
comm [-1] [-2] [-3] file1 file2
```

Compares two linewise presorted files. Without additional options the output is in three columns: the first column contains the lines that occur only in *file1*, the second column displays all lines that occur exclusively in *file2*, and the third column contains all common lines.

-1   suppresses column 1

-2   suppresses column 2

-3   suppresses column 3

```
csplit [-f prefix] [-b suffix] [-k] [-n n] [-q]
       [-s] [-z] file [expression]
```

Splits the specified *file* into multiple smaller files and displays the sizes of the generated files. If the specified file name is -, then data are read from the standard input device. The locations for the splitting can be specified by an optional *expression* of the following form:

number   specifies the number of lines after which a new output file is to be created

/regexp/[offset]   regular expression that specifies the splitting locations; an optional positive (+) or negative (–) line offset can be defined

%regexp%[offset]   like the above expression, but in this case the specified section is skipped rather than written to a file

{repetitions}   induces the repeated application of an expression to which it is appended. If an asterisk (*) is specified instead of a number, then the expression is applied until the end of the input file is reached

Options:

-f *prefix*   specifies the prefix for the generated output files

-b *suffix*   changes the suffix of the generated files; the format of suffix is based on the format commands of printf(); %d sets the number of the output file in decimal form, while %x results in hexadecimal representation

-k   already generated files are preserved, even if the command is aborted

-n *n*   length of the sequential number in the name of the output files (default 2)

-q   suppresses screen output

-s   see -q

-z   suppresses the generation of files of length 0

Examples:

```
golem:~> csplit -k linux.txt '%cut%' {30}
```

splits the file linux.txt at positions cut into at most 30 output files

```
golem:~> csplit -k list.txt 10 '{100}'
```

splits the file list.txt into at most 100 files with 10 lines each

```
cut [-b list] [-c list] [-d c] [-f list] [-s]
    [files]
```

Cuts a series of fields or columns from a line of the input file. One of the options -b, -c, or -f must be specified. Each of these options expects a list that can contain numbers separated by commas or fields defined by hyphens.

-b *list*   selects the character at the position defined in *list*

-c *list*   selects the columns specified in *list*

-d *c*   is output together with -f to specify the field delimiter character (*c*)

-f *list*   selects the fields (separated by tabulators or the delimiting character) from *list*

-s   restricts output to lines that contain the field separator

Example:

```
golem:~> cut -d: -f1, 3 /etc/passwd
```

outputs the login names and user IDs of all users

```
diff [-a] [-b] [-B] [-c] [-C n] [-d] [-D name]
     [-e] [-f] [-h] [-H] [-i] [-l] [-n] [-N]
     [-q] [-r] [-s] [-S file] [-t] [-t] [-u]
     [-w] [-xpattern] [-y] file1 file2
```

Compares two files or all files in two directories. If one of the two paths is specified as -, then the files are expected from the standard input device. The output of diff lists all lines that occur in only one file or that are different. This output can be used by patch to make changes in files. Another alternative for comparing or merging files is the Emacs Lisp program ediff.

-a   treats all input files as text files and compares linewise

491

-b   ignores differences in the number of blanks (at the end of a line as well)

-B   ignores blanks

-c   generates output with three lines of context around each difference

-C *n*   like -c, but *n* lines of context are output around each difference

-d   uses a better, although slower, algorithm for file comparison

-D *name*   mixes the two files and inserts appropriate preprocessor instructions (#ifdef *name*) to make the two versions distinguishable. If *name* is defined during compilation, then the version is output to *file1*, otherwise to *file2*

-e   outputs instructions for the ed editor to be able to generate *file2* from *file1*

-f   like option -e, but reversed, yet it cannot be used as an ed script

-h   is ignored

-H   uses heuristics to increase the speed

-i   ignores differences in upper/lower case

-l   (only when comparing whole directories) the output can be processed with the command pr so that each file begins on a new page

-n   generates output in RCS format

-N   in comparing two directories, missing files are considered as existing, but empty

-q   simply reports whether the files are different

-r   (only when comparing whole directories) subdirectories are handled recursively and all files are compared

-s   reports whether two files are identical

-S *file*   starts comparing directories with a certain file

-t   replaces tabs with blanks

-T   outputs a tab instead of a blank at the start of every output line

-u   generates output in GNU-specific "unified" format

-v   displays the version number

-w   ignores blanks and tabs when comparing lines

-x *pattern*   ignores files and subdirectories that match the specified *pattern* (when comparing whole directories)

-y   outputs in easy-to-read, two-column format

```
diff3 [-a] [-A] [-e] [-E] [-i] [-m] [-T] [-v]
      [-x] [-X] [-3] file1 file2 file3
```

Compares three files linewise.

-a linewise comparison treating all input files as text files
-A inserts all changes between *file2* and *file3* in *file1* and marks conflicts
-e generates a script for the ed editor that integrate all changes from *file2* to *file3* in *file1*
-E like option -e, but the output is less verbose
-i generates w and q commands at the end of a generated ed script
-m applies the edit script to *file1* and displays it
-T outputs a tab instead of a blank at the start of every output line
-v outputs the version number of the command
-x like option -e, but only overlapping changes are output
-X like option -E, but only overlapping changes are output
-3 like option -e, but only nonoverlapping changes are output

```
expand file
```

Replaces tabs with blanks (default: 8).

```
gawk
```

The awk clone from GNU.

```
grep [-b] [-c] [-h] [-i] [-l] [-n] [-s] [-v]
     regexp [files]
```

Searches *files* or data from the standard input device linewise for a regular expression (regexp) and outputs the found lines to the standard output device.

-b additionally outputs the byte position where the expression was found

493

-c   outputs only the number of lines in which the expression was found

-h   suppresses the output of file names

-i   ignores differences in size and (upper/lower) case

-l   outputs only the names, but not the lines, of files in which the expression was found

-n   outputs the line numbers of found lines

-s   suppresses error messages in case a file does not exist or cannot be opened

-v   searches for lines that do not contain the regular expression

```
head [-n] [-c n[b¦k¦m]] [files]
```

Displays the first 10 lines of the specified (text) *files*. On specification of multiple files, the file name precedes the file contents in the output.

-n   changes the number of lines to be output to the specified value

-c *n*[b¦k¦m]   outputs the first *n* bytes, where the specification can be made in bytes (b), kilobytes (k), or megabytes (m)

-q   suppresses the output of file name

```
join [-a n] [-e string] [-jn m] [-o] file1
     file2
```

Joins two alphabetically sorted ASCII files via a key. Lines with identical keys are joined and written to the standard output device. Keys must be separated by blanks or tabs. If no further options are specified, the first column is used as the key.

-a *n*   adds an empty line to the output if one line of file *n* (1 or 2) does not have a matching key in the other file

-e *string*   replaces empty output fields with the specified character *string*

-j*n* *m*   uses column *m* of file *n* (1 or 2) as the key

-t *z*   uses character *z* as field delimiter (input/output)

```
sdiff file1 file2
```

Compares two files and outputs the differences in two columns (also   sdiff
see diff). This output is easier to read than that of diff. Lines that
are not contained in one of the two files are marked with <or >. A
pair of lines that differ are indicated with ¦.

```
sed [-e commands] [-f file] [-n] [files]
```

Modifies without interaction with the user. This command is usually
used in shell scripts to replace, delete, or insert text. If no file is
specified, then sed works with the standard input device.

-e commands   appends commands to the command list
-f file   reads the edit statements from script file
-n   suppresses the echo of input lines on the screen

```
golem:~> cat speech ¦ sed '/Eurasia/s//East Asia/' > newspeech
```

Greetings from Orwell... All occurrences of "Eurasia" are replaced
by "East Asia."

```
sort [+n -m] [-b] [-c] [-d] [-f] [-i] [-m] [-M]
     [-n] [-o file] [-r] [-t char] [-u] [files]
```

Sorts the lines in the specified files. If no files are specified, the
standard input device is processed.

+n -m   sets the sorting key between fields n and m
-b   suppresses leading blanks
-c   checks whether the specified files are already sorted; if so, the
       program terminates with an error message
-d   ignores punctuation marks during sorting
-f   case-sensitive (upper/lower)
-i   ignores nonprintable ASCII characters

495

-m   mixes two input *files*

-M   interprets the first three characters as a month name (JAN, FEB, ..., DEC) and sorts by month

-n   sorts numerically

-o *file*   redirects the standard output device to a file

-r   inverts sorting order

-t *char*   specifies the delimiting character for columns (default: blank or tab)

-u   removes duplicate lines

Example:

```
golem:~> sort +2n -t: /etc/passwd
```

sorts the password file numerically according to the third column

```
strings [-a] [-f] [-n] [-o] files
```

Searches for character strings in binary and object *files* or programs. A character string is considered to be any sequence of four or more printable characters terminated with null.

-a   normally for object files, only the code and data segments are searched; this option assures that the whole file is processed

-f   each character string is preceded by the corresponding file name

-n   specifies the minimum length of the character string (default: 4)

-o   outputs the position of a character string in bytes

```
tail -c [b¦k¦m] -f -n -v [files]
```

Outputs the last 10 lines of the specified *files*.

-c *[b¦k¦m]*   outputs the last *n* bytes in blocks (b), kilobytes (k), or megabytes (m)

-f   does not terminate after outputting the last lines, but waits until the *file* is written to; as soon as new lines are appended to the *file*, they are output; in this mode the program is terminated with break ([**Ctrl**]+[**C**]); this mode proves especially suitable for monitoring log files

-n   outputs the last *n* lines

-v   outputs the file name as title line

```
tr [-c] [-d] [-s] [string1 [string2]]
```

Copies the standard input device to the standard output device and in the process replaces or deletes characters. If a character from string1 is found in the standard input device, then it is replaced with the corresponding character from string2.

-c   outputs the complement of the set of characters in string1

-d   deletes characters that appear in string1

-s   suppresses repeated sequences in the output

```
uniq [-c] [-d] [-u] [-n] [+n] [-w] [file1
      [file2]]
```

Deletes successive identical lines in the linewise sorted *file1* and outputs these to *file2* (or the standard output device).

-c   outputs the number of repetitions

-d   outputs only lines that occur redundantly

-u   outputs only lines that occur uniquely

-n   skips a number *n* of fields (with tabs and blanks as delimiters) before comparing two lines

+n   skips *n* characters before beginning to compare

-w   specifies the number of characters to be compared

```
wc [-c] [-l] [-w] [files]
```

Counts the number of characters, words, and lines in a text *file*.

-c   only the number of characters

-1   only the number of lines

-w   only the number of words

16.12   Text formatting

```
dvilp
```

Converts .dvi files to PCL (HP Deskjet).

```
dvips
```

Converts .dvi files to PostScript.

```
groff [-a] [-e] [-E] [-h] [-m macro] [-p] [-s]
    [-t] [-Tformat] [-v] [files]
```

groff is the GNU variant of nroff and troff. The command serves to format Manual pages and other documents that are available in the appropriate format. Additional preprocessors such as eqn or tbl are integrated in groff and can be activated with options. The results can be stored in ASCII, DVI, or PostScript format. In formatting documents, it is important to specify the macro package used. For Manual pages, for example, the option -man would be specified. The formatted file is written to the standard output device.

-a   outputs pure ASCII format

-e   activates the eqn preprocessor

-E   suppresses error messages

-h   outputs help text

    -m macro   uses a special macro package for formatting

    an   macros for Manual pages

    s   ms macro package

-p   activates pic preprocessor

-s   activates soelim preprocessor

-t   activates `tab` preprocessor

-T *format*   specifies output *format* (ascii, ps, dvi)

-v   outputs the version number

Example:

```
golem:~> groff -man -Tps ls.1 > ls.ps
```

formats the Manual page `ls.1` with the corresponding macro package and outputs the result in PostScript format to the file `ls.ps`

```
nroff files
```

Formats *files* that contain corresponding format statements for output on the screen or the printer (see also `groff`).

```
pr [-column] [+page] [-a] [-c] [-d]
    [-e[chars[width]]] [-f] [-h]
    [-i[chars[width]]] [-l] [-n[chars[width]]]
    [-o] [-r] [-t] [-v] [-w] [-x] [files]
```

Prepares text *files* for printing. The *file* contents are prepared pagewise and provided with a title line containing the date, the file name, and the page number.

+*page*   begins printing starting with the specified *page*

-*column*   produces multiple-*column* output

-a   prints columns alongside rather than under one another

-c   outputs nonprintable characters in ^ notation

-d   double-spaced printout

-e[*chars*[*width*]]   replaces any number of *characters* with a number of blanks; the default value for tab characters is 8 blanks

-f   produces a form feed at the end of a page instead of generating a series of blank lines

-h *text*　　replaces the file name in the title line with the specified
　　　text

-i[*chars*[*width*]]　　reverse effect of option -e

-l *length*　　determines the *length* of a page (default 66 lines)

-n[*chars*[*width*]]　　outputs a sequential number before each
　　　line; optionally, a *character* that separates the number from the
　　　text and the *width* of the number can be specified

-o *width*　　creates a left margin of specified *width*

-r　　suppresses error messages for files that cannot be opened

-t　　suppresses the header and footer

-v　　outputs nonprintable characters in format

-w　　specifies page width in characters (default 72)

-x　　displays the processes that are not assigned to a terminal

```
troff
```

Formats files for printer or linotronic machine (also see nroff and
groff).

16.13　Time

```
at [-b] [-d] [-f file] [-l] [-m] [-qQ] [-V]
    time
```

Executes commands at a certain *time*. The commands are entered
at the standard input device and terminated with EOF (⎡Ctrl⎤ + ⎡D⎤).
Option -f permits alternative input from a shell script. A Bourne
shell (/bin/sh) is used for execution.

Via the option -q individual jobs can be assigned to different
queues (a-z, A-Z), where letters later in the alphabet reflect
decreasing priority.

The *time* can be specified in numeric form (HHMM, HH:MM)
or with a keyword such as noon, teatime (16:00), or midnight.
Alternatively, the *time* can be specified as a difference such as
now +3 hours. Minutes, hours, days, weeks, months, and years are

permissible units. If the job is to run on a certain day, then the month (Jan, Feb, Mar, ...) and the year (97, 98, ...) are specified additionally.

-b   equivalent to the command `batch`
-d   removes the specified jobs from the queue (`atrm`)
-f *file*   executes the commands in *file*
-l   lists the current user's jobs (`atq`)
-m   sends an e-mail to the user when the commands have been completed
-q *Q*   assigns a job to a particular queue specified in *Q* (a-z, A-Z)
-V   returns the version number

```
atq [-q Q] [-V] [-v]
```

Displays the jobs that are yet to be executed by the user's `at` commands.

-q *Q*   restricts output to the contents of a specific queue *Q*
-V   displays the version number of the command
-v   displays a list of jobs that have been executed, but not deleted

```
atrm [-V] jobs
```

Removes the specified at-*jobs*. A *job* is identified by its job ID, displayed by the `at` or `atq` command.

-V   displays the version number

```
atrun
```

This program is invoked regularly by `cron` to process the queued `at` jobs.

```
batch [-f file] [-m] [-q] [-V] [time]
```

Behaves like the at command. However, it only executes the specified commands when the system load is low. (Also see at.)

-f *file*   executes the commands specified in *file*

-m   sends an e-mail to the user when the commands have been completed

-q *Q*   assigns the job to the queue specified in *Q* (a-z, A-Z)

-V   displays the version number

```
cal [-j] [-y] [[month] year]
```

Displays a calendar for the current *month* or a specified *month* or *year*. The number of the *year* must be given in long form (e.g., 1997) and the *month* as a number (1–12).

-j   displays a Julian calendar (with days numbered sequentially)

-y   displays a calendar for the current year

```
cron
crond
```

The cron daemon (or sometimes crond) executes certain commands in the background at certain times. This might include backups on magnetic tape overnight or every 15 minutes collecting data for load statistics. cron is generally started automatically on booting. Which commands are executed when is recorded in /var/cron/ or in /var/spool/cron/crontab/—there each user has a file (with a matching name) containing the user's *cron-Jobs*. The jobs can be changed with the command crontab.

```
crontab {file|-|-l|-e|-d|-c} [-u user]
```

Replaces, edits, lists, or deletes a user's `crontab` file. The administrator can process any user's `crontab` file by using the option `-u`.

-e   edits the `crontab` file in the default editor (environment variable `EDITOR`)

-l   lists a user's `crontab` file

-r   deletes the `crontab` file

```
date [+format]
date [-d] [-s date] [-u] [string]
```

In the former form, the current date and time are returned in a `format` that can be provided optionally. With the second form, the system administrator can set the system time.

Output `format`:

%%   percent sign

%n   new line

%t   tabulator

%H   hour (00..23)

%I   hour (01..12)

%k   hour (0..23)

%l   hour (1..12)

%M   minute (00..59)

%p   AM or PM

%r   time in 12-hour format (hh:mm:ss[AM|PM])

%s   seconds since January 1, 1970, 0:00

%S   seconds (00..59)

%T   time in 24-hour format

%X   time in local format

%Z   time zone, if defined, else empty

%a   local abbreviation of day name

%A   local name of day of week

`%b`   local abbreviation of month name (Jan. . . Dec)

`%B`   local month name (January. . . December)

`%c`   local date with time and time zone

`%d`   day of month (01. . 31)

`%D`   date (mm/dd/yy)

`%h`   identical to `%b`

`%j`   sequential day of the year (001 .. 366)

`%m`   month as number (01 .. 12)

`%U`   week as number (0053) where Sunday is the first day

`%w`   day of week as number (0 .. 6)

`%W`   week as number (00 .. 53) where Monday is the first day

`%x`   local representation of the date (dd/mm/yy)

`%y`   last two digits of the year (00 .. 99)

`%Y`   year (1997 . . .)

Format of the *string* to set the time:

`DD`   day of month

`hh`   hour

`mm`   minute

`CC`   first two digits of year (=century)

`YY`   last two digits of year

`ss`   seconds

Options:

`-d` *date*   outputs the specified date (which can contain the month name, time zone, ...)

`-s` *date*   sets the date in arbitrary format (which can contain the month name, time zone, ...)

`-u`   ignores time zone and uses UTC (Universal Coordinated Time)

```
sleep time
```

Sleeps the specified *time* in seconds. This command is usually used in shell scripts.

```
time command [arguments]
```

Executes the specified command and then displays the execution time.

```
touch [-a] [-c] [-m] [-r file] [-t value] files
```

Changes the last access date/time and the last modification date/time of *files*. If a specified *file* does not exist, it is created as empty.

-a   changes only the time of the last access
-c   disables the creation of empty files for nonexistent ones
-m   changes only the time of the last modification
-r *file*   transfers the time from a specified reference *file*
-t *value*   sets the file date and the system time to the specified *value* with the format MMDDhhmm (month, day, hour, minute)

16.14   Internet and communication

```
arp
```

Outputs the kernel ARP table, or sets or deletes entries. In most cases the kernel resolves IP addresses independently, so that arp is not needed.

```
dig
```

DNS server query.

```
finger [-l] [-m] [-p] [-s] [user]
```

Provides information on users. *user* can be in the form of *name*, *name@host*, or *@host*. In the first two forms the names of the users, the times, the last logins, and additional information are output. If the file .plan or .project exists in the *user*'s home directory, then it is also displayed. If only one host is specified with @*host*, then all users are listed who are currently logged into that system.

-l   forces verbose output (at @*host*)

-m the specified *user* must exactly match the user name; without this option the specified name is also compared with the full name of the user as stored in the file /etc/passwd

-p the files .plan and .project of the respective *user* are not displayed

-s forces brief output format

```
ftp [-d] [-g] [-i] [-n] [-v] [host]
```

This program is for transferring files with the ftp protocol. The *host* can be specified by name or IP address. If no *host* is specified, then the program responds with a prompt that allows entry of ftp commands. Entering **help** evokes a help text.

-d debug mode

-g toggles off the use of wildcards for file names

-i   turns off queries (mget, mput)

-n suppresses automatic login on computer listed in the file .netrc

-v displays all the ftp server's messages

```
host hostname
```

Resolution of host names; dig is more multifaceted.

```
ifconfig
```

For configuration of network adapters (Ethernet, ISDN, ...) and kernel network interfaces.

```
golem:~> ifconfig eth0 141.7.11.12
```

Directs the kernel to use IP address 141.7.11.12 for Ethernet adapter eth0.

```
mail addresses
```

This program is for reading and sending e-mail. Users should instead use the program pine or a graphical mail reader. However, mail proves superb for simply sending text files because the contents can be transferred via the standard input device.

Example:

```
golem:~> mail linux@fh-heilbronn.de < critique.txt
```

```
mesg [y¦n]
```

Determines whether other users can write messages on the terminal with write. If mesg is invoked without options, the current status is displayed.

```
netdate [tcp¦udp] host
```

Synchronizes the local host's clock with the specified hosts.

```
netstat [-i¦-r¦-t¦-u¦-x] [-n]
```

Outputs network Infos:

-i   statistics and setting of the various network interfaces
-r   routing table
-t   displays all TCP sockets and connections and their status

-u   displays all UDP sockets and their status

-x   displays all UNIX domain sockets and connections (local interprocess communication primitives, not network connections)

-n   prevents resolution of IP addresses in DNS names; recommended if a DNS server cannot be reached due to network problems

```
nslookup [options]
```

Query to DNS servers.

```
golem:~> nslookup
> set type=A
> lem.stud.fh-heilbronn.de
Server:   urmel.Informatik.RWTH-Aachen.DE
Address:  137.226.112.21

Name:     lemming.stud.fh-heilbronn.de
Address:  141.7.11.12
Aliases:  lem.stud.fh-heilbronn.de
```

A records are host addresses.

```
ping host
```

Each second, sends an ICMP echo request packet to the specified host. This helps to diagnose packet losses (if only some of the packets are echoed) on the network connection or a crashed target host (if there is no echo at all).

```
rarp
```

Ouputs the kernel RARP table or complements or deletes entries.

```
rcp [-r] [-p] sources target
```

Copies files between computers. The sources and the target are in the form user@host:path, whereby user@ can be omitted, in which case the current user name is used. For local files only the path is specified.

-r   recursively copies subdirectories and their contents

-p   retains the file attributes (date, permissions) during copying

```
rlogin [-l name] host
```

Similar to telnet, this command provides a connection to the specified *host* and logs in there. If the current user is entered on the remote *host* in the files .rhosts or /etc/hosts.equiv, then no password is required.

-l *name*   uses *name* as the user name on the remote host

```
route
```

Outputs or manipulates the kernel routing table.

```
golem:~> route add default gw 141.7.11.1 dev eth0
```

"Send all IP packets to which the other routing rules do not apply to gateway 141.7.11.1. This is on the same Ethernet cable as our Ethernet interface eth0."

```
golem:~> route add 127.0.0.1 dev lo
```

"Route IP packets for 127.0.0.1 through the loopback device lo."

```
rsh [-l user] [-n] host [commands]
```

Executes commands on a remote *host*. Access must be permitted via an entry in /etc/hosts.equiv or ~/.rhosts.

-l *user*   attempts to execute the specified command under another user name

-n   redirects the standard input device to /dev/null (works around problems with csh)

Example:

```
golem:~> rsh -l uhl zeus.demo.de ls
```

executes the command ls as user uhl on the host zeus.demo.de

```
talk user[@host] [tty]
```

Sets up a talk connection to the specified *user*. If this *user* is logged in on multiple terminals, then the terminal to be used (*tty*) can be entered in the command line. A talk connection splits the terminal screen in two parts, with local input shown in the top half and remote input in the lower half. The connection is terminated with [Ctrl] + [C]. Unfortunately, there are two incompatible versions of talk, so that connection to a different platform does not always succeed.

```
telnet [host [port]]
```

Opens a connection to the specified *host* using the telnet protocol. A *port* number can be specified optionally. This program is often used to test services that are available for connections on certain ports. If no host is specified, then telnet goes into command mode, where telnet commands can be entered. The command help lists all important commands.

```
traceroute host
```

This tool for analyzing network problems determines the route that IP packets to *host* take, including waiting time.

```
uudecode [file]
```

Decodes a *file* encoded with uuencode using its original name, owner, and permissions.

```
uuencode [file] name
```

Encodes binary files so that they can be represented as ASCII files and sent via e-mail. An encoded file is 35% larger than the original. The result is written to the standard output device. The specified *name* corresponds to the file name after the file is unpacked by its recipient.

```
wall
```

Like write, only the message is written to all terminals.

```
write user [terminal]
```

Outputs a message on a certain user's *terminal*. The message is read   write by the standard input device until it encounters EOF (**Ctrl** + **D**).

```
write [user] [tty]
```

Outputs a text from standard input on one of the terminals at which *user* is logged in, assuming that the user has not suppressed message output with **mesg n**. The end of the text is indicated by **Crtl** + **D**.

16.15   Shells and shell tools

```
alias [alias=command]
alias [alias command]
```

Defines a command *alias*. The shell expands an alias in place of a command name (but not at other locations in a command) to the full command text. Options can be specified. The first syntax is used in the C shell, the second in the Bourne shell. C shells interpret the rest of the line as alias value, while sh and bash require the alias value to be in quotes (see Section 2.7). The first syntax is used by sh and bash, the second by csh and tcsh. Using alias has a drawback: A command shortcut is only accessible in one kind of shell. It is better to realize shortcuts with scripts.

```
golem:~> alias lsfd='mount -t auto /dev/fd0 /mnt; ls /mnt; umount /mnt'
```

shortcut for "display diskette contents"

```
basename pathname [suffix]
```

Clears the path and optionally a specified file extension and outputs the remaining file names to the standard output device. It is usually used in shell scripts.

```
bash
```

A command interpreter similar to Bourne shell and Korn shell.

```
csh
```

Command interpreter with a syntax based on C.

```
dirname pathname
```

Extracts the directory part of a complete path specification (counterpart to basename). If the path does not contain a file at the end, then . is returned.

```
echo [-n] [text]
```

This command is usually built into shells. It outputs *text* to the standard output device.

-n   suppresses the output of the newline character

-e   Interpret "n," "a," and other sequences as "end-of-line," "beeper," etc.

```
env [-i] [-u name] [variable=value] [command]
```

If invoked without parameters, this command produces a list of all environment variables. In addition, this command permits starting *commands* in a modified environment. In the command line, new variables can be defined or existing ones removed.

-i   ignores the inherited environment

-u *name*   removes the specified environment variable

```
expr arg1 operator arg2 [operator arg3 ... ]
```

Evaluates an expression and outputs the result to the standard output device. Expressions can be numeric, logical, or relational. This command is usually used in shell scripts.

Arithmetic operators
+, -, *, /, % (modular remainder)

Relational operators
=, !=, >, >=, <, <=

Logical operators
¦ (or), & (and), : (seek arg2 as a regular expression in arg1)

Examples:

```
golem:~> expr 7+8/2
```

evaluates to 7 (integer arithmetic, left to right!)

```
golem:~> expr $s="hello"
```

evaluates to 1 if s contains the string "hello," else 0

```
false
```

This command does nothing and returns *false* (not 0). (Also see true.)

```
ksh
```

See bash.

```
nohup command [arguments] &
```

This command is usually integrated into the shell. It prevents termination of the shell when the specified *command* terminates.

```
printenv [variable]
```

Shows all or a particular environment variable.

```
pwd
```

Outputs the complete path of the current directory.

```
tcsh
```

The expanded C shell.

```
tee [-a] [-i] [files]
```

This program is used as a filter. It copies the standard input device to the standard output device and the specified `files`.

-a   appends the data received from the standard input device to the end of the `files` instead of overwriting them

-i   ignores interrupt signals

```
test condition
```

Evaluates the specified `condition` and returns zero if the result is true, else a nonzero value. Alternatively, the `condition` can be put in square braces, which is primarily used in shell scripts.

Files

-b `file`   `file` is a block device

-c `file`   `file` is a character device

-d `file`   `file` is a directory

-f `file`   `file` is a normal file

-g `file`   set group ID bit (SGID) of `file` is set

-G `file`   effective GID matches owner's group

-k `file`   sticky bit of `file` is set

-O `file`   effective UID matches the file owner

-p `file`   `file` is a named pipe

-r `file`   `file` exists and is readable

-s `file`   `file` is larger than 0 bytes

-S `file`   `file` is a socket

-t [n]   file descriptor n (default 1) corresponds to a terminal

-u `file`   set user ID bit (SUID) of `file` is set

-w `file`   `file` exists and is writable

-x `file`   `file` exists and is executable

d1 -ef *d2*   *files d1* and *d2* are linked
d1 -nt *d2*   *file d1* is newer than *file d2*
d1 -ot *d2*   *file d1* is older than *file d2*

Character strings

-n *z1*   length of character string *z1* is greater than zero
-z *z1*   length of character string *z1* is zero
z1   character string *z1* is not null
z1=*z2*   *z1* is equal to *z2*
z1 != *z2*   *z1* is not equal to *z2*
z1< *z2*   *z1* is lexicographically smaller than *z2*
z1 > *z2*   *z1* is lexicographically greater than *z2*

Numeric conditions

n1 -eq *n2*   *n1* equals *n2*
n1 -ge *n2*   *n1* is greater than or equal to *n2*
n1 -gt *n2*   *n1* is greater than *n2*
n1 -le *n2*   *n1* is less than or equal to *n2*
n1 -lt *n2*   *n1* is smaller than *n2*
n1 -ne *n2*   *n1* is not equal to *n2*

Combinatoric conditions

! *a1*   true if expression *a1* is false
a1 -a *a2*   true if *a1* and *a2* are true
a1 -o *a2*   true if *a1* or *a2* is true

Examples

```
golem:~> if [ -f /etc/shadow ]
```

tests whether file /etc/shadow exists

```
golem:~> if [ "$res" != "j" ]
```

Does the content of the variable res equal "j"?

```
golem:~> while [ -z "$res" ]
```

Does the variable res contain an empty string?

```
umask [value]
```

Outputs the current value of the file generation mask as an octal number or sets this value. This mask determines the maximum permissions that a newly created file can receive. Here the umask value is subtracted from the permissions of the file to be created.

```
which [commands]
```

Outputs the file path of the specified commands (usually an internal shell command)

```
xargs [-0] [-e] [-l n] [-n n] [-p] [-s n] [-t]
      [commands]
```

Executes a command with the (multiple) arguments read from the standard input device. This enables passing lists of any length of arguments to commands.

-0   file names are terminated by the character null
-e string   ends processing as soon as the specified character string appears in the list of file names (default is _)
-l n   executes the command with n arguments
-n n   executes the command with at most n arguments
-p   interactive processing where the user must respond with [y] before a command is executed
-s n   each argument may contain at most n characters
-t   displays the command before its execution

16.16   Printing

```
lpc [command [argument]]
```

Serves to control printer spoolers. It enables the activation and deactivation of individual printers and their printing queues, shifting printer jobs within the printing queues, and outputting status information. Invoking `lpc` without an argument produces an interactive command modus. Alternatively, these commands can also be passed to `lpc` on invocation.

Available commands

abort {all¦*printer*}   terminates active spooler(s) and disables the corresponding *printer*(s)

clean {all¦*printer*}   removes all incomplete files from the specified *printer* queue(s)

disable {all¦*printer*}   disables the corresponding *printer*(s)

down {all¦*printer*}   turns off the specified queue, disables *printer*(s), and writes the specified *message* in the printer status file. This message is output on invocation of lpq.

enable {all¦*printer*}   enables the specified printer queue(s) and permits the addition of new jobs

exit, quit   ends the lpc program

help   displays a list of available commands

restart {all¦*printer*}   attempts to restart *printer* daemon(s)

start {all¦*printer*}   activates *printer*(s) and starts *printer* daemon(s) for the specified *printer*(s)

status {all¦*printer*}   outputs status information on currently active *printer* daemon(s) and queue(s)

stop {all¦*printer*}   stops the *printer* daemon on completion of the current job and disables the *printer*

topq *printer* [*job#*] [*user*]   places the specified job at the head of the queue up {all¦*printer*}　　　activates queue(s) and starts *printer* daemon(s)

```
lpq -1 -P name [jobs] [user]
```

Provides information on the current status of printer queues.

-1　verbose status report on each job
-P *name*　selects a printer queue

```
lpr -#n [-C text] [-h] [-J job] [-m] [-P name]
    [-r] [-s] [-U user] [files]
```

Sends *files* to a printer queue. Alternatively, data can be printed　　lpr
via the standard input device. Invocation without options outputs to
the queue *lp*.

-#*n*　creates *n* copies of the specified documents
-C *text*　prints a job classification on the title page
-h　suppresses the output of a header before a print job
-J *job*　prints a *job* name on the title page
-m　sends a mail to the user on completion of the job
-P *name*　selects the specified printer queue
-r　deletes the file after printing (with option -s)
-s　file is not spooled but linked. Thus the printer file must not be deleted during printing.
-U *user*　prints the *user* name on the title page

```
lprm - -P name [job numbers] [user]
```

Removes entries from a printer queue. *Job numbers* or *user* names can be specified as selection criteria. If no argument is specified, the active job is removed.

-　removes all entries from a queue

-P *name*   selects the specified printer queue

16.17   Miscellaneous

```
bc [-l] [-s] [-w] [files]
```

Interactive program for computation or converting numbers to another base. bc has its own language, which supports the definition of new functions, for example. bc also supports floating-point numbers; you need only set the variable SCALE to a different value: **SCALE=10**.

-l   makes the functions of the mathematics library available

-s   causes POSIX-compatible behavior

-w   displays warnings that conform to POSIX

Example

```
zeus:/home/uhl> bc
bc 1.02 (Mar3, 92) Copyright © 1991, 1992 Free Software
Foundation, Inc.
This is free software with ABSOLUTELY NO WARRANTY.
For details type 'warranty'.
a=5
b=3
a*b
15
quit
zeus:/home/uhl>
```

## Chapter 17

Error and error localization under Linux

One of the most forbidding chapters in UNIX, as with computers in general, is error localization. However, often the difficulties arise simply from a lack of information—the various programs take different approaches to outputting error messages, and often a highly interesting message lands in a quiet grave in some file deep in the Linux directory tree. This need not be the case: in the following we describe the various log files and mechanisms as well as frequent errors and error messages.

The standard error output `stderr` of each process is generally of relevance. This is a file or a terminal to which the process outputs status and error messages while it is running. Each process has its own definition of `stderr`. Just what `stderr` is depends on the specifications of the user or a shell script; in general it is the terminal where the process is running, but it could be a file on disk. Processes can also change `stderr` autonomously. If a process forks a child process, then the child inherits `stderr`—assuming that the child does not select a different standard error output, it uses the same file or the same terminal for error message output.

17.1   Where to find error messages

Terminal processes

> Processes that were launched on a terminal (one of the virtual consoles, an `xterm` window or a `TELNET` terminal), generally output error messages to `stderr`. Certain programs write their error messages in dedicated log files; these files are noted in the Manual pages (usually under `FILES`).

X-Windows; fvwm

> For programs launched from `xterm`, the comments above apply. If a program was launched via the `fvwm` menu or the `fvwm` toolbar, then its standard error output matches that of `fvwm` (see `fvwm`).

fvwm

> `fvwm` writes its own error messages and those of programs that were started from its menus, toolbar, or configuration files to `stderr`. What that is depends on how `fvwm` was invoked, usually in `/usr/lib/X11/xdm/Xsession` or `/usr/lib/X11/xinit/xinitrc`. If `stderr` was redirected (e.g., with `2> /somewhere/fvwm-errors`), then error messages can be found there. Otherwise standard error output is identical with that of `xdm` or `xinit`—depending on whether X-Windows was launched with `xdm` or `startx` (see below).

xdm

`/usr/lib/X11/xdm/xdm-config`

> `stderr` for `xdm` is specified in the configuration file `/usr/lib/X11/xdm/xdm-config (.errorLogFile)`.

xinit

> `stderr` for `xinit` is the terminal from which `xinit` or `startx` was started. If X-Windows starts automatically on booting, this is the first virtual terminal, reached with `Ctrl` + `Alt` + `F1`.

Daemon

`/etc/syslog.conf`

> Linux's various daemons (such as `cron` [see below], `lpd`, or especially the numerous Internet daemons such as `inetd`) use the `syslog` system for error messages. A special daemon named `syslogd` handles this, accepting messages from various sources and distributing them according to its configuration file `/etc/syslog.conf` to a handful of log files. Alternatively, it is possible to forward messages to another host on the network, so that error messages for a whole LAN can be collected and evaluated on a central log host. For configuration, see `man syslogd(8)` and `syslog.conf(5)`.

cron

> Output from cron jobs are sent as mails if the respective crontab has a MAILTO= entry specified. In fact, the variant crond has no other possibility.
>
> syslogd usually manages its log files under /var/adm or /var/log. Important files include /var/log/messages (which collects all messages) and /var/log/syslog (which collects only error messages, including warnings). Over time, the log files become quite inflated. This encourages regular archiving (e.g., with a cron job) and deletion of old files. In addition, for evaluating the files, the command tail proves useful: it reads only the last lines, i.e., the chronologically newest messages. For configuration of syslogd, see Section 6.3.

Kernel

> Kernel messages, inasmuch as they regard erroneous behavior, are written to the first virtual console. For this purpose, the kernel has a small circular buffer that contains the last handful of messages. This buffer can be read with dmesg. The use of klogd is recommended—it reads kernel messages and passes them to the syslog system.

17.2   Some errors and their possible causes

Output on a terminal is suddenly frozen; even ^C does not work.

> Perhaps you unintentionally pressed [Ctrl] + [S]; this key combination halts the foreground process and terminal output. Press [Ctrl] + [Q] to continue.

mkfs fails on a partition over 2 GB.

> You are using an old version of the ext2 tools. Install the newest version of the package e2fsprogs.*

The command df gets stuck at a certain position.

> One of the file systems has problems (e.g., floppies or NFS file systems). You can only try to correct the problem (e.g., restore connection to NFS server).

*Sunsite: system/Filesystems/ext2

A process cannot be terminated with Ctrl + C.

Many processes make use of the possibility of intercepting and then ignoring the signal SIGINT triggered by Ctrl + C. Determine the PID of the processes with **ps -ax** ¦ **grep** *name* and try **kill** *PID* instead. If the process continues to run, then it has also ignored the signal SIGTERM. The signal **kill -KILL** *PID* cannot be intercepted. If the process still continues to run, then it is dormant in a system function—uninterruptably. ps displays this state with a D in the STAT field. Usually the process is carrying out disk operations (processes in other system functions can indeed be interrupted). Wait for a while to see if it returns from this state by itself. If not, an error has occurred. Perhaps the process is attempting to access a file in an NFS file system while the connection to the NFS server has broken down. If you cannot correct the cause, the problem can be corrected only by waiting or by rebooting.

make reports no makefile found, although there is one in the current directory.

Your make version no longer works with newer libcs. At the end of the file release.libc-5.0.9 is a patch for make sources; in newer make versions this error should already have been corrected.

On booting, the message LILO appears distorted or not at all; this is followed by curious error codes or nothing.

/usr/lib/lilo/doc/user.tex

The boot sector has been damaged by some accident. Boot from diskette and install the boot sector with lilo. An overview of error sources can be found in /usr/lib/lilo/doc/ user.tex (depending on the distribution, the file might be

/etc/lilo.conf

elsewhere). Clear the option compact in /etc/lilo.conf.

root cannot carry out a write operation in an NFS directory mounted as read/write.

On the NFS server in the file /etc/exports, set the option no_root_squash for this directory. Its counterpart, root_squash (contrary to the specifications in the /etc/exports Manual pages) is the default value and ef-

fects handling access by `root` via NFS like local access by
the user `nobody` (with few privileges).

17.3   Frequent error messages and possible causes

Kernel panic: VFS: Unable to mount root fs...

>   The kernel boots, but cannot mount the first file system.
>   This can have various causes:
>   – The kernel is missing a hardware driver for accessing the
>   hard disk, diskette, etc.: compile a new kernel.
>   – The kernel does not properly support the file system:
>   compile a new kernel.
>   – The diskette or partition contains a damaged file system
>   or none at all: boot from diskette and try to repair the file
>   system with `fsck`.

Directory not empty.

>   The directory to be deleted is not empty. It might contain
>   hidden files (name beginning with .); display these with **ls
>   -a**.

Connection reset by peer.

>   The other host has terminated the network connection (e.g.,
>   TELNET or FTP) at its end.

Connection timed out.

>   After a certain time without data transfer, network connec-
>   tions can terminate autonomously.

`command`: unable to open display '`display`'

>   On launching of the X server, `xdm` generates an access
>   code. All commands sent to the X server must be provided
>   with this access code in order to be executed. This prevents
>   manipulations by a user other than the one who is currently
>   working under X-Windows. The key is stored in the user's
>   home directory in the file `.Xauthority`. If you log in
>   to an `xterm` as `root` (from a shell with the privileges of
>   some normal user) (e.g., via `su`), then you cannot launch
>   X-Windows programs from this shell because they cannot
>   find the access code. The simplest (but somewhat insecure)
>   solution is to turn off access control:

```
golem:~> xhost +
access control disabled, clients can connect from any host
```

If you want more security, you instead need to transfer the access code in `root`'s `.Xauthority` file as follows:

```
golem:~> xauth extract -f ~X-Windows-User/.Xauthority - :0 | xauth merge
-
```

Now you can open additional `xterms`, etc. Also see `xauth(1)`.

Permission denied

When trying to execute a command, you might not have the necessary permissions to invoke the corresponding program file. Check permissions with **ls -l /path/command**. If you do not know the location of the file, use **which command**. You need a set x flag. If you are the owner of the file, the first flag is important; if you belong to the user group, the second; otherwise the last. Read and write permissions are not needed.

If the message occurs in a process that is already running: the process attempted to execute an operation that is not allowed with your permissions.

service/*protocol*:unknown service

For some Internet services, the corresponding entry in `/etc/services` needed for resolution of "service name to port number" is missing.

Unable to connect to remote host: Connection refused.

There is no daemon running on the remote host to receive a connection at the corresponding port. Possibly this host does not offer the desired service. Possibly the daemon was not launched or terminated due to an error.

Service not available, remote server has closed connection.

`inetd` is running on the specified host on the corresponding port; however, its attempt to launch a subserver (such as `in.telnetd` for TELNET connections or `in.ftpd` for FTP sessions) has failed for some reason. If you are maintaining

this server, check the entry in /etc/inetd.conf. Always
specify the full path of the daemon—inetd has a different
PATH variable than its shell and possibly might not find the
program file. This message can also occur during a running
session (e.g., FTP); in this case the daemon terminated with
an exit status unequal to 0.

service/protocol: bind: Address already in use

An Internet server was launched, but could not reserve its
usual port. Either such a server process is already running or
a server has crashed and could not properly release the port
(in this case the port remains blocked for a certain time to
avoid phantom packets; wait or reboot to solve the problem).

Network is unreachable

Your host does not know where to send packets for a certain
IP address. Which packets are sent where is recorded in
the kernel routing tables. In any case they should contain
a default entry: any packets whose IP addresses does not
correspond to the preceding entries are forwarded to this host.

The routing table can be output and modified with route.

Command not found

Here there are quite a number of alternatives:

– A typing error has occurred or the command does not exist.
– The command exists, but it cannot be found immediately.
  This can be checked with **which** *command*. If needed,
  complement your PATH variable with the directory where
  this command resides, or invoke the command with the full
  path. Do you have permission to execute the command? In
  its search, the shell does not consider files without a set x
  flag.
– The command is in the current directory: the shell does not
  necessarily search in the working directory for a program
  file! Precede the command name with **./**.
– If the command exists and the shell can find it: The above
  message is also output (confusingly) when the program file
  was found, but not one of the shared libraries necessary for
  its execution. Check this with **ldd** *file*. If not found
  occurs in one line, this shared library was not found;

`/etc/ld.so.conf` enter the current directory in `/etc/ld.so.conf` and then invoke **ldconfig**.

umount: *device*: device is busy

> Some process still has a file open in this file system or has its working directory there.

No more space left on device

> Hard disk capacity is exhausted. **You absolutely need to make space; processing files with a full disk can lead to their loss!** Many programs do not consider a full disk as an error and crash without an appropriate error message.

Error writing to "elv..."

> You apparently wanted to process a file with `elvis`. The file system in which `/tmp` is located is full. Make space immediately!

Broken pipe

> A generally harmless message.

Loading failed! The module symbols (from linux-*version*) don't match your linux-*version*.

> On trying to load a kernel module, an error occurred. If the version numbers are different, recompile and reinstall the kernel modules or activate the option CONFIG_MODVERSIONS on kernel compilation. If the version numbers are the same, another error has occurred. For example, the module that should have been loaded with `insmod` might require another module that also has not been loaded. Use `modprobe` instead.

> The new 2.0 kernel also requires the `modules` package version 2.0.0, since the system invocations have changed. The package can be found on most Linux FTP servers along with kernel packages.

Exec format error

> Usually a program file has the format `a.out` or `ELF` which the kernel does not support. The program package must be recompiled and reinstalled. However, it is best to include support for these formats during kernel compilation.

No such device

> A process has attempted to use a certain device file; however, there is no device with the corresponding number

in the kernel. Possibly an upgrade to a new kernel changed device numbers; they are listed in linux/Documentation/ devices.txt. Often, under /dev you will find the script MAKEDEV, which updates device files after kernel upgrades. Invoke it with

linux/Documentation/
devices.txt
/dev

```
golem:~> /dev/MAKEDEV
```

If you cannot find the script, delete the device file with **rm** **/dev/**device and re-create it with **mknod** **{**b¦c**}** major minor **/dev/**device.

Text file busy

This error occurs on compilation of programs or on editing shell scripts if the program file is being used by a process. To avoid excessive disk access, Linux loads parts of the program file into memory when a process needs some part of it. The prerequisite is naturally that the file not be modified while the process executes. The solution is to copy the file, delete the original, rename the copy to the original, and then edit/compile. Internally Linux has not yet deleted the original file; only the link to it in the file system has disappeared.

Read-only file system

A write operation is impossible because it was invoked in a file system mounted as readonly. Even with root permissions there is nothing you can do; the file system must be remounted as read/write.

## Chapter 18

Appendix

18.1   Contents of the proc file system

`cmdline`

> The boot options with which the running kernel started.

`cpuinfo`

> Information on the processor: CPU type, manufacturer, BogoMIPS, ...

`devices`

> All (active) device drivers and their numbers (i.e., the major device numbers of the devices they serve).

`dma`

> Information on the DMA controller.

`filesystems`

> File systems supported by the kernel.

`interrupts`

> The various PC interrupts and their (apparent?) users. After each interrupt is a number indicating how often it was triggered (if your Ethernet adapter, despite incoming frames and a flickering control LED, has a 0, then the cause is an interrupt conflict). This is an important source of information for problems with extension boards.

`ioports`

> IO ports and their (apparent?) users are likewise interesting when hardware problems arise. IO ports are those that are *assumed* by various drivers; in reality the hardware can use another port.

kcore

A memory image of the kernel. It can be debugged with gdb, but just read-only.

kmsg

Here you can read the kernel messages.

ksyms

The kernel symbol table; here ps can determine in which kernel function a process is sleeping.

loadavg

Kernel load: average number of running processes in the last 1, 5, or 15 minutes (first three numbers), number of processes running currently, and total processes including the number of processes launched since booting.

locks

Currently effective file locks.

mdstat

Status of metadevices.

meminfo

Information on memory use; displayed by free.

misc

Character devices with major number 10: e.g., real-time clock /dev/rtc. Numbers before names are minor device numbers.

modules

The presently loaded modules, the number of memory pages they occupy and the number of kernel parts by which they are used (precisely: the number of locks that the kernel has set on a module; a module can only be removed if all locks have been removed).

mounts

The currently mounted file systems with type and options.

net/

Information concerning network support:

alias_types

The various types of network address aliasing (see Section 9.4). In Linux 2.0 there is only one (aliasing for IP addresses).

aliases

> Active IP aliases.

arp

> Contents of kernel ARP cache (see Section 9.3).

dev

> Statistics of network interfaces (sent and received packets, errors, collisions, . . .).

ip_acct

> Rule list for IP accounting.

ip_forward

> Packet filter rule list for packet forwarding (see Section 9.3).

ip_input

> Packet filter rule list for incoming packet (see Section 9.3).

ip_masq_app

> Information on IP masquerading status (see Section 9.3), referring to a certain service (FTP, IRC, . . .).

ip_masquerade

> Information on IP masquerading status (see Section 9.3).

ip_output

> Packet filter rule list for outgoing packets (see Section 9.3).

raw

> Information on RAW sockets.

route

> Routing tables of the kernel; they can be displayed and modified with route.

snmp

> Various SNMP variables of the kernel. SNMP (Simple Network Management Protocol) is a protocol for monitoring and configuration of networks and network components. This file serves to export values that are interesting for SNMP; SNMP is realized by a corresponding daemon in user mode.

sockstat

> Information on socket structures in kernel.

tcp

> Information on existing TCP connections; they can be displayed with **netstat -t**.

udp

> Information on UDP sockets; they can be displayed with **netstat -u**.

unix

> Information on UNIX domain sockets (only for local communication between processes).

pci

> Information about PCI bus (attached devices and device parameters).

PID/

> The *PID* is the PID (process identification) of a process; this directory contains information on this process.

cmdline

> How the program that the process is currently executing was launched (e.g., **/bin/bash -login**).

cwd

> "Current working directory": a link pointing to the current working directory of a process.

environ

> Environment variable of a process: between the individual variables **cat environ** returns null bytes (which the terminal suppresses to make them invisible).

exe

> The code of the program that the process is currently executing: If process 81, e.g., is a Bourne shell, then **less /proc/81/exe** returns the contents of /bin/bash.

fd

> This directory contains links to all files that the process currently has open. The links have the numbers of the corresponding file descriptor. **ls -**

1 /proc/_PID_**/fd/**_fd_ returns a number in square
brackets and (delimited by a colon) a second number.
The first number identifies the block device on which
the file is located (0303, e.g., means /dev/hda3); the
second number stands for the i-node number. If the
first number is zero, then it is not a file but a socket,
a pipe, or something else.

maps

With cat you can read from this pipe, which files
the process currently has mapped to a (virtual) main
memory address with the system call mmap(). The
range specification at the start of the line is the virtual
address space. This is followed by the permissions
on this memory space. The last flag can be p or s,
depending on whether the address space is private
or shared (for file mmaps: shared regions are saved,
private regions are not saved).

mem

Memory image of the process; currently you cannot
do anything with this.

root@

The root of the directory tree as viewed by this
process. The root is not the same for all processes;
it can be changed with the system call chroot().

stat

Some status information, which is better viewed with
·ps. The structure of this information is specified in
the Kernel Hacker's Guide.* The current version 0.6
is somewhat antiquated, however.

statm

Similar to stat.

status

Some readable information about the process,
including status ("sleeping," "ready," ...), effective,

*Sunsite: docs/linux-doc-project/kernel-hackers-guide

535

real and saved UID/GID, PID of the parent process, memory allocation, and signal masks.

rtc

Information on real-time clock. Here you can read time and date and more. The information comes from the battery-driven RAM of the real-time clock.

self@

For every process that reads it, this link points to the status directory (i.e., for process PID 437 to /proc/437/).

scsi/

Information about the SCSI subsystem.

adapter/

For every (known) SCSI adapter there is also a corresponding subdirectory with additional information.

scsi

If the kernel supports SCSI, this lists all recognized SCSI host adapters and the connected devices.

stat

General kernel status infos.

sys/kernel/

General kernel information.

domainname

The domain name currently set in the kernel.

file-nr

Number of open files.

hostname

The host name currently set in the kernel.

osrelease

Linux version.

ostype

Always returns Linux.

panic

Values other than zero indicate kernel panic.

version

Build number and date of build.

```
golem:~> cat /proc/sys/kernel/version
#4 Thu Dec 12 15:26:06 MET 1996
```

uptime

> The first number is the time elapsed since the last boot in
> seconds; the second is that part thereof spent in idle task. (=
> all processes sleeping).

version

```
golem:~> cat /proc/sys/kernel/version
#4 Thu Dec 12 15:26:06 MET 1996
```

> Linux version, time when kernel was compiled, gcc
> version used, host where compiled ...

18.2   Overview of /etc files

Most configuration files reside in the directory /etc. This section
gives an overview of the most important of these configuration files.
Our list refers primarily to the Slackware distribution, which does
not completely comply with the new Linux File System Standard
(FSSTND).

/etc

aliases

> Aliases and alias lists for e-mail; see **man aliases**.
> After any modification, **newaliases** must be invoked to
> create/update the files aliases.dir and aliases.pag.

apsfilterrc

> Configuration file for apsfilter, created automatically on
> installation. In the file you can use the variable FEATURE to
> set the conversion of ASCII files.

at.deny, at.allow

> If at.allow exists, then only users entered there can use at.
> If at.deny exists, any users entered there are denied the use
> of at.

bootptab

> Configuration file for bootpd daemon.

boot

conf.modules

Here you can define aliases for kernel modules and specify which options a module is to be given automatically on loading.

csh.cshrc

The commands in this file execute the C shell on booting.

csh.login

The commands in this file are executed in addition to those in csh.cshrc if the C shell is a login shell (see Section 2.7).

diphosts

SLIP List of machines permitted to make a SLIP connection.

DIR_COLORS

ls colors Configuration file with color settings of the ls command.

disktab

hard disk File for determination of nonstandard hard disk parameters for LILO.

exports

NFS Defines the directories to be exported by NFS.

fdprm

floppy disk Parameters for floppy disk drives.

fstab

file system and swap Contains the file systems and swap partitions to be mounted or activated on booting.

ftpaccess

FTP Configuration file for the FTP daemon; allows the definition of access restrictions and messages for wu-ftpd or diku-ftpd.

ftpusers

Configuration file for the FTP daemon. Users listed in this file cannot log in per FTP.

gateways

File with a list of routers.

gettydefs

Configuration file for getty.

group

This defines all user groups with their GIDs and their member users.

`host.conf`

> See Section 9.10.

`hosts`

> This file contains the names and IP addresses of other
> computers. Depending on the settings in the file `host.conf`, network hosts
> this file is searched before or after the name server to find the
> IP address of a host.

`hosts.allow`

> Lists computers with permission to access local network
> services (used by `tcp_wrapper`, see below).

`hosts.deny`

> Lists computers that are denied access to local network ser-
> vices. Both files are used by Wietse Venema's `tcp_wrapper`.
> In `/etc/inetd.conf`, before the invocation of various
> subdaemons the respective `tcp_wrapper` (command name
> `tcpd`) is started. If the remote host does not have access,
> `tcp_wrapper` does not invoke the server, but breaks the con-
> nection. Non-`inetd` services such as NFS or Secure Shell are
> not affected by these files.

`hosts.equiv`

> Defines trusted users/hosts for services with the Berkeley   trusted users
> r-utilities.

`hosts.lpd`

> Lists computers with permission to use local printers.   printers

`inetd.conf`

> This configuration file for the daemon `inetd` establishes a   Internet
> one-to-one correspondence between a connection to a certain
> port and the daemon to be started.

`inittab`

> This configuration file for the `init` process contains the
> assignments of shell scripts to run levels.   run level

`issue`

> This text file is displayed before the login prompt. Normally   login
> it contains the name of the host and a greeting message.

`ld.so.cache`

> File with configuration data for dynamic linker.   dynamic linker

539

ld.so.conf

shared libraries
>File with paths to shared libraries.

lilo.conf

LILO
>Configuration file for Linux Loader (LILO). See Section 5.5.

localtime
>Here date records the host's time zone (see **man date**).

magic

file type
>This file establishes the correspondence between byte patterns at the beginning of a file and the respective file type. A file's type can be determined by searching magic for the file's starting byte pattern. The command file is used for this.

mdtab
>Configuration file for metadevice utilities; see Section 6.6.

motd

login message
>This text file (message of the day) is normally automatically displayed after each login.

mtab

file systems
>This internal table for mount lists all currently mounted file systems.

mtools
>Configuration file for MTools.

named.boot

name server
>Boot file for the name server; see Section 9.10.

networks
>Contains the IP addresses and names of known networks.

nntpserver
>Here some News readers expect the name of the NNTP server (if it exists).

passwd

users and passwords
>Users are defined in this file by specifying each user's ID, user name, login shell, and primary group. The actual passwords are stored in the file shadow, which, unlike the passwd file, can only be read with root permissions.

printcap

printer queue
>Configuration file for printer queues, see **man printcap**.

profile

> If the Bourne shell bash is launched as login shell (by
> /bin/login, with **su -** or directly with **bash -login**),
> then it first executes /etc/profile, where primarily
> important environment variables are set.

protocols

> Translates IP protocol name to protocol number (e.g., TCP to
> 6).

psdatabase

> With the help of this database ps determines in which queue
> a sleeping process is located.

rpc

> Configuration file for RPC server.   RPC

securetty

> Specifies on which TTYs the superuser can log in.

sendmail.cf

> Configuration file for sendmail.

sendmail.st

> Here sendmail stores statistics that can be queried with
> mailstats. However, sendmail must be compiled with
> a corresponding option.

services

> Contains the assignment of TCP/IP ports to corresponding   port assignment
> names of services (programs).

shadow

> File with encrypted user passwords.

shells

> This file contains the valid system shells. When the user logs
> in as anonymous or ftp, the FTP daemon checks whether
> the user's login shell is entered in this list. If not, the login is
> denied.

syslog.conf

> Configuration file for the syslog daemon (see Section 6.3).   syslog

termcap

> Configuration file for the termcap library defining the
> control characters of the various types of terminals.

`ttys`

> Determines which `terminfo` file is to be used for which terminal.

`utmp, wtmp`

> Log file of all user logins and logouts.

`xmmounttab`

> Configuration file for `xmmount`.

`xvmounttab`

> Configuration file for `xvmount`.

18.3   Overview of /etc directories

`default/`

> Stores the default values of parameters:

> `useradd`

new user
>> Default values for `useradd` command.

> `getty.XXX`

port
>> Configuration of `getty` program for port *XXX*.

> `uugetty.XXX`

>> Configuration of `uugetty` program for port *XXX*.

`bind/`

> Subdirectory with DNS databases for the name server `named`.

`lilo/`

LILO
> Contains LILO installation program.

`ppp/`

> PPP daemon configuration scripts.

`skel/`

new user
> Contains files that, on execution of `useradd` , are automatically copied into the home directory of a new user.

`rc.d/`

> Scripts executed on system startup.

> `rc.0`

shutdown
>> Script for run level 0 (system shutdown).

> `rc.6`

>> Script for run level 6 (login via `xdm`).

> `rc.K`

single-user mode
>> Script for single-user mode.

`rc.M`

    Script for multi-user mode (run levels 1 to 6).   multi-user mode

`rc.S`

    Script that activates swapping and checks consistency   consistency
of file system on booting.

`rc.keymap`

    Script for loading country-specific keyboard layouts.   keyboard

`rc.local`

    Script to start local daemons.   daemon

`rc.inet1`

    Script to initialize network interfaces.   network

`rc.inet2`

    Script to start network daemons.

`rc.serial`

    Script to configure serial interfaces.   serial

18.4   Hidden files in home directories

`.ICEauthority`

    ICE is part of the X server. It serves to distinguish the individual X11 clients (i.e., the various X-Windows programs) by assigning them access codes. This file contains the corresponding keys.

`.abbrev_defs`

    This Emacs Lisp file defines shortcuts for the various Emacs modes. Users can enter their own shortcuts here.

`.addressbook*`

    These files contain the `pine` e-mail address book.

`.amaya/`

    This directory contains configuration and data files for the Amaya browser.

`.bash_history`

    Here `bash` records the last couple of dozen commands that the user has entered in past sessions.

`.bash_profile`

    These commands are executed by a login `bash` at the start (see Section 2.7).

`.bashrc`

> These commands are executed by `bash` at the start of a session (see Section 2.7).

`.cshrc`

> These commands are executed by a C shell at the start of a session (see Section 2.7).

`.emacs`

> Here the user can enter Emacs commands to be executed when the editor starts.

`.forward`

> In this file a user can specify that e-mails are to be forwarded to a certain address or passed to a UNIX program for processing.

`.gimprc`

> Configuration file for the graphic tool `gimp`.

`.history`

> Here a C shell records the last command lines entered by the user.

`.inputrc`

> Configuration file for the GNU Readline Library, which is used by `bash` and many other GNU utilities (see `readline(3)`).

`.login`

> These commands are executed by a login C shell at the start of a session (see Section 2.7).

`.logout`

> This file is executed by a login C shell at the end of a session.

`.lyx_lastfiles`

> List of the last TEX files that the user opened in LyX.

`.mc.ini`

> Configuration file for Midnight Commander, a file manager similar to the popular Norton Commander for MS-DOS.

`.mcwd`

> Here the mtools record the working directory that is used when the full DOS path name is not specified on invocation of one of the mtools. `mcd` allows you to change the current directory.

.netrc

If this file contains a user name and a password, ftp attempts an automatic login with these values; see Section 10.5.

.netscape/

This directory contains configuration, lock, and cache files for Netscape, as well as bookmarks and the history (user's last visited URLs).

bookmarks.html

User's bookmark file.

history.db

Last visited URLs.

preferences

Configuration file.

cache/

WWW page cache.

.netscape-cache/

Older Netscape versions stored cached WWW pages here.

.netscape-history

Last visited URLs for older Netscape versions.

.netscape-preferences

Configuration file for older Netscape versions.

.pgp/

PGP records the user's public and private keys here along with public keys of communication partners. .pgp/rand-seed.bin is a default value for the PGP random number generator.

.pinerc

pine configuration file.

.plan

The contents of this file are displayed when someone requests information about the user via finger.

.profile

These commands are executed by (any) login bash or login sh at the start of a session (see Section 2.7).

.project

Like .plan.

`.rhosts`

>In this file the user enters which login name he/she uses on other hosts. Then the user can log in there with `rlogin` without a password and execute commands in `rsh` without a password. The file is structured in lines. At the start of the line is the host name of the remote host, then the user name (blank delimited). This method of logging in without a password is extremely insecure and makes it easier for hackers to intrude into your system.

`.ssh/`

>Directory for secure shell `ssh`:
>
>`identity`
>
>>User's private key.
>
>`identity.pub`
>
>>User's public key.
>
>`known_hosts`
>
>>Here the user stores the public keys of other hosts on the network. If the user creates an `.rhosts` file and the system administrator has correspondingly configured `sshd` (secure shell daemon), then the user can log in from a remote host without entering a password—the same login name on both hosts suffices.

`.tclshrc`

>Tcl commands that are executed by a `tclsh` on startup.

`.tcshrc`

>These commands are executed by a `tcsh` at the start of a session (see Section 2.7).

`.tkined`

>Configuration file for the dsa network monitoring tool `tkined`.

`.Xauthority`

>Contains keys that the programs of the current X-Windows users use for accessing the X-Windows server. Without these keys, no graphic or window operations can be executed. This access protection prevents manipulations by other users or hackers.

`.xvpics/`

> The graphic tool `xv` stores information in this directory
> when the image browser Visual Schnauzer is used. Visual
> Schnauzer searches the current directory and generates
> overview sheets with stamp-sized images of all recognized
> graphic files, which facilitates looking for images in large
> directories (see Section 10.8).

18.5   List of known SunSite mirrors

- Africa
  - South Africa
    Stellenbosch:
    > `ftp.sun.ac.za:/pub/linux/sunsite/`
    Johannesburg:
    > `ftp.is.co.za:/linux/sunsite/`
- Asia
  - Hong Kong: `ftp.cs.cuhk.hk:/pub/Linux/`
    `sunsite.ust.hk:/pub/Linux/`
  - Japan
    Tokyo:
    > `ftp.spin.ad.jp:/pub/linux/`
    > `sunsite.unc.edu/`
  - Korea
    Seoul:
    > `ftp.nuri.net:/pub/Linux/`
  - Malaysia: `ftp.jaring.my:/pub/Linux/`
  - Republic of Singapore: `ftp.nus.sg:/pub/unix/Linux/`
  - Thailand
    Bangkok:
    > `ftp.nectec.or.th:/pub/mirrors/linux/`
- Australia
  - Brisbane: `ftp.dstc.edu.au:/pub/linux/`
  - Canbera: `sunsite.anu.edu.au:/pub/linux/`
  - Melbourne: `ftp.monash.edu.au:/pub/linux/`
  - Sydney: `ftp.sydutech.usyd.edu.au:/pub/linux/`
- Europe

- Austria

Vienna:

>   ftp.univie.ac.at:/systems/linux/sunsite/

- Czech Republic

Brno:

>   ftp.fi.muni.cz:/pub/UNIX/linux/

- Finland

Espo:

>   ftp.funet.fi:/pub/Linux/sunsite/

- France

Angers:

>   ftp.univ-angers.fr:/pub/Linux/

Belfort:

>   ftp.iut-bm.univ-fcomte.fr:

Nancy:

>   ftp.loria.fr:/pub/linux/sunsite/

Paris:

>   ftp.ibp.fr:/pub/linux/sunsite/

- Germany (Deutschland)

Aachen:

>   ftp.dfv.rwth-aachen.de:/pub/linux/
>   sunsite/

Dortmund:

>   ftp.germany.eu.net:/pub/os/Linux/
>   Mirror.SunSITE/

Dresden:

>   ftp.tu-dresden.de:/pub/Linux/sunsite/

Erlangen:

>   ftp.uni-erlangen.de:/pub/Linux/
>   MIRROR.sunsite/

Göttingen:

>   ftp.gwdg.de:/pub/linux/mirrors/sunsite/

Karlsruhe:

>   ftp.rz.uni-karlsruhe.de:/pub/linux/
>   mirror.sunsite/

Mannheim:

    `ftp.ba-mannheim.de:/pub/linux/`

    `mirror.sunsite/`

Paderborn:

    `ftp.uni-paderborn.de:/pub/Mirrors/`

    `sunsite.unc.edu/`

Rostock:

    `ftp.uni-rostock.de:/Linux/sunsite/`

Stuttgart:

    `ftp.rus.uni-stuttgart.de:/pub/unix/`

    `.systems/linux/MIRROR.sunsite/`

Tuebingen:

    `ftp.uni-tuebingen.de:/pub/linux/`

    `Mirror.sunsite/`

Ulm:

    `ftp.rz.uni-ulm.de:/pub/mirrors/linux/`

    `sunsite/`

– Hungary

Budapest:

    `ftp.kfki.hu:/pub/linux/`

– Italy

Casale Monferrato:

    `linux.italnet.it:/pub/Linux/`

Naples:

    `ftp.unina.it:/pub/linux/sunsite/`

Padova:

    `giotto.unipd.it:/pub/unix/Linux/`

Pisa:

    `cnuce-arch.cnr.it:/pub/Linux/`

Rome:

    `ftp.flashnet.it:/mirror2/sunsite.unc.edu/`

– Netherlands

Amsterdam:

    `ftp.nijenrode.nl:/pub/linux/`

    `sunsite.unc-mirror/`

Leiden:

    `ftp.LeidenUniv.nl:/pub/linux/sunsite/`

549

- Norway
  Trondheim:

      ftp.nvg.unit.no:/pub/linux/sunsite/

- Poland
  Warsaw:

      sunsite.icm.edu.pl:/pub/Linux/
      sunsite.unc.edu/

- Spain
  Barcelona:

      ftp.upc.es:/pub/sistemes/linux/

  Madrid:

      ftp.rediris.es:/software/os/linux/
      sunsite/

  Madrid:

      sunsite.rediris.es:/software/linux/

  Oviedo:

      ftp.etsimo.uniovi.es:/pub/linux/

  Seville:

      ftp.cs.us.es:/pub/Linux/sunsite-mirror/

  Tarragone:

      ftp.etse.urv.es:/pub/mirror/linux/

  Valladolid:

      ftp.luna.gui.es:/pub/linux.new/

- Switzerland
  Zurich:

      ftp.switch.ch:/mirror/linux/

- Turkey (Turkiye)
  Ankara:

      ftp.metu.edu.tr:/pub/linux/sunsite/

- United Kingdom
  Canterbury:

      unix.hensa.ac.uk:/mirrors/sunsite/pub/
      Linux/

  Coventry:

      ftp.maths.warwick.ac.uk:/mirrors/linux/
      sunsite.unc-mirror/

Greenwich:

> `ftp.idiscover.co.uk:/pub/Linux/`
> `sunsite.unc-mirror/`

London:

> `sunsite.doc.ic.ac.uk:/packages/linux/`
> `sunsite.unc-mirror/`

Mildenhall:

> `ftp.dungeon.com:/pub/linux/`
> `sunsite-mirror/`

- North America
  - Canada

    Toronto, Ontario:

    > `ftp.io.org:/pub/mirrors/linux/sunsite/`

  - United States

    Atlanta, GA:

    > `ftp.cc.gatech.edu:/pub/linux/`

    Chapel Hill, NC:

    > `sunsite.unc.edu:/pub/Linux/`

    Concord, CA:

    > `ftp.cdrom.com:/pub/linux/sunsite/`

    Dallas, TX:

    > `ftp.siriuscc.com:/pub/Linux/Sunsite/`

    Fayetteville, AR:

    > `ftp.engr.uark.edu:/pub/linux/sunsite/`

    Flagstaff, AZ:

    > `ftp.infomagic.com:/pub/mirrors/linux/`
    > `sunsite/`

    Laurel, MD:

    > `ftp.linux.org:/pub/mirrors/sunsite/`

    Minneapolis, MN:

    > `ftp.cs.umn.edu:/pub/Linux/sunsite/`

    Norman, OK:

    > `ftp.uoknor.edu:/linux/sunsite/`

    Pasadena, CA:

    > `ftp.fuller.edu:/mirror/sunsite/`

Raleigh, NC:

> `ftp.redhat.com:/pub/mirrors/`
>
> `sunsite.unc.edu/`

Rochester, NY:

> `ftp.rge.com:/pub/systems/linux/sunsite/`

Salt Lake City, UT:

> `ftp.pht.com:/mirrors/linux/sunsite/`

San Jose, CA:

> `ftp.yggdrasil.com:mirrors/sunsite/`

Sunnyvale, CA:

> `ftp.drcdrom.com:/pub/linux/sunsite/`

Urbana, IL:

> `uiarchive.cso.uiuc.edu:/pub/systems/`
>
> `linux/sunsite/`

Waukesha, WI:

> `ftp.wit.com:/unix/linux/`

- South America
  - Brazil

    Campinas:

    > `ftp.fee.unicamp.br:/pub/Linux/mirrors/`
    >
    > `sunsite.unc.edu/`

    Rio de Janeiro:

    > `ftp.iis.com.br:/pub/Linux/`

    Sao Paulo:

    > `linux.if.usp.br:/pub/mirror/`
    >
    > `sunsite.unc.edu/pub/Linux/`

    Unknown:

    > `farofa.ime.usp.br:/pub/linux/`

Bibliography

1. Andeleigh, Prabhat K. *UNIX System Architecture* Prentice-Hall [1993].

2. Carl-Mitchell, Smoot, and Quarterman, John S. *Practical Internetworking with TCP/IP and UNIX* Addison-Wesley [1993].

3. Cheswick, William R., and Bellovin, Steven M. *Firewalls and Internet Security* Addison-Wesley [1994].

4. Comer, Douglas E. *Internetworking with TCP/IP, Vol. 1–3* Prentice-Hall [1991].

5. Flanagan, David. *X Toolkit Intrinsics Reference Manual, Vol. 5.* O'Reilly [1993].

6. Gilly, Daniel. *UNIX in a Nutshell* O'Reilly [1992].

7. Gulbins, Jürgen. *UNIX* Springer [1988].

8. Heller, Dan. *XView Programming Manual, Vol. 7* O'Reilly [1991].

9. Heller, Dan. *Motif Programming Manual, Vol. 6* O'Reilly [1992].

10. Hewlett-Packard. *Ultimate Guide to the Vi and Ex Text Editors* Addison Wesley [1990].

11. Kehoe, Brendan P. *Zen and the Art of the Internet* Prentice-Hall [1993].

12. Krol, Ed. *The Whole Internet: User's Guide and Catalog* O'Reilly [1993].

13. Lippmann, Stanley B. *C++ Primer* Addison Wesley [1991].

14. Maurer, Rainer. *HTML und CGI-Programmierung - mit einer Einführung in Tcl* dpunkt Heidelberg [1996].

15. Middendorf, Stefan. *Java - Programmierhandbuch und Referenz* dpunkt Heidelberg [1996].

16. Mui, Linda, and Pearce, Eric. *X Window System Administrator's Guide, Vol. 8* O'Reilly [1993].

17. Nemeth E., Snyder G., Seebass S., and Trent, R. H. *UNIX System Administration Handbook, 2nd Ed.* Prentice Hall [1995].

18. Nye, Adrian. *Xlib Programming Manual, Vol. 1* O'Reilly [1992].

19. Nye, Adrian. *Xlib Reference Manual, Vol. 2* O'Reilly [1992].

20. Nye, Adrian, and O'Reilly, Tim. *X Toolkit Intrinsics Programming Manual, Vol. 4.* O'Reilly [1990].

21. Open Software Foundation. *OSF/Motif Programmer's Guide* Prentice-Hall [1993].

22. Open Software Foundation. *OSF/Motif Programmer's Reference* Prentice-Hall [1993].

23. Open Software Foundation. *OSF/Motif Users' Guide* Prentice-Hall [1993].

24. Quercia, Valerie, and O'Reilly, Tim. *X Window System User's Guide, Vol. 3* O'Reilly [1991].

25. Schneier, Bruce W. *Applied Cryptography, 2nd Ed.* John Wiley & Sons [1996].

26. Schoonover, Michael A. *GNU Emacs—UNIX Text Editing and Programming* Addison-Wesley [1992].

27. Stevens, W. Richard. *Advanced Programming in the UNIX Environment* Addison Wesley [1992].

28. Stevens, W. Richard. *UNIX Network Programming* Prentice-Hall [1990].

29. Stoll, Clifford. *The Cuckoo's Egg: Tracking a Spy Through the Maze of Computer Espionage* Doubleday, New York [1989].

30. Tanenbaum, Andrew S. *Distributed Open Systems* Prentice-Hall [1995].

31. Young, Douglas A. *X Window System, Programming and Applications with Xt* Prentice-Hall [1990].

Index

—I—